MW00803901

TRYING TO M

TRYING TO MAKE IT

The Enterprises, Gangs, and People of the American Drug Trade

R. V. Gundur

CORNELL UNIVERSITY PRESS ITHACA AND LONDON

Copyright © 2022 by Cornell University

All rights reserved. Except for brief quotations in a review, this book, or parts thereof, must not be reproduced in any form without permission in writing from the publisher. For information, address Cornell University Press, Sage House, 512 East State Street, Ithaca, New York 14850. Visit our website at cornellpress.cornell.edu.

First published 2022 by Cornell University Press

Library of Congress Cataloging-in-Publication Data

Names: Gundur, Rajeev, author.
Title: Trying to make it : the enterprises, gangs, and people of the American drug trade / R. V. Gundur.
Description: Ithaca [New York] : Cornell University Press, 2022. | Includes bibliographical references and index.
Identifiers: LCCN 2021044473 (print) | LCCN 2021044474 (ebook) | ISBN 9781501764462 (hardcover) | ISBN 9781501764479 (paperback) | ISBN 9781501764486 (pdf) | ISBN 9781501764493 (epub)
Subjects: LCSH: Drug traffic—Social aspects—United States. | Drug traffic—Social aspects—Mexico. | Drug dealers—United States. | Drug dealers—Mexico. | Drug control—Social aspects—United States. | Drug control—Social aspects—Mexico.
Classification: LCC HV5825 .G86 2022 (print) | LCC HV5825 (ebook) | DDC 364.1/770972—dc23
LC record available at https://lccn.loc.gov/2021044473
LC ebook record available at https://lccn.loc.gov/2021044474

To Vishwanath, Josephine, Juan el Bueno, and José

Some people deserve to be in prison; but we were never that mean.
—Interview with Bruce, a member of Barrio Azteca, March 2014

Contents

Preface

What follows is a story of the banalities of the drug trade in America and the struggles many of the people involved face. The story is the result of my observations, court documents, and interviews with 129 people. These people included law enforcement, professionals who worked with marginalized communities, residents of those communities, and current and former participants in the drug trade.

Many of the names of the respondents have been changed to grant them anonymity. Sometimes respondents picked their pseudonyms, but when they elected not to do so I assigned them a name of my own choosing. All people who are presented mononymously have been given pseudonyms. No composite characters appear; each person described is a unique, real individual. All the firsthand events described within did occur; however, the events I observed did not necessarily occur in the order presented. I have done my best to validate the historical events recounted by respondents to ensure accuracy of the claims.

The quotations within this text are either the direct words from recordings with respondents, taken always with their full consent and knowledge, or, in cases where I could not record, reconstructions of conversations from notes written during or made shortly after the events occurred. Recordings were transcribed intelligently, meaning that tics, pauses, and filler phrases were excluded. I have edited some quotes to clarify pronouns and to omit repetition. Where the respondents spoke in dialect, I have kept their speech true to what they said, with most explanations of slang and translations in the notes. The quotations selected are often representative of what other respondents expressed. I have also endeavored to include as wide an array of respondent views as possible. Translations from Spanish to English are mine, as are any errors within the text.

A brief explanation about the terms used to refer to groups that traffic drugs as well as different types of gangs is necessary. The language used to describe these groups varies considerably among law enforcement practitioners, the news media, and the members of such groups. In this text I use a mix of official and colloquial terms, particularly when the latter provides a sense of nuance that the former does not.

Finally, I realize that some readers will bring their own predispositions to the table and flatly reject some or all that I have to say. And I realize that other readers will argue that I have understated, overstated, or misrepresented the problems explored within this work. My goal has been to minimize my own prejudice so that the individuals I interviewed can read what I have written and say that I have understood the kernel of what they were telling me. I did not expect many of the stories within and what I learned often challenged the perspectives I held before conducting my study. I have great respect for the people who kindly gave me their time and their experiences. I have done my best to represent them accurately.

Acknowledgments

Many people made this book possible, and I thank each of them. First and foremost, there were the people who participated in my research. Without their willingness and honesty, I could not have written this book. I'm grateful to the people who have believed in me as a scholar: Maureen Shea and Jimmy Huck at Tulane University, Paul Keal and Andrew Phillips at the Australian National University, and Martin Innes and Michael Levi at Cardiff University. Martin Innes gave me the opportunity of a lifetime when he helped me develop this topic and apply for the Economic and Social Research Council studentship at Cardiff University.

The Economic and Social Research Council paid my fees and funded a generous travel grant, without which I could not have undertaken the research for this book. The late Tom Horlick-Jones helped me through the ethics approval and made sure that I thought about my own safety. Michelle Valencia and Shaun Bauer proofread my Spanish documents so I wouldn't embarrass myself.

During my fieldwork, I was hosted by many people through Couchsurfing. Octavio, Chuckie, Chris, Laney, Lulu, and Gina helped me adjust quickly to each new place and provided me with a great wealth of local insight. In El Paso, several people helped me hit the ground running. Sandra Garabano, then the director for the Center for Inter-American Border Studies at the University of Texas at El Paso, provided me with a wonderful workspace where I interviewed many of my respondents. Brad Larkin opened his house to me when I needed a change of scenery. Charles Bowden, who died way too soon, plugged me into a network of well-informed individuals, including Bill Conroy, José "Raulio" Fierro Rivera, and Molly Molloy. And Marcus Felson provided great advice on how to proceed and complete this book.

I was equally fortunate in Juárez. Leobardo Alvarado and Cesar Olivas at the Universidad Autónoma Ciudad Juárez provided me with excellent connections, a sense of safety, and help in finding transcriptionists who did a fantastic job transcribing my notes.

In Phoenix at the Arizona State University School of Criminology and Criminal Justice, Cassia Spohn facilitated my stay, and the administrative staff, Linda Bork and Shannon Stewart, made things easy. Scott Decker provided me with invaluable connections including Jeffeory Hynes and Natividad Mendoza, who introduced me to many of my respondents. My many colleagues at Arizona State

University made going into the office a pleasure. Mario Cano made me feel welcome from the start, and Rick Moule Jr. challenged me intellectually and supported me after I was burglarized. Many friends—Daniel Alati, Katie Dunn, Molly Arenberg, and Steve Jennings—helped to get me on my feet after that incident.

Mark Coburn put me up in Denver, which allowed me to visit the courts there. José Rivera and his family hosted me for a brief visit in Nebraska, where José provided me with invaluable insight into the birth of Barrio Azteca.

Back in Illinois, I could not have been successful without assistance from David Olson and Loyola University Chicago's Department of Criminal Justice and Criminology and from Mike Vecchio, who welcomed me to the department. Wesley Skogan and Guadalupe Cruz introduced me to the Violence Interrupters. And Gulnaz "Gulu" Saiyed and Neema Nazem hosted me in Chicago as I finished my study.

I thank Jim Lance for believing in my book and giving me the opportunity to present my work to a wider audience. I thank those who helped me get to the end: Adriana Chavez for research assistance, Florence Lourme for designing the figures, Denise MacLeod for providing editorial assistance, and Kate Mertes for doing the index. I thank the professionals who helped deliver the book in its final form: Clare Jones and Mary Kate Murphy at Cornell University Press, and Michelle Scott, Kate Gibson, and their team at Westchester Publishing Services. I especially thank Nicola Cockburn for providing feedback on my alt text.

Finally, I thank the people who have read my work, engaged with it, and made it infinitely more readable and accessible: Maya P. Barak, Derek Dalton, Tom Hall, Mark Halsey, Travis K. Henry, Martin Innes, Timothy Lauger, and Michael Levi. A special thanks to those who read complete drafts: William J. Clark, Isobel Scavetta, and the three anonymous reviewers.

Abbreviations

AB	Aryan Brotherhood
BA	Barrio Azteca
BD	Black Disciples
CASS	Central Arizona Shelter Services
CAT	Convention Against Torture
CBP	Customs and Border Protection
DEA	Drug Enforcement Agency
DoJ	Department of Justice
FBI	Federal Bureau of Investigation
GD	Gangster Disciple; later Growth and Development
GIITEM	Gang and Immigration Intelligence Team Enforcement Mission
HIDTA	High Intensity Drug Trafficking Area
LA	Los Angeles
PAN	Partido Acción Nacional
PRI	Partido Revolucionario Institucional
RICO	Racketeer Influenced and Corrupt Organizations Act
TDC	Texas Department of Corrections

TRYING TO MAKE IT

HOME

He was named Vishwanath. Wish. Wa. Nut. But it was a name too hard for Westerners. He let people call him whatever made them comfortable. So, his colleagues called him Vish. His patients called him Doc. I called him Dad.

Behind the name was a man who had been on both sides, sometimes simultaneously, of a thin line: on one side, Dad was the professional, a psychiatrist who specialized in addiction, and on the other side, he was the patient, a man who struggled with depression and addiction. Like so many in America—immigrant and citizen alike—he was simply trying to make it. He went to work, put in long hours, and did his best to provide. And he chased success, the quintessential but elusive element of the American dream.

When the pressures Dad faced were too much to bear, he drank. A lot. Sometimes, he put down an entire handle in a sitting.[1] Scotch was his favorite, but bourbon would do. And at times it was vodka, which he carried with him in water bottles. He kept working for years before he was finally caught drinking on the job. But his downfall wasn't his own doing. At least, that's what he told himself. It was the woman who reported him. Without her, he could have gone on functioning. Without her, he could have kept pursuing his dreams.

Dad was a respected doctor, and his patients loved him. Drunk, sober, it didn't matter. He could motivate some of them to do the things he himself struggled to do: be honest with themselves, confront their demons, get it together. His work put him in the middle of a world of substance abuse that ran parallel to his own. For most of his career, he saw patients from rural America who struggled with drug misuse. His patients came from all around the country and from all walks of life. Some abused amphetamines made from ingredients available locally. Others abused opioids made overseas, bought from pharmacists or pushers.

Both pharmacists and pushers—if we're honest—are in the same line of business. They exist on a spectrum of enterprise in which one vendor is legally sanctioned while the other is not.[2] Both pharmacist and pusher are sellers of mind- and body-altering products that travel along supply chains across the globe. Consumers buy from whichever retailer they can access. The transaction is a simple, banal process that features in the lives of everyday people, including those who button up their starched shirts to go to an office, those who lace up their steel-capped boots to go to a building site, and those who tie the drawstrings on their name-brand sweatpants to go to a college seminar room.

Across campus, the name of a young woman was on everybody's lips. She had always been popular but now she had suddenly become famous. She wasn't there, however, to enjoy her moment of fame; fresh to death, her warmth had departed this world. A sophomore in college, she had just turned twenty. The chatter echoed through the quads. Her friends remembered her laugh, her beauty, her spirit. Those who didn't know her just knew she had taken too much Oxy.[3] It was an accident. She came from a good family and had a bright future. God, no, she wasn't an addict. She wasn't meant to die so young. It was so very sad.

Then the talk stopped as quickly as it had begun. Everyday students went back to their everyday lives. Some kept using, just as she had done, and most went on to graduate. But even as her name faded from memory, her experience echoed in obituaries throughout the country as America grappled with her story, repeated by others just like her, tens of thousands of times over: ephemeral faces in fleeting spotlights.[4]

And there were the tens of thousands, now long forgotten, who had died before her. They're the ones who had perished in the shadows of dilapidated apartments or on cold streets in cities such as Chicago, New York, and Baltimore, far from the dormitory where she had died, surrounded by warm, green grass and a future worth living.

Optics make the public care, worry, and demand action.[5] But the dominant images of the drug trade have long depicted it and the people involved with it as members of a nefarious underworld far from the lives of decent people, such as the folks I grew up with among the corn and soybean fields of middle America.

When I was growing up in 1990s Springfield, a small city of about 120,000 people in central Illinois, drugs and gangs were things I saw mostly on TV or heard about on the radio. Television dramas painted these issues in stark terms, and sometimes the anchors on the WGN-Chicago news would cover stories of violence in the Windy City. Occasionally, my hometown news would cover the presence of drugs in central Illinois when a sporadic meth lab was busted. One story in particular made headlines: some people from one of the rural towns nearby tried to steal anhydrous ammonia from a tank in a farmer's field.[6] Their goal was to make "crank," a homemade amphetamine that is less pure than crystal meth, but they burned themselves badly in the botched attempt to procure the ammonia and ended up in the hospital. These bungling idiots were a far cry from the slick and organized drug lords of Hollywood dramas. But less clumsy people, otherwise like them, helped keep a number of folks in rural America high.[7] As a result, from the 1990s to the early 2000s, meth use grew twofold in Illinois before plateauing.[8]

Despite the demand, meth production in central and southern Illinois is largely a homemade affair, outside the control of the notorious drug cartels. The optic that features the Brown faces of "violent" Mexicans and, before them, "malevolent" Colombians, which continues to be among the principal images that define the villains of the drug trade, couldn't be further from the truth. Unseen are the contemporary largely White, small-scale Illinois meth producers who mostly barter their goods not to get rich but instead to feed their habits.[9] But even so, as it was during my childhood, now those problems were concentrated in the rural counties, hidden from my community, invisible from our consciousness.

Nevertheless, as a boy I was constantly reminded of the dangers of drugs. As was the experience of many schoolchildren throughout the United States, a local police officer periodically visited my grade school classroom to deliver the Drug Abuse Resistance Education (D.A.R.E.) program.[10] He reminded us to resist those naughty peers who might tempt us with drugs, nicotine, and alcohol. The D.A.R.E. officer told us of the harm those substances would do to our bodies and our minds. He showed us videos that warned of the shadowy dealers who would offer these forbidden fruits destined to turn their users into tragic figures destroyed by addiction. The message was clear and unambiguous: drugs were bad, and to use them was unequivocally stupid. As I grew up I knew some kids who smoked weed, obtained from an older sibling, or took Ritalin, scored from kids with ADHD.[11] The images of disfigured methamphetamine users and emaciated heroin addicts had no tangible touchstones in my lived experience.

Central Illinois was, of course, no drug-free utopia. There were people who used and abused drugs of all types; my father's work was evidence of their existence and their need for support. Yet in my neighborhood, people whose lives had been affected by drugs hardly ever talked about their experiences and the impact drugs had on them or their families. Sometimes, there was gossip: a neighbor's son overdosed on heroin; a local lawyer lost his license for buying cocaine. But the stigma of addiction meant that most people kept those issues as private as possible, since neither help nor empathy was forthcoming. Though drugs existed in small-town America where I lived, the street corner hustle, selling nickel and dime bags to make a buck, evoked in Biggie's "Ten Crack Commandments," Prince Paul's *A Prince among Thieves*, and Clipse's *Hell Hath No Fury*, and the wholesale drug trade, selling kilos to make a million, portrayed by Al Pacino, Johnny Depp, and Denzel Washington in, respectively, *Scarface*, *Blow*, and *American Gangster*, were not part of my youth experience.

In fact, the first time I saw the 'hood was in the spring of 2001. My father was looking for a new job and had interviews far from Springfield. His driver's license had been suspended, and as a newly minted driver I offered to drive him to his interviews. The first was in East St. Louis, Illinois. All that I knew about the place was that it was impoverished and violent.

After I dropped my dad off at the hospital for his interview, I noticed that the needle on my fuel gauge was pointing to empty. So, I started looking for a gas station. When I went to fill up, there was no credit card reader on the pump—a first for me—so I figured I could just pump my gas and then pay the clerk. I put the nozzle into my fuel tank, selected the fuel grade, and squeezed the handle. Nothing happened. Thinking the pump was broken, I pulled the car around the other side and tried again. Once more, nothing happened. I went inside the gas station to ask the clerk, who was sitting behind a plexiglass window, what was wrong and, if the pump was broken, where the closest gas station would be. Package liquor and cigarettes featured prominently behind and around her.

"You ain't from around here, huh baby?" asked the clerk, a bubbly Black woman in her twenties.

"No, I'm from Springfield."

"What brings you here?" she asked me, raising an eyebrow. She seemed surprised that a teenager from upstate was in her gas station.

"My dad has an interview at the hospital, and I brought him down. I just wanted to fill up the tank. I tried to, but the gas wouldn't pump."

"You got to pay first. *Then* you pump your gas. How much do you want to put in?"

"I don't know; I really wanted to fill it up for the drive home. What do you think? Twenty-five?" I had absolutely no idea how much a full tank would cost.

With my twenty-five dollars spent, I checked the fuel gauge again. The tank wasn't full, but there was enough gas to get home.

With the interview over, my dad and the hospital administrator came out to meet me. I asked the administrator about the violence in East St. Louis. The tales of shootings were all that I knew about the place.

"It's gotten a lot better recently. We're down to one shooting victim a week. When I got here a few years ago, we had at least one almost every day."

My dad's second interview was at the state prison in Gary, Indiana, another of the most violent cities in the country. Like East St. Louis, all I knew about

Gary was that it was violent and that Michael Jackson was from there. The trip took us past Chicago. On the way home, my dad fell asleep. I had never driven from Gary to Springfield, and with no map or GPS (this was before the ubiquitous presence of smartphones), I was relying on him for directions. I took a wrong exit and ended up driving into the south side of Chicago. It was run-down, and I knew I was in the wrong place. My dad woke up as I stopped for a red light. He looked around and asked me, somewhat panicked, where we were. I wasn't sure, and I wasn't sure how to go back.

"Why don't I just pull over and ask for directions," I naively suggested as dusk fell.

"No, son. Don't pull over here. It's not safe. Just keep going," my dad said, clearly alarmed at the part of town we were in. We eventually hit a street that my father was familiar with and got back on the road home. Like many people who had never been to these communities, my dad viewed them as unequivocally dangerous.

Thirteen years later during another cold and icy winter, I again found myself in parts of Chicago where my father would have been uncomfortable. This time I meant to be there. Chicago was the final stop of my journey that had begun at the Mexican border. It was a journey that started with a desire to learn about how the drug trade worked within the communities that had been demonized by the media. The danger of drugs and the drug trade were topics that had colored my entire life, as officials panicked and spun a narrative to criminalize drugs and protect the public against this violent and pervasive threat.

Indeed, that narrative predated my lifetime and even my parents' lifetimes. The criminalization of recreational drugs accelerated during the 1930s when Harry Anslinger, the first commissioner of the US Treasury Department's Federal Bureau of Narcotics, reported on the "harms" of marijuana.[12] Subsequently, criminalization of marijuana and certain other mind-altering substances escalated with President Richard Nixon's declaration of the infamous war on drugs in 1971. In 1982 President Ronald Reagan reemphasized the government's commitment to the war on drugs, and with this began the antidrug campaigns that came to define drug use as an unmistakable evil in the public consciousness, with one of the most memorable campaigns being First Lady Nancy Reagan's "Just Say No" initiative.[13] The prohibitionist position adopted and universalized by the war on drugs has been the driving force behind most of the drug rhetoric in the United States. Prohibitionists often characterize the drug trade for the American public in a simple, unnuanced way: drugs and the people who sell and use them are bad.[14]

Since Nixon's declaration of a war on drugs, in the United States alone the federal and state governments have spent a trillion dollars ($1,000,000,000,000) and counting in a fruitless attempt to "win" that "war."[15] All of this expenditure

FIGURE 1. Winter in central Illinois.

Photo by R. V. Gundur.

occurred while opium was being smuggled within Southeast Asia on the Central Intelligence Agency's airline Air America and onto American shores upon military aircraft in the 1970s.[16] Then in the 1980s the US government, notoriously led by Lieutenant Colonel Oliver North, armed the Contra guerrillas in Nicaragua who, in turn, trafficked Colombian cocaine, supplied by Pablo Escobar's infamous Medellín Cartel, to the United States.[17] Moreover, US government support extended to propping up Panamanian dictator Manuel Noriega, who likewise trafficked cocaine from Medellín.[18] These images have been brought to the fore of the public consciousness time and again on television and in the movies.

Less visible are the works of investigative journalists, such as Gary Webb, Charles Bowden, and Bill Conroy, who shed light on the hypocrisy of the government's rhetoric in light of its actions vis-à-vis the war on drugs.[19] Their reporting has been often obscured by the dominant narrative that the mainstream press presents, a narrative in which out-of-control users and evil dealers are juxtaposed against the brave souls who fight against the scourge of drugs to protect the innocent.[20] Policymakers, in turn, use such coverage to justify the domestic policies that have contributed to the burgeoning incarceration rate in the United States, particularly of people of color.[21]

The focus on illegal drugs and the people who buy and sell them is not just domestic, given that the provenance of most illegal drugs is outside the United States. The Colombian bogeymen of the 1980s slowly gave way to Mexican drug trafficking organizations—colloquially known as cartels—in the 1990s.[22] Various media outlets have claimed that Mexican drug trafficking organizations flood the United States with heroin and fentanyl (among a litany of other drugs), leading to the epidemic of opioid abuse that the country has witnessed since the 2010s, while expanding their organizational apparatus into the United States and taking control of the local drug markets, resulting in violence.[23] Although heroin's devastating effects on American communities are not new, the violence associated with its wholesale trade is not and never has been significant in the United States. There is no foreign invasion of large organized criminal groups waging guerrilla war to control US retail drug markets. The public discourse insists on naming bigger-than-life villains, and foreign drug cartels fit the bill perfectly, despite a truth running counter to that narrative.

Perhaps the most notorious drug trafficking organization of the early part of the twenty-first century has been the Sinaloa Federation, the organization once led by Joaquín Archivaldo "El Chapo" Guzmán Loera whose net worth was once reported by *Forbes* to be over US$1 billion.[24] Prior to Guzmán's 2016 arrest and extradition to the United States, law enforcement at several levels primarily blamed the Sinaloa Federation for much of the US drug trade.[25] It was a singular focus despite the presence of several drug trafficking organizations in Mexico, where, starting in 2008, competition resulted in years of heavy bloodshed.[26] Moreover, the Drug Enforcement Administration (DEA) has consistently shown that there are several Mexican drug trafficking organizations supplying the various drug markets in the United States and that the cartels that supply different cities and states have not been the same over time.[27]

The public discourse reflects how conversational entrepreneurs: politicians, talking heads, community leaders, and other public figures, frame problems and propose solutions. In this context, the drug trade is defined by images of violent drug cartels, unauthorized immigrants, gang members, and drug traffickers, who are all agents of the drug trade, working to control the drug markets of various US cities and are destroying innocent American lives. While Mexico has undoubtedly suffered widespread drug-related violence, there is little evidence to indicate that such violence is common in the United States or that Mexican drug trafficking organizations control spaces by using violence to maintain their presence in US drug marketplaces.

Nonetheless, when I started this project in 2012, many American politicians and commentators—particularly those who didn't live near the US-Mexican border—seemed alarmed that some of the safest cities in the United States were only a bridge crossing or a pedestrian checkpoint away from cities plagued by the worst of Mexico's violence. There was fear that a border city such as El Paso, Texas, could fall into chaos, since only a bridge separated it from Juárez, Chihuahua. At the time, Juárez was one of the most violent cities in the world. The drug-related violence, characterized by beheadings and other grisly acts, shocked viewers globally.[28] Policymakers and politicians publicly worried that the narco violence would spill over and that the casualties suffered in Mexico would soon become commonplace in the United States.[29] That never happened.

Those worries were founded in a set of images taken from analysts who all too often looked down at the violence of Mexico from a perch far away. That view from above obscured the everyday existence of the drug trade in America, ignoring the people and the enterprises that underwrite it. What follows is a "history from below," constructed from conversations with people who have participated in, policed, or simply been around the drug trade.[30] This is a history drawn from the voices of people in Ciudad Juárez, El Paso, Phoenix, and Chicago, places that have featured in the optics of the drug trade.

Ciudad Juárez, El Paso's sister city, was a place where drug cartels fought each other for prime point of access to the American market. It was a place where thousands of people had been reported shot, victims of drug trade–related violence. Juárez had one of the highest murder rates in the world at that time. El Paso was on the other side of the border. And although it was a place where large quantities of illicit drugs passed through, El Paso was conspicuously absent of violence.

Phoenix, the largest city in Arizona, had made the news as a place where drug traffickers were supposedly breaking into people's homes, tying them up, and robbing them—a narrative that was later disproven. Nonetheless, Phoenix had also become the epicenter of a political discourse that focused on unauthorized immigrants, associating them with criminality.[31]

And Chicago was Chicago. A place that for the past century has been a social laboratory. A place with a long-standing history of drugs and gangs that sell them. A place where violence is conducted by those gangs to the point that it attracts national attention.

My journey through these communities, separated by hundreds of miles but united by the public scrutiny of their roles in the drug trade, provided me with a better understanding of the drug trade in the United States and the knowledge that informs this book. It was a journey that had certain obstacles. I was not from nor had I ever lived in any of these cities. And I didn't have the time (or the money) to develop the relationships and *confianza*—trust—necessary to conduct the long-term, embedded ethnographic studies that other researchers had under-taken.[32] Nonetheless, I did my best to blend into each community as quickly as possible, to give myself a chance to get to know the communities that had often been demonized by the optics of the drug trade and build relationships with people who knew how the drug trade impacted those communities and could provide an account uncolored by the sensationalism needed to sell a story.

In each location, I visited the low-income neighborhoods that the press and sometimes local authorities identified as problematic; the immigration courts, given the narratives surrounding the criminality of unauthorized immigrants; and the spaces that the people I interviewed felt were important to the drug trade either at that time or historically. I spoke with members of the community, law enforcement, and academics who could help me, an undertaking that produced limited but helpful contacts that gave me access to journalists, members of law enforcement, field-workers, and community leaders who helped me understand the communities and the issues from a straightforward, even-keel, local perspec-tive. But I wanted to go beyond these contacts and meet people who had been involved, so I did what a lot of Millennials who are looking for stuff do: I placed ads on Craigslist.[33]

The ads were bilingual, given that when I first placed them I was in El Paso, where I heard Spanish everywhere I went. The ads solicited people who had been convicted of crimes related to the drug trade. People started calling a few hours after I posted the initial ad. But after a couple of days the calls stopped, so I placed another ad. I did this in each place, and I found people who, at some point in their lives, had been involved with the drug trade. The forty people who re-sponded to the ads included former drug users who had crossed into Juárez to score dope directly from shooting galleries and individuals who identified them-selves as either current or former prison gang members.[34] I was able to substan-tiate people's stories from the gang tattoos they showed me; the track marks on their arms, indicating intravenous drug use; or the intimate knowledge of the operations of gang or prison life that was remarkably consistent, thereby allow-ing me to develop confidence in the narratives that I heard.

But why would anyone want to talk to me? By listening, I gave people an op-portunity to be heard or, as many said, an opportunity to contribute to society in a positive way. Many of my respondents wanted me to *know* what was true and what was not. Much like the people whom anthropologist Philippe Bour-gois encountered in Spanish Harlem, my respondents would remind me, "You know, twenty dollars ain't shit. I'm doing this to help you out, man, because somebody needs to be doing what you're doing."[35]

These vivid conversations transported me to their lived experiences. I didn't need to see my respondents in their "native" environment. I treated the people

I studied who shared their knowledge of the drug trade with me as my equals and received them as my guests. With that approach we were comfortable with each other, and they spoke openly as I listened. One respondent named Breeze, a man in his early fifties, told me that he had been interviewed once back in the 1980s while he was incarcerated by someone interested in prisons and drugs. "That guy was a real jerk. It seemed like his mind was already made up, that prisoners couldn't be fixed. His questions were real pointed. He wasn't at all like you. You just sit and listen to what I have to say. It's real open here."

Various people had told me to never trust gang members. "They exaggerate everything," one gang intelligence officer offered as I attended a capital murder trial of a Barrio Azteca gang member.[36] I heard this advice again from José Rivera, the man who founded the Barrio Azteca prison gang. Nonetheless, I seldom felt as if I was being spun a tall tale, particularly by those who had any time behind them. Mature gang members and former gang members were not boisterous and fanciful. Many respondents pointed out where others might exaggerate their claims, referred to the fantastical portrayals of gang life in popular media, and presented their actions in undramatic, matter-of-fact ways.

Some might suspect that the respondents were engaging in impression management, that they presented their histories in such a way as to make themselves appear favorably, but this notion should be dispelled given the degree of self-reflection that my respondents with criminal histories often expressed in tandem with their accounts of prison life or roles in the drug trade.[37] Moreover, I was a nobody to them. They had little to gain by impressing me; my respondents did not likely believe that I could garner them an audience or further their ambitions, be it a signal to competitors or a story to impress the general public. With me, respondents expressed the evolution of their views and behaviors toward prison and criminal life. And where the drug trade was concerned, respondents contextualized their accounts, pointing out and detailing why fantastic accounts as portrayed in the media were unrealistic or implausible, an experience consistent with sociologist Rebecca Trammell's interviews with former prisoners.[38] Such context helped to create a relative sense of what actors in these communities deemed to be serious.

Furthermore, drawing on the expertise of my transcriptionists, I am confident that I was successful in getting respondents to be comfortable and to be mostly truthful. Two women transcribed my interviews: Lois, who transcribes for police departments throughout the United States, particularly ones in California that deal with gang issues, and Ruby, who worked in a police department following her conviction and incarceration for selling crack cocaine. Lois remarked that she felt that the cops were "as straight with you as they could be within the limits of what they could share, even anonymously."

Lois further remarked that when I was interviewing cops, even the ones who were the most defensive with me at the start of an interview, "I saw what I always see. The cops make you fight for their trust at the beginning. That's normal. As you went on with the interviews, the trust level got deeper. I felt they were honest with you; you know, as a transcriptionist, we hear so many tapes. You definitely hear some recordings where you just feel like the speaker isn't telling the truth." Ruby would often note in the transcripts that the content rang true based on her experiences in the drug world and that most, though not all, of the events described seemed to be within the realm of possibility.

My experiences with the online respondents, coupled with my increasing familiarity with each place over time, quickly gave me the confidence I needed to venture off into the communities I was studying. I learned how to occupy space inconspicuously and engage the denizens of those spaces without making them uncomfortable with me. By managing my role in a new space properly, by appearing as if I belonged, I was able to take advantage of spontaneous opportunities. This "gonzo research" emerged from pure luck and was not systematically cultivated; nevertheless, it depended on my being immersed and engaged in the communities that feature in this book.[39]

These principles proved useful in both formal and informal spaces. For instance, I gained atypical access to members of immigration and criminal courts. During my time in the Southwest, I attended several immigration court hearings and the murder trial of a Barrio Azteca gang member. By showing up and becoming part of the fabric, I could speak to lawyers, judges, court clerks, journalists, and others in the court setting. I also learned from people who were part of my normal routine: my neighbors and members of the community. These spontaneous conversations allowed me to visualize the world that many had told me about. They put faces onto people and facades onto buildings, setting the scenes in the stories that my respondents recounted to me and indicating what was plausible and what was not. Sometimes, these opportunities presented insights that I never would have been able to get had I been looking.

Hanging out at the Tap, an El Paso institution, and striking up a conversation with a guy who was enjoying his last night out before beginning a prison sentence resulted in my learning about the margins of the drug trade and the role of prison gangs in the eastern part of Texas. On another occasion, accepting my participants' invitations to ride along and see what they considered the real side of what I was studying took me around El Paso and helped me understand the paucity of overt gang activity. In Juárez, even within the limits I placed on myself, opportunities presented themselves, and I ended up in shooting galleries and brothels.

Phoenix gave me the chance to participate directly in the lives of former gang members. Initially, my contact was skeptical of my work but was swayed to give me access when I offered something he needed more than money: my skills as a teacher. Next thing I knew, I was teaching basic job skills to people who were associated with gangs. When a student's brother was murdered, helping the family raise money through the "funeral car wash" gained me credibility within the community. Open ears allowed me to learn about different players in the principal gang and to conduct better interviews later. In Chicago, an unexpected invitation by a member of the Violence Interrupters—a team of former gang members who work within the community to stop gang retaliations—to shadow him as he went about his job granted me access to several people who played different roles within their street gang.

This gonzo research exposed me to knowledge that I never imagined I would access and allowed me to meet several marginal and integral people of the drug economy and learn how that economy is socially organized. The lessons were many, but one constant was present: the drug trade that existed in El Paso, Phoenix, and Chicago was part of an unremarkable, everyday existence and had little to do with the salacious portrayals associated with the people and organizations most often held responsible for the presence of illicit drugs in America. There is no archetypical person who sells or traffics drugs, just as there is no archetypical person who buys and uses drugs. There were no illicit corporations controlling the drug trade throughout the United States and dictating the retail trade. For most people involved in the drug trade, it is a small business that functions like many others: people buy and sell products in search of income or pleasure. Most are ordinary folks just trying to make it from one day to the next.

THE SOUTHERN BORDER

A day after leaving Springfield in the red pickup, I found myself cruising down the highway, westbound past Dallas and then through the vast emptiness of Texas. Daylight illuminated the unending plains and oil fields that the highway cut through. It wasn't my first time in the state—I was born there—but I left as an infant and only returned for brief visits. As I drove south and west, I wondered just how I would fit in on the border, but as it turned out, my ethnic ambiguity allowed me to blend in easily.

Usually my accent immediately betrays my American roots, but even before I open my mouth people make assumptions. Rarely does someone come up to me and correctly identify either my Indian or Italian heritage. In places where White people are the majority, I've been identified as all sorts of nationalities. And when I'm identified as Maghrebi, Middle Easterner, or Gypsy, it's often accompanied by an attempt at intimidation. In places where Latino people are the majority population, I've been mistaken for Latino or Brazilian, identities that typically carry positive connotations.

The first time I was suspected of being Latino was when I was a baby. It was September 1985. My dad had gone to Mexico City to sit a multiday exam, and my mom and I followed a few days later.

"Back then, you could cross the border with just a birth certificate if you were a child," my mother explained. For my first international trip, all I had was "a slip of paper; it wasn't even an official birth certificate, but it sufficed." At the airport in Mexico City, for the return flight to Dallas, my mother checked her bags and, inadvertently along with them, that little slip of paper.

"At that time, there was trafficking in babies in Mexico, across the Mexican-American border," my mother noted. "And you being a Brown baby with a White, blue-eyed mother, and the fact that your father and I had entered Mexico separately raised concerns. So, essentially, we began this process of how to board the plane without your documents, without any documentation for you. And several men got involved, different agents in the airport, and they were trying to decide whether you were a Mexican baby we had purchased or whether you were truly my child.

"They talked amongst themselves, and they asked totally ridiculous questions, from my perspective, such as, 'Was I a good Catholic?' Of course, this is all going on in Spanish, and your father, who was holding you the whole time, didn't know what was going on. And they were making different observations, such as you were very comfortable with your father and very comfortable with me. And it just went on, and we were about to miss our flight. But my biggest concern was that they were going to take you and how would we ever find you in this legal maze that would develop. But one of the men prevailed and decided that you must be our child."

Had I been screaming or crying, that story could have ended quite differently. But I was comfortable, and my comfort was contagious. And being comfortable is paramount to establishing and maintaining a good rapport with others.

In most places where I have lived for any significant length of time, I have been a Brown man in a White society, a fact that became clearer and clearer to me throughout my twenties as I dealt with unfriendly looks and random stops by authorities. Such experiences, as aggravating as they were, taught me that when people are not comfortable with me for any reason, they create trouble for me. I have felt the gaze of racial mistrust even in the security of my own middle-class life; I never needed to go to the 'hood to understand that phenomenon personally. So, as an adult I've always tried to make people comfortable because in the odd instance when people cease to be comfortable with me, I quickly find myself in situations that I really don't want to be in.

I didn't know it yet, but in El Paso, for the first time in my life, I would be living in a place where most people in the community would accept me as I am, as somebody who could well be a local and not an anomaly in their world. I wouldn't be alien to the community or represent a feared population. Though I would always feel like an outsider because of my nonnative Spanish accent and my lack of a personal history there, I would be more at home on the border than anywhere else I had ever lived.

With the sun's western descent, the brush and the oil pumps that pepper West Texas's part of the Chihuahuan Desert turn into silhouettes. And after the sun sets, the lights of the few towns in the distance and the flames, burning natural gas, atop beacons that dot the middle of nowhere break the darkness. Immediately before El Paso, civilization returns in the stretch of Interstate 10, which is first adorned by strip clubs and then gives way to several shopping malls. The interstate passes the central business district, where there are a couple of the bridges to Juárez, and then passes through the western part of the city, where the University of Texas at El Paso is located, before continuing on to New Mexico.

The room I first rented was in a house in the historic Sunset Heights neighborhood of El Paso, next to the university. Sunset Heights has been around since before the Mexican Revolution (1910–1920), a violent conflict that began on November 20, 1910, when a call to arms came to overthrow longtime dictator Porfirio Díaz.[1] The violence lasted over a decade. Supposedly, José Doroteo Arango Arámbula, famously known as Pancho Villa, owned and lived in a property in the neighborhood. During the revolution, according to one of the locals whose family went back several generations in the Paso del Norte area, many people fled the violence and settled in Sunset Heights because it was just outside the reach of the conflict.

FIGURE 2.   View into Mexico from Sunset Heights, El Paso, Texas.

Photo by R. V. Gundur.

Today, the neighborhood has a great variety of housing. The streets are haphazard, rarely forming a clean grid. Intersections provide a view of the Franklin Mountains to the north and Mexico to the south. Parts of Sunset Heights still have the massive houses that indicate its affluent past. Yet some streets, such as the one I lived on, are packed with apartment buildings and small single-family dwellings, some of which have been split up into several apartments, each unit housing an entire family. The sidewalks are littered with glass and trash, the yards are home to barking dogs of varying degrees of viciousness, and the streets are filled with children playing in the evenings, a sight unseen in places where more affluent kids are plugged into their videogame systems.

The northeastern part of El Paso, where I later moved, is home to the headquarters of Fort Bliss, a US Army base with a history that dates to the nineteenth century. During the Mexican Revolution, Fort Bliss became a cavalry post and was called upon to secure the border from spillover violence and border violations. Its largest involvement in the Mexican Revolution came in 1916 when General John J. Pershing led the Punitive Expedition in pursuit of Pancho Villa. Pershing failed to capture the elusive Villa but successfully deployed airplanes in the field of combat for the first time in American military history.[2]

Shortly after I arrived in El Paso, my friend Mikey drove me around town so I could get a feel for the city. Riding around, I realized just how large El Paso is. In 2020 it was the twentieth-largest city in the United States by population, home to roughly seven hundred thousand people.[3] The city is also expansive, covering over 255 square miles. To drive from one end of El Paso to the other can take more than half an hour even on the freeway. Looking out the window as we snaked through El Paso's many neighborhoods, I noticed that the houses seemed to be mostly ranch-style, though some two-story residential dwellings could be seen from time to time. The affluent parts of town presented houses that were bigger and fancier. As one person told me, El Paso is a brown city—a reference not only to its majority Hispanic population but also to its earthy tones—which is unsurprising given that the Rio Grande that separates El Paso from Juárez runs dry.[4] Indeed, there is very little by way of grass and greenery particularly in the middle of winter, when I arrived.

To show me Paso del Norte's beauty, Mikey took me up Scenic Drive, past the police training center, to a magnificent view of El Paso and Ciudad Juárez, a high perch along the south spur of the Franklin Mountains. From above, what distinguishes the two cities are the buses and flashing lights. In Juárez, old school buses, painted in Technicolor hues instead of their familiar orange monochrome, roll along the streets looking for passengers. Sometimes the Policía Federal trucks, with their lights flashing on top, hurry from one point to another. Traffic is piled up behind the bridges that cross over to the United States. No such chaos is apparent in El Paso, at least from the view above. From that height one cannot see what happens "underwater," where, as one local gang member described it, crime tends to happen to avoid the gaze of the police.

In El Paso, food and culture are important. As dawn breaks, tamale vendors sell their fare to the early-morning workers who pick up lunch for later that day. At night, restaurants throughout the city's neighborhoods feed hungry patrons with food that stays with them in their dreams. A burgeoning music scene invites the city's youths to come out and enjoy themselves. People meet up for a night out at a bar to chat, switching effortlessly between Spanish and English.

The city's nickname, El Chuco, is derived from the *pachucos*, the youths who brought zoot suits into fashion in the 1940s in both El Paso and Juárez, a style that then spread to Los Angeles.[5] People who have lived in the area for years view El Paso and Juárez as a unified metropolitan area with a shared people, history, and culture. Longtime El Paso residents, regardless of race or ability to speak Spanish, recall how they used to go into Juárez frequently to catch a movie, go out to eat, or go shopping. But that was before the violence started in Juárez in the early 2000s. Despite the lull in violence that occurred at the time I was visiting in 2014, only El Pasoans with strong family ties in Juárez still dared to venture over to visit relatives. Too many innocent people had been killed, and for many the trip was not worth the risk.

The inverse was a little different; Juarenses talked about going into El Paso to buy goods they couldn't get in Mexico or to work at better-paying jobs. Despite the long lines to cross the border into the United States and the hassles of crossing that hadn't existed before, some continued to cross daily to work or study. Most civilians I met lamented the changes brought by the violence and the construction of the towering metal border fence. For instance, my housemate Ricardo, who grew up between Los Angeles, El Paso, and Juárez, noted that the fence was an icon of division that was strange to people such as him who grew up in a unified community with fluid traffic between the cities.

"See, I didn't grow up with that icon," Ricardo said. "To me it was just like— you just crossed the bridge. That's it. Now, it's like so fucking militarized; it's like *Total Recall* kind of shit, really sci-fi, you know.[6] Homeland Security, whatever they want to call it, have to check everyone. But when I was a kid, that wasn't much to worry about."

As someone who didn't grow up in El Paso or Juárez, to me the fence seemed to separate two culturally similar but physically different places. The streets of Juárez are dustier and more crowded than El Paso's. During the day, the streets bustle with some of Juárez's one and a half million people rushing to their next destination, passing through downtown where cigarette and taco vendors hawk their goods.[7] Beyond downtown, Juárez features neighborhoods of all types: slums for the dirt-poor, functional dwellings for blue-collar factory workers, modest single-family homes for the middle class, and compounds with opulent mansions for the wealthy.

Compared to El Paso, the houses in Juárez are closer together and smaller than their American counterparts, often side by side almost like row houses. In prime areas of the city, ostentatious mansions sit on expansive grounds. Large and small, houses in Juárez are equipped with metal bars that separate every pane of glass from the outside world. Though these bars wouldn't stop a well-placed bullet, they might deter a person from breaching the threshold they protect. As I walked down the Juárez roads, I noticed the endless twisting barbed wire that adorned fences and some rooftops even on modest homes as well as the broken glass that was mixed into the concrete that crowned the security walls. In these Juarense neighborhoods, I wasn't always sure whether I was looking at a prison, a military compound, or somebody's home.

The border fence is also a symbol of separation between two sets of prospects: those that are available in Mexico and those that are available in the United States. Juárez, in its own right, is a city of opportunity. Yes, it is a transshipment point for drugs, and some people engage in the drug trade to make a buck. But many more people are attracted to Juárez for the opportunities provided by the maquiladoras, the factories that line the border, which produce or assemble products destined to be shipped north to the United States and beyond. The border is a place of significant economic importance for Mexico, with Juárez being the largest city in that economic ecosystem. The jobs in Juárez afford workers, especially women working in maquiladoras, wages that are higher than what is frequently available elsewhere in Mexico, allowing internal migrants to earn enough to support their families far away.[8]

For many, however, Juárez is not a destination but rather a transit point. For those people, the journey north represents an opportunity to escape poverty and sometimes violence. Success is dependent only on a desire to work hard. But getting into and staying in the United States is not a straightforward task; access to visa applications is highly unequal.[9] Those who struggle to get visas innovate to chase their dreams, putting themselves on one of several paths that may bring them in contact with the immigration system. Some seek asylum. Some cross clandestinely. Others overstay their visas. Most who end up before an immigration judge have no criminal history except for immigration-related offenses. Yet the American press, as it often continues to do, talked constantly about "criminal aliens" who were, among other things, facilitating the drug trade. On the airwaves, it sounded as if drug dealers and traffickers who were going through the immigration courts were a dime a dozen. If that were true, I thought I should be able to see them there and start learning about the people of the drug trade immediately.

IMMIGRATION COURT

Alien threat narratives—stories that promote a fear of the outsider—are nothing new; politicians, in an effort to develop political capital, push their favored policies, or create an electoral boost, have long been telling their constituents to fear the unknown. In the United States, many immigrant populations, from the Irish and the Italians to the Mexicans and the Syrians, at some point have been cast by political actors as what sociologist Stan Cohen called "folk devils."[1] These narratives are eerily similar regardless of the object of their ire, and they ebb and flow according to political and practical convenience. When times are plentiful and labor is in short supply, policymakers seek to augment the workforce with cheap labor. When times are difficult and labor outpaces demand, immigrants morph into "Schrödinger's immigrants"—who simultaneously steal jobs and lounge about unemployed, collecting welfare and leeching off society—or into deadly killers: vectors of disease, gangbangers, and assassins of ruthless drug cartels.[2] It's a narrative that conveniently links immigrant threats and the pernicious presence of organized crime.[3]

For the better part of the twentieth century and into the twenty-first, US alien threat narratives have disproportionately targeted Latinos, casting Latin American migrants, particularly from Mexico and Central America, as "'illegals' . . . who take jobs from natives, depress wages, burden taxpayers, increase crime rates, and pose a threat to national unity and regional identity."[4] These decades-long narratives have fostered a sense of resentment and underwritten a slew of anti-immigrant projects ranging from the 1980s and 1990s English-only education movement, which sought to restrict Spanish-speaking immigrants' access to education, to the emergence of the "crimmigration" movement in the late 1990s, which sought to impose criminal penalties on unauthorized immigrants and brand them as "criminal aliens" rather than mere civil offenders.[5] Undoubtedly, the political use of these criminalizing terms and narratives has fostered among some Americans a sense of sustained hostility toward unauthorized immigrants and turned them into convenient political scapegoats.[6]

With the September 11, 2001, attack of the World Trade Center in New York, US territorial security became a central political issue, widely used to justify reallocation of spending and diminution of liberty, while the prevailing narratives turned a widening gaze of suspicion upon immigrants in general. The threat discourse that emerged from 9/11 presented all unauthorized immigrants as a danger to both the domestic economy and the security of the United States.[7] Accordingly, the actual failure to secure the borders against the Al-Qaeda attackers (and later against the purported imminent threat from ISIS attackers) led to domestic anxieties that a genuine personal, physical security threat from immigration existed.

Yet in that climate of more general anti-immigrant sentiment, the Latino scapegoats of previous decades were not forgotten. As narco violence in Mexico increased and the US government prioritized border security, elements of the news media, political pundits, and politicians broadly attributed to the Latino migrant population the worst kind of criminals—kidnappers, drug dealers, rapists, murderers, and terrorists, echoing the contemporary anxiety that foreigners were coming to the United States to commit unspeakable acts of violence.[8] The discourse created "policy and practice [that] equate[d] illicit crossings with national-security risks and the ever-present threat of terrorism."[9]

Given that backdrop, I decided that I needed a real-world sample of the people immigrating to the United States, one that I could compare or contrast with the politically constructed scapegoat. To extend a metaphor, I needed to crack open Schrödinger's box and find out what sort of immigrant was really inside. And that box turned out to be the Department of Justice's (DoJ) Executive Office for Immigration Review, what most people refer to as "immigration court." These courts are administrative in nature: the judges don't have the same power or discretion as judges in criminal courts but do process the removals—that is, the deportations—of thousands of immigrants every year. I hoped to cast a line and see whether I could fish out some of the violent, dangerous drug trafficking types that, according to the political press and rhetoric, were supposedly threatening America's security. Being in the American Southwest and next to the border, I was in as good a place as any to see who the Border Patrol detained. Throughout my trip I expanded my observations to include various immigration courts to see if they were any different, hoping that such observations would reveal whether those peddling the Latino threat narrative were oracles or Chicken Littles.[10]

I called in advance before my first visit to the El Paso Immigration Court. The woman on the phone told me that I could come in and observe the immigration proceedings; I would have no problem. I would need identification to enter. I couldn't record anything, but I could take handwritten notes. I would be excluded from some cases, but generally speaking, I could attend so long as court was in session. Expecting no barriers to observation, that afternoon I drove to "The Camp," the detainee immigration court located at the migrant detention center in the eastern part of El Paso. As I pulled in, the armed private security guards checking vehicles as they entered the compound were completely taken off guard by my request to observe: "No one told us you were coming."

"I called ahead and was told I could just come down," I responded.

"Who did you talk to?"

"I don't know. I called the public number on the DoJ website, and the woman on the other end said I could come whenever I wanted to."

The guards told me that I should always take down a name and contact number to get authorization. I pulled aside to let the other cars pass through as the guards called in my authorization. As I waited, a torrent of vehicles arrived bearing Department of Homeland Security license plates. All around me was a sea of hundreds of border patrol vehicles. The single-story beige buildings of the complex were islands protruding from an ocean of white and green.

The guards were friendly enough. They chatted with me about the size of the county, the different roles that law enforcement bodies in the borderlands play, and the other detention facilities nearby.

"You should check out the facility up at Otero County—up along US 54," one of the guards said. "It has US Marshalls and ICE [Immigration and Customs Enforcement] together. It's totally different from here."

The guard's comment was something I hadn't considered earlier, but he was right: there would certainly be some variance in cases depending on venue; the contexts that landed immigrants in various immigration courts varied throughout the country, so observing different courts would be necessary to get a bigger picture. Eventually the guards' phone rang with the permission for me to observe the immigration proceedings, and I thanked them for their kindness and went to the Executive Office of Immigration building where the courtroom was located.

The actions of the guards at the El Paso detention center were incongruent both with the legal code outlining public access to hearings and with the relevant section in the *Immigration Court Practice Manual*.[11] To be fair, any individual hearing can be blocked if the judge chooses; it is the judge's statutory right, but by default hearings are open to observation. The guards' actions closed the proceedings by default and thus undermined the exercise of discretion by the judges, who, without exception, welcomed me to observe their courts. The judges' attitudes echoed the sentiment expressed at the time by the Administrative Office of the US Courts: "By conducting their judicial work in public view, judges enhance public confidence in the courts, and they allow citizens to learn firsthand how our judicial system works."[12]

Nevertheless, security—at least in immigration courts and the detention centers associated with them—is subcontracted, and those subcontractors seem to be able to make their own rules and restrictions, irrespective of the policies published on the DoJ's website. Such was the case in El Paso, and no matter how well-intentioned, the guards' actions certainly added opacity to a process intended to be transparent.

Sometimes the guards' actions not only obscured the judicial process but also infringed on the rights of the respondents. On that same day, an attorney from California representing a respondent detained in El Paso was denied both entry and guidance as to where to register for his court appearance. When the judge, William Lee Abbott, heard about the denial, he turned to the bailiff, who had been working there for several years, and said, "Can you tell those knuckleheads the rule? We need to make this process as transparent as possible. If someone wants to observe, they can do that. They can come right in. It's supposed to be open to the public."

Similar events recurred at other immigration courts particularly in detained settings, where detainees are held as they await their hearings and security tends to be heavier, and even at the same court when different guards were on duty.[13] There were always house rules to be obeyed, which meant widely variable access and transparency inconsistent with published guidelines.

Once I was inside the courts, various administrators provided different explanations of the rules.[14] Some would tell me that I could observe what I wanted to observe so long as the judge didn't close the hearing. Others would say that access would depend on whether the respondents or, if they had representation, their counsel would allow it. It was clear to me that outside visitors were unusual: I was often asked who I was and what I was doing or was mistaken for an attorney, a law student, or, sometimes in the nondetained dockets—which heard cases of people who were living in the community on bond—as a respondent. I seldom saw other observers. Once there was a journalist, and once there was a group of law students. Sometimes it wasn't rules or procedures impeding access: in Phoenix, the courtrooms were so full of respondents waiting for their cases to be heard at the start of the day that at times it was hard for an observer to find a seat or even enter the courtroom. But generally, the barriers I faced involved private security and their inconsistent understanding and acceptance of the rules that allowed observers into the courtroom.

Once past security, I observed immigration hearings that usually occurred in small rectangular rooms. The courtrooms were weirdly analogous to casinos: windowless places where some strike it lucky but most do not. The large clock on the wall offers a sense of time under unforgiving florescent lighting. Behind the judge's bench there is wood paneling, a Department of Justice seal, and an American flag. The other walls are all white and bare unless the judge chooses to decorate the room. The tasks are repetitive. Sometimes a case comes along that deviates from the monotony, but many of the cases follow a similar pattern, dictated by the realities of immigration.

The simple fact is that many people who come to the United States do so for similar reasons and in similar ways. Moreover, once they enter the immigration system, they discover that they have a very limited set of legal alternatives to choose from. Consequently, the immigration cases they appear in do not vary significantly. By and large, immigrants who come to the United States without a visa in hand that authorizes entry make the journey to escape poverty, violence, or both. Generally, migrants without visas arrive at the border without a clear path to long-term residency or citizenship. Some go to the points of entry along the border and ask for asylum. Others attempt to cross the border without authorization.

Some make this crossing successfully; others are caught and turned back—sent back across the border immediately—or detained and processed through immigration court. Those unauthorized migrants who avoid capture are generally subject to apprehension and detention at a later date. These are broad strokes, and many exceptions apply; however, these broad strokes dictate what types of cases dominate immigration proceedings.

Immigration proceedings involve respondents who want to immigrate and the state that argues for their removal. There are two types of respondents: detainees and nondetainees. Detainees are people detained after being apprehended during an unauthorized entry, usually by Customs and Border Protection (CBP) agents, or at some point after an unauthorized entry, perhaps by Immigration and Customs Enforcement or even by local authorities who have discovered their unauthorized status. Nondetainees are people who live in the community on bond but can be placed in detained proceedings if they are caught behaving badly. Detainees and nondetainees alike seek to avail themselves of the limited legal avenues to long-term residency within their immigration proceedings. By and large, detainees and nondetainees appear on separate dockets.

This state of affairs creates a common flow chart–like timeline (see figure 3) for immigrants facing an immigration case. First, migrants make contact with the immigration system. If they are apprehended and released or are not detained, they likely will be served with a notice to appear in immigration court.

Simplified Removal Proceedings

1 **Contact with the Department of Homeland Security (DHS)**

Non-citizen presents at the border or is detained with unlawful status or following a criminal conviction

2 **Process**

DHS initiates action (removal/deportation proceedings)

↓

Notice to appear in court (immigration violation charging document)

↓

Master calendar hearing

↓

Individual merits hearing

3 **Immigration judge decision**

Relief (from removal)

Termination of proceedings (immigration charges dismissed)

Removal/deportation

Voluntary departure

4 **Outcome**

Respondents remain in the US lawfully

Respondents are forced to leave the US, if they stay, they do so unlawfully

5 **Appeals**

Appeal may be made by DHS, respondent, or both to the Board of Immigration Appeals. Respondents can further appeal to Federal Court.

UNITED STATES COURT OF APPEALS

FIGURE 3. An overview of the removal proceedings process.

Source: Department of Justice, Executive Office for Immigration Review. Diagram by Florence Lourme.

If they are detained, a court date will be set. Thus, they become respondents in an immigration case. The first appearance a respondent typically makes before a judge is called a master calendar hearing. At the master calendar hearing, the charges, if any, against the respondent, such as unauthorized entry or overstaying a visa, are made, and the respondent has the opportunity to begin an application for relief from removal, such as asylum; to ask for a continuance, perhaps to obtain more time to find an attorney; or, if eligible, to agree to voluntary removal. If the respondent's case requires additional process, a later individual hearing, often on the merits of a case for relief from removal, will be scheduled. Common among such individual hearings are "credible fear" hearings in which the respondent must present evidence that he or she has a well-founded fear of persecution due to being a member of a certain race, political group, or other category. These are particularized proceedings, focusing on the merits of a single case. By contrast, master calendar hearings are often conducted with multiple respondents present, each being called forth one at a time.

An immigration judge makes life-changing and sometimes life-shattering decisions at such hearings. As one immigration judge put it, they are "paid the big bucks to make hard decisions that many others would not want to make." It seems that at times no matter what the judges do, they cannot please anyone—not the public, the respondents, the politicians, and sometimes not even themselves—particularly when they must reject people whom they would prefer not to reject. That being said, the same judge underscored that immigration judges are not pressured to deport people: "We're not. We—especially those of us appointed since 2008—just try to follow the rules. . . . When people fail to get relief, it's usually because their reason doesn't qualify them for it."[15] The judge's comment was likely accurate at the time when he said it, during the Barack Obama administration, but those pressures changed under the Donald Trump administration, which implemented case quotas in order to seek faster deportations, thereby showing how the executive branch can change the reality for migrants unilaterally.[16]

The average court scene varies little in the detention setting. A bailiff ushers in the detained respondents for their hearing. The respondents are not handcuffed or otherwise restrained. Sometimes the detainees are separated by gender; other times they are separated by whether or not they have legal representation. They are almost always unified by their silent, still demeanor. They sit together in their colored, single-tone jumpsuits, and these colors tell a story in and of themselves. In the El Paso court, navy blue uniforms indicate that the respondents have no association with crime. People who are detained at a point of entry are invariably dressed in this color, as are those who have never been accused or convicted of a criminal offense in the United States. Orange indicates that the individuals so dressed may have charges pending against them or may have been convicted of a minor crime. Red, which isn't terribly common in the detention center, designates a person who has been convicted of a serious crime, such as a Class A misdemeanor (the most serious misdemeanor) or any felony conviction that might result in removability. Other courts use similar coding schemes but with different colors. This color coding made it easy for me to identify one constant: relatively few people were dressed as serious offenders.

The scene in Judge Abbott's El Paso detention center courtroom was typical of what I would see time and again during the months I spent observing master calendar hearings on detained dockets in both Texas and Arizona. First, the judge summarized the process for the respondents. Addressing the respondents directly, he went through their rights. He was explicit and clear, leaving ample time for the translator to do her work efficiently. He told the respondents that they had a right to have an attorney but at no cost to the government. Judge Abbott went on to tell them that if they did not have an attorney, they should have received a list of attorneys who might help them pro bono; nonetheless, there were no guarantees that they could find one. That first day, nearly all of the detainees were having their first hearing. The judge told them that they had the right to reschedule their hearing in order to have time to find an attorney or prepare their cases. They also had the right to testify (or not) on their own behalf. And finally, they had the right to appeal to the Board of Immigration Appeals if they were dissatisfied with the judge's decision.

His lips hidden behind a Texas-sized moustache, Judge Abbott spoke calmly and evenly. He remained so throughout the entire afternoon, regardless of the outcomes of the cases or how many times he was asked to repeat or rephrase what he had just said. Abbott had a warmth to his voice and seemed to express empathy for each person whose case he decided, always leaving them with the phrase "Be careful and good luck to you." As the afternoon went on, he kept to schedule but did not seem hurried. He smiled and occasionally joked. At times, for the benefit of the attorneys present, he would comment on the legal limitations that bound his decisions and, for the detainee whose case he was considering, he would present the legal reasoning behind his decision.

Not all the judges had Abbott's warmth or his patience or engaged in explaining the legal reasoning behind his decisions, but all judges appeared committed to being clear and to upholding the law. A critic would rightly point out that appearances aren't everything. Some justices serving were appointed prior to 2008, when immigration justices were generally appointed without public competition for the position, often based on political ties, and without regard to past immigration law experience.[17] Certainly liberal and conservative appointees' decisions differed, but their actions were constrained by the law, which is "broad and rigid" in its determination of whether a respondent is removable and has as its only penalty removal.[18]

Nonetheless, due process was important to all the judges I spoke to. Despite their massive workloads and, in El Paso, their internal goals of case completion, there were several instances at master calendar hearings when a judge refused to proceed with a case because the court did not have an interpreter in the native tongue of a respondent who spoke neither English nor Spanish. Some, but not all, of the judges seemed aware that many indigenous people who come from Latin America do not speak Spanish natively. Occasionally, the interpreters would identify issues in communication and flag these issues to the judges. Overall, a majority of the immigration judges I observed seemed to have the respondents' best interests in mind, given the limits of the law. What Judge Guadalupe Gonzalez told me was echoed by other judges who talked to me and was supported by what I often saw in court. "It is the responsibility of the court to ensure due process. We need to explain to the respondents the nature of the proceeding. We need to be proactive in protecting their rights. But once someone is represented by an attorney, the attorney takes all of that responsibility. The attorney is obligated by the attorney-client privilege to protect their client's rights."

I asked, "Does it happen that an attorney fails to protect their client's rights? If so, what do you do?" Another judge had commented on the low quality of many of the immigration attorneys, saying bluntly that many were lousy.

"I've had situations when attorneys are not as well versed in the law as they should be. Sometimes I, or even the government counsel, will tell the respondent's counsel about the relief available. It's the attorney's ethical duty to know the law required to represent someone fully. Sometimes not everyone is adequately versed in the law necessary to represent their clients successfully," Judge Gonzalez explained. "I try to maintain an atmosphere in court where respondents are comfortable. They need to feel like they can tell their story fully."

Yet despite such precautions, it seemed that anywhere from a fifth to a third of the respondents in the detained setting—typically middle-aged Mexican men in the proceedings I observed—simply asked to be deported, even when they had legal alternatives available. One such alternative, voluntary departure, allows respondents who meet certain criteria to be quickly repatriated while avoiding some of the legal repercussions of involuntary removal. Other alternatives, such as asylum, claims under the Convention Against Torture (CAT), and withholding of removal, entitle respondents to stay in the United States but require them to provide evidence of an imminent threat of violence or persecution in their native countries, often in a credible fear hearing or a similar proceeding.

The claim that I heard from some of the immigration attorneys that such respondents just wanted to leave the camp didn't always make much sense when Mexicans requested to be deported from El Paso: voluntary departure, in such cases, would be neither more expensive nor more involved than deportation. Even in the face of such requests, judges would exhaust their protocol to ensure a respondent made the request for removal knowingly and with complete understanding of its future consequences before issuing a deportation order. Occasionally, the judge's repeated questioning of the respondent to determine whether he or she wanted to be removed would reveal that the respondent had failed to understand his or her situation. In such situations, the judge would rule for a continuation of the case rather than issue a deportation order.

One judge, reflecting on respondents' requests for deportation, said that "we go wrong if we pretend we know what's better for them. Our job is to tell the respondents what their options are and what the consequences of their choices are. Who are we to tell them to sit in detention a while longer if they don't want to because *we* think it is in their best interest?" More importantly, when every single day a high percentage of respondents ask to be repatriated immediately, judges find it difficult to believe that individuals face imminent threats upon returning.

However, risk is individualized, and that specific, individualized risk is a task for respondents to demonstrate. It's a difficult task, even in the best of circumstances, and the Trump administration's changes to immigration courts made it even more so.[19] Nonetheless, the end of the 2010s saw a dramatic increase in the rates of families and unaccompanied children attempting to apply for asylum. Respondents requested humanitarian protection as they recounted experiences of "torture, gang recruitment, abusive spouses, extortionists and crooked police."[20]

I watched these respondents seeking asylum face the difficulty of drawing an intelligible narrative from the morass of violence, corruption, and political instability they were attempting to leave behind. For example, in San Antonio, where many of the respondents were Salvadoran, attorneys often claimed that the MS-13 and Barrio 18 gangs, implacable historical enemies, were somehow in cahoots with one another and with the leftist government of El Salvador to boot and that all three were threatening the respondent. The underlying truth was more complicated: rival Salvadoran political parties, the Farabundo Martí National Liberation Front and the Nationalist Republican Alliance, courted both gangs in an effort to persuade them to reduce gang violence, hoping to build political capital.[21] But for an inexpert attorney, often without the resources to bring in expert testimony, it was clearly difficult to construct a coherent, persuasive narrative—one that would also fulfill the strict requirements of statutory bases for relief from removal—on the uneven foundation of the political and social turmoil of the respondents' home countries. As the attorneys struggled to explain a complicated political reality in a foreign country and to clarify the connections between government action and the respondents' persecution, the judges struggled to make informed and fair decisions, often expressing doubt about the attorneys' claims.

Though members of gangs and drug trafficking organizations seldom appeared in person during immigration proceedings, they were often discussed and clearly impacted many respondents' lives. Nearly all of the Latin Americans I observed who attempted to lodge an asylum claim cited threats from drug trafficking organizations or gangs, respectively, depending on whether they were from Mexico or Central America. (I never saw a respondent from South America.) Despite the frequency of these tales and their importance in lodging a successful asylum claim, respondents were often vague when describing to the court the threats they had experienced.

Unfortunately for many respondents, establishing grounds for relief from removal usually requires specificity. For example, to seek asylum, one must demonstrate a well-founded fear of persecution on the grounds of race, religion, nationality, political opinion, or membership in a particular social group. But such a showing requires specific knowledge of the persecutors and their motivations, which can be difficult for respondents to know. Even if that information is known, it can be difficult to articulate in front of an immigration judge. In one such instance, a detainee, a man named Herberto, had attempted to establish that he and his family faced a credible physical threat if he were to return to Mexico. He had been interviewed by an asylum agent, who had rejected his claim, so now he appealed for a hearing in front of Judge Sunita Mahtabfar, who was to reexamine that decision and determine whether Herberto would be subject to deportation.

At the opening of the hearing, Judge Mahtabfar, as a courtesy, allowed Herberto's attorney to make a brief statement before the facts of the case were reviewed. In addition, Herberto had an opportunity to respond on his own behalf. The attorney simply said that given the recent social history in Mexico, he hoped the court would side with his client. Then the judge went through the claimed facts.

One day out of the blue, some six masked men came to Herberto's home and asked him to work for them. He refused, so these masked men began to beat him. After about ten minutes, they fled when someone outside the house called out that the military was approaching. After the incident Herberto called the local police, who said they would respond in about two hours. Rather than wait, he immediately packed up what he could and fled with his family. Battered and bruised, he drove to the border, where he requested entry. In the days after his departure, neighbors told his family members that men had come and looted his house, taking everything away. Through it all, Herberto did not know who the men were; their masks had concealed their identities.

Herberto's claim was vague, and he did not choose to go into further detail. The judge asked him several times to elaborate on who he thought the men were, but Herberto did not offer any additional information. Like the asylum officer, the judge ruled against the man's claim. Herberto had failed to meet the burden of proof necessary to establish that he faced a credible threat should he be deported back to Mexico.

One judge would later tell me that the law does not allow an immigration judge to read into the facts. The description Herberto gave is consistent with the actions of criminal actors affiliated in some way with drug trafficking organizations in Mexico.[22] His account of the police's time frame is consistent with reports that the police lollygag to give assassins time to kill. None of these details was presented to the court.

The decision resulted in the man moving a step closer toward deportation. After the ruling was handed down, Herberto's attorney chatted with the judge briefly. He asked the judge if the court views that kind of violence as a credible threat, with all that's been going on in Mexico.

"No" was the judge's response. The respondent was vague; there weren't enough details to establish Herberto's case.

The attorney alleged to the judge that his client, the respondent, gave a lot more detail when speaking privately with him. Important details had not come out in court. "There was no opportunity for me to cross-examine him, so that stuff remained outside of the court."

The judge explained that recruitment is not a valid basis upon which to establish a credible threat, and Herberto had failed to show that there was anything else going on beyond an attempt to recruit him into a criminal group. Moreover, Herberto had a criminal record and had been deported several times before, which made it difficult to find relief for him.

This episode had several hallmarks I noticed in cases of Mexicans seeking asylum. First, there was a claim that some organized criminal group, usually one of the better-known drug trafficking organizations or a group assumed to be associated with such organizations, was attempting to harm them. Second, the details of the threats or past events were vague, with no positive identification or clear motives disclosed. Sometimes the respondents would blame the state as being complicit. Third, should the claim be evaluated in full, there was some element in the case that would result in an unsuccessful asylum claim, given the strict requirements for asylum.

Immigration attorney and University of Texas academic Denise Gilman explained to me why vagueness is so common in Latin American asylum claims. "These are very truncated procedures. I really, truly have seen a lot of cases that look really bad at the beginning, and then, once we spend hours and hours and hours with people, you know, going through their stories, by the end the judges—when we present [the cases]—the judge is like, 'You guys take all the easy cases.' I'm like, 'No, that's not the way it works.' People don't know what's relevant. People don't know what kind of specificity [is needed to be successful in their claim]. People don't know what kind of documents the judges are expecting to get. They don't necessarily narrate in Western-style chronological order. So, that's one thing.

"And then . . . sometimes those credible fear interviews take place pretty quickly, so people are still out of it. They don't really understand what's going on. They may have suffered trauma. So, they're not really in a very good position to be able to tell their story."

The need to effectively tell the story is important. "Harm alone is insufficient to grant asylum" Judge Abbott told me after a woman had presented her case pro se (i.e., without an attorney representing her) and attempted to request asylum on the basis that she was being extorted by the Caballeros de Templar, a notoriously violent criminal organization in her home state of Michoacán. According to Abbott the case law is clear, and the accepted reasons to substantiate asylum claims are narrow and specific. For instance, the law considers victimization from "common crime" insufficient grounds for granting asylum. Also, respondents have a responsibility to move within their home countries to avoid their problems before they can seek asylum in the United States.[23] Such nuances of asylum law are not known to most respondents, who therefore cannot know the importance of providing any detail that might fall into a favorable rule or exception.

The clear majority of the immigration court proceedings that involved people accused of a crime, on both the detained and nondetained dockets, involved respondents who had committed only immigration-related crimes or misdemeanors. Many had been picked up shortly after unauthorized crossing attempts but long enough after crossing to warrant an appearance before an immigration judge rather than a mere turnback.[24] Others had been detained after a DUI arrest or some petty offense. On any given day on the nondetained docket, I saw nothing to suggest that the respondents were criminally involved on any regular basis or with any illicit enterprise, which made sense since they had made bond. Even on the detained docket, on any given day I would see one or maybe two respondents out of twenty-five dressed in a jumpsuit that indicated that they had committed a removable offense. When the judges drilled down into the respondents' histories, they learned that some had committed violent criminal offenses, but few seemed to be players in the drug trade or some other criminal enterprise.

Once I was observing a "reason to believe drug trafficker" hearing with a respondent who had been brought in from the Otero County Processing Center.[25] He needed to have his hearing in person since the communications system that links into the El Paso court was down. During a break in the proceedings, the Otero guards who had accompanied the respondent to El Paso struck up a conversation with me, asking me about my research. They told me that a few months earlier they had Sandra Ávila Beltrán, known as the Reina del Pacífico, and another high-ranking member of the Sinaloa Federation in their custody.[26] Ávila Beltrán and her associate had been quickly and quietly deported back to Mexico.

"The Reina was a woman in her late forties, early fifties," one of the guards recounted.[27] "She looked good for her age, but after lots of plastic surgery. I guess with that kind of money [from drug trafficking] you can buy your looks. People said that we shouldn't say anything to her. With just a phone call, she might be able to get us killed."

The guards' apprehensions were hyperbole; the killing of any federal agent would start a firestorm that drug trafficking organizations would prefer to avoid, considering the cost to business. Nonetheless, the guards are not supposed to know who they are transporting. Moreover, they receive no additional training to deal with sensitive persons, as everyone in custody is to be treated equally.

"We were told to drive them and not ask questions. We handed them over to the Mexican authorities. After that, they are the Mexican government's business. We never did find out what happened to them."

The guards managed to learn that the woman they had been guarding was Ávila Beltrán because colleagues in the detention facility whispered that she had been there. Later her presence was confirmed in the press.[28] She was deported after serving time as part of a plea deal, avoiding a cocaine trafficking conspiracy charge; upon her return to Mexico, she was arrested, tried, and convicted on money laundering charges.[29]

"Her quick departure," the guard opined, "is typical of big players in the drug game. They never stick around. Their cases are always quick. They ask for deportation and get the order over with. That way, there is less of a chance for the FBI or whoever else to interrogate them or even watch them. Maybe in Mexico they have enough reach that their money can buy their freedom or at least a comfortable amount of space in order to live without too many restrictions."

During my time in immigration court, I never saw any big shots of the criminal underworld appear—at least based on the court proceedings I witnessed and the information that was disclosed within them. It would appear that the big players were targets of the Federal Bureau of Investigation (FBI) and the DEA and that their only involvement in the immigration process occurred when they were ordered removed after serving their sentences; I doubt that any big players got picked up by Border Patrol and circumvented the scrutiny of law enforcement by asking to be deported.

Minor players and their activities were infrequent orders of business in immigration court: out of the hundreds of cases that I observed, only one case revealed significant details regarding the drug trade. The respondent, a former legal permanent resident, had been caught with six kilos of meth in his vehicle as he tried to cross into the United States from Mexico. Such a quantity didn't make him a Chapo Guzmán or anything close to a drug kingpin. The respondent could have been a typical cross-border drug trafficker or wholesale supplier who on the grand scale of things would be a small- or medium-level player depending on the frequency with which he actually trafficked drugs, or he could have merely been a decoy used to draw attention from a bigger load being trafficked behind him.

More commonly, respondents convicted of a felony would be simply ordered deported. It is possible that some of these men were large-scale traffickers, but if they were they weren't big enough to warrant press coverage like Ávila Beltrán. Most accepted deportation, for they had few realistic options to remain in the United States, and the details of their crimes were not reviewed. Only once did I see someone in a nondetained setting be accused of drug trafficking. The respondent in question, a middle-aged Mexican man, was trying to apply for political asylum. The Department of Homeland Security attorney indicated that the respondent was not eligible for asylum or withholding of removal because there was reason to believe he was a drug trafficker. All the man could lodge was a CAT claim, which is often even harder to obtain than asylum and withholding of removal, considering the need to demonstrate that the persecution one might experience falls under the government's definition of torture.[30]

It seemed curious that the Mexican man whom the government alleged was a drug trafficker had been granted bond and that the bond had not been revoked despite such a finding. The man's attorney contested the idea that the man had committed a "particularly serious crime" that would bar him from asylum. The attorney wanted time to prepare a defense of that claim. The judge decided to ask for briefs from both parties in which they would present their cases in writing; he would decide on the merits of the case in a future hearing. The respondent walked out of the courtroom still on bond.

One judge explained to me that to constitute a valid CAT claim, "torture has to be *by* the government." The number of involved government agents it takes to bind the whole government to complicity in the torture is a point of current debate. Part of the consideration judges make in these circumstances involves the steps that a government takes to crack down on such abuses. Nationals who come from countries where a good faith effort is being made to tackle such abuses typically do not qualify for protection under the CAT. Respondents must show a 50.1 percent risk that they will be tortured *by the government* of the country to which they will be deported. This provision doesn't cover criminal groups. However, a 2009 decision by the 8th Circuit Court of Appeals, *Ramirez-Peyro v. Holder*, suggests that even one government actor can bind the government if that person acts under the "color of law," that is, if that actor uses official government resources to commit an act of torture even when the state does not condone or sanction the act.[31] But as the judge noted, many immigration attorneys fail to present such cases and the necessary arguments in court.

By removing respondents with felony records, immigration courts have played a role in the emergence of American-style street and prison gangs in Mexico and Central America. Modesto, a born-again Christian and a former Sureño gang member who was in Los Angeles in the 1980s, recounted how the notorious Barrio 18 and MS-13 gangs were born in the streets of LA. As these gang members, following felony convictions, were deported back to El Salvador, they regrouped and started to gangbang again.[32] With no rehabilitation and no realistic opportunities for licit employment, it was natural for these men to return to the only life they had known since adolescence: being a cog in illicit enterprise. And since they were familiar with the structure of gangs, they re-created them in the streets of El Salvador and Guatemala.[33]

Gangs with foreign membership soon became transnational, with their members maintaining ties in both the deporting and receiving countries. Special Agent Diana Apodaca, the public information officer for the DEA in El Paso, told me that this was the case with the Mexicles, the gang associated with the Sinaloa Federation in Juárez, who "upon their release and deportation . . . continued their criminal activities in Mexico, eventually forming an alliance with the Artistas Asesinos, aka Doble A's and Doblados, in Ciudad Juárez."

My housemate Ricardo, who spent part of his childhood growing up in Los Angeles, El Paso, and Juárez, likewise saw the effects of these deportations during his boyhood after some gang members were deported back to Mexico from Texas.

"Once the Ortiz brothers got out of jail, the US authorities tossed them into Juárez," Ricardo recalled. "And six months later, all I see all over the Juárez streets is Ortiz gang, Ortiz gang, and I was like fuck—Juárez is going to start getting all gangster like I saw it in LA. And sure enough, the cartel blew up, and I saw a lot of little gangsters running around."

However, when I did see alleged gang affiliations come up in immigration court, it seemed that Department of Homeland Security attorneys mischaracterized respondents as being involved with drug trafficking or gangs. Héctor, a man in his late twenties who had been brought from Otero, fit this bill. He was facing drug possession charges, but his attorney said that those charges would be dropped. As the case unfolded, the judge in the case, Stephen Ruhle, seemed skeptical that Héctor was a drug trafficker, telling the government attorney that "the respondent has only two arrests and no convictions. He's been here for seventeen years. If he was involved with bad things, it's unlikely that he would be in the US for such a long time without getting into any trouble." After interviewing the respondent and evaluating the facts of the case, the judge eventually ruled that there was no reason to believe that Héctor was a drug trafficker and granted him bond so he could attend to his criminal court case.

Another case in front of Judge Ruhle involved a respondent named Loreto dressed in an orange jumpsuit, indicating that he had some conviction that could subject him to removal. Judge Ruhle started the hearing, as he commonly did with respondents dressed in orange or red, by asking what Loreto's criminal history was. The government attorney responded by saying that Loreto had a gang affiliation, not just any gang but Mara Salvatrucha 13, often known as MS-13, a name that conjures a ruthless reputation nationally.[34] But the attorney's claim didn't make sense. MS-13 has a nonexistent presence in the El Paso area, and its members aren't players in the drug trade along the border, despite the gang being formally designated as a "transnational criminal organization."[35] Why would Loreto be a player in a gang that had no presence in the area in which he lived? Judge Ruhle looked at Loreto's file and saw that he had been granted bond previously. In fact, Ruhle was the judge who had granted it. The judge turned to the government attorney and explained that if he had granted bond previously, he did not believe Loreto was criminally involved with anything. Loreto spoke in his own defense, repudiating the government attorney's claim. Yes, he had a juvenile record. As a boy, he had associated with his brother, who is in fact a gang member. But Loreto said that he never got seriously involved. Plus, he had a family and a job now, not to mention the fact that he hadn't heard from his brother for more than three years.

Loreto had his bond revoked for disorderly conduct and possession of marijuana. The judge told him that most people don't get bond initially and (almost) nobody gets it twice. Loreto was scheduled for a hearing at the end of the month, so the judge decided that it would be in Loreto's best interest for him to remain in the detention center so he could have his case heard and decided upon quickly. Had Loreto been bonded out, it would have taken about two and a half years for his case to be heard on the nondetainee docket.

Loreto accepted Judge Ruhle's decision without protest. The judge advised Loreto to have his wife and anybody else show up to support his character; however, the judge warned the respondent that he shouldn't "bring them if they don't have status—they won't leave. You have two possible conclusions that have very different connotations. If the judge believes you, then it will be positive, and if she doesn't, then it won't. The more people you have to support your character the better; it carries more weight in court than just you or your wife."

Loreto thanked the judge for his advice and left the courtroom. After he left, the judge lightly scolded the attorney: "I didn't believe he was a gang member; your case was 'the apple doesn't fall far from the tree.' I'm not buying that argument."

Sporadically, there would be a respondent who had been convicted of a drug crime or some other felony barring relief from removal. Yet as these crimes were discussed in the court, it became clear that these people were at best low-level distributors, individuals who may have been involved in a gang but weren't on the corner pushing dope on the street. One such case in Judge Gonzalez's El Paso court featured a young Mexican man, likely brought to the United States as a baby or a child, who spoke perfect English with a midwestern accent. He had been convicted on two separate occasions, once for credit card fraud and a second time for possession of marijuana with intent to distribute. The judge examined his records and told him outright that he had no relief available because he had been convicted of two separate crimes, one an aggravated felony. The man accepted his deportation but asked about his prospects for return.

"If you accept my order as final, you will receive a lifetime ban to return," Judge Gonzalez told him. Resigned to his fate, the young man accepted the judge's decision. The bailiff led him back to the detention center to await imminent deportation.

And that trickle of cases featuring small-time crimes characterized what was visible to an immigration court observer. From my observations, it seems that the sky is not falling; it's just a handful of acorns, or bad apples if it were. The overwhelming majority of respondents are ordinary people with no felony criminal history. Most with criminal histories appeared to have convictions related to being unauthorized in the United States, crimmigrants who in past decades would have been mere civil offenders.[36] Only a sliver of respondents had any criminal record that could be related to the drug trade. The broad brush of violent criminality that colored—and continues to color—the perception of immigrants within parts of the public discourse is inaccurate, conflating status offenders, whose crimes are approximately as legally significant as speeding, with drug traffickers and money launderers.

Yet it was clear that some of the professionals working for the government, including some of the judges, felt that of the individuals who came before them, a high proportion must be criminals. This belief manifested in the charged and accusatory language of some of the government counsel, even absent supporting evidence. While most of the Department of Homeland Security attorneys I observed approached their job impassively, presenting facts in a straightforward, neutral manner, there was a subset of government attorneys whose choice of words indicated a clear disdain for the respondents and whose aggression seemed better suited to a criminal court rather than a civil one. Their aggressive pursuit of victory was sometimes admonished by the judges, though usually only in the most over-the-top situations. For instance, I once saw a judge remind a government attorney, who was scarlet with rage, that if the respondent was not answering her questions to her satisfaction, she needed to rephrase the queries. The incident was noteworthy because the simultaneous translation was failing to convey the full response from Spanish to English, piling confusion onto aggression and frustration.

At the same time, the judges swore that criminal actors were common. Given that I failed to see suspected criminals frequently in immigration courts, I made an effort during the breaks to chat with the judges; some of them were happy to answer a few questions, but many were not. One judge at the Eloy, Arizona, facility assured me that "we see drug traffickers all the time." Shortly before this conversation, a respondent, a woman who had been convicted of possessing drugs with the intent to sell, appeared in court. What seemed unclear to me was the extent to which large-scale traffickers were going through the court and what "all the time" meant. It is possible that anyone who had been convicted with possession with the intent to distribute is considered a trafficker. But from the off-the-record conversations I had with judges, some of them indicated that they routinely see respondents convicted for large trafficking loads. Yet my efforts to see such cases came up largely empty.

It is also possible that cases involving true drug traffickers stick out in the judges' minds because they deviate from the mountains of routine cases the judges also see. Moreover, those who are convicted of serious crimes have little relief available to them, outside a CAT claim, and many are likely deported directly from prison or shortly after serving their time, with the details of their cases never coming into play as their hearings unfold. Even if the majority of these deportees were drug traffickers, they represent a small proportion of people ordered to be removed to Mexico (or anywhere else). In addition, it certainly does not mean that those individuals were part of a drug trafficking organization, nor does it indicate that those individuals were anything like the notorious villains whose names grace the headlines. When illegal drugs did come up, the amounts were in the tens of pounds of marijuana or a few kilos of hard drugs. Even if there were a respondent in every group who was a drug trafficker, the number overall would be around 5 percent.

However, I failed to see anywhere near that number, even using the loosest definitions for what a trafficker could be, even in Arizona at the Eloy Immigration Court, which processes a higher proportion of criminal respondents than an average detained-docket immigration court. The mundane, standard proceedings clearly indicated that any talk of drug traffickers needed to be kept in perspective. Relative to the population, the number of people involved in serious and organized crimes is small.[37] That a similar pattern should emerge in immigration court proceedings is unsurprising. Nonetheless, at this point in the Obama administration, deportation orders were at an all-time high, with the rhetoric justifying the rate by arguing that most of the deportations were removing criminal aliens.[38]

Yet, serious criminals do not seem to represent a large proportion of the cases where criminal history came up. Based on what I saw, the clear majority of such respondents were in the system purely for immigration offenses, with a minority arrested for misdemeanor criminal offenses and an even smaller number convicted for felony criminal offenses. That being said, the number of cases is so large that the immigration system is overwhelmed, so much so that the cases cannot be dealt with in a timely manner, especially when cases need to be referred to the nondetained docket.

In terms of the drug trade, the most common stories I heard were recounted by those seeking relief from removal as they described the threats and violence they encountered in their home countries; they were escaping the criminals who were part of the cartels that had captured the imagination of the media and the public. Unfortunately for most, they were victims of "common criminality" and ineligible for asylum.

"Roughly 2 percent of those who were seeking asylum from Mexico in 2012 received it. So, that tells you that just not here in El Paso, but across the nation, how folks from Mexico who are seeking asylum are viewed," explained Katie Hudak, the outgoing director of Las Americas Immigrant Advocacy Center. "There have been things in the US Congress—you know—some people feel that some Mexicans are coming in asking for asylum but are really seeking some other form of immigration relief, so [some politicians may believe that] folks are playing the system. We hear things like 'Mexico's a democratic country, so why would anybody be seeking asylum from Mexico?' 'They're one of our biggest trading partners; they're trying to do something about the violence that is occurring in Mexico.'"

The perception that Hudak described characterizes the position of many politicians and remains a significant hurdle for Mexican asylum seekers. One judge, speaking to me anonymously, explained that immigration judges must rely on State Department reports to assess the quality of governance of a foreign state, and as such it is unlikely that any given judge will consider Mexico as being anything other than a democratic nation attempting to maintain the rule of law and fulfill its sovereign responsibilities. Given the relatively recent democratization of Mexico, marked by the end of decades-long run of Partido Revolucionario Institucional (PRI) rule in 2000, I asked the judge how the court determines "democratic countries," since in 2014 when we were speaking, it could be claimed that Iraq and Afghanistan were democratic countries, despite continued unrest.[39] The judge explained that the State Department seems to recognize shortcomings in the Iraqi and Afghan democracies, since they don't observe the due process expected in the United States.

Despite the stated apolitical nature of immigration courts, their use of State Department reports to inform their decisions betrays indirect political bias underwritten by the foreign policy interests of the US government. For example, the US State Department reports a high standard of due process in Mexico's judicial system, an assertion that has been challenged by several high-profile trials. One such trial involved Israel Arzate Meléndez, a man who was falsely accused in the Villas de Salvárcar case in which a group of young Juarenses with no gang or drug affiliation whatsoever was gunned downed by masked men, reportedly associated with the Barrio Azteca gang, on January 31, 2010.[40] Arzate was severely beaten by his arresting officers and presumed guilty until proven innocent. Though Arzate was eventually exonerated, his case is one of many examples of due process being ignored in Mexico's judicial system.

Despite the shortcomings of the State Department reports, it would be impractical to require judges to make independent assessments of every asylum seeker's country of origin. And it would be difficult for respondents to afford expert witnesses, who would have to be hired at their expense. Therefore, within the immigration courts, the State Department reports become a standard of information. Some judges do make interpretations, defining individuals as members of a social group when they are threatened by criminal actors, so that the individuals may qualify for asylum, but the judges' ability to do so is governed by precedents established in their respective Circuit courts.

While the ins and outs of the drug trade certainly weren't going to come to the fore in immigration court, observing the arguments set forth in the courts, a juxtaposition between how Mexico is painted rhetorically and how it is treated politically emerged. Rhetorically, Mexico is painted as a place where pernicious drug trafficking organizations are, at best, beyond the control of the government or, at worst, in cahoots with the government; moreover, over the past ten years or more, drug trafficking organizations have been responsible for the deaths of thousands upon thousands of individuals. However, politically, America's relationship with Mexico is still important for trade. The US Department of State "warns U.S. citizens about the risk of traveling to certain places in Mexico due to threats to safety and security posed by organized criminal groups in the country," noting that "U.S. citizens have been the victims of violent crimes, such as kidnapping, carjacking, and robbery by organized criminal groups in various Mexican states."[41] Nevertheless, the US government evidently still maintains that its Mexican counterpart behaves within the rule of law and upholds its responsibilities, capturing the culprits behind drug violence, prosecuting them effectively, and keeping them under lock and key, which is ironic considering the US government's insistence on extraditing and prosecuting Mexican drug kingpins, some of whom have never set foot on American soil.

THE SANTA FE STREET BRIDGE

The face of Joaquín Archivaldo "El Chapo" Guzmán Loera, perhaps the most storied drug lord since Pablo Escobar, stared bleakly out through the windows of the newspaper stands as I walked down the streets of El Paso to the Santa Fe Street Bridge, one of several bridges that connect the city to Juárez. Guzmán had been recently arrested in a joint operation of US and Mexican forces. Famous for his short stature and chronicled in song and folklore, Guzmán was the moral leader of the Sinaloa Federation, often considered the most powerful and among the most violent of the drug trafficking conglomerates operating in the Western Hemisphere.

The timing of Guzmán's capture was conspicuous. President Barak Obama had gone to Toluca, Mexico, to meet with Mexican president Enrique Peña Nieto and Canadian prime minister Stephen Harper in a North American summit. Earlier in the week, *Time* magazine had announced that its February 24, 2014, international issue would feature Peña Nieto as "Savior of Mexico," specifically claiming that his reforms had "changed the narrative in his narco-stained nation."[1] The *Time* cover was widely spoofed by Mexican critics, who opined on social media that Peña Nieto had no part in any reduction in drug-related violence. They argued that *autodefensas* (vigilante groups) had been contesting drug trafficking organizations and their violence by killing drug dealers and corrupt cops, freeing kidnapping victims, and running the drug trafficking organizations out of town; these actions, the critics maintained, deserved more praise than anybody in government.[2]

At the time, the news of Guzmán's capture fueled intense speculation regarding possible consequences. In the United States, armchair pundits suggested that violence associated with the drug trade would increase in Mexico and possibly spill over into the United States, while the flow of heroin and cocaine into the United States would decrease. By contrast, those of us who had been keeping a close eye on drug trafficking organizations were quick to note that Guzmán's capture needed to be kept in perspective: El Chapo had not been the operational leader of his cartel for some years. Operational control of the Sinaloa Federation had long since been passed to Ismael "El Mayo" Zambada García.[3] The fall of Guzmán thus was unlikely to trigger the territorial wars and infighting that followed prior upheavals. Despite El Chapo's capture, leadership of the Sinaloa Federation would remain stable. So, what seemed likely—and indeed what happened—was a small decrease in the perception of insecurity in Mexico and an increase in the popularity of Peña Nieto. Little additional empirically observable change occurred that could be rightfully attributed to Guzmán's arrest.

Still, newspapers on both sides of the border floated questions: What legal consequences would El Chapo face? Would he be tried in Mexico? Would the United States demand extradition? If so, would Mexico allow it? Would there be infighting or power grabs, despite El Mayo's established leadership in the Sinaloa Federation? Would the accusations that the governments of the United States and Mexico were propping up the Sinaloa Federation fade?[4] Or would the groans of graft and corruption increase? Would any political boost in favor of Peña Nieto subside, as quickly as his American counterpart's, following the killing of Osama bin Laden? Oh, and would Guzmán escape again?

After the initial buzz washed out of the news cycle, some of their questions began to receive answers. El Chapo escaped from prison on July 11, 2015, in dramatic fashion, disappearing through a hole in his prison shower connected to a mile-long tunnel that proved to be his ticket back to freedom.[5] He remained free until January 8, 2016, when he was arrested near his Sinaloa base. Just over a year later in January 2017, he was extradited to the United States to face charges of conspiracy to import cocaine. In 2019 in a federal courtroom in New York, Guzmán was convicted and sentenced to life in prison. He was remanded to the United States Penitentiary, Administrative Maximum Facility in Florence, Colorado, where some of the most notorious inmates in America, including former Gangster Disciple leader Larry Hoover, Black P. Stones founder Jeff Fort, and former Gulf Cartel boss Osiel Cárdenas Guillén, have been incarcerated. Throughout this period of escape and recapture, the drug trade continued unimpeded, and the media continued to spin sensational reports about the Sinaloa Federation's prowess.

In 2009, just five years before my visit, Juárez was rated the most violent city not in an active warzone in the world due in large part to the conflict between the Sinaloa and Juárez Cartels.⁶ The city of Juárez then held this dubious accolade for three years running. During the height of the violence, various sources attempted to keep track of the death toll, and though their numbers differed, the message was the same: too many people were dying in Juárez. Undeniably, the drug trade was to blame for thousands of lives lost annually.⁷ At the same time, across the border El Paso was ranked one of the safest cities of its size in the United States.⁸

By 2014, Juárez seemed to be on the upswing. Violence persisted, but its frequency declined. I was invited out one night by Esmeralda, an academic at the Universidad Autónoma de Ciudad Juárez. She was leading a research project examining the reclamation of the city's social spaces. Around 8:00 p.m., I walked across the Santa Fe Street Bridge and jumped into the back of her car.

"Two years ago, I would never be out driving at this time," Esmeralda explained. "During the height of the violence from 2008 until 2011 or 2012, nobody went out at night unless they really had to or had some specific business. We had here in Juárez something that hadn't really existed in the town's history— people going home after work and spending time with their families."

"How did people decide it was safe to go out again?" I asked.

"There wasn't a single thing that caused people to go out again all of a sudden. The government tried to change perception. Government officials would go on the news and say that there was less violence. Officials would parade statistics on the news saying there were fewer killings. And as people started to go out little by little, more people followed suit. And now, as you'll see, families will be out on a Friday night once again."

We went to several venues that evening to witness that phenomenon. We started the night in an Applebee's, where middle-class Mexicans can afford to eat. The prices were comparable to those of an El Paso Applebee's. However, considering that the average monthly wage in Mexico was at the time just US$200, the prices seemed downright exorbitant. Nonetheless, the restaurant was reasonably well attended by groups of friends and couples enjoying a Friday night.

The next stop was a fun fair where we met up with some of Esmeralda's students. It was already dark when we arrived. Parking was a struggle. At the fair, live musicians played oldies as families lined up to buy pizza, hotdogs, churros, and *elotes*. Fathers took their sons and daughters on the carousel while the older kids piled into the bumper cars. On the adjacent baseball field, teams of kids were playing in the oldest continuing youth league in the city.

We left to visit a row of clubs in the Zona Pronaf. Bouncers with thick necks and wrinkled faces sat at each club door, asking for IDs. At the first club, some of the men in our group were frisked before we were allowed to enter and enjoy the promise of good music and atmosphere that was floating out the door. But this

FIGURE 4.   Clubs in the Zona Pronaf, Ciudad Juárez, Chihuahua.

Photo by R. V. Gundur.

club, like the parking lots across the street, was empty, so we left. The next three places told the same story, albeit sans frisking—empty seats stagnated in darkness. Americana decorated the walls in almost every location—a poster of a Rolling Stone magazine cover, a Confederate flag—as tunes played over thumping sound systems to empty dance floors. With nothing to see, we shared a liter bottle of beer and headed to another nearby area. We walked past more empty parking lots and darkened nightclubs that had not yet reopened or found new owners after businesses collapsed when the violence started keeping people home. Many of the local establishments that were open seemed empty as we peered through the windows, wondering how they could even make enough to keep the dim lights on.

Eventually we came to a place where parking was indeed scarce. The San Martín Cantina Tradicional is, according to Esmeralda, "the most Mexican place in Juárez." Not a table was empty. Two bands alternated, playing mostly classics. Few patrons bothered with conversation. Most folks were busy eating, drinking, or singing along to the music.

Slowly but surely the city was rebuilding its image. Refurbishment of the main drag, Avenida Juárez, was under way. Near the Santa Fe Street Bridge, the old repurposed school buses, with tinted windows and hand-painted signs indicating their routes, waited for passengers. Street vendors and cabbies hawked their services along the road leading up to the bridge. Sometimes if they realized someone was American, they offered drugs or access to paid sex.

As one exits the Santa Fe Street Bridge on the Juárez side, a couple of blocks up on the right side of the street is the Kentucky Club, the birthplace of the margarita. The iconic bar serves as a reminder of the history of smuggling and bootlegging in the Paso del Norte area extending at least back to Prohibition.[9] With the right kind of guide, know-how, or cojones and luck, you can still satisfy all kinds of prohibited vices.

While shadowing Facundo, a harm reduction worker who supplied clean needles to drug users to help curb the spread of hepatitis and AIDS, I was taken to a shooting gallery, a spot where you can buy heroin and use it. When we arrived, a gaunt man who went by the apt name of Flaquito invited us in. He darted out to buy his fix and left us with his cousin, who was rooted to a nearby couch. The cousin's abuse of *agua celeste*, a type of shoe glue commonly huffed by poor Juarenses to get high, had left him with permanent brain damage.

After a few minutes, Flaquito returned with two tiny packages wrapped in tinfoil. Each was about the size of a pinkie nail, perhaps a quarter inch in diameter. He sat down on the dilapidated couch to begin the preparation process and placed a crushed beer can upside down on his knee.

"The heroin users are called *tecatos* because they used crushed beer cans to prep their fix, and Tecate is probably the most commonly consumed beer, at least up here," Facundo later explained.

Flaquito carefully unwrapped his two tiny packages and put the contents in the well of the can. The little balls of heroin were a dark brown color, almost black. From the package Facundo gave him, Flaquito took out a syringe. He removed the plunger and used it as a pestle to crush the tiny balls of *chiba* in the little well that the upside-down beer can offered. After about a minute, he took a package of distilled water and added it to the well. After another three to five minutes of mashing, the heroin was finally fully incorporated into the water, and the solution could be drawn with a needle. Flaquito took two syringes and drew half of the liquid into each, handing one to his brother, who disappeared into the other room.

In one fluid motion, Flaquito suddenly stood up, lifted up his baggy shirt, and dropped his pants, exposing his pubic area. He then plunged the needle into his skin in the area adjacent to his pubic hair. On one side of his groin, there was significant keloidal scarring from this practice. The scar ran vertically about three inches. He initially tried the other side of his body but could not hit a vein. His plunger would not budge. He withdrew the syringe and plunged it into the bottom of his scar tissue, sticking himself twice before finding a vein successfully on the third attempt. He pushed the plunger in with a look of gusto on his face. He let the depressed syringe remain in his body for a few moments before removing it and throwing it casually away in the trash. He then tended to the bleeding wound he had just created for himself.

"That's it," Flaquito told me, with a grin on his face fitting of Gollum.

"That will hold you over for the rest of today?" I asked him.

"No. I'll try to inject myself seven, eight times if I can. I'll do whatever it takes to get that."

"How much did each of those little *curas* cost you?"

"Each one is sixty pesos." That's about five dollars, a bit short of the daily minimum wage in Mexico.[10]

"So, you spend about forty bucks a day? How do you get the money?"

"I do what I need to get it."

Flaquito didn't elaborate. Undoubtedly, few licit options were available to him. Had he been a woman, Flaquito would likely have turned to prostitution to raise funds, which is quasi legal and visible in red-light districts and in brothels in several Mexican border cities.[11] It took me a while to recognize the sex workers; many looked like nothing more than ordinary women, going about ordinary business, but made their vocation known by loitering in certain doorways. Several of the women working the streets of Juárez were on the needle and had track marks visible on their arms. The most desperate were there throughout the day, some with pregnant bellies and sunken faces on full display, trying to pick up johns.

One night at the Kentucky Club I met a retired American trucker named Sam. I struck up a conversation with him, and we started talking about women of the night and the toll their heavy drug use appeared to exact. Before I knew it, Sam and I were heading to a brothel where he said there were pretty girls. As we walked to the establishment, Sam gave me some background. The place in question, strictly speaking, was a bar. It used to be located somewhere else but was shut down for some reason. It was "definitely controlled" by criminal interests—though exactly who, Sam wasn't sure. And it was a great place to go to pick up a young, attractive woman for a price, of course, if your heart so desired and your wallet allowed.

The place had a doorman, but unlike the Pronaf bouncers, he didn't ask for ID or check us over. We walked in and found a medium-sized crowd. The music was loud but not so that we couldn't talk over it. The middle of the room featured a stripper pole where the women who plied their trade there would take turns dancing. However, there was no nudity; at most we would see a bikini underneath a woman's outfit. All the women there were dressed in the same way—in skintight dresses that emphasized their figures without showing too much skin.

The bar extended over one entire wall. Sitting there were all kinds of men— Black, White, Latino—and judging by their clean-shaven faces and tightly cropped haircuts, some were probably American soldiers from Fort Bliss. Speaking to each of them was a young, attractive woman.

Sam and I walked up to an unoccupied corner of the bar, ordered a beer, and chitchatted for a while.

"So, how much would someone expect to spend on a girl here?" I asked.

"If you went straight up to them, it would be about eighty bucks. The girl would get about twenty and pay the rest to the crime people. If you come in with a 'tour guide,' that is, someone who has brought you here for a fee, then you'll likely get a discount and pay somewhere between forty and sixty bucks. The girl's cut would be about the same, but here it's reasonably good money. What did I tell you, though? They're pretty good-looking, right?"

They were indeed. Unlike the sex workers on the street, these women did not have track marks on their arms from heroin abuse. Their faces weren't covered in pancake makeup to hide damaged skin. An outsider could be forgiven for confusing them with any number of young women on a university campus in College Town, USA. They looked just like the type of girl that a shy undergraduate might spend an evening working up the nerve to talk to. But here even wallflowers got prompt attention. The girls approached and chatted with anyone and everyone who walked through the door.

After about two sips of beer, a young woman approached Sam and me to see if we were interested.

"I've seen you around here before," she said to Sam.

"Yes. I come in from time to time. I'm just showing my friend 'Ted' around. Do you want a drink?"

She nodded yes, and Sam bought her a beer. It was a little twenty-milliliter bottle that the bartender promptly served. Sam went on to ask the escort about herself. Her name was Tiffany, a gringa name chosen by her father, who was apparently Canadian. She was only twenty years old and already had a child. As her attention was called elsewhere, Sam pointed out one of her colleagues behind me.

"See that girl over there? She's an E-ticket. Do you know what an E-ticket is?"

"No idea."

"Well, when I was a kid and I went to Disneyland, you'd get a book of tickets: A, B, C all the way down to E. And guess what? You wanted that E-ticket because that got you on all the *best* rides. So, my friend, check her out. A *bona fide* E-ticket!"

"She looks awfully young. Is she as young as the other girl?"

"Well, the E-ticket is thirty-one. I've known her for ten years. The others are probably in their twenties."

Tiffany returned to us and chatted with Sam a bit longer. She was polite and charismatic, but Sam told her that he might be interested some other day. He finished his beer, and we got up to head back to Avenida Juárez for me to cross the bridge and for Sam to hit up another bar.

As we walked the three or four blocks back to the main street, a police patrol crept up the street. We could tell without looking not because of their sirens but because of the flashing lights that reflected on the buildings in front of us.

"Keep walking at a good pace," said Sam.

As we walked, the patrol approached us.

"Whatever you do, don't look at them. If you look at them, they'll definitely stop us and throw us up against the wall."

The patrol passed us and turned left on the block ahead.

"Slow down. Let's make sure they get ahead of us," Sam said. "It's a one-way street, so they ain't going to backtrack. Oh, okay—they're around the corner. Let's get on with it."

We turned down Avenida Juárez and walked toward the bridge, pulling up shy of the bar Sam was about to enter.

"I'm going to go to the Yankee Bar. I'll tell you something, given your interests and all. You see that bar up a bit further?"

"Yeah." Sam was indicating the Chess Discotheque.

"Well, let me just say that I used to go there, but I won't anymore. Let me just say there is a lot of action here. All you have to do is look at what's gone down in the different clubs. Over there, the Chess Club, there were all kinds of murders. When that shit goes down, normally the clubs get shut down. Did the Chess? Fuck no!

"One last piece of advice. If you see some guys riding their bikes around you and they've got walkie-talkies, watch out, 'cause they are going to fuck you up. Any case, that's all I've got to say. Good luck, kid."

And with that Sam walked into the Yankee. I walked across the bridge, got into the red pickup, and drove home.

Five years later I walked along the same streets that I had navigated with Sam, and I barely recognized them. The repairs that had been under way in 2014 were finally completed, but the renovations alone did not explain the transformation. The city was crowded, with lots of people out for the evening packing in bars and restaurants, some of them recently opened. Salsa, new to the scene, played along with the norteño that had always been a fixture. The streets were better lit than ever before. Hotels that, for longer than anyone could remember, had served guests who stayed only a few hours now had guests who were staying for days and weeks. Also new was an encampment of people living in tents right at the entrance to the pedestrian bridge to El Paso, huddling together as winter descended.

The city's transformation was partly driven by the Trump administration's "Asylum Protection Protocols" policy, which forced asylum seekers to remain in Mexico as they waited for their hearings.[12] Those who could afford hotels to wait for their asylum hearings stayed in them. Most of the hotel residents were Cubans whose destination had shifted from the shores of southern Florida to the borders of southern Texas. Many of those in hotels were fortunate to have the financial support of US-based Cuban communities. With American dollars to spend and an infectious, almost relentless, positivity, the Cuban residents invested in their temporary homes, sprucing up hotels and opening Cuban restaurants, redefining business as usual, and forcing Juárez's downtown to reopen. On the other hand, the people in the tents were typically impoverished migrants from Central America or elsewhere in Mexico who were just waiting, often with no clear understanding of how the asylum process would unfold. They were scared about crossing the border, worried their families would be ripped apart.

There was no evidence that more criminal actors were trying to get into the United States than before. Migration was down, but that wasn't the point of the Trump administration's immigration policy. Cruelty was. The threat narrative continued to stream from the administration's mouthpieces, who sought and found political capital therein. It was a narrative that inspired a gunman to drive over nine hours from Allen, Texas, an affluent suburb of Dallas, to El Paso, likely past the same flares and pumpjacks I had seen, to shoot up a Wal-Mart on August 3, 2019, where he killed twenty-three people and injured twenty-three more, knocking El Paso off the safest cities ranking for the first time in over a decade.

BUSINESS AS USUAL

As fabled as he once was, Joaquín "El Chapo" Guzmán Loera was not the first of his kind; he followed a long line of drug barons, including the original Jefe de Jefes, Miguel Ángel Félix Gallardo, the leader of the Guadalajara Cartel and the man who schooled Guzmán in the drug trade. Although Guzmán willingly engaged in and perhaps raised the stakes in the violent games that came to characterize the drug trade in the 2000s, "business as usual" was established long before he became a top-level player.[1] Guzmán was just one of several leaders and figureheads of violent, semiautonomous illicit enterprises that emerged from historical processes that evolved over nearly a century. The fables woven around Guzmán and other drug lords before and since evince an almost hypnotic human fascination with power, violence, and independence; however, this fascination often obscures the truth.

Understanding the roles that men such as Guzmán play in the drug trafficking business, separating those roles from the press frenzy surrounding them, and comprehending how those roles play out within the tangled web of illicit enterprise in the Paso del Norte region require a historical inquiry that starts with the years just after the Mexican Revolution, a war fought in part within view of the Sunset Heights neighborhood in which I stayed. What I learned from that inquiry was that the historical forces that shaped contemporary drug trafficking organizations could be reduced to a few simple constants: the people and organizations' need for security and protection, the power and independence that grow from being able to provide that security and protection, and the powerlessness that results from the inability to do so.

The recent history of protection in Mexico is bound with the country's struggle with liberal democracy. The Mexican Revolution led to the promulgation of Mexico's present constitution. Written in 1917, it is a revision of the 1857 constitution, which attempted to establish Mexico as a liberal democratic state. The 1917 Mexican Constitution offered liberal democratic rights that were not afforded under the regime of Porfirio Díaz, the military dictator who governed Mexico for thirty of the thirty-four years (1876–1910) preceding the Mexican Revolution.[2] However, the 1917 constitution alone was not sufficient to achieve the ideals it codified.

While the revolution was ushered in along with a stated desire for democratic elections, any true sense of democracy in Mexico proved elusive for the better part of the next eighty years.[3] From 1929, when the party that later became the Partido Revolucionario Institucional won its first presidential election, up to the beginning of regime liberalization in the 1980s, Mexico was largely under the PRI's sole control. During this period, which came to be known as the Priísmo, the PRI established and maintained itself as the largest electoral force in the country.[4] The PRI left no space for legitimate democratic elections or popular control of government; it acted as an autocracy—not so blatant an autocracy as Diaz's but an autocracy all the same.

Despite its stranglehold on Mexican politics, the PRI did not publicly advertise its dominance. Whereas other autocratic regimes in Latin America justified illiberal actions by modifying their legal codes without the consent of their citizens or by relying on coercive tactics to generate apparent popular support, the PRI, in contrast, sought to maintain a relatively high degree of popular legitimacy by adopting policies that created the appearance that it was responding to the demands of Mexico's citizens and operating in their best interests.[5] Perhaps most importantly, the PRI government portrayed itself as providing economic and physical security to its citizens, thus fulfilling its most critical responsibilities to the public.[6]

Not satisfied with its initial dominance, the PRI then sought to entrench itself by consolidating control. It did so by asserting a monopoly over the protection market. Protection, at its core, is the capacity to set rules and enforce them; it is the chief parameter delimiting the boundaries of one's behavior. The PRI correctly understood this dynamic as being the keystone to extended political dominance, whereby the PRI, in both licit and illicit contexts, determined protected behaviors that were acceptable and unprotected behaviors that were not.

Colloquially, the idea of "protection rackets," where protection is imposed on customers regardless of their demand for it, evokes images of predatory regulation of behavior: a thick-necked mob lackey shaking down a store owner for an envelope full of cash because "it would be a shame to see such a nice place burn down."[7] However, protection rackets are not necessarily criminal products; they are simply mechanisms that provide protection to a given range of actors. Protection rackets are common in licit settings, international and domestic politics, and individual, familial, and group activities.[8]

Protection sets limits on how people may be impeded or controlled by others. Store owners who pay the mob for illicit protection are buying the right to operate a shop without the risk of being coerced out of the market, violently and unjustly, by one of the mob's competitors. In a licit protection scheme, fire sales are actions allowed by the state, but arson is not. Accordingly, when criminal groups show up and successfully impose protection on an unwilling customer, they successfully undermine the licit protection arrangement. Similarly, illicit businesspersons, such as drug dealers, may be extorted by a criminal gang as they attempt to ply their trade. Drug dealers, after all, are mortal beings. However, in the case of the drug dealer, the extorting gang may also provide protection from police or even be the police themselves. Thus, impositions of protection can both contest and undermine the licit protection norms that the state otherwise imposes and allow criminal actors a space for engaging in unlawful behavior.[9] Everyone needs protection, and the ability to provide or impose it comes with power and control.

A state's power and control are predicated on its sovereignty, which is defined as how a government organizes and effectively exercises its public authority.[10] In principle, sovereignty means that "states are subject to no external earthly authority."[11] States—and states alone—are supposed to decide which behaviors are protected and which are not. Although this principle is sometimes violated when a more powerful state (or group of states) exerts its will on another, states strive to maintain it. Accordingly, a fundamental sovereign duty of the state is to protect its people from criminal impositions of protection. This underpins the arrangements we generally expect in liberal democracies: Each state is entirely responsible for protecting its own people, and no other state or organization has either the right or the duty to do so. In ordinary circumstances, the state exercises complete control over protection within its borders. Other countries and other organizations should not interfere.

Thus, the state affords protection to people and organizations within its territory so that they may enjoy the ability to pursue opportunity within a set of rules that govern the limits of acceptable behavior. However, when criminal organizations undermine or seek to replace the state-sanctioned protection arrangements, they impinge on the state's sovereignty and the power and control that accompany it. Consequently, when the PRI identified the protection market as key to its political dominance and longevity, it understood that it also needed to control the illicit protection market to maintain true dominance over Mexico.

Identifying protection as a function of the state is the observation of sociologist and historian Charles Tilly, who wrote, "If protection rackets represent organized crime at its smoothest, then war making and state making—quintessential protection rackets with the advantage of legitimacy—qualify as our largest examples of organized crime."[12] Tilly's analogy rightly illustrates that the protection rackets that states establish are, in theory, legitimate, all-encompassing, and preeminent. However, I offer a slight correction to Tilly's claim: protection rackets do not represent organized crime at its *smoothest* but rather at its most *fundamental*. When the state is unable to enforce its rules effectively, as is often the case at the margins of society where the state finds its denizens unwilling to cooperate or its policing bodies corrupt or disinterested, organized criminal enterprises are able to make their own rules. When criminal organizations are able to run protection rackets governed by their own rules rather than the state's rules, the state no longer presents a hazard to criminal organizations' operations; as a result, criminal organizations can easily develop and expand business. In short, successful criminal organizations provide (and impose) protection, which allows them to ignore both the state's rules and its efforts to enforce those rules.

Mexican drug cartels did not have effective protection rackets for most of the twentieth century, which created a growth ceiling that limited the magnitude of their success. Instead, the PRI maintained a virtual monopoly of protection, using the Mexican military to enforce the norms it established.[13] The protection imposed by the PRI was both "comforting and ominous."[14] It was comforting in that for the majority of the Priísmo, Mexico enjoyed a relatively high level of economic stability and national security.[15] It was ominous in that over that same period the PRI established hegemonic, vertical control, integrating nearly everything, including businesses, unions, and criminal enterprise, into a corporatist patronage structure that it deftly administered.[16] Among those criminal enterprises was, of course, illicit trade.

"Juárez has always been a city, throughout history, that has had organized criminal activities revolving around smuggling, and a lot of its economy has depended on them," Carolina, a longtime Juárez journalist, explained to me as we sat in a restaurant not far from the newspaper where she worked. "We're talking about decades where smuggling was concentrated through here. Even Al Capone trafficked his liquor through here. After that, Juárez remained, due to our geographical position, located between bonanza and disgrace, a transit point for everything."

While no laws existed that allowed drug trafficking organizations to operate legally, a set of de facto rules, defined by the PRI government, maintained order in the criminal underworld. These de facto rules dictated the number of drug trafficking organizations in existence; designated so-called plazas (territories with logistical importance, those in proximity to a border, port, or, less commonly, significant local drug market) that each drug trafficking organization controlled; and determined the volume and kind of product (illicit drugs) each organization trafficked.[17] These rules established which drug trafficking organization behaviors would be protected by the government, particularly as these behaviors related to other drug trafficking organizations and the public.[18] The PRI's effective monopoly in providing or withholding protection allowed it to augment its constitutionally conferred authority (the ability to make de jure or de facto rules) and to institutionalize control (the ability to enforce those rules).[19] The PRI's unquestioned authority and effective control ensured that drug trafficking organizations would largely obey the PRI's rules.[20] Accordingly, drug trafficking organizations were restricted to specific territories, which forced them to concentrate on the "transactional" aspect of the drug trade rather its "territorial" aspect, given that territory was not contestable for the time being.[21]

Initially, PRI-defined and guaranteed protection for criminal actors benefited both the government and drug trafficking organizations. On the one hand, PRI-governed protection provided drug trafficking organizations with uncontested plazas by minimizing threats and limiting disputes over territory, market share, and resources among competitors, including other drug trafficking organizations and law enforcement. The arrangement compensated drug trafficking organizations for potential revenue foregone due to the inability to freely compete in the drug market by saving them the expense and trouble of competition. On the other hand, the PRI used the knowledge it gained through its provision of protection to undertake selective arrests, which not only reinforced the public illusion that the government was providing security to its citizens within the confines of law but also led to increased "credit, praise, and promotions," political currency that allowed the PRI to underscore its authority and consolidate its control with an air of democratic legitimacy.[22]

Through its monopoly of the protection market, supported by its military superiority relative to the drug trafficking organizations of the era, the PRI could easily constrain any criminal organization that operated within its territory, thus guaranteeing obedience to its de facto rules. Drug trafficking organizations that engaged in non–PRI-approved acts, violent or otherwise, were easily squelched.[23] By co-opting drug trafficking organizations and condoning their illegal activities during the Priísmo, the PRI discarded any internal semblance of democratic legitimacy despite keeping up an external charade of "democratic" elections.[24] Heavy-handed control tactics against criminal actors who failed to abide by the terms of play buttressed the government's authority and allowed the PRI to sustain the popular support necessary to remain in power and attend to the state's affairs. Drug trafficking organizations paid corrupt politicians to remain in good political graces and to keep their illicit business interests free from catastrophic government interference, and corrupt relationships between several of the state's many law enforcement bodies and drug trafficking organizations flourished.[25]

However, during the late 1970s, a fundamental change began. The liberal democratic ideals of the Mexican Constitution had a gradual and increasingly destabilizing resurgence in Mexican politics. As regime liberalization commenced, the PRI dominance and the long-existing "gentleman's agreement" between the PRI and drug barons started to deteriorate. Political pressure exerted externally from the United States and internally from opposition parties called the PRI's democratic bluff. Actual democratic legitimacy, rather than the PRI's sham, was reintroduced as a rightful component of Mexican sovereignty. The PRI's critics called for a transition toward a liberal democratic governance model. But the push to legitimatize the government via a more democratic process necessarily weakened the de facto illegitimate protection scheme that had for decades underpinned the PRI's operations.

With the crumbling of the protection scheme on which the PRI built an era of stable, behind-the-scenes autocracy, Mexico's transition to a modern liberal democracy was not seamless. In the words of political scientist Francis Fukuyama, Mexico transitioned from a "well-governed" authoritarian regime to a "mal-administered" democracy.[26] Despite the appearance of relatively smooth democratic transitions, it remains questionable whether any Mexican government during or since this transition period had or has the capacity to govern effectively. Large swaths of the population lack confidence in the government's ability to provide security, and the country remains subject to ongoing corruption, massive inequality, and severe outbreaks of violence. Governance after democratization has been less effective than it was during the Priísmo.[27]

The destabilizing regime liberalization of the 1980s brought with it a similarly destabilizing liberalization of Mexico's illicit markets. The 1982 elections eroded the PRI's political monopoly and introduced a legitimate competing party. The undermining of PRI-sponsored protection rackets and PRI-centralized control only grew as the main opposition party, the Partido Acción Nacional (PAN), won gubernatorial victories in Baja California in 1989 and Chihuahua in 1992.[28] With the PAN in control at the state level, the protection racket monopoly the PRI once held disintegrated, and the territory-limited, transactionally focused drug trafficking organizations of the Priísmo quickly became obsolete. By the early 1990s, drug trafficking organizations needed to overhaul their business model completely to survive in a newly competitive protection market.[29]

Just as protection is the foundation of a state's ability to operate freely and expand its sphere of influence, a protection racket is the foundation that gives illegal entrepreneurs the ability to develop and expand their enterprises and to maximize control over their own affairs.[30] For that reason, when the opportunities to compete with the state in the protection market increased in Mexico in the 1980s, crime bosses, such as Miguel Ángel Félix Gallardo, Rafael Caro Quintero, and Ernesto Fonseca Carrillo, saw an opportunity to reach levels of power, wealth, and influence undreamed of under the hoof of the PRI.

Criminal actors who had long existed under PRI rule quickly and efficiently leveraged the organizational strength, formed by market share, connections, and operational know-how gained during the restricted-market years, to challenge the government in the protection market. They finally moved beyond their transactional focus and began to compete for territory. The first drug trafficking organization to take advantage of the liberalization of the underworld was the Guadalajara Cartel founded by Félix Gallardo, Caro Quintero, and Fonseca Carrillo after the 1982 elections.[31]

However, the drug trafficking organizations that emerged in the 1980s lacked the strength and interest to topple their governments. Instead, they created parallel protection structures to compete with governmental authority and control in their specific plazas of operation, smoothing drug trafficking operations by circumventing or undermining government efforts to provide or impose protection or, in market terms, to regulate their business.[32] These new drug trafficking organizations can be located midway along a continuum of power seeking from "banditry, piracy, gangland rivalry, policing, [to] war making."[33] Though more subversive than mere pirates and interested in establishing and enforcing rules within their operational corridors, these organizations were not interested in entirely supplanting governance and taking responsibility for the provision of services.[34]

Thus, even as drug trafficking organizations become more sophisticated and diversified in their interests in the twenty-first century, there is little evidence to suggest that they have sought to assume the responsibilities of governing or supplanting the state's government. They do not want the challenges that come with running an entire country. What they want is more profit, and to increase profit they need to expand market share by outcompeting or eliminating rival drug trafficking organizations, occupying their plazas, and absorbing their suppliers and markets. Under the PRI, such competition and potential expansion was not permitted. With the PRI's decline, drug trafficking organizations in Mexico can and do aspire to become part of a few much larger, much richer players in the oligopoly of the wholesale drug trade. To make such aspirations a reality, they neither need nor want to assume the Mexican government's myriad additional roles and responsibilities; they need only a limited space in the margins of society where they can operate and grow.

To that end, such criminal actors undermine the government's legitimacy and authority to operate and to establish laws and norms. They employ corruption and bribery, and they contest the government's ability to enforce its rules by either compromising law enforcement or intimidating the public so that they refrain from calling law enforcement.[35] Evidence of these tactics to undermine state sovereignty became apparent in the earliest stages of Mexico's democratic transition. The Mexican government quickly found itself unable to effectively control the new breed of drug trafficking organizations, which rejected the old rules of engagement, based primarily on exchanging corruption and patronage for PRI protection, and ventured toward establishing their own protection rackets.[36] Forward-thinking drug trafficking organizations were evolving into efficient, illicit enterprises that sought to maximize profits and dominate the wholesale drug market without paying others for protection and without limiting their aspirations of expansion.[37]

By contrast, even as the opportunity to expand quickly presented itself, the cautious old-school bosses favored corruption over violence to facilitate business, an arrangement that had become normalized in Mexican political society.[38] After all, the newly developing protection rackets filling the vacuum left by the waning PRI were nascent and untested. Bosses were unsure whether these new protection rackets would be competitive and effective products capable of establishing security within a system clearly in flux. The old-school bosses were likely unsure whether the amount of control they had over their plazas, the strength of their protection rackets, was sufficient to contest the Mexican state outright. Thus, in that period of uncertainty, many bosses continued to rely on corruption to allow their businesses to proceed with less risk of interruption by the authorities. Although there are many ways to corrupt government entities, some are more effective than others. One of the best ways to ensure that corrupt practices will provide priority access to premium markets is to infiltrate law enforcement institutions with a double agent, such as Rafael Aguilar Guajardo.

In the 1970s Rafael Aguilar joined the Dirección Federal de Seguridad, the Mexican federal secret police responsible, under the PRI, for organizing and administering the drug trafficking organizations' plazas.[39] Aguilar remained a member for fifteen years until the Dirección Federal de Seguridad was disbanded in the wake of the 1985 murder of DEA agent Enrique "Kiki" Camarena Salazar. As the PRI ceded its monopoly and the Dirección Federal de Seguridad was dissolved, Aguilar used his know-how and connections to gain control of the Juárez plaza, which was valuable as one of the largest inland ports in the United States.[40] When the breakup of his organization eliminated his role as a cop on the take, Aguilar became a drug trafficker, a full-time narco.

"Aguilar was the one who maintained the peace between the cartels in the area. Then, when he no longer held his law enforcement position, he paid [Gilberto] "El Greñas" [Ontiveros Lucero] for the right to run the plaza," Jacob, a former Aguilar employee, explained to me.[41] "El Greñas was the one who managed the plaza for the Juárez Cartel," Jacob added.

As Jacob's cocaine habit grew, so too did his relationship with the criminal underworld. Ultimately, he was recruited for his skills in finance. Paying Ontiveros Lucero, noted marijuana smuggler and one of the Juárez Cartel's founders, to run the plaza was an investment that would earn Aguilar millions of dollars, which Jacob laundered through various business fronts, shell companies, and dead-end investments. Initially, Jacob handled only payments for Hotel Silvas in Juárez. The hotel, which has long since burned down, was an establishment owned and operated by Aguilar entirely as a front to launder some of his many proceeds from crime.

"The first time I was asked to launder money, I took about 180 thousand dollars to a *casa de cambio* that doesn't exist anymore, and they gave me checks.[42] And it was up to me to do the bank transfers to pay the hotel's bills and employees," Jacob recounted. "Eventually, they sent me about a million dollars to deal with. I was tempted to steal it, but where was I going to go where the boss wasn't going to find me? I drove my pickup to the hotel, and I knew that there was always somebody behind me. So, they continued to give me larger and larger quantities. First, 180 thousand, then 200 thousand, until it was a million dollars. From then on, it was only millions of dollars." With those quantities, Jacob learned diverse strategies to launder money, often in ways that seemed, at face value, to drive investment. Some of the scams Jacob explained, such as establishing a construction company to build maquiladora workers' housing and never finishing the project, continue to be used.

Jacob reminisced about how different—namely less violent and outwardly gruesome—the drug trade was when he was involved during the 1980s and early 1990s: "Everyone knew there was a lot going on in Juárez because there were those in the government who let it happen. There were lots of dive bars and cheap hotels that were open twenty-four hours a day and full of government employees, US military guys. There was a lot of cash flow. The narcos set up businesses, and they were successful. It was all built on the power that the narcos had, and it was why they kept a low profile."

The men involved in the drug trade as well as the journalists who covered it recalled a time long gone. "In those days, Juárez was full of all kinds of people: *gabachos*, Italians, Puerto Ricans, et cetera.[43] The border was beautiful. It was rare that, in a bar, somebody would kill someone with a gun," said Jaime, a former assassin, as he compared the 1980s and 1990s to the violence and bloodshed of the late 2000s and 2010s.

When there was violence in the old days, those involved viewed it as targeted against people who were part of the trade. "I used to always say that if you aren't

FIGURE 5.   Maquila worker house, Ciudad Juárez, Chihuahua. Abandoned construction projects, such as this house designed for maquiladora workers, serve as money laundering schemes. Construction companies launder money by funneling it to criminal entrepreneurs via the acquisition process during construction.

Photo by R. V. Gundur.

in debt, you don't have anything to worry about," explained Lucas, a former Juárez gang member, implying that people who failed to pay in a timely manner would be the most likely targets of violence. But the role of the narcos in terms of controlling day-to-day life in the drug trade was undeniable. "All of the violence that was erupting was the cartels; the victims weren't average people. The innocents killed were people who had seen or heard something," Lucas continued. "I always managed to never see, never hear, and never speak." It was all part of a code that the narcos usually abided by, rules that were designed to keep unwanted attention at bay.

"There weren't executions in the street," Jacob explained. "If there were people who tried to sell drugs within the plaza, the narcos picked them up and told them that if they wanted to sell, there wouldn't be a problem so long as they paid *cuota*.[44] The narcos would take their drugs away and let them go. They would give nonpaying street vendors one other warning. Then, the third time, they would kidnap them and kill them outside of Juárez. There was a code that said you couldn't kill people in front of children or women. It wasn't good to draw unwanted attention; the narcos kept a low profile."

Carolina, a journalist who had been working the narco beat for more than twenty years, corroborated Jacob's account. She recalled that in the 1980s and 1990s, "the violence wasn't perceptible because the narcos' way of settling their debts was to disappear people, who were never heard from again."

For those who lived in Juárez at the time, the drug-related violence was confined to the realm of the narcos; gangs didn't play a big part. There was a normalcy to everyday life, completely free from the threat of being caught in the cross fire. The economy was based heavily on tourism and the maquiladoras, manufacturing plants that made products from steering wheels to computer components to clothes destined for the US markets. Tourists and workers alike went freely about their business without much worry, besides the normal concerns of having a good time or making rent.

Even for children growing up in the rough parts of Juárez, street life in the 1970s and 1980s was not folded into anything that resembled the omnipresent and all-absorbing drug trade of the 2000s. Life was unremarkable: young people did things that were commonplace in many cities of the same size. Hidalgo, who grew up poor in Juárez in the 1970s, described his youth as one where he "drank, smoked pot, went dancing, went out with his friends, and, when he needed to, looked for work to get money to be able to have a good time with his friends." Drugs were not as easy to come by either. Hidalgo, who now uses heroin regularly, talked about huffing *pegarey*, a kind of shoe glue that was a popular high. Heroin was not easily procured in Juárez until he became an adult.

Lucas spent his youth as a 1980s street child, sniffing glue and committing petty theft and robberies to make some money. Like Hidalgo, he became a regular drug user until he was born again into Christianity and gave up using. His first trip on heroin was across the border, in Segundo Barrio in El Paso, a place where he liked to go to hang out with his friends. As he got older, the kids he ran with operated more like a street gang; they didn't answer to any prison gang, and they weren't controlled by the narcos. His first contact with a prison gang occurred when he was incarcerated in the Juárez prison for car theft.

The life of petty delinquency and neighborhood street gangs was also familiar to Modesto, a native-born Juarense who went on to become a Sureño prison gang member in southern California. Like Lucas, Modesto described the gangs of his youth during 1980s Juárez as being organized along neighborhood lines and not interested in expanding. "We just wanted to be in the neighborhood, selling weed on the corner, drinking some beers. If some kids from another neighborhood came, we'd fight them just to keep the neighborhood safe." Although delinquent, it was a life distinct and separate from that of being part of the wholesale drug trade. Only later, when their world was absorbed by the interests of the cartel bosses, who saw the utility in subsuming street gang members into the fold, did Modesto's and Lucas's worlds become firmly intertwined with the world of drug trafficking organizations.

Jacob, Jaime, Modesto, and Lucas lived and worked in the drug trade, and Carolina reported on it during a time of transition that spanned over fifteen years from the mid-1980s until the late 1990s. They saw changes in the drug trade that eventually gave rise to the circumstances that would foment the violence for which Juárez would become infamous. At first, cash, not violence, remained the principal building block of the drug trade. But over time, in Juárez those involved in the drug trade realized that violence was cheaper than paying bribes. The cost of most human lives in Mexico was negligible. And with that realization, violent conflict became more commonplace.

In 1993 Jacob's boss, Rafael Aguilar, was murdered, shot to death as he vacationed in Cancún. Aguilar's killing happened days after US intelligence intercepted a communication in which Aguilar had complained to his protectors, likely Mexican law enforcement, about the amount of money he was being forced to pay.[45] Aguilar's murder happened in broad daylight, a signal that Amado Carrillo Fuentes, Aguilar's former business partner, had arrived.[46] In some respects, Aguilar's assassination departed from the code to leave those not involved unharmed: a tourist from Denver was caught in the gunfire and died; his wife and son were wounded in the attack.[47] This was emblematic of the emerging violence of the time: infighting began to escalate into violent disputes as a number of emerging drug lords attempted to take over their rivals' plazas.[48]

Carrillo Fuentes, known as "El Señor de los Cielos" (The Lord of the Skies) expanded business more than anyone before him with a fleet of airplanes to traffic increasing quantities of drugs.[49] Carrillo Fuentes also used targeted violence to protect against losses and treachery, exterminating hundreds of victims. However, as an old-school boss, he primarily relied on extensive payoffs to grow his business; he had an estimated "payoff budget between $500 million and $800 million a year flowing to his protectors in government."[50]

Jaime, a man who had worked as a *gatillero* (triggerman) for the Juárez Cartel, echoed this account. Jaime's job was to eliminate problems within the organization and to ensure that in doing so he did not create new ones.

"Today, '*gatilleros*' are known as '*sicarios*,' the difference only being the word used to describe them," Jaime explained. But killing was undertaken differently in the past; violence was controlled. Jaime noted that there used to be "respect" for violence: "A narco, for example, would have people killed, but he would always say, 'Be careful with the children; don't kill anybody in front of the children. Wait until children are gone to kill people.'"

Several of the journalists I interviewed corroborated Jaime's view on violence. These journalists, who had covered drug trade–related violence in Juárez since the 1990s, noted that there was a time when children were not harmed and were not allowed to engage in harmful activities, such as shooting heroin or firearms. In addition, children were not employed as soldiers because violence was not rampant. However, in the 2010s when the proxy war pitted gangs representing different drug trafficking organizations against one another, gangs recruited children to fill the voids caused by the many casualties.

In the past, the narcos used their wealth to their advantage. "The narcos had power because they had lots of money. In those days, it was because they came from wealthy families or got rich by trafficking drugs. They could buy chiefs of police, prison guards, customs agents," Jaime explained. "There were prisoners who could leave the penitentiary but had to return by a certain date and had to make sure they didn't get into trouble or get media attention."

In the old days, money greased the wheels that kept illicit enterprises turning in Mexico.[51] But the continued pressure from the US government's ongoing war on drugs forced Mexican law enforcement operations to target specific drug trafficking organizations more heavily than others in an effort to create the perception that they were sincerely trying to stop drug trafficking. This move, coupled with the conflicts within and between drug trafficking organizations, resulted in the incarceration or death of many old-school, negotiate-first drug trafficking organization bosses—including, notably, Félix Gallardo—throughout the late 1980s and 1990s.[52] Despite these operations, the complicity between law enforcement and drug traffickers continued, albeit with different people acting out the roles.[53]

The resulting cultural sea change saw a rising tide of new bosses, often former *sicarios*, who favored confrontation and violence over the diplomatic patronage system of old.[54] These new bosses included Vicente "El Viceroy" Carrillo Fuentes, who joined his brother Amado in running the Juárez Cartel; Osiel Cárdenas Guillén, who headed the Gulf Cartel; and, of course, Joaquín Guzmán Loera, who came to be a leader of the infamous Sinaloa Federation upon Félix Gallardo's incarceration and the resulting dissolution of his Guadalajara Cartel. The conflicts among these emerging leaders tested their protection rackets, which had been developing as the old-school bosses continued to compromise government and law enforcement officials, a practice that remains a part of Mexico's political landscape.[55] Although government officials continued to enjoy fattened wallets, they no longer possessed the power they once held over the narcos. They were unable to recoup the PRI monopoly or develop dominance in the protection market. Ultimately, the government could no longer hold the drug trafficking organizations in check; the people who lived in areas where the drug trade was a significant part of daily life would now be subjected to involuntary private protection imposed by illicit enterprises operating outside the government's control.

The new days of the drug trade were on the horizon. In Juárez, this era was marked with Amado Carrillo Fuentes's 1997 death on a Mexico City operating table. "After Amado Carrillo was already dead, the first mass killing happened in a restaurant called Maxi. Seven people—all innocent—died that day in an attack directed against people who were associated with Amado Carrillo," Carolina recalled. "From then on, other violent acts happened. The next one was in a bar called Gerónimo where the director of the jail and the boss of the establishment were both killed. These acts showed a new behavior that had to do more than anything with the new cartel leadership, who began to behave more aggressively, disappearing a whole host of people, including police commanders, businessmen, and people, who in some way, had crossed the narcos."

In this new era, to increase their territories and so realize the greatest potential profits by dominating transactions in a larger set of spaces, drug trafficking organizations turned to violence on an expanded scale. Money alone no longer sufficed. Drug trafficking organizations' protection rackets were proving strong enough to guarantee their survival in the face of competition from other organizations and without protection from the Mexican state. They had developed effective violent self-help mechanisms that provided for "the handling of a grievance with aggression" and could allow a criminal entrepreneur the means necessary to protect illicit activity.[56] To further dominate the emerging protection market of the 1990s, the new drug bosses of the era continued to move further and further beyond the corruption of law enforcement and into the development of armed branches of their organizations, which would buttress their emerging protection rackets and underwrite an expanding capacity to participate in the wholesale drug trade.[57]

Osiel Cárdenas Guillén, the boss of the Gulf Cartel, which operated primarily in the eastern part of Mexico in the state of Tamaulipas, was the first to introduce such a group. In 1996, Cárdenas recruited soldiers from the Grupos Aeromóviles de Fuerzas Especiales, a commando unit of the Mexican armed forces, and formed what was to become known as the Zetas.[58] Cárdenas, without access to the government protection that his predecessor Juan García Ábrego had enjoyed, eschewed low-visibility, focused violence and replaced it with a widespread brutality that allowed him to consolidate power.[59] The Zetas embraced and revolutionized the role of internal protection, bringing a high level of violence to their trade. This violence was critical in eroding the government's ability to operate effectively against the Gulf Cartel on its turf.

Highly visible violence served as a signal to competing drug trafficking organizations, the state, and the general public that there would be consequences for trespassing on someone's plaza.[60] Such public violence also showed competitors that their own plazas required protection. Accordingly, competing drug trafficking organizations saw little choice but to emulate the Zetas's successful use of violence and began to establish their own armed groups, such as the Juárez Cartel's creation of La Línea, which included a motley crew of local and federal police as well as members of the Mexican Army.[61]

These developments effectively put the Mexican government on notice: corruption alone would now be insufficient; moreover, corruption would no longer be optional. The watchwords became *plata o plomo*, meaning "take a bribe" (*plata*) or "take a bullet" (*plomo*). With the protection market effectively privatized among drug trafficking organizations, the Mexican government could no longer unilaterally regulate the drug trade or its associated violence, and a new business as usual emerged.

The new business as usual has five primary components. First, drug cartels want to ensure that the government is unable to control them by interfering in their business. To speak in terms of political science, Mexican drug trafficking organizations contest the sovereignty of the state: they undermine the government's authority with corruption and confront the government's control with violence.[62] If we consider the drug cartels' actions in terms of market dynamics, contesting the government's authority and control is a strategy that, in theory, can drive down costs by removing unwanted government regulation and de facto taxation.

Second, the drug cartels want to ensure that insecurity keeps the public from interfering. When the public is too scared to report or react to criminal acts, most criminal acts, including murder, do not result in a law enforcement response. *Autodefensas*, vigilante groups that have developed to contest the dominance of drug trafficking organizations in some places, have emerged to attempt to contest drug trafficking organizations;[63] however, their efficacy, and thus their impact on the protection market, is still uncertain.

Third, the cartels want to ensure that their protection providers do not turn against them, conducting something akin to a military coup. As an El Paso police sergeant named Patricio explained, drug trafficking organizations seek to control their affiliated gangs "through the use of intimidation and violence, even up to death."

Fourth, drug trafficking organizations diversify their risk. With protection, drug trafficking organizations can employ many underlings, such as gang mem-

bers, to do relatively small tasks. The success of each individual task is unimport-
ant so long as the aggregate pays out. For instance, narcotics could be trafficked by
a process of smurfing whereby several small loads are pushed through over a period of time, with the assumption that some underlings will be captured or even
killed, while enough will get through to still make a profit.

Fifth, drug cartels want to control the published narrative, a desire manifested
in the deaths of journalists and average citizens in Mexico. Under the threat of
retribution, journalists came to fear covering illicit activity and organizations.
The 2008 killing of Armando Rodríguez Carreón, a journalist for the Juárez
broadsheet *El Diario*, rattled many of his peers and contributed to the insecurity that plagues those who cover the drug beat.[64] Journalists covering this space
engage very cautiously, publishing their bylines as "Staff." I had been shadowing a journalist called Isidro, but something spooked him, and he was no longer
able to help me. He wrote me an email that read like a telegram:

> DEAR RVG, A WARM HELLO. ALLOW ME TO TELL YOU THAT JEALOUS AND
> MALINTENTIONED PEOPLE HAVE CAUSED ME TO GET IN TROUBLE WITH
> MY DIRECT BOSS. THEY TOLD HIM THAT I WAS WORKING FOR A FOREIGN
> MEDIA OUTLET, WHICH IS NOT TRUE, REFERRING TO YOU. AS A RESULT
> WITH SADNESS I ASK THAT YOU EXCUSE ME BECAUSE I CAN NO LONGER
> HELP YOU. IN ANY EVENT, I WILL BE THERE FOR YOU IF I CAN AND I OFFER
> MY SINCERE FRIENDSHIP. I REPEAT, A THOUSAND TIMES SORRY. ISIDRO.

I didn't see it coming, that sudden severance of our communications; we had
been hanging out for a few days, and things were easy. The only plausible explanation was that somebody had threatened him or otherwise caused him to feel
fear for helping me. Marco, a journalist who once covered the narco beat, noted
that "like all of the citizens, Juárez-based journalists feel the *inseguridad* in their
bones." *Inseguridad* roughly translates to "insecurity" but is a multifaceted concept.[65] It involves not only the feeling that one is unsafe but also the conviction
that the government is failing to protect its citizens from the violent actors of
the criminal underworld. It is the perception that the government is incompe-
tent. It is the feeling that government is colluding with the very criminals from
whom they are meant to be protecting the public. It is the government's failure
or unwillingness to pursue meaningful outcomes within the justice system and
the fear that one will become a victim of crime.[66] *Inseguridad* is how approximately 70 percent of Mexicans describe the security status of their city, while
nearly 60 percent of all Mexicans say it is their principal worry.[67]

One former Juárez journalist, Elena, who covered the drug trade extensively
in her career of twenty-plus years, identified two important elements that allow
the drug trade to exist as it did then and does now in its contemporary form.

"One element is impunity, and the other is that the cartels have a social base. Impunity has to do with the poor procurement of justice. The social base is characterized by certain illegal activities that have permeated into society and have become normalized." The most notable activity is the institutionalized corruption in the practice of paying *mordidas* (bribes) to the police. Nobodies can buy their way out of minor infractions; somebodies can buy their way out of larger ones.

Another journalist, Pedro, furthered Elena's point by noting that the major criminal players were well known. "I think that the majority of journalists know who the bosses of the drug trafficking organizations in Juárez and the dirty politicians are. But, obviously, you can't say their names, much less publish them. The sins of politicians are untouchable, because if you were to say something, people in government have many ways they can put pressure on you. They go over your taxes, over every little thing that you are accountable for, and they find something, you know?"

Certainly, the fear of being harmed by violent criminals and even the corrupt cops and officials who were in their pocket was felt in corners of Juárez beyond journalistic circles. Members of the public came to fear reporting illicit activity to law enforcement, since the public now believed that those in law enforcement were either inept or colluding with drug trafficking organizations. The public reacted to these "signal crimes," which demonstrated that the criminals feared no reprisal, with forced silence, in part because the state—the Mexican government—was unable to respond to the public's demand for improved public safety.[68] In short, drug trafficking organizations normalized silence in the wake of crime in Mexican society.

The historic and present inability of the press and the public to report consistently and transparently on wrongs and to see appropriate responses, without being threatened or harmed, means that the line between government actors and the criminals was, and for many still is, blurred. The inability to criticize officials without repercussions appears to be a holdover from the opacity instituted by the PRI during the twentieth century.[69] For criminal entrepreneurs in the protection market, this situation is optimal: it reduces the control and authority of the government while buttressing drug trafficking organizations' violent, self-help mechanisms that allow them to act according to their interests.[70] In essence, drug trafficking organizations affected society by changing how society (generally) responds to criminal acts. That change is the reason many of the respondents in immigration court refused to report their assaults to Mexican authorities. It also explains why those respondents viewed moving within Mexico as dangerous and therefore impossible, since a government they do not and cannot trust is present throughout the territory.

Yet, almost every time I walked from El Paso to Juárez, photos of accused narco criminals graced the front pages of the afternoon tabloids. Whenever someone of the narco world was arrested, a media circus ensued. Isidro once took me along to see a perp walk, where the accused were paraded in front of journalists representing a half dozen or so media outlets. The suspects, sometimes bearing signs of having been battered, were standing behind a table on which were displayed the tools they had allegedly used to commit their crimes. Reporters barked questions at the accused, seemingly convinced of the suspects' guilt. The suspects always confessed their guilt with short, clear sentences that they repeated until the questioning was over. There was no regard for due process, no right to remain silent, and no attorney present. The accused whom I saw were peons in the new business as usual: a few of the many gang members, who, besides their gang affiliations, were otherwise rather ordinary people of the border, now serving as minions for the narcos, the people who established the logistics of the transnational drug trade.

FATHER AND SON

On the last day of 1973, sixty-three-year-old Miguel Rivera lay frozen to death somewhere in a New Mexican culvert not too far from where New Mexico, Texas, and Mexico all come together. He was a son, a husband, a father—just like my dad. Like most people, perhaps, Miguel Rivera could be described in less flattering terms as well. His own son, José Raul "Raulio" Rivera Fierro, called him a "drunk" and an "ex-con," but the boy also called him "Dad." Miguel, like millions of people in America and indeed the world, abused a substance—in his case, like my dad, alcohol—on a regular basis.[1] And when Miguel drank he often became violent, which landed him in trouble with the law. In another time and place, Miguel could have been one of my father's patients, their lives separated by the thinnest of lines.

José was fourteen years old when his father died.[2] José's relationship with Miguel wasn't one of father and son bonding over fishing and camping trips or playing catch. Instead, Miguel dragged his son to church and then took him from El Paso to Juárez to go bar hopping, chasing the night. On a violent day, Miguel would just beat José. In that respect, Miguel's death meant José's freedom. But even before Miguel's death, José's childhood was free, in a sense. Growing up in poverty meant that his mother worked whatever jobs she could find whenever they were available; there weren't many grownups around to watch him or his siblings. So, for a time José and his brother, Buck, spent their childhood running around barefoot and playing among the natural beauty of the banks of the Rio Grande. Unlike today, it was then unmistakably a river, and even if the water was contaminated by runoff from the Asarco smelting plant, it still flowed.[3]

However, José's innocent, youthful, adventure-seeking days riding feral horses and climbing barefoot in the Franklin Mountains quickly gave way to a very different life, one that diverged from those of his siblings. José started huffing glue and getting into trouble at school. He got a reputation as the "bad" Rivera child and was often accused of wrongdoing, although he was only sometimes responsible. And he started to get high outside of school. As a branded troublemaker, José joined Los Diablos, a gang based out of the Sandoval housing projects where he lived. Los Diablos was run by young Vietnam War veterans. These vets, like many other returning soldiers, found few prospects waiting for them at home. Some became addicted to the opiates, amphetamines, or barbiturates they used to treat the physical and mental trauma of their military service.[4]

Retired El Paso police lieutenant Harry Kirk documented the rise of gangs in El Paso.[5] He recounted a history of groups in El Paso that could be characterized as gangs dating back to the 1960s. These groups were located in neighborhoods in the city's downtown such as Segundo Barrio, also known as the Second Ward, where some of the poorest people in El Paso lived. The end of the 1960s brought policies that led to the construction of public housing throughout the city. Along with the city's poorest residents, those neighborhood groups moved to housing projects far from downtown, such as the Sandoval homes in the far west reaches of El Paso where José lived.

In the 1970s during José's youth, El Paso street gangs, already woven into the fabric of the city, began fighting each other and so became a more noticeable part of its pattern. But despite increasing visibility, gang members were always only a small proportion of El Paso's more than half a million inhabitants. By the early 1990s when the first estimates of gang populations were made, the total number of gang members was at most maybe a bit more than four thousand total, including hangers-on at the periphery of the gangs. While young men often led street gangs, most of the members were just boys, still in school. Their crimes were mostly petty: vandalism, property crime, and small-time drug sales. For many members, gangs were spaces where they found belonging. And that belonging is what drew José in.

For José, being part of a gang meant comradery, having people to party with, accomplices in mischief, and a shared purpose, such as protecting the neighborhood from outsiders. The gang didn't "like people that weren't from my neighborhood coming into my neighborhood, especially messing with our girls and stuff like that," José explained. "You just couldn't do that. So, in that respect, I guess it was a sense of honor that we're bad, we're better than you."

A few months after José's dad died, small parties, mischief, and petty crime gave way to more lavish parties, heroin, car theft, burglary, and violent clashes fought with knives and chains. It was a path of criminality that José easily embraced. "The better the criminal you were, the more prestige you had, the more respect you had. I was already respected. The older guys would say, 'Man, you're bad, dude. You and Güero, man, you take care of business.'"[6]

Sometimes José got caught, and as a boy he was frequently sentenced to reform school, but he never reformed. He would run away from home to continue to live his preferred life of burglarizing, partying, and using heroin. Eighteen was a year of firsts: he became a father and was sentenced to prison. José did his first stretch of time on a prison farm called Clemens, located in Brazoria County, Texas, not too far from Houston. In José's day, most of the inmates were men under twenty-one. As a young man, José continued to get into trouble and was frequently sentenced to serve additional time at Clemens, but the Department of Corrections utterly failed to "correct" José. At twenty-one, José, by then a repeat offender, was sent to the Coffield Unit near Tennessee Colony, Texas, about a hundred miles southeast of Dallas. Coffield was Texas's largest prison and housed only adults.[7] It was there that José founded Barrio Azteca in the early 1980s. The group was initially formed to provide solidarity to inmates from the Paso del Norte area so they could avoid being caught up in conflicts between other prison gangs. From this limited role, long after José left its leadership, Barrio Azteca evolved into one of the largest and most violent prison gangs in the Texas prison system.[8]

José was never attracted by the allure of power and riches that higher echelons of the drug trade and other illicit enterprise could offer. As he once told me, he never met any big-shot drug dealers, nor did he want to. Fresh out of prison, José's primary focus was getting high. The respect he earned in the joint meant easy access to drugs, particularly as Barrio Azteca expanded into the streets. As its members returned to the blocks where they had grown up, Barrio Azteca took control of the Latino street gangs' operations and centralized much of the city's drug trade. And despite José's best efforts to quit using heroin, such easy access allowed his addiction to retain a tight grip.

"I would try to quit all the time. I'd go get cold turkey, doing for three days, *la malia*, the cold turkey," José recounted.[9] "I tried working, and that didn't work out. I couldn't make it to work; overdosed one time, I pulled an Elvis: overdosed in the shitter one morning, ended up in the hospital. Had a good job at Fort Bliss, lasted one night; another job and it lasted one night because I needed a fucking fix. I'd just call somebody, and they'd bring the heroin. So, how easy was that? That would be impossible for a junkie to say, 'you know what, I'm done.' You could say, 'I'm done,' but as long as it's there, you're not going to quit. I had to change my environment."

And so, José tried to leave it all behind, first via a failed suicide attempt and eventually via a Greyhound bus. He left El Paso and everything and everybody he had there for the cornfields of Nebraska, where he found religion, which he later abandoned, and romance, which he held onto for the rest of his life. He left behind him not only his drug addiction but also his son, Emiliano, who never had a father to guide him through his childhood.[10] José's radical departure from the environment where he had committed most of his crimes mirrored the stories told by most of the few others I met who had truly left gang life behind them.

Just like his father, José, Emiliano joined his neighborhood street gang as a young boy. And just like José, Emiliano got into trouble. Like José, he was the only one of his siblings who did, and when trouble came it was always big. Emiliano was ten years old the first time he got arrested for participating in a drive-by shooting, an activity that his dad would not have condoned. But for Emiliano, his father's approval mattered little. He was trying to step outside his father's shadow and become his own man, even as he joined his father's gang. Unlike José, Emiliano engaged in activities that would position him well in the gang both on the street and in prison. He engaged in violent activities in prison to become a respected gang soldier. As a stand-up guy, a man with respect within Barrio Azteca, he had credibility within the gang that allowed him to manage a piece of territory to sell drugs once he was released from prison. But ultimately, like his father, Emiliano realized that the gang life wasn't for him, and he sought an exit. The hard part wasn't leaving his old life behind him—nobody threatened him to stay—but instead was figuring out what his new life ahead and the opportunities or lack thereof would look like.

"I don't really consider myself part of society," Emiliano said, reflecting on his inability to get employment at a hospital. He had trained to be a phlebotomist, a job he didn't realize that he could never assume because of his felony record. "I don't know if it's because of all the doors that have been slammed on my face just because of what I used to be—they see me with tattoos or my prior convictions. So, it's not like they give you a chance to do something different."

Frustrated but not undeterred, Emiliano kept looking for work, trying to sell himself as a person who could work well and work honestly; finally, one woman gave him a chance, which he hasn't squandered.

"I told this lady—the one I'm working for in the cleaning business—I told her since the beginning, 'I'm a convicted felon. I used to do this. I used to do that. Now all I want is a chance, for you to give me a chance so I can work for you. You're going to see that I'm a hard worker,'" Emiliano explained. He had to sell himself because he knew that any employer he approached would likely have doubts. But his boss is happy with him.

"She trusts me so much. She gives me the keys to her house and everything. She's been telling me, 'You know what? I'm thankful that I gave you a chance.' She said, 'I ain't gonna lie. I thought about it, but something told me to give you the chance.'"

And though Emiliano has a wife and children who have not followed his or his father's footsteps into a life of trouble, crime, and gangs, he still doesn't feel that he's a part of society. It was a feeling that his father felt for the entirety of his life. Being at the margins of society is a struggle that many in Emiliano's position face: the felony record embroiders a scarlet letter on their chests and makes it difficult to find honest work.[11] And with stable employment elusive, the gang life, which these men long to leave in their past, beckons.

That was the fear that Pancho had. Like Emiliano and José, Pancho had been a gang member since he was just a boy. As Pancho grew older, he too became a member of Barrio Azteca. And despite its being the life he knew best, he too wanted to leave it behind him. But Pancho had less confidence in his ability to do so; he saw a return to prison as his destiny. He feared that he would be a bad role model to his children, so he stayed away from them, praying that their destiny would be different from his. He wanted nothing more than to break the cycle of violence and criminal activity that his life had continued. He cut grass in an effort to make an honest day's wage from an honest day's work; however, the better economic opportunities that the gang life and its access to the drug trade offered along the border remained great temptations.

LA CARRUCHA

El Paso's status as a prime transshipment point makes the city valuable for any business that needs to ship products, legal or not, from Mexico to the United States. Compared to Juárez, which has become known for its violence in the twenty-first century, El Paso is a sleepy city with little violent crime. As Pancho noted, any illicit business that happens in the city these days happens mainly "underwater," avoiding the gaze of the eyes of law enforcement, who could disrupt important business opportunities. Although Pancho's characterization rings true, the concerns that violence could spill over from Mexico into the United States persists in the news and in the rhetoric of politicians. Notable examples include former Texas governor Rick Perry's false claim that there were car bombs in El Paso and Texas senator John Cornyn's unsupported claim that the threat of spillover violence was real and escalating.[1]

For drug trafficking organizations, bringing visible violence to the US side of the border would increase risk and undermine business. Investigative journalist Bill Conroy, who has covered narco violence for several years, discredited the notion that drug-related violence would cross over into the United States; even during the worst of the violence in Juárez, no evidence suggested that there was spillover into El Paso or any other US border town.

"Nonetheless, there are a few rural pockets where the murder rate shot up," explained Bill. "And that, to me, was kind of interesting. The way it was explained to me is that if someone wants to murder you in San Antonio, the assassins are smart if they take you out to a smaller county and kill you because the rural police force is not used to dealing with those crimes."

It appears that when violence does happen in the United States, it happens in a way that minimizes risk to illicit business interests.

"You have to remember, [drug traffickers] are businessmen," Elizabeth Kempshall, then director of the Arizona High Intensity Drug Trafficking Area (HIDTA) but who had previously worked extensively in Texas, told me.[2] "They don't want to do anything that is going to cost them more money to do their business. If they start having that violence that's occurring in Mexico occurring here in the United States, then the United States is going to rise up and get more committed to stopping that type of activity from coming across the border. So, when [Americans] rise up, put more forces on the border, [and] shut the border down . . . , the cartels, in effect, are hampered in making money. So, they don't want to encourage that type of activity."

Consequently, despite the presence of Barrio Azteca—the city's most notorious drug trade "businessmen"—El Paso continues to be recognized as particularly safe. The various gang members and law enforcement personnel I interviewed noted that Barrio Azteca has a clear presence in El Paso's underworld, even though violence was not commonplace in the city. Violence is not typically necessary because Barrio Azteca has maintained a near monopoly in the regional wholesale and retail trade since at least the turn of the century, a position, along with its historical presence in the Texas prison system, that has allowed members of the gang to set the rules of the street. And since violence in El Paso almost certainly brings unwanted law enforcement attention, everything happens underwater to ensure that business keeps chugging along.

The same cannot be said on the other side of the bridge. Barrio Azteca remains associated with the violence of Juárez, having been involved in two of the most violent and publicly covered events in the city. In January 2010 Barrio Azteca members massacred innocent university students, whom they mistook for members of a rival gang, at a subdivision called the Villas de Salvácar.[3] In March of the same year members of the gang, apparently on the orders of the Juárez Cartel, shot and killed US consulate worker Lesley Ann Enriquez Catton and her husband Arthur H. Redelfs as well as Jorge Alberto Salcido Ceniceros, the husband of another US consulate worker.[4] The Barrio Azteca lieutenant, Arturo Gallegos Castrellón, who ordered the slayings, was sentenced to life in prison in 2014.[5] Because the violence in Juárez is both real and frightening, the people of Paso del Norte see Barrio Azteca as a violent force. Even when a violent reputation does not translate into violent or visible action, it can still underpin a real fear. After all, only bridges and steel fencing separate El Paso from Juárez and its high rates of crime and violence.[6] The border may separate the two cities, but both cities have been affected by the history of Barrio Azteca. To understand this history, one must venture far from the Paso del Norte area to the medium- and high-security prison farms in the eastern part of Texas and examine the evolution of the Texas Department of Corrections (TDC).

A Brief History of Corrections in Texas

In some ways, the circumstances in which Barrio Azteca formed and evolved within the TDC parallel the circumstances in which drug trafficking organizations formed and evolved in Mexico. In both cases, an established, stable system of security and protection, based on institutionalized cooperation between administrative entities and criminal actors, began to deteriorate as pressure to embody a more liberal set of ideals grew. In both cases, the resulting instability created both the need and the opportunity for criminal groups to establish their own systems of security and protection. And in both cases, the emergence of such systems marked an opportunity for illicit businesspeople to expand the horizons of their criminal enterprises.

The Control System

From the early 1800s until 1983, Texas prisons made use of a "control model" that employed punitive, plantation-style prisons with inmate guards, known as "building tenders" or "turnkeys."[7] Although the use of building tenders had fallen out of fashion in most state penal systems throughout the United States by the mid-twentieth century, George J. Beto, who was the director of the TDC from 1962 until 1972, championed the system. Beto continued to employ inmate guards to keep costs down, since discontinuing the practice would have required the construction of more single-unit cells and the hiring of more corrections officers.[8] Beto's successor, Ward James "Jim" Estelle Jr., likewise continued with the system.[9]

Building tenders were selected by the prison administration to control other inmates.[10] Prison administrators incentivized building tenders to enforce prison policy by affording them special privileges, such as having their cells unlocked at all times, being able to eat whenever they wanted, keeping pets, possessing weapons, and having the keys to other inmates' cells.[11] Building tenders maintained control by brutally and violently repressing uncooperative inmates and by deputizing friends to inform on their fellow inmates.[12]

Through the 1970s, the building tender system was the primary provider of security within the prison walls and helped the prison administration control the majority of inmates.[13] Prison officials relied on the building tenders to "effectively maintain order among the inmates (frequently through the use of force)," and to serve as their "intelligence network."[14] The building tenders kept inmate violence at a minimum and discouraged the formation of organized prisoner groups.[15] This control strategy made Texas prisons "perhaps the most orderly prison system in the country."[16] Prison administrators willingly turned a blind eye to the building tenders' abuse of their fellow inmates so long as the building tenders kept order.

However, in the late 1970s Texas experienced an incarceration boom that more than doubled the inmate population.[17] With this influx, other inmate groups such as the Texas Syndicate and the Aryan Brotherhood, prison gangs that had formed in California and whose members were now getting locked up in Texas, gained significance in the Texas prison system.[18] The building tender system kept these inmate groups in check until the system's demise.[19] It was during this transition period that José Raul Rivera Fierro started to get locked up.

No matter how bad prison was, José was, in some ways, happy to be there. "My plan was at last coming to fruition," he said. "I was following in the footsteps of my role models." When he entered prison for the first time in 1978, José was a scrappy, still-growing five-foot, three-inch nineteen-year-old kid who realized that in order to be left alone, he needed to outcrazy most people by playing the role of the maniac tough guy. Later in 1981 when José was transferred to the Coffield Unit, he cultivated a more refined image of himself: likable but tough enough to take care of himself, a necessary characteristic if he was to defend himself from the unwanted advances of the building tenders, who looked for smaller inmates to exploit.

"Every unit was run by 'politicians,'" José explained. "They worked both sides. They were inmates that worked for the man, and they pretty much had authority. They could tell the man things and could get you hurt. They were running the show still when I got to Coffield. I felt small. I hadn't felt that small in a long time."

One of the building tenders attempted to "Ike and Mike" José, in other words, attempted to turn him into his "punk," his sexual object.[20] José played along just enough to extract favors but without prostituting himself. His intuition and charisma allowed him to make the alliances necessary to survive and to gain the trust and respect of his fellow El Paso inmates. And even though he was in prison, his life was steady once he got past the initial learning curve of unit politics.

Ruiz v. Estelle: Transitioning from Building Tenders to Corrections Officers

In 1983, prison politics changed. In 1972, inmate David Ruiz petitioned the Federal Eastern District Court to examine the TDC's policies regarding solitary confinement, arguing that he was being subjected to cruel and unusual punishment, a violation of his constitutional rights.[21] The judge in the case, William Wayne Justice, combined the Ruiz case with complaints from seven other inmates, making it a single civil class action filed under the name *Ruiz v. Estelle*.[22] The case finally went to trial in October 1978, and upon its conclusion, "Judge Justice found the [TDC] in violation of inmates' constitutional rights in six major areas: (1) overcrowding; (2) security; (3) fire safety; (4) medical care; (5) discipline; and (6) access to the courts."[23] Accordingly, Judge Justice ordered the TDC to undertake several extensive organizational changes to address these violations and set a deadline of 1982 to phase out and eventually abolish the building tender system.[24]

Judge Justice's decree created three significant problems for the TDC, given the short, two-year timescale provided for institutional change. First, since the building tenders could no longer fulfill their security role, the prison administrators faced shortages in security staff. Between 1979 and 1984, the number of guards tripled to about six thousand across the state prison system.[25]

Second, new staff lacked the experience to effectively control the inmates' behavior and were hesitant to intervene in violent inmate-inmate confrontations, which building tenders would ordinarily have suppressed.[26] The transition resulted in a power vacuum whereby the prison administration, without the building tenders to maintain order, no longer had a monopoly on violence within the prison grounds.[27] Both inmates and guards felt that the balance of power, or the ability to control the prison yard, had shifted to the inmates' favor. The lack of control within the prison became obvious in 1984 when the number of inmate homicides reached twenty-five, a rate of seven per ten thousand inmates, which "was well ahead of all other systems [and] more than double the number (twelve) of the previous two high years, 1981 and 1982."[28] That number would be eclipsed the following year.[29] Most of the killings were gang-related.[30]

Third, without the building tenders, the prison administration no longer had the insider intelligence that had allowed it to keep tabs on prison developments.[31] In short, the decree ensured that the protection market within the prison walls was now open for competition. Ready to fill the protection void were several inmate groups that organized themselves along racial and national-origin lines.

In writing about similar turmoil within the California prison system, which occurred in the 1950s, 1960s, and 1970s as the California Department of Correction lost its dominance in the prison yards, former prisoner John Irwin described how the prisoners formed pseudofamilial structures to mediate disputes among themselves. However, as racial hatred reached a high level among the inmates, "cliques increasingly became organized for their own members' protection."[32] This evolution of organization was echoed in the TDC. In the decade following the downfall of the building tender system, several inmate groups formed and grew large enough to be classified by the TDC as "security threat groups," the prisons administrations' technical term for prison gangs.

Among the Latino inmate community in Texas, the only inmate group to pre-date the fall of the building tender system was the Texas Syndicate.[33] The Texas Syndicate is a long-standing organization that developed in the 1970s in the Cali-fornian penitentiaries Folsom and San Quentin in response to the harassment of native Texan inmates.[34] The Mexican Mafia, forming in the early 1980s, was the first Latino inmate group to appear in Texan prisons after the Texas Syndicate. Also referred to as the Mexikanemi or Eme, Texas's Mexican Mafia is not to be confused with organizations in California, Arizona, and elsewhere that bear the same name.[35]

According to José, the Eme and the Texas Syndicate initially coexisted, given the instability that occurred as the prison transitioned out of the building ten-der system and as Latinos needed unity among themselves to counter the Black inmates. "As soon as that suit hit and the TDC had to get rid of the building ten-ders, it caught the prison administration with their pants down because they weren't expecting it. During that transition period, all hell broke loose," José re-called. "It started in 1983. It continued for about two years. The TDC had to train a bunch of guards. They just needed bodies in uniform. They were inexpe-rienced and the guards were getting beat up." José went on to say that "the guards were scared, and some of them would kind of like hang out with us because we treated them well. We weren't being assholes to them, but the Blacks—a major for the prison guards got stabbed, and the Black inmates were just scary for the guards as well as for everybody else. It was out of hand, out-of-control chaos. Chaos was the rule of the day."

Regardless of whether José's claims about the violence undertaken by Black inmates is accurate, the guards did fear the inmates; in the aftermath of the fall of the building tender system, assaults on the prison staff skyrocketed system-wide from 4 in 1981 to 129 in 1984.[36] Moreover, inmates fought among them-selves more frequently. Wars between the prisoner groups that had been suppressed by the building tenders were openly waged. In 1984 and 1985 the Aryan Brotherhood, a White supremist prison gang, fought the Mandingo War-riors, a Black inmate group, out of racial spite, and with the honeymoon period of uncertainty in the prisons over, the Texas Syndicate fought the Texas Mexi-can Mafia over control of Latino inmates and the prison drug trade.[37]

According to José, "The Texas Syndicate went to the upstart Mexican Mafia at the Darrington Unit where the Eme were selling weed and told them, 'You know what, we want a cut. You got to pay taxes.'[38] Now, the Texas Syndicate thought the Eme would be scared of them, that they were just going to lay down.

But the Eme were no punks either. They were standup, too; they were somebody to be reckoned with."

As prisoners were transferred, "catching the chain" to other prison camps throughout the state prison system, the word of the conflict spread. Violence escalated between the Eme and Texas Syndicate, which had become the two largest prison gangs in the Texas prison system; however, the violence drew the unwanted attention of the prison administration. The prison guards responded by placing every Eme or Texas Syndicate leader they could identify in administrative segregation (i.e., solitary confinement).[39] With leadership weakened and in need of replacements, both the Texas Syndicate and the Eme now vied for recruits to replenish their ranks and effectively challenge each other for dominance in the penitentiary. In their efforts to recruit, both the Texas Syndicate and the Eme relaxed their entry requirements.

"They said, 'Man, you don't have to kill anyone to get in or all that stuff,'" José recounted. "I said, 'Still, I don't think so.' They told me, 'Man, if you join, there's a lot of people who are going to follow you.' I said, 'No.' I just put a stop to it. Between 1984 and 1985, the prison administration just started locking gang leaders up because it got out of hand."

By 1985 at least eight prisoner groups had formed, which included Latino, Black, and White groups.[40] These groups, along with a now more experienced prison staff, were able to reestablish an effective social order within the prison walls that remained through the latter half of the decade. As a result, the chaotic scenes of interracial conflict that characterized 1983, 1984, and 1985 dissipated. Nonetheless, the established prisoner groups were actively recruiting to fill out their ranks, since depleted in the conflict, in case further conflict should occur.

For their part, the "boys" of El Paso had remained mostly neutral, respecting each organization. But when the Texas Syndicate and the Eme began to ask the Chuco crew to pick sides, neither José nor his fellow El Pasoans wanted to be part of any bloodbath, and most rebuffed the advances. Eventually José decided to start his own organization to provide enough of a structure to preclude other groups from recruiting the El Paso boys.

The Birth and Growth of Barrio Azteca

One day José was smoking a joint with his pal Benny Acosta when the idea to start a *carrucha*, "a ride," for the El Paso and Juárez boys occurred to him. "We were talking about all of the shit that had been happening on the unit. A couple more of our homeboys had joined the gangs, and I was not feeling too happy about it. El Paso had always been sort of a pseudogang, and now we were about to get swallowed up by bigger fish," José recounted.

"I told Benny, 'You know what, man? Vamos a comenzar una carrucha. ¿Cómo ves? Pues, toda la gente está puesta.'[41] And he said, 'No estuviera mal Raulio. Aquí vamos a hablar con la gente en la yarda en la tarde.'"[42]

José called a meeting in the yard that evening to poll interest in starting a ride: a gang for the inmates from El Paso and Juárez. José was likable and had the respect of his El Paso peers, and they were already hanging out together. "Most of us from El Paso knew each other from the free world, and being locked up together was just like hanging out in the barrio." That relationship meant that José knew that the others wanted no part of the conflict between the Texas Syndicate and the Eme, and he liked his chances of getting a group going. He was right: most of the El Paso and Juárez people who had been called to the meeting joined his upstart group. José instituted a rough hierarchical order, placing himself at the top with four or five captains under him (he could not remember definitively if there was a fifth). The rest were put on the ride as "soldiers," emulating the structure of the other organizations in prison.

Moreover, to join the gang "there was no blood in, blood out," José explained. Membership was informal. "There was just, 'Yeah, I'm in the gang,' just by saying it." During the meeting José suggested using the name "Barrio Azteca," in reference to his Mexican heritage and the nickname of a neighborhood in El Paso; the name stuck. The next day, he used his job pushing a broom throughout the unit to go around and get the word out. Barrio Azteca had been born.

Despite the hierarchical organization of the group, José described the initial objectives to be twofold: to provide solidarity for the guys who were from El Paso and Juárez when they entered the prison system and to ensure that the group would not be part of or be victimized by the other prison gangs. The most common way to show support to incoming inmates is to provide basic goods, such as coffee and hygiene products, that incoming inmates do not have and to back each other up in the face of conflict in the yard.

Giving such support is an exercise of soft power. "Soft power" is a term coined by political scientist Joseph Nye Jr. to describe, in the context of world politics, a state's ability to attract and persuade as a foil to hard power, which is the ability to coerce.[43] In prison politics, inmate groups, rather than states, exercise these forms of power. The soft power of inmate groups is their ability to entice new inmates to join their ranks under the banner of brotherhood, which underpins the maintenance of protection. An inmate group's ability to attract recruits, through gifts, promised solidarity, reputation, or potentially a preexisting association with a street gang, is at play here; there are no direct threats to encourage recruitment, and many inmates choose not to join an inmate group.[44] Prison gangs reserve the exercise of hard power to forcefully carve out a place in the criminal underworld within and beyond the walls of corrections facilities. And though José did not start Barrio Azteca with this goal in mind, it soon evolved from a group that sought to avoid war within the prison walls to a group that sought to establish its preeminence among prison gangs in the TDC.

Barrio Azteca managed to avoid significant attention from the prison administration for the rest of the 1980s. José downplayed the role of violence during the early incarnation of Barrio Azteca, particularly on the streets, but he acknowledged the gang's growing authoritarian streak as it quickly evolved and grew from a self-protection group trying to avoid violence to a predator group inflicting violence on others.

José also downplayed his role in Barrio Azteca's development, saying he was unaware of the group's evolution into a hard-nosed prison gang as it happened in part due to his heroin use and his general lack of interest in the gang while he was not incarcerated. But Barrio Azteca began to emulate the Eme and the Texas Syndicate quite early on and, by the time of José's final stint in prison, from 2006 to 2008, had completely evolved into a prison gang that was as big as and often bigger than either the Texas Mexican Mafia or the Texas Syndicate in the units within the Texas Department of Criminal Justice (TDCJ)—which the TDC came to be called in 1989—that had many El Paso and Juárez inmates. Like its predecessors, Barrio Azteca created a presence that allowed it to establish rules both within and beyond the prison walls.

Inside prison, one of Barrio Azteca's early predatory actions resulted in the establishment of the Mexicles in 1987. The Mexicles started as a group of *paisas*, or Mexican nationals, who had grouped together for probably many of the same reasons José formed the Aztecas.[45]

"The Mexicles were an upstart group. They formed because we alienated and shunned them when they wouldn't join us. They were a very small group," Jose explained. It's not an incidental development: today the Mexicles, who are primarily based in Ciudad Juárez, are the chief adversaries of the Aztecas there, having allied themselves with the Sinaloa Federation. The violence between the two groups has been possibly the largest driver of the city's exorbitant body count over the past decade.[46]

And thus, history repeated itself: now as a predator group, Barrio Azteca preyed on weaker cliques for their members. This recruitment effort was met by formalized resistance from the Mexicles. The Mexicles, however, were never assessed by the Texas Department of Public Safety to be a preeminent risk, probably because most of its members, being foreign nationals convicted of felonies, were deported upon completing their sentences and accordingly were less likely to return to the Texas jail and prison systems en masse.[47]

For Barrio Azteca, having control within carceral settings meant having control on the streets. For instance, establishing control over the county jail allowed José to reduce drive-by shootings in El Paso by making sure anybody who was sent to county jail for committing a drive-by would be punished.

"I was at my sister's house, and this was in '89, like the third or fourth time I got out, and I'm watching the news and there's a drive-by: little girl gets shot in the head," José said. "She was just sitting doing her math homework, and somebody drove by and shot at the house and shot and killed her. It tore me up, but I knew that I ran the county jail, that all my people, it's all Azteca. I let it be known, you know what, 'Ponga la palabra, que no va a ver drive-bys. Al otro güey que caiga por un drive, le tumba por un cantón.'"[48]

The enactment of this policy marked the beginning of Barrio Azteca's power over the streets of El Paso. From what current gang members told me, the policy remains in effect to this day and explains why drive-by shootings in El Paso are unusual. Its continued enforcement, however, may have more to do with keeping unwanted attention from law enforcement at bay rather than with any altruistic purpose.

As José's influence faded and his ambitious captains took over, Barrio Azteca became increasingly violent. By some accounts, the gang had a written constitution, formalizing its structure, code of conduct, and objectives, though no gang members I ever met referred to any constitution.[49] Undoubtedly, the new captains helped transform Barrio Azteca from the inmate solidarity group that José established into one of the most notorious prison gangs in the TDCJ.

As the Aztecas grew, they expanded their recruitment efforts from prison to the county jail. Street gang members locked up in county jails were vetted to see whether they had any "jackets," such as a history of being a snitch or a child molester.[50] If no disqualifying jackets appeared, these prospects, known as *flechas* (arrows) or *coras* (hearts) were sometimes offered the opportunity to join the gang. Prospective members were and continue to be vetted through a system of communication using *wilas* (kites) that inmates use to transfer information when they cannot come in physical proximity with one another.[51]

In an effort to gain information on a possible prospect, *wilas* are sent to members in neighboring cells or in administrative segregation. In some cases, these notes are smuggled outside jail or prison for outside vetting. In addition, prospects have to "put in work" by engaging in risky behavior that their superiors order them to do, such as keeping the shanks for the gang or assaulting another inmate. Ideally, the gang wants to recruit only members who are fully committed to gang life.

Today, people who attempt to leave the gang may be stigmatized, as is the case with most prison gangs. Membership in the Aztecas is a lifelong commitment with ex-members, or *equis*, being deemed persona non grata, with a standing "green light" on them should they leave the organization without getting old or finding religion.[52] In this instance, a green light indicates that at least in theory, existing members have a duty to attempt to kill ex-members who leave the fold. In practice, a green light is usually a threat of assault and is not likely to occur in situations that would bring unwanted attention to the gang. Accordingly, ex-members understand the risks of being an *equis*, so they do their best to avoid situations that place them at risk of an attack. For example, they avoid going out on the town and committing crimes that could see them incarcerated again. When avoiding trouble is not possible, ex-members might be forced to go on the offensive.

"As an *equis*, if you come across a young guy who is active, you have to beat his ass, because you know they are supposed to kill you," Alberto, a Barrio Azteca *equis*, explained. "You have to assert yourself. If you don't, you'll end up dead."

From Barrio Azteca's point of view, such a ruthless attitude was necessary to effectively contest the established Texas Syndicate and Eme for dominance of the protection market within prison, to assert control over the El Paso county jail, and to establish Barrio Azteca's criminal bona fides on the streets of El Paso and Juárez and beyond. It was an organizational attitude that eventually caught the attention of the prison administration and resulted in the gang being designated as a security threat group—a verified prison gang—in 1993. Barrio Azteca became just one more prison gang that upheld and enforced the politics of Texas's prisons and El Paso's jails.[53]

Most inmates never join a prison gang. Criminologists David Pyrooz's and Scott Decker's study of Texas male inmates reported that only about 20 percent join a prison gang.[54] But staying out of the prison political system, which is largely dictated by the prison gangs, is difficult.[55] All prisoners, regardless of their race, are offered the opportunity to join some sort of solidarity organization within prison—though not necessarily a prison gang—as a means to navigate and participate in the politics of inside. Recruitment featured in nearly every first-day story I heard, and the details of the various first-day stories were remarkably consistent. Only the players involved, depending on the respondent's race or street gang affiliation, and the terms used for the various roles within the prison order differed. Nonetheless, these distinctions underscore the importance that race plays in the social order of prisons.[56] Although racial segregation within prisons has been banned, prisoners in Texas—as in many other states—typically self-segregate by race.[57]

The TDCJ evaluates and classifies inmates and then transfers them to an assigned unit, where they face three options. In the first option, new inmates can join the lowest ranks of a prison gang's political structure; members of street gangs are obligated to join a specific prison gang should they decide to join one.[58]

Returning inmates reenter at the rank they previously held or higher. Whether an inmate climbs the hierarchy remains his choice; he can remain at the bottom and enjoy the fringe benefits of protection offered to him by the overarching structure to which he pertains.

Cultural exceptions to the racial polices of prison politics occur when someone, such as an Asian man, does not identify with any of the dominant racial groups or when an atypical street gang association exists, such as being a White member of a Black street gang. Such associations typically override racial considerations, though not without conflict, specifically when one's race is typically associated with an existing prison gang.

"Being White caused a big problem for me, especially in prison, especially the fact that I'm a GD, too," said Bradley, a White member of the Gangster Disciples, often referred to as the GDs, a gang that originated in Chicago and features a primarily Black membership. "First off, I had Aryan Brotherhood come after me. Aryan Brotherhood came after me, and I told them, 'Look, I'm just here to do my time.' That's what I told them, and I tried to be respectful about it. I ain't trying to cause no problems with them. I'm just here to do my time. 'Alright, we'll see you around, 'Wood.'"

The Aryan Brotherhood expected Bradley, an obvious street gang member who was therefore likely to join a prison gang, to be at least a Peckerwood, a non–gang-affiliated White person in prison, if not a member of the Aryan Brotherhood. When he refused to acknowledge that designation, the Aryan Brotherhood attempted to assault him; his gang, the Gangster Disciples, helped him defend against the attack.

The second option that a new (or returning) inmate has upon entering prison is to attempt to ride his time out on his own by becoming a *solano*, or a "neutron"—someone who is not involved with the prisoners' political structure—while still observing the rules of racial segregation imposed by the prison gangs.[59] Riding solo is a tough life; an inmate cannot depend on the other members of his race in the event of a one-on-one conflict with another inmate. It also means fewer rights within prison's social order.

"*Solanos* don't have no privileges. Families come first," Pancho explained, referring to the preeminence of prison gangs. "If you don't run with nobody, you don't get a chair to sit or nothing like that. You sit in your bunk if you want or you can sit on the floor, but only the families have the table."

"You can just roll *solano*, but you're a fucking nobody," said Joey, a former inmate who had associated with Chuco Tango, the prison gang formed of El Paso inmates, while he did his time. "You're up for grabs, pretty much. Everybody can fuck with you, and nobody's going to see anything."

"It's not like you have very many options," Alberto noted. He echoed the perception of most of the Latino prison gang members I interviewed in that being a *solano* was an unusual choice. "You can join a gang to gain protection, or you can be extorted by them. Some people can be *solanos*, but it's hard. You still have to follow everybody's rules. The *solanos* are few and far between. So, what happens is that you help the prison gangs fill their ranks."

The third option is to find religion. In prison, religious groups do not require protection from the other inmate groups, even those that are very predatory in nature. The physical protection that religious groups enjoy is conferred on them by the high levels of respect that religious figures, including clergy, lay preachers, and strict adherents, enjoy within prison society. In many ways, this practice echoes the respect that Christianity holds in American society. Thus, religious groups include individuals who might otherwise wish to remain *solano* or who are looking to exit a prison gang without the usual violent or deadly repercussions. Generally speaking, so long as a person declares a religious lifestyle and consistently upholds what is considered to be pious behavior—not using or selling drugs, not cussing, and not engaging in violent behavior, among other typically gang-associated activities—then that person is off limits to the prison gangs as a target for extortion.

Effectively, the restrictions imposed by the nonpious prisoners on the pious ones mean that religious organizations, like prison gangs, trade in protection, albeit on slightly different terms. Unlike prison gangs that offer comfort and physical security veiling an implicit threat, the religious groups offer comfort and physical security along with spiritual healing and redemption in the eye of the Almighty should physical security fail. Religious groups' protection market share expands by evangelizing other inmates. The members of the religious community enjoy several benefits: they develop comradery, enjoy a certain degree of personal security, and, upon release, have no mandatory responsibilities to fulfill on behalf of those who are still incarcerated. According to the code of the underworld, however, they are required to maintain their pious lifestyle in the free world and will lose their protective status should they return to prison for a crime committed since finding God.

With these three options available, joining a prison gang, even at its lowest levels, is perhaps the most attractive option for inmates who don't want to be by themselves or live a life of evangelical penance. For inmates from El Paso, in El Paso jails or in the state penitentiaries, joining Barrio Azteca was the best option available in the 1990s and early 2000s.

"I became an *esquina*, in other words, a prospect," Bruce, a Barrio Azteca member who first went to prison in the 1990s, recalled.[60] "I started doing dirt.

In ISF,[61] they had a lot of sex offenders. So, we started preying on sex offenders; as far as if you had a child sex crime, you'd have to pay at least a hundred and fifty a week. I didn't care how you got it. Either call your mom, call your dad, call somebody—shit, a hundred and fifty dollars."

Prospecting is not unique to the Latino gangs. Ian, a member of the Aryan Brotherhood, described the expectations that a prospect must meet when he decides to join the gang. "When you prospect, whatever they tell you to do, you *have* to do. The gang leaders will get you and a couple of other prospects, or even by yourself, and tell you go discipline that person for whatever reason, and you go, and you beat them up. Or they put an S.O.S.—which is "smash on sight"—on them. And if you see them, regardless—it could be in front of the major or the—it could be in front of anybody. You could be on the side of the walkway or the causeway, you'd have to run across and just start smashing them. If you don't, you get smashed on and you are no longer prospecting."

Asking recruits to engage in violence on behalf of the gang is an inexpensive way to reinforce the protection offered by the gang. The protection model instituted by the prison gangs that came into existence in the 1980s in the Texas prison system was not challenged effectively until the rise of the Tangos in the early 2000s (though some Tangos were founded in the 1990s).[62] The Tangos, sometimes collectively referred to as "Tango Blast," sought system-wide control by replacing the vertically organized prison gangs with horizontally organized groups.

Like Barrio Azteca, the Tangos formed to contest the protection status quo among inmates. According to the people I interviewed who claimed to be affiliated with a Tango while incarcerated, the Tangos are organizationally distinct from the traditional vertically organized prison gangs.[63] Whereas prison gangs have strict rules and permanent associations of hardened individuals, "Tangos are people like—you and I," Joey said. In prison slang, *tango* means "place," and the Tango organizations are organized by the cities their members represent.[64] Today, in addition to the El Paso–based Chuco Tangos, there are several other Tangos throughout the TDCJ, Joey explained, including, "D-towns [from Dallas], San Antone [aka Orejón, from San Antonio], and West Texas that is a bunch of ghost towns that come together, and they make a set, which is like Odessa, Plainview, Brownsville."[65] Other notable Tango sets include the eponymously named Fort Worth; Capirucha, from Austin; Charcos, from Corpus Christi; and Vallucos, from the Rio Grande Valley.[66] Collectively, they have become the largest prison gang in the TDCJ, numbering an estimated twenty-two thousand to twenty-five thousand members, or about four times the size of the next largest prison gang, the Texas Mexican Mafia; however, it's important to remember that the various Tangos don't always cooperate with one another.[67]

"When you became a member of Mexican Mafia, Texas Syndicate, Barrio Azteca, it's a lifelong commitment," Patricio, and El Paso police sergeant who focused on gangs, explained. "You're going to report; you're going to be doing for the gangs when you came out. Slowly but surely, people began saying, 'You know what? I don't want to have to report to anybody when I leave prison.' So, that's when the mentality of the Tango Blast came to be. You become Tango Blast while you're in prison. When you come back out, you go back to whatever normal life that you came from."

Though some scholars state that the various Tangos served as *esquina*, or backup, for established Latino prison gangs, the members of Chuco Tango whom I interviewed never mentioned that role, perhaps because the Tangos were a dominant force in the prison and likely had long abandoned the need to assume that function.[68]

The rise and continued presence of the Tangos can be explained by analyzing shifts in the protection market. First, as Patricio noted, individual inmates who were going to prison were wary of the required lifelong commitment that the established prison gangs demanded of them. Membership in a Tango allows less commitment; identity is fluid as members return to their street gangs and reassume that identity upon their release, unlike most other prison gangs.[69]

Second, in the twenty-first century, the TDCJ has been successful in identifying and isolating the leadership of hierarchical gangs.[70] By putting gang leadership into "super-max" conditions, the prison administration sought to reduce "prison social order to its lowest possible relevance by increasing the level of isolation of the inmate from both other inmates and the staff toward the theoretical limits . . . of total segregation."[71] Given the established prison gangs' paramilitary system of hierarchical order, isolation is effective in limiting a gang's ability to promote new leadership, recruit new members, and engage in the visible violence that the hard power of coercion requires to be effective; members of the traditional hierarchical prison gangs operated outside their gangs' structure and declined leadership roles to avoid the prison administration's attention.[72] Nobody wants to spend his time incarcerated in solitary confinement. Consequently, as was the case in California, when the Texas prison administration broke the monopoly that established organizations held on protection, a space for new inmate organizations, in this case the Tangos, opened up.[73]

"Barrio Azteca is in lockdown right now," Frank, a 19th Street Gang member who associated with Chuco Tango when he was incarcerated, told me. "But, before, in '07 when I would go to county for some crimes or whatever, Barrio Azteca was up there, and they would try to recruit you, and they would tell you, 'Hey, you're a cora—¿Quieres ser cora?'[74]—that means to be like their maids, in other words."

"Right now, Chuco Tango and the GDs run the El Paso county jail annex," said Bradley with a certain degree of bombast that seemed suspiciously to big-up his own gang, the Gangster Disciples. "If the other inmates find out you're Barrio Azteca over in Sanchez, the state jail here, ooh-wee, I'm sorry to hear that! Actually, statewide across prisons—I've heard this, time and time again—if you're Barrio Azteca, you're getting put in lockdown. Off the bat, they're going to lock you down because Barrio Azteca ain't shit. They really ain't shit other than here in El Paso. Nowhere else. And nobody else gives them any clout anywhere in Texas. In prison, you don't see them anywhere. You don't see any 2-1 tattoos.[75] You don't see any of that shit."

The Tangos have managed so far to avoid being locked down by employing a horizontal model, evidenced by their impressive numbers. Instead of having a vertically controlled organization with strict rules, the Tangos recruit members who are given equal status among the group. Unlike hierarchically organized prison gangs, they do not have clear shot callers.[76] Instead, norms are enforced by mob rule. This strategy has been successful in recruiting members, potentially expanding to the point where without a clear leadership system to target, the TDCJ may have limited options in terms of breaking the Tangos' control within the prison system.[77] Nonetheless, Patricio suspects that it is only a matter of time before the Tangos, like Barrio Azteca in the 1980s, depart from a mission of solidarity through a convenience-based model of membership, which allows members to join and leave without consequence, and adopt a mission that requires a more formalized structure, with the objective of establishing a street presence that competes in the drug trade. If history is any indication, Patricio may be right yet: the groups that control the prison yards are often the ones to control the street corners.

While it is true that Barrio Azteca isn't what it once was in the Texas prison system, it is still considered a Tier 1 (top-level) threat by the TDCJ.[78] This status has not been continuous, with the group being downgraded by the TDCJ to a Tier 2 organization briefly in the mid-2010s. Undoubtedly, Barrio Azteca's status within the carceral system allowed it to use the norms of prison to recruit and expand its membership base.[79] With growth, the organization expanded within the prison system and transferred into the free world effectively.[80] Consequently, even though Barrio Azteca may not be as dominant in the prison system today as it once was, it continues, at least for the time being, to maintain strong links to drug trafficking organizations in Mexico and also continues to dominate the drug trade in El Paso.

Upon release, the Aztecas of the 1980s returned to the Paso del Norte area and encountered lucrative criminal enterprises associated with the drug trade at both the wholesale and retail levels. The connections made in prison and the geographical advantage of the Paso del Norte area allowed the Aztecas to become players in the drug trade on both sides of the border. In the streets, the transnational relationships that were commonplace in the Paso del Norte area, along with the improved connections that gang members obtained via incarceration, facilitated involvement with the drug trade.[81] For budding drug entrepreneurs, going to prison provided networking opportunities comparable to those that an MBA might offer budding businesspeople seeking lucrative careers in various industries.

The groundwork that Barrio Azteca laid in the late 1980s continues to pay dividends some thirty-five years later. On the street, the Aztecas control the retail market in both Juárez and El Paso through a retail outlet system consisting of *tiendas*, or houses from which drug dealers sell their product. Each Azteca is entitled to one *tienda*, which allows members to generate money upon their release when few other prospects are available.

"The gang leaders give you whatever you want to sell," explained Emiliano. "If you want to sell some coke or heroin or whatever, they'll give you a piece and you can start selling for some money and get on your feet. So, that's what I did when I was released from prison to El Paso. I started selling."

In Juárez, life as an average Barrio Azteca member—one who could no longer simply cross back into El Paso—developed somewhat differently and in some respects separately, indicating that settings and circumstance do influence illicit entrepreneurial decisions.[82] In the Texas prison system, Barrio Azteca did recruit Mexican nationals—typically men from Ciudad Juárez—into its ranks, but as with almost all criminal aliens, these men were deported back to their countries of origin upon completion of their criminal sentences in the Texas prison system. The deportation of Aztecas effectively exported the prison gang and its organizational traditions, connections, and criminal behaviors to the deportees' home city of Juárez. The deportation and transplantation of prison gangs is a phenomenon that has been seen elsewhere, perhaps most famously with the Mara Salvatrucha 13s, MS-13s, who were deported from Los Angeles to El Salvador and Guatemala.[83]

Nonetheless, while some outlets report that "Barrio Azteca" in El Paso is an organization distinct from "The Aztecas" in Juárez, this distinction is not accurate.[84] Barrio Azteca is transnational, even though all its members are not: El Paso–based Barrio Azteca members can enter and leave Juárez with only a passport or a passport card. No visa is required, and if one, like most who cross the bridge into Juárez, avoids pressing the button present at the end of the bridge that entrants are meant to press to determine if they should be randomly searched or not, one can enter Juárez from El Paso with no passport check or scrutiny of one's criminal record. That means that El Paso-based Barrio Azteca members

FIGURE 6. The Santa Fe bridge. Pictured is the pedestrian portion of the bridge. The border lies between the Mexican and US flags. Notice the customs officers on the US side (the men in the dark uniforms) and the differences in construction on either side of the divide, which is a mirror of the resources available in Juárez and El Paso.

Photo by R. V. Gundur.

are not impeded from entering. This capacity for some members to go back and forth across the border legally through the controlled checkpoints is a net benefit for the gang, especially since rival Juárez gangs do not have an equivalent setup of transnational operatives in El Paso, thus limiting their business opportunities. Most Juárez-based gang members are geographically restricted, and the progression of their criminal careers is impacted by that constraint.

Like their American counterparts, many of the Juárez-based Aztecas returned to prison, albeit in Mexico. Prison life in Ciudad Juárez is distinct from that in Texas. Juárez's municipal jail and Chihuahua's state prison are both known as a Centro Readaptación Social, colloquially referred to by the acronym "Cereso." The state Cereso is a high-security prison governed by criminal organizations, including Barrio Azteca.[85] According to Human Rights Watch, 65 percent of

Mexico's prisons are under inmate rule.[86] Several journalistic reports indicate that the criminal organizations that control the Juárez Cereso have established livable communities that are distinct and separate from one another, with amenities including restaurants, bars, and sex workers.[87]

As in Texas, Chihuahuan prisons are places where prison gangs recruit new members. Lucas, who spent time in the Cereso as a young man, described his recruitment in the 1990s by the Hermandad Pistolera Latina 45, a smaller prison gang that also exists in the Texas prison system and at the time was feuding with the Mexican Mafia in the Cereso. Like many recruits, he joined for protection and was asked to put in work: "We had to do a mission: beat up two Emes." It was the way forward to being recognized as a carnal and becoming part of the gang.

Dominant prisoners exercise violence to subjugate their fellow inmates, and the general population wing is viewed as a dangerous place to do time.[88] The rival factions have access to weapons and have rioted and fought each other in the past, resulting in several deaths.[89] Like their American counterparts, the Juárez-based Aztecas sought to take advantage of the protection rackets they maintained in order to earn money through illicit enterprise.

As the Barrio Azteca gained manpower, the Juárez Cartel recruited the gang to be its muscle. That arrangement allowed Barrio Azteca to grow and reach its organizational pinnacle while specializing in different activities on each side of the border. In Juárez, Barrio Azteca became an effective enforcer, entrenched itself in the burgeoning retail drug market, established itself as a reliable heroin wholesaler, and became an undisputed presence in the local Juárez penitentiary.[90] In El Paso, Barrio Azteca members became the kings of the underworld and controlled the retail drug market, facilitated a significant amount of the wholesaling of heroin, dominated the protection markets inside county jails, provided weapons to their Mexican counterparts, and maintained a competitive presence in Texas state prisons.[91] At its operational apex from the 2000s through the mid-2010s, the different parts of the mature Barrio Azteca organization—the prison gang, the drug trafficking organization, and the enforcement crew—worked well and in concert with each other to exploit comparative advantages enjoyed on either side of the border, at least for a time.

VIOLENCE

When the dead become numbers, they lose their humanity. The body count in Juárez is commonly reported as a daily, monthly, or annual toll. Absent from these numbers are the stories of the people such as Facundo, the man who once showed me around Juárez. Facundo was shot dozens of times as he left his home in a modest Juárez neighborhood one autumn morning in 2018. He was a man of few words. He found his mission later in life, after conquering addiction. He spent his days reducing the harm of drug use and sex work among the vulnerable who engaged in those activities. As with thousands of other people killed in the drug violence of Juárez, the reason for Facundo's murder remains unknown; his assailants, who were almost certainly involved in the drug trade at some petty level, will never be captured.

While the numbers of the dead ebb at times, violence and conflict seem always to reappear. This persistence arises from the fact that drug trafficking organizations in Mexico generally continue to compete for market presence and dominance. For most drug trafficking organizations, protection against outside threats, including the state and especially the organizations' competitors, remains a problem. In Mexico, one solution has been to recruit military and law enforcement personnel to deploy military tactics.[1] The Juárez Cartel opted for this solution when it formed La Línea to be its armed branch.[2] Another solution is to recruit the gangs that developed throughout the 1990s following the deportation of prison gang members from the United States to Mexico. La Línea, in turn, opted for this solution to expand its operational capacity by partnering with Barrio Azteca.

Drug trafficking organizations throughout Mexico and their armed branches, or gang enforcers, employ violent tactics to establish dominance over their smuggling routes to fend off competition and to ensure that the state cannot reestablish control over security and protection in these spaces. Occasionally the drug trafficking organizations' efforts backfire, especially when their contracted muscle becomes autonomous and establishes itself as a competitor in the drug trade.

The first example of such a split was the emergence of the Gulf Cartel's armed branch, the Zetas. Over the course of a few years, the Zetas used the efficacy of the violent tactics they pioneered to distance themselves from the Gulf Cartel and to establish themselves as their own separate, full-fledged drug trafficking organization and a preeminent player in the wholesale drug marketplace in eastern Mexico.[3] A war between the Zetas and their former masters, the Gulf Cartel, started in 2010. Eager to make a name for themselves and to assert control over the Gulf Cartel's areas of operation, the Zetas used terrorist-inspired tactics, such as beheadings, kidnappings, and bombings, to gain control over rivals and to intimidate local society, media, and law enforcement.[4]

This left the Gulf Cartel in an unenviable position. It had failed to control either its anointed protection providers or the Mexican state and consequently was targeted by both, losing all forms of available protection.[5] On the one side, the Zetas were exacting high casualties; on the other, returning to the government for protection was no longer an option: the Calderón administration had enacted a public policy designed to hit drug traffickers hard.

By all appearances, the Juárez Cartel and La Línea have had better luck in their partnership with Barrio Azteca. Special Agent Diana Apodaca, then the public information officer for the El Paso DEA office, stated that "since the mid-2000s, the Juárez Cartel has used members of the Barrio Azteca gang to oversee its retail-level drug sales in Ciudad Juárez and to assist in fighting rival cartel members. [Barrio Azteca] members subsequently expanded their role to include enforcement, providing additional personnel and firepower against the Sinaloa Cartel and fighting a proxy war with the Sinaloa-aligned street gangs known as the Artistas Asesinos and the Mexicles."

Indeed, it seems that in certain cases gangs have evolved to work more smoothly with drug trafficking organizations. While the "street gangs" Apodaca referred to have elements of the "traditional street gangs" of Chicago, Los Angeles, and New York that come to mind in popular culture, in that "they are territorial in the sense that they identify strongly with their turf, 'hood, or barrio," they are not the youth street gangs that Lucas and Modesto joined in their adolescence in 1980s Juárez.[6] Lucas's and Modesto's crews focused on controlling the block, having fun, and getting high. Those street gangs—like the most commonly seen street gangs in the United States and Mexico—recruited and developed primarily youth members and did "not have extensive transnational connections or connections to large Mexican drug trafficking organizations."[7] Gangs that do have such connections, such as Barrio Azteca, the Artistas Asesinos, and the Mexicles, differ from traditional street gangs in three significant ways.

First, most of these gangs are groups that were founded in jails and prisons. Their leadership is often located, at least partially, in the prison system. While some of these gangs may be accurately termed "prison gangs," they also have an active role in the street.[8] Plus, in Mexico, recruitment may occur without being incarcerated first.

Second, they typically have an older age range. The gangs initially recruited their members primarily in jails and prisons, meaning that the members were likely to be older. As recruitment moved to the street, it was a function of need often linked to physical capability. Consequently, the gangs do not include "peewee" ranks of preteen members.

Third, in Juárez, these gangs associate themselves with and thus defer to a drug trafficking organization operating in their community, meaning that they do not claim their turf as "theirs alone," an attribute that is typical of street gangs.[9] The association with drug trafficking organizations means that gangs such as the Barrio Azteca, the Artistas Asesinos, and the Mexicles commit relatively serious crimes.

Yet, these gangs are not "specialty gangs" that "narrowly [focus] on a few offenses" and "tend to be small."[10] They tend to engage in a range of offenses and be quite large. Accordingly, these gangs may oversee the retail operations of street gangs in the emerging retail drug market in Mexico.[11] Nonetheless, their primary business interests—and means of making money—include facilitating midlevel wholesale drug operations and engaging in tasks that contest the control and authority of the state and establish operational control in plazas where rival drug trafficking organizations may attempt to operate.[12]

Notably, these gangs are not themselves drug trafficking organizations as we have come to understand the term. While the Zetas developed the network necessary to replace the logistics previously undertaken by their employers, the Gulf Cartel, this development is not the norm. Most drug trafficking organizations appear to have structured the ways in which gangs provide protection and assume trafficking tasks in order to constrain them. Gangs typically engage in only intermediary trafficking activities and do not have access to suppliers in countries from which precursor products originate. This arrangement generally benefits both gangs and drug trafficking organizations: gangs generate income while using the skills they already possess, while drug trafficking organizations defray risk to themselves by accepting a modest cost for having gangs assume riskier roles. To young men thirsting after money and a sense of power, it is an easy sell.

"You don't have to convince gang members to take risks, because most of the soldiers . . . don't care much because they're already taking risks, themselves, just by being in a gang.[13] So, they don't have worries," Frank explained to me. He was a member of the 19th Street Gang, a Juárez-based street gang with four generations of members. "So, to them they are actually fighting to get cartel work, saying 'Hey! Me, me, me. I want that money. I want to be your guy.' So, it's not really convincing somebody. It's more like finding the right person: someone that is not going to snitch on you, someone that is not going to be a rat or that is going to just disappear with everything. That's what you have to worry about—finding the right person and making the right decisions—because otherwise your business is going to drop, and then the drug cartel is going to come after your head."

On occasion, the gang members involved in such activities are convinced that being a fall guy is simply part of their job description. One former Barrio Azteca member, Alberto, told me that when he got caught for smuggling drugs, he knew that he was going to be caught on that day. "Everyone would take their turn being a possible fall guy with a small load to distract customs from the larger shipment behind. The first time I went to prison, I knew that I was going to get busted. It was all arranged, and it didn't matter to me at the time."

For drug trafficking organizations using this new business model, which involves co-opting gangs and swelling the numbers of operatives at their disposal, the value of any single actor decreases. It is a clever strategy, considering the success the Zetas had in deposing their masters. No contracted protection provider now has sufficient know-how to run an entire drug trafficking operation on its own, thus rendering the protection providers more controllable. Nonetheless, as the number of protection providers has multiplied, competition in the protection marketplace has grown fiercer. Violence has supplanted cash reserves and corrupting officials in terms of importance. In short, the liberalization of the protection market resulted in a reconfiguration of the priorities and mentalities within the drug trade in Mexico.

Cartel bosses were no longer content to earn only the money that corrupting officials alone offered. They knew that despite a larger human cost, more money could be made by developing a presence in the protection market either through their own organizations or by proxy through subcontracting armed groups, such as the Zetas, or gangs, such as Barrio Azteca. Protection allows drug trafficking organizations to better compete in the wholesale drug trafficking market, and by developing their own armed groups, drug trafficking organizations can compete directly with one another, allowing for the possibility of exponential expansion of their criminal enterprises. Effectively, drug trafficking organizations created their own best-case scenario. By controlling their own protection, drug trafficking organizations have less need to respect the government's threat of violence.

Therefore, so long as they can maintain an effective protection racket, which insulates them from not only state interference but also annihilation by their competitors, and so long as the demand for their products continues, they do not need to fear their collective demise; they just need to fear each other.

In Mexico, the apex of the drug violence, underwritten by clashes between drug cartels and their associates, occurred between 2010 and 2011; however, after 2015 violence increased once again. Violence brings unwanted attention to the drug trade, so keeping heat from the plazas is a logistical concern for drug trafficking organizations whose profits are, after all, driven by their ability to move their illicit commerce across the US-Mexican border. By the numbers, violence dipped from those blood-soaked years but remained still comparatively high in many plazas throughout Mexico, and violence appears to be on the uptick again.[14] A reduction in violence associated with the drug trade in a given site reflects a parallel trend regarding competition in the protection market. Less violence can be the result of four outcomes, all indicating a change in the degree of competition in the protection market.

First, a drop in violence may be caused by the unlikely event that the government has reasserted control over the market. Though it appears that government actors still heavily promote a culture of corruption, there is little evidence to suggest that the government, even upon returning to PRI rule, regained control over any sizable proportion of the drug market in Mexico.[15]

Second, the Mexican government could be implementing legal changes that are causing drug trafficking organizations to make greater efforts to hide their previously visible violence, which in turn results in the perception that there is less violence.[16] Judging by the information I collected while in Juárez, this practice of hiding violence, together with collusion between corrupt government actors and criminal entrepreneurs, appears to be the most reasonable explanation for the decrease in the visibility of violence in Juárez. In essence, the criminal-political arrangements are returning to those resembling the days of PRI dominance when overt violence was suppressed by the effective control exercised by the state.

Alberto noted the concerns that violence presents for criminal organizations. "Violence is a problem. It leads to discovery by law enforcement. In the past when you could negotiate with other gangs, it was easier to keep unwanted attention away. For a long time, the Mexican law wasn't equal. As long as you did things quietly, you could get away literally with murder. If you did get caught, the sentence was lenient. Now, with all of the violence, the laws are changing. The Mexican government is looking for ways to send murderers to the US to get punished."

Alberto's functionalist argument alone cannot explain when violence escalates.[17] We must understand whether law enforcement's ability to investigate effectively or the public's ability to demand a law enforcement response so that an investigation happens affects the presence of violence. When the state is unable or unwilling to investigate, the performance of violence becomes a powerful tool to intimidate opponents or witnesses. Sometimes states need help to improve or supplement its capacity to respond. With the successful extraditions and US convictions of Edgar "La Barbie" Valdez Villarreal, Jesús Vicente "El Mayito" Zambada Niebla, the son of Ismael "El Mayo" Zambada, and, perhaps most famously, Joaquín Archivaldo "El Chapo" Guzmán Loera, among many others, it appears that the Mexican government is making an effort to show that despite its ongoing struggles, it can maintain control well enough to deter future ostentatious drug traffickers from drawing too much attention to themselves or risk arrest and prosecution. Nonetheless, the ongoing violence in Mexico indicates that these efforts remain ineffective to a degree.[18]

Pancho, a current Barrio Azteca member who enjoys an intermediate status in the gang hierarchy, commented that acts of violence are now less blatant in Juárez. "Well, there is violence, but not like it used to be. Like leaving the bodies out on the street. Now they bury them. Now it's like back in the days; they do it underwater."[19]

"What caused people to change that behavior?" I asked.

"The US government was about to go in over there. They just wanted to take the heat off the bridge [that connects El Paso and Juárez]. Everybody was losing money."[20]

"Everybody, as in everybody who?"

"All the cartels." Pancho explained. "All the people that was moving something. They were losing money because of all the heat they brought to the bridge. They needed to stop that."

Third, violence can drop when one group asserts a monopoly over protection in a plaza.[21] This was the case in Ciudad Acuña, Coahuila, a town that is uncontested and under the control of the Zetas, according to "Cartel Maps" that the DEA and think tanks such as Stratfor produce in an attempt to map drug trafficking organization presence within Mexico. While visiting the area I met an American woman named April, who lived in the sleepy border town of Del Rio, Texas, but worked across the border in Acuña as an engineer in one of the maquiladoras owned by a major American company.

"I work in Acuña every day, and we don't really have any problems there either. The Zetas control the area, yes, and sometimes there might be a dustup, so we work for a day or two in our warehouse in Del Rio until the story of what happened comes out. But it's never for very long," April explained. "Violence has never affected me directly. I think that there isn't a whole lot of criminal activity or drug trafficking or even drug use around here because it's hard to do those activities. There are all of the military guys, and there are lots of Border Patrol agents. There is the DEA too."

April noted that Mexican police aren't a problem for her, and that was the case even before the corrupt local cops were replaced by *federales*. Moreover, she was not convinced that the *federales* were any less corrupt than the local smokies had been. "Having Texas or Coahuila plates will usually ensure that the Mexican police will leave you alone. Sometimes, our workers get transferred in from another Mexican state and they don't change their plates. That's when I've heard of people getting into a bind not with the police but with the Zetas, who are afraid their foreign plates belong to spies from another criminal organization. We tell new employees that they need to change their plates over for that reason." In short, the main concern that her workers faced was being subjected to drug trafficking organization efforts to assert control.

Fourth, violence may drop when competing drug trafficking organizations engage as an economic cartel and collude with one another.[22] This practice serves two purposes. First, it minimizes the human, monetary, and security costs of violence, which after a certain point become so expensive, when taken in the aggregate, that an enterprise cannot survive and grow. Second, it allows the drug trafficking organizations to work more efficiently in terms of trafficking.

The people who are closest to the criminal action—the gang members and the police—doubt the dominance of the Sinaloa Federation in the Juárez plaza, which is the predominate narrative presented by most law enforcement outside El Paso.[23] El Paso–based law enforcement and gang members alike thought that the plaza was still in contest; the violence was being controlled either through an understanding among the drug trafficking organizations or a cease-fire that was in fact a period of retooling. The view that the Sinaloa Federation dominates the drug market is tenuous given the lack of Sinaloa-affiliated outlets present in El Paso to offload product into the United States. Nonetheless, the organizational dynamic of criminal enterprises in the Paso del Norte region is in constant flux. Leaders come and go, their exits usually due to arrest or death, and those changes in leadership sometimes change organizational strengths and alliances.

There have been several high-profile arrests of Mexican cartel bosses, including the October 2014 arrest of Juárez Cartel boss Vicente Carrillo Fuentes and the April 2015 arrest of his successor Jesús "El Chuyin" Salas Aguayo.[24] Additionally, 2014 saw the conclusion of a three-year-long law enforcement operation that led to the indictment of fifty-five Barrio Azteca members in El Paso. Eighteen were ultimately arrested and tried in El Paso. Of those, seventeen were eventually convicted for crimes prosecuted via the Racketeer Influenced and Corrupt Organizations Act (RICO), with sentences ranging from one year to twenty-five years.[25] Since then, the federal government has continued with its strategy of charging Barrio Azteca members and their associates under RICO in an effort to disrupt the gang's operations.[26]

Despite prosecutorial successes in the United States, there are still bursts of significant violence within Mexico, which are often credited to drug trafficking organization infighting or to "high-intensity criminality" related to the drug trade.[27] There is evidence to support these claims, such as the factionalization of Barrio Azteca in Juárez in 2018. The Juárez leadership of Barrio Azteca changed in June 2018 when authorities arrested Eduardo "Tablas" Ravelo Rodríguez, who reportedly had been the elusive leader for the gang for some time. However, Emiliano and José remembered Ravelo as a heroin addict rather than a kingpin.[28] Nonetheless, Ravelo was indicted in 2008 and again in 2011 in El Paso on federal organized crime charges connected to the 2010 killings of consulate workers in Juárez and placed on the FBI's "Most Wanted" list in 2009.[29]

Barrio Azteca's second-in-command, Juan Arturo "El Genio" Padilla Juárez, was arrested along with Ravelo. Padilla Juárez was murdered in a Chihuahua City prison a month after his capture, allegedly on the orders of the man who replaced him, René Gerardo "El 300" Santana Garza. Santana's ascension to power was facilitated by Barrio Azteca's old Juárez Cartel–sponsored ally, La Línea, which did not consult the gang's veteran leadership about who should be next to head the gang.[30] The decision to elevate Santana led to a division within Barrio Azteca. Although Barrio Azteca remained the gang, supported by La Línea and led by Santana, a rival faction, La Vieja Guardia led by Jesús Alfredo "El Fredy" Martínez Mendoza, emerged.[31]

Despite the turmoil in Juárez, Barrio Azteca's power struggles have not manifested in El Paso. The calm that Barrio Azteca maintains in its US operations reflects how the organization understands that the violence it uses in Juárez cannot be used north of the border, where violence could easily destroy its steady and profitable business activities. It's a business sense that most drug trafficking organizations appear to share. In Mexico, clear hot spots of violence have appeared in mid- to large-size cities on or near the US-Mexican border. However, on the US side of the border, port cities and transportation hubs that import drugs or the precursor products used to synthesize them from South America and Asia are not hot at all; in fact, most of the time they aren't even lukewarm.

One day in late May 2014, the five o'clock news panned to a shot of a billboard with a graffiti tag that boldly stated "Plata o Plomo," a threat that had been publicly issued by drug trafficking organizations in the past via *narcomantas*, blankets hung from freeway overpasses, in Mexico.[32] Take the bribe or take a bullet. The local TV press misreported the message as saying "Pay or take the bribe," which was an unexpected mistranslation given how many people speak Spanish at home in the Paso del Norte. At first glance, I thought the message was just more of the same threats that had been made throughout the hot spots of drug-related violence in Mexico, but this time the billboard was not south of the border. It was in El Paso. And such billboard messages had never appeared in El Chuco before. There was another billboard with a message written in English: "Dying for Drugs." Both of the billboards had dressed mannequins hanging from nooses dangling from the platforms.

The messages had appeared mysteriously overnight in the far eastern part of the city, and nobody could make sense of them. The press seemed to latch onto the *plata o plomo* message, and a moment of panic ensued. The heavy coverage of violence across the border fed an ongoing latent fear that the violence might actually spill over from violent Juárez into peaceful El Paso. Theories abounded: Was it gonzo advertising for a movie? Or, *holy shit*, had the violence finally crossed over? The month of May had been an especially deadly one in Juárez. But for some time already, the border had been completely militarized and closely scrutinized, so the possibility of violence suddenly crossing over into El Paso seemed unreasonable. Plus, what the hell did "Dying for Drugs" mean? That didn't seem like a cartel threat.

Some in the media as well as people I knew in El Chuco were skeptical that anyone would put up these billboards for a prank. But then came the news report that the police had arrested a suspect and had linked him to the crime scenes with fingerprints. Graffiti artist Ryan Edward Jean of Las Vegas, Nevada, was arrested as he tried to fly back home after a fingerprint found on the scene matched his record in a national police database.[33] Jean said that he vandalized the billboards to make a political statement. On the border, it was clearly lost in translation.

The billboard prank forced a discussion about the possibility that the drug violence in Mexico might for the first time spill over the border. The Mexican government's inability to control violence and to provide security to its citizens is of little concern to US border inhabitants whose day-to-day lives are in cities and towns with murder rates far lower than those in their Mexican counterparts across the border.[34] Despite claims to the contrary made by commentators and politicians who insist on a narrative of impending catastrophic violence, the US side of the border remains safe. In fact, any spillover effect is felt solely on the Mexican side of the border, as guns are smuggled into Mexico from the United States, bought in states such as Texas and Arizona where firearms are easily purchased.[35]

One concern regarding border security is corruption. Customs agents are the custodians of the points of entry along the border and Border Patrol agents are the custodians of the stretches in between. But within an organization made up of thousands of individuals, some are corruptible and represent a compromise to border security. One Border Patrol agent, who was giving me a border tour, told me that the George W. Bush administration's call to double the size of the Border Patrol was a mixed blessing.

"We were ten thousand agents in 2005. By 2008/2009 we were up to twenty-one thousand agents. We doubled in size, and the George W. Bush administration wanted to get it done in two years. It's a good thing in that we got people, personnel; we got some infrastructure. The bad thing is that we got a lot of bad seeds that made it through. Some of the cartel families, they have their kids or their associates run a clean life. These people don't get arrested, don't get pulled over, and don't even get involved in drugs. They just go to school. Then they might join the police force, but they actually work for the cartels. The authorities busted a lot here within El Paso sector; crooked agents were escorting drug lords around or selling our secrets or the way that we work."[36]

These concerns were echoed by James Tomsheck, who served as head of Internal Affairs at CBP from 2006 to 2014. Tomsheck believed that between 5 and 10 percent of CBP agents had been corrupt at some point in their careers. Customs and Border Protection leadership ordered him to redefine corruption to reduce the number of cases, and when Tomsheck refused, he was forced out of his internal affairs role.[37] In 2017, the Trump administration expanded the Border Patrol to support its constant narrative that the border was under threat. The expansion failed to heed the lessons of the past and occurred with weakened oversight in terms of its hiring practices, given the agency's difficulties in maintaining, much less expanding, operational capacity.[38] CBP has a long-standing history of corrupt agents in its employ. From October 2004 through March 2018, there were over two hundred corruption case resulting in legal action due to CBP agents engaging in rape, drug smuggling, human smuggling, bribery, and sharing top secret government data.[39] Corrupting law enforcement officers, rather than deploying violence, was straight out of the old-school cartel playbook: criminal entrepreneurs had to respect the state's ability to respond forcefully and interrupt business, and a few compromised agents would obviate the need to go against an entire agency and keep the goods moving.

A few compromised agents, however, does not account for the crossing of all of the illicit goods that transit the border. Many, if not most, drugs enter via licit points of entry despite the best efforts of honest Border Patrol agents. Given the need to keep licit trade moving through, Border Patrol agents have limited time available to search for illicit goods. Had the *plata o plomo* threat been genuine, it would have marked a serious escalation of outward rhetoric, driven by drug trafficking organizations, in the United States and would have provoked a firestorm of law enforcement and a possible shutdown of the border. Such a swell of police presence would greatly reduce the value of the Juárez plaza, since its logistical advantages in terms of its ability to transport assets, whether they be clothes, food, and cars or drugs, money, and weapons, would be compromised. Such an increase in law enforcement would be, frankly, bad for business. Instead, the drug trade churns along in El Paso as it has for decades, largely outside the public view and without visible violence.

THE STREET

The day after the billboard news broke I was back in the red pickup, driving through the streets of El Chuco with Emiliano. He had promised to show me the old haunts where the action used to go down. Like his dad, José, Emiliano had decided that the gang life was no longer for him; he had children and was no longer interested in slinging drugs to make ends meet. But his firsthand experience running a *tienda* for the preeminent drug trafficking and retailing organization in El Paso only a few years earlier would help paint a picture of the way the drug trade unfolded in the city.

Everyone, from journalists to gang members to my neighbors to current and former police, described a time when El Paso was far less peaceful—though never anywhere as violent as Ciudad Juárez had gotten. These days, El Paso by and large seemed to live up to its peaceful reputation; there were rarely news reports of violence, much less gang- or drug-related incidents.

"From the late '50s to the late '80s or '90s, we had a lot of different gangs throughout the city, a lot of membership, but they were more focused on protecting their blocks and not so much into profiteering, selling drugs, prostitution, and things of that nature. Most of them were copycatting and they just went around the city and graffitied their areas," explained Harry Kirk, a retired El Paso police lieutenant who worked on gangs in the 1980s and 1990s. But by the end of that period there had been, according to Kirk, "a proliferation of drive-by shootings and retaliation events."

Several people who had been involved in gangs in the 1980s described how much their scene changed in that decade alone. Miguel, who had done over twenty years in prison for murdering a rival gang member when he was a teenager, talked about the Nasty Boys, the group he associated with as a youth. At first the Nasty Boys was just a "party crew," made up of a hundred or so kids whose primary goal was to go out to party and dance. They drank underage and smoked marijuana, but they were hardly up to anything that could be considered more than usual teenage mischief. Eventually that changed; violence came into the picture, and the group needed to protect itself from others who attempted to disrupt their parties.

Miguel described the initial stages of the group's transformation from a party crew into a street gang. "We had seen that other party crews wanted to jump so-and-so at a party or at a club.[1] And we had seen a lot of—this was '83, '84, and '85—that's when I saw a bunch of guns, stabbings, and fights, of course."

"Why would somebody want to jump somebody in your crew?" I asked.

"I think it's just the jealousy," Miguel responded. "I even got to know many other people from other gangs. And they were like, 'We don't know why we started shit with you all. I guess it's because you guys had more girls in your crew.' I guess it's just a jealousy issue. So, for protection, along with my brother, we started carrying guns."

"Why did you decide to get weapons?"

"Because all of the other gangs started getting weapons or guns, and they wanted to shoot at us. We did have a lot of circumstances where they would shoot at us at parties or at get-togethers or even when we were just chilling at the apartments or whatever. They would just go and do a drive-by. Back in '87, they killed one of my homies. Then out of the hundred that were with the Nasty Boys, about twenty-five of us, we just went berserk or something. Out of the twenty-five, I think like maybe twenty of us went to prison. Murders, attempted murders, aggravated assault, attempted murders of police officers."

In the impoverished parts of town, street gangs ran with a goal to "protect" their blocks. Pancho recounted his youth as a member of the Diablos street gang. When his housing project was torn down, he was forced to relocate into unfriendly territory. "Nobody liked us. Every one or two blocks in Segundo, it used to be a different gang, and nobody liked us.[2] Every day when we went to school and everything, it was an adventure."

Eventually Pancho started getting into more serious activities with the Diablos. "We would steal, you know? Do different things, go to other 'hoods just to fight, to represent, to let them know we were there."

Patricio, who started his career in the El Paso Police Department in the early 1990s, noted how different the gang scene was then compared to the mid-2010s. "When I first got here, we were mostly dealing with turf issues between street gangs. Most of the problems that we saw back then was, again, issues on turf, issues of disrespect where they were disrespecting each other—hand signs, mad-dogging—that's what was sparking off a lot of the gang violence."[3]

By the 2010s, however, significant violence in El Paso was a thing of the past. Everyone I spoke to had a different idea as to why El Paso had become peaceful. Harry Kirk and Patricio credited the efforts of the police department, especially community policing and community outreach programs. My housemate Pablo speculated that it was due to the influx of soldiers at Fort Bliss as a result of the US involvement in foreign wars. Bruce, an *esquina* for Barrio Azteca, claimed that Barrio Azteca, in controlling the politics of the streets, ensured that its members did not draw police attention to themselves. Whatever the cause, the streets of El Paso were mostly devoid of obvious delinquent activity.

As I cruised around with Emiliano, we looked for anything that could possibly be gang-related. To my untrained eye nothing looked obvious, so I was hoping that Emiliano could point some action out to me. Our first stop was his childhood neighborhood, Sandoval. Here were the same tenement houses where José had spent part of his childhood some thirty years before. The blue housing projects appeared to be a tranquil working-class apartment complex.

"That's the first spot I did a drive-by. I was ten," Emiliano told me as we passed a rundown house near the projects. Little, if any, remains of the violence that characterized his childhood days running with the local street gang, Puro Barrio Sandoval.

"It ain't the same as it used to be when I was with Puro Barrio Sandoval. You don't see all the people hanging around the corners like we used to. Or at the park. It's not like in the early '90s, with all these different gangs doing drive-bys. You don't hear that no more."

The absence of violence in El Paso remained a running theme during our drive through the city. We passed all the old hot spots. After visiting the west side we went downtown, where a lot of the drug dealing used to happen. The area was mostly empty and under reconstruction. On the back end of the main downtown area, Segundo Barrio, which once had a rough reputation, was quiet too. The real estate next to the brand-new baseball stadium, home of the El Paso Chihuahuas, was being snatched up for redevelopment. Central appeared to be a middle-class residential area of El Paso. The east side of town, where empty fields used to be, now offered new shopping malls. Throughout our drive, the only potential evidence we saw of the drug trade was one disheveled woman who was staggering down the street, possibly high on something.

"Wow. *Nobody* is posting up; I can't believe it," Emiliano observed. The corners, parks, and streets were devoid of the gang culture, the loitering and tagging, that Emiliano remembered and lived. That life simply didn't exist publicly anymore anywhere in El Paso except possibly within a few bars that Emiliano said were local hangouts for Barrio Azteca members. We didn't go inside because Emiliano was unwilling to check them out, perhaps due to his *equis* status.

But those empty streets likely belie a steady, quiet stream of illicit activity in and through El Paso, out of the public eye. The El Paso Police Department sergeant who runs the Stash House Unit said that a lot of product and payment is stored in El Paso for further transportation.[4] Stash houses for northbound drugs, including marijuana, cocaine, heroin, and methamphetamine, as well as southbound currency are scattered throughout the city. Before the violence escalated in Juárez, the stash houses in El Paso held multikilo quantities of cocaine and heroin, but the stash house unit was reasonably successful in rooting out these properties. "Because of that, drug traffickers started changing their strategy," Patricio explained. "They stopped keeping all their eggs in the same basket." Contemporary traffickers stash smaller quantities to protect against loss, but outside of that there does not seem to be a predictable pattern to the stash houses. They have been found throughout the city and, as Patricio noted, "can seem almost abandoned to having a family living inside."

When a stash house bust does happen, there is rarely violence. After all, the traffickers don't want their neighbors to live on edge, since the residents of El Paso, with their safe communities and relatively good opinions of the police, are more likely to report suspicious activities than the residents of Juárez. This does not mean that there aren't any killings anymore, Emiliano warned, echoing what Pancho had told me about things happening underwater.

"You don't hear about killings, but it's happening. You got to be a part of it—be a part of the streets or something so that you can hear what's really going on the streets. For example, the cops recently found two bodies, and one of them was an Azteca," Emiliano recounted. "The other guy was a White dude. I don't know what he was doing. He had been in prison himself. So, I don't know [exactly] what was going on, but I know because Ismael used to sell for me when I was over on the west side. He used to sell heroin for me. So, I don't know what he did or didn't do, but they found him dead. But they never did too much about it like reporting it on the news every day when he got identified or none of that. They just said they found two bodies and that's it. You never heard about it again."

In the six years that Emiliano had been out of prison, he had heard of approximately six men affiliated with the gangs who had been murdered. According to Emiliano, people who are affiliated with the drug trafficking organizations in El Paso prefer to keep those affiliations quiet. "Right here in El Paso, it's like cartel members just want to be family people. They want to be with their families and stuff. They don't want to call attention to themselves or anything like that."

An editor for the *El Paso Times* corroborated Emiliano's claim, telling me that the paper had run stories on "cartel members on this side of the border, but they don't do anything in El Paso." In short, if any territorial claim is to be made for El Paso, Barrio Azteca is the only drug trafficking group that can make that claim. Other than that, there are only a handful of street gangs in El Paso that claim territory, and the territories include just the small districts in which the gangs are concentrated.

The majority of the Latino gang members I spoke to had two gang-related identities: one on the street and another in prison. One of the two identities trumped the other. Those who joined Barrio Azteca were Aztecas for life (unless, of course, they abandoned the gang and became *equis*). Those who were part of Chuco Tango identified with whichever gang they identified with before going to prison. The distinction is not incidental; the roles and allegiances forged in the context of the street are different from those hammered out in prison. Pancho contrasted the responsibilities and relationships that came with being a member of the Diablos, a street gang, with those that came with being a member of Barrio Azteca, a prison gang.

As a member of a street gang, you have "to take care of an area, to take care of your 'hood. It's just like a friendship, binding together, bonding together," Pancho explained. "But a family inside the prison is forever. You cannot turn your back on that or you cannot get out of it; you cannot leave. If you're going to go somewhere to work or something, you need to let them know where you're going to be so they can let you know if there's homeboys around that area where you can just clique together."

There is a difference in status, too, between being identified primarily as a member of a "family"—a prison gang—or being identified primarily as a member of a street gang. Once someone becomes an Azteca, he has more clout on the streets of El Paso. He shoots up the hierarchy of his street gang's control structure. By allowing for dual identities to exist in a clear hierarchy, Barrio Azteca was able to unify several street gangs under an overarching political structure, which was one of the factors that reduced violent conflict among El Paso's street gangs. Plus, there were no prison gangs competing with Barrio Azteca in El Paso for the better part of twenty years, so the structure the Aztecas imposed was accepted without much opposition. Consequently, turf wars were and are forbidden in an effort to avoid unwanted law enforcement attention. Accordingly, several street gangs have become part of an enterprise that has focused on moving drugs, accepting the rules handed down to them by their Azteca bosses in accordance with their business interests.

Moreover, the few established gangs that remain active prevent emerging groups from becoming anything more than party crews. Frank, who is a member of an established Juárez-based gang, said that when party crews end and most of those kids leave the area to go to college or to work, the remaining members are forcibly incorporated into his gang.

"Some of the youngsters from our gang, they recruit those guys from party crews," Frank explained. "They tell them, 'You're not going to be with this party crew anymore. You're going to be with us, all of you guys.' And the youngsters go and fuck them up and make sure that they stop with that party crew bullshit."

Most of the men I spoke to who had joined street gangs did so after hanging out with existing gang members for a protracted period of time. Their accounts were similar, always tales of seeking acceptance or the love that they felt they had failed to receive at home as children. In every instance, the men who had joined street gangs were from poor backgrounds and had parents who were absent because they were working multiple jobs to make ends meet, were on drugs, or were just gone.

Without a parent or any other authority figure to guide them, these kids began to hang out with other kids who provided the acceptance they craved. They would party with them and hang out with them until the kids who were already part of the gang would say that hanging out time was over: it was time to get jumped in.

"I was nine years old; that's when I got jumped into my gang," Pancho said. "At that time, I was a follower. I was a little boy looking up to older guys. I just liked the situation, the relationship everybody had."

Joey was jumped in during middle school, just for hanging around the gang too much. "I didn't want to get into that gang; I just wanted to kick it and then, yeah, we started messing up, started hanging around, started robbing stereos, started robbing Walmart, just jacking Disney movies to get money, and then, yeah, I started messing up," Joey recounted. "Then I got jumped into the 'hood eventually, because they said, 'No, you're kicking it with us too much,' or whatever; I got put in the gang. I didn't want to, but I got jumped in."

My housemate, Pablo, a man who left gang life completely behind him by joining the military, recounted how he got jumped in during his sophomore year in high school. "It was kind of one of those things where I lived in this apartment building, and there were some people there who were all part of this gang. I ended up spending a lot of time with them and hanging out with them. One day it was just time to jump me in. Four guys came up on me and beat the crap out of me, and I was in. They put me in the hospital."

As a member of a street gang, it is easier to fade away from *la vida loca*, gang life, than when one becomes a member of a prison gang. The obligations owed to the street gang are not typically as concrete as those owed a prison gang. Some street gang members, such as Pablo, move away or move on with their lives, finding interests beyond the delinquent behaviors of their childhood. For others, such as Pancho and Frank, the street gangs serve as a springboard into prison as their criminal activities become more and more serious. Once a man spends time in a medium-security or higher prison, he becomes part of prison politics whether he wants to or not.

"What happens is that you have your street gang members. They get arrested for a violent crime or for narcotics. They can't make bond because, obviously, it was something pretty serious that they did. So, they end up at the El Paso County jail," Patricio, the gang sergeant, explained. "At the El Paso County jail, depending on how long you're there, you'll stay at the downtown facility or get transferred to the jail annex. If you're going to be incarcerated for a certain period of time and you're a state jail inmate with state charges, you're most likely going to end up at the annex. For protection from other gangs that are there, I would say there's a very high percentage—probably in the 90s—that those people are going to join one gang or another for protection.

"But this is where Barrio Azteca starts their recruitment, in that they want people that are going to be loyal to the gang. They're going to want people that will strike for the gang at any given time, even kill for the gang. A lot of times, a lot of these street gang members, they already know what they can do. They've pretty much already proven themselves, and by just getting to the jail, that's where the recruiting process starts."

A prison gang will recruit members from street gangs in cities where it wants a street presence, allowing it to assert control outside the prison walls. When recognized members who have gone up the gang hierarchy eventually leave prison, they typically return to the cities they came from and are expected, per the norms of the prison gang, to impose a supragovernmental structure over the street gangs of those cities.

"When folks come out of jail they are completely changed, though not necessarily reformed. It is a system that runs on money and doesn't pause to think about the monster it feeds," Alberto said. "When people go to jail, their new connections lead them to taking risks they never imagined taking." On the outside, the status gained from being in prison demands respect within the underworld.

The concept of respect is fundamental to members of a gang. Respect, at its core, indicates an understanding and reverence for the rules and social stations within the structure of the underworld. Minding one's own business is the key to respect at the most basic level. One should not try to engage above one's own station.

"Out here, when you talk to a person, you make eye contact, right?" Pablo explained. "In prison, you cannot make a lot of eye contact with a person. You need to mind your own business."

Much like the military, the respect one commands in a gang depends on his status within the organization. "In a gang, the lower ranking you are, the less you have to say about anything. You get respect in a gang by being consistent, that you're always there, that you're always down to throw down and whatever needs to be done to keep people safe or whatever," said Pablo, who had spent several years in the US armed forces. "In the military, the same thing. If you go in there and you work hard and you do your job well, you get respect for it."

Accordingly, respect is synonymous with power. "I was tempted to join Barrio Azteca, to try to get a little bit of respect, more respect, I mean, to feel more powerful," explained Alonzo, a man convicted of human smuggling but who, like many inmates, did not join a gang. "I would hang around with the Aztecas, but those guys, usually, that you meet in prison that are in gangs, they don't care; they're not in a hurry to come out. If they have to stab somebody, they'll stab him. They'll get more time, but they don't care."

Critically, respect is earned and not given for nothing. Traditionally, a gang member earns and maintains respect by understanding and abiding by the rules of the underworld. He increases it by "putting in work," such as stabbing someone or engaging in other high-risk behaviors within the prison. Putting in work is the traditional way to rise up through the ranks of a prison gang. As a gang member elevates his station, respect changes. Ian, who called shots for the Aryan Brotherhood in his prison unit, defined respect at the highest level as "knowing you can go whip somebody's ass and ain't nobody can do anything about it. People deferring to you. People asking your permission to do something. Being able to put out a hit. That's a respect power thing."

Being able to return to the free world and to control the street—that is, demanding respect—are part of what make prison gangs influential in the underground economy. From a market viewpoint, it is in a prison gang's best interest to engage in a realpolitik of the street, in which a prison gang attempts to minimize the number of competitive organizations not only within the city or cities where it operates but also within the prison system as a whole.[5] In prison, just as in the free world, establishing a monopoly that eliminates competing enterprises and emerging groups, which could become potential competitors, results in the maximization of earning potential.

For a time, Barrio Azteca was able to sustain its monopoly. When the organization dominated the county jail, rival gang members needed to be careful not to fall into its bad graces. If Barrio Azteca's rivals found themselves incarcerated and refused to abide by the organization's mandated social order, they would be subjected to significant violence, which limited rival gangs' potential for growth. However, once Barrio Azteca no longer had a monopoly in the county jail, rival gang members feared retaliation less; they knew Barrio Azteca no longer owned every corner of the jail system. As Frank explained, he refused to follow the Barrio Azteca's orders when he got locked up in county. "They would kick my ass right there, and I would ship myself out of that tank to another one where it was more Chuco Tango."

Despite a diminution of Barrio Azteca's presence in the prison system, the gang's continued domination of the retail drug market is one factor that contributes to the lack of street-level intraracial violent conflict in El Paso. By most accounts from users and gang members alike, despite its waning influence in the prison system, Barrio Azteca continues to control the retail market. Historically, the Aztecas have forced other gangs to pay *cuota*, a tax, for the right to sell drugs unmolested within most of El Paso, though some people claim that the Aztecas' diminished dominance in the prisons has meant that *cuota* is no longer consistently or effectively imposed.[6]

When Barrio Azteca undisputedly controlled the jails, they exacted retribution when someone refused to pay *cuota*. "It's just that if you're going through the wrong way, you're going to get caught sooner or later," said Emiliano.[7] "Even if it's not you, it can be one of your family members or somebody you know that's close to you.[8] And that's the way Azteca is going to set an example.

"When your people go to county jail, the Aztecas will say 'So, these people don't want to pay us? And you're related to them? Okay.' And the Aztecas will beat them up. They'll rough your people up pretty good and stuff. Your people are going to tell their family members, 'Hey, this happened to me when I was in there.' So, it makes nonpayers think twice because they're thinking 'Even if I don't go to jail, one of the family members will or one of the gang members will, and something's going to happen.'"

Cara, a woman originally from Appalachia and a recovering heroin user, distinctly remembered and feared Barrio Azteca's guarantee of violence. Though she felt safe from the Aztecas because she was a good customer, Cara knew a woman named Jenny who had been threatened for not paying her *cuota*.

"I started living with a girl that was a drug dealer," Cara said. "She wasn't an Azteca, but her husband was Texas Syndicate. She was selling up here in El Paso. She had an apartment on Oregon Street, and she was selling heroin. And she would go across the bridge each day and get her heroin, but she was paying the Aztecas what they call a *cuota*. Apparently, she was behind on her *cuota*, so they sent this man here.

"I knew the man. I knew him very well. He was what I considered a friend of mine. And he told her, 'Look, Jenny, they sent me down here to tell you that if you don't pay this, you know what's coming. They said you're not going to sell it in their territory and them not profit from it. You're not going to make profit from their territory. This is their territory. They're allowing you to make a little money so you can get by, but you're basically taking money out of their hands. So, they're pissed.'"

Cara used to accompany Jenny to the bridge to Juárez to go score crack, Jenny's drug of choice. They would cross the bridge to Juárez where the drugs were cheaper and come back. One day Cara's friend, the Azteca member, pulled her aside and said, "Cara, I'm telling you, *do not* go to the bridge with Jenny tonight. Do not go to the bridge with her because if she hasn't paid that money by then, they're going to be waiting on her. They know exactly the way she goes. They're going to kill her; and when they kill her, they're not going to leave a witness. If you're there, you're dead too. They don't care who you are. They don't care. They're not from here. They ain't going to have to worry about the consequences from here. They're not worried about it. It's just going to be as easy as that. You're just going to be another nobody."

Amid Barrio Azteca's recent difficulties recruiting and replenishing its ranks in prison, some members of non-Azteca–allied gangs reported that they had refused to pay *cuota* without facing any real consequences; respect for Barrio Azteca's authority on the street had declined. Some Barrio Azteca members have noted that the gang has started to recruit directly from street gangs, allowing individuals to join without the traditional vetting processes and without putting in work. The biggest complaint that *equis* members make is the deterioration of the *carnalismo*, or brotherhood, that initially enticed them to join.

Prospects are no longer required to go to county jail or prison before being allowed to join. New members are being blessed into Barrio Azteca while they are still on the street. When someone is blessed in, however, they do not have to put in work. Respect is gained and accorded to them via their organizational association. Older members, who went through the traditional process, lack trust in these newer members, whom they often blame for making rash decisions that undermine the overall well-being of the organization. When established leaders are incarcerated, these youngsters are left to assume leadership positions even though they lack the connections, trust, and respect to lead as effectively as their predecessors.

"Back in the day, the gang was all about *carnalismo*," Alberto lamented. "Being an Azteca was about respect and educating people, so they knew what they were getting themselves into. Now it's all rumors and obstruction; nobody is straight up. The youngsters have started to falsify everything. They don't know shit. There is a lot of show and poor management. The guys who are all tatted up aren't the hardest. When you've done something serious, you're going to be segregated. Those guys won't have tattoos because they don't have the opportunity to get tagged. It used to be that if someone screwed up, everyone dealt with the consequences together unless you did something you weren't supposed to do, that wasn't spoken for; then you got punished personally.[9] People aren't standing up for their brothers anymore."

In addition, the El Paso side of the gang appears to be overseen differently than the Juárez side, a difference that Alberto attributes to the life-and-death stakes in Juárez's violent environment. "In Juárez, the Aztecas are different, in part because they are dealing with a life that has serious consequences by comparison. Over there, they go to war to kill and not to let the others on your side die. It's serious. But with the power that came from the war is the negative. They just became assassins, which is bad. Before, gangs used to talk to each other. But not anymore. Violence is now what you have to do in Juárez if you are to survive."

The need to stay sharp and to back-up one's compadres leads to strict anti-drug policies for gang members in Juárez, who might be otherwise tempted to use the products they sling on the street. "Over in Juárez, you can't be strung out on heroin," Emiliano explained. "The gang will give you a couple of chances. They even put you in rehab centers so you can clean yourself and stuff. If you don't listen, then it's a different story. But over there, it's like being in prison because they're taking care of each other. They don't want to see you struggling or all raggedy or all hooked up on heroin. They don't like to see that. So, they do it themselves and put you in a rehab center and stuff to help you out. Over here, it's nothing like that."

"In Juárez, Barrio Azteca give drug-using gang members two opportunities to go through a drug program," Patricio told me. "If they fail to succeed after the second time, the Aztecas kill them. They just do away with druggies because they want their members to be sharp." The same cannot be said in El Paso, where many Azteca gang members use heroin, creating an air of weakness that leads to disrespect in the Paso del Norte criminal underground.

The change in the way respect is conceptualized among the members of the underworld from being earned to being relational or attributional is an indication of the changing dynamics of the protection racket in the same space. As potential competitors no longer viewed the previously dominant Barrio Azteca as fearsome, the respect paradigms shifted so that Barrio Azteca no longer held the hegemonic status required to back up its authority and force competitors' assimilation or subjugation. Nonetheless, the violence that liberalization of the protection market in Mexico created in Juárez was not replicated in the streets of El Paso, partly because gang members believe—correctly, given the evidence—that they face more scrutiny from US law enforcement. And more scrutiny results in an increased likelihood of being caught.

Gang members' perception that they will be caught by law enforcement squares directly with economist Gary Becker's thesis that the best deterrence against crime is the credible threat of capture.[10] The perception of probable capture and punishment in the free world explains why, despite emerging competition from growing prison gangs such as Chuco Tango and lingering street gangs such as the Gangster Disciples, in the retail drug trade little free world violence manifests publicly in El Paso. Nor can rivals violently contest Barrio Azteca's monopoly over the protection market by openly challenging its members in prison, because doing so would allow the prison administration to identify and segregate those who did so. In the absence of such challenges, the Tangos have been able to grow due to the prison administration's targeting of established gangs' leadership. Nonetheless, Chuco Tango does not appear to have a significant market share of street dealing. Its members do not operate as a unit yet, and those who deal appear to have a small clientele that may allow them to fly under Barrio Azteca's radar. So, even though weakened in prison, Barrio Azteca remains the most common—though by no means the only—wholesale and street suppliers of powder cocaine and black tar heroin to El Paso's drug users.

In El Paso, you are never too far away from someone involved in the drug trade if you know where to look. Across the street from my house in Sunset Heights was a duplex owned by a woman who was always wacked out of her head, high on God knows what. Big, snarling dogs guarded the yard. In an inconspicuous apartment at the rear of the property lived a drug dealer. I never saw him in all the time that I was there, but everyone in the neighborhood knew about him. It was an open secret, and so long as he didn't cause any trouble, nobody really cared. Random, usually beat-up cars would pull up from time to time and sometimes park next to my house. Their drivers or passengers would quickly cross the street and disappear into the back of the duplex. A few minutes later they would reemerge, bounty in fist, and climb back into their jalopies and drive off. This arrangement is common in El Paso's retail drug trade.

El Paso is divided into several different markets, where various gangs and some independent sellers hawk different products based on comparative advantages. The far northeastern part of the city features the White boys, selling the little bit of meth consumed in El Paso mostly to other White people. Those who sold meth claimed that their meth came from small domestically produced batches and not from the Mexican drug trafficking organizations. The market for meth in El Paso was tiny, with most drug users there appearing to prefer cocaine and heroin, so it's possible that the meth sold there was a local product, while the Mexican large-batch meth was shipped farther inland for use in rural America where demand was and is high and good quality can be hard to come by.

Southwest of Fort Bliss is the Devil's Triangle, an area where Bradley's gang, the Gangster Disciples, sells crack cocaine. The market they serve is also small. They get their product from a "plug," someone who has a connection with one of the Mexican drug trafficking organizations. Rarely did anyone in Bradley's gang, which has few if any Latino members, come into contact with anybody who was a full-fledged member of a Mexican drug trafficking organization. The lack of connections that non-Latino gang members have within the drug world curtails their ability to go into business for themselves and increases the cost of their supply. Because the Gangster Disciples process powder cocaine into crack, something the Latino dealers generally don't bother with in El Paso, they are able to sell enough to stay in business without facing any real competition.

The remaining street drug markets are interspersed throughout the rest of the town and are primarily run by Barrio Azteca gang members who specialize in selling cocaine and heroin. Of course marijuana is available, but it is so commonly available that the Aztecas don't even bother taxing the dealers. The real money is not in retail sales on the street but rather in the transnational wholesale opportunities that being on the border provides.

"It's mostly the gangs—the prison gangs—that run the drug trade in American border towns," Emiliano explained. "Once you go up to Mexico, you as a gang member don't have no authority to go and claim respect. It's like, over there the gangs—like if it's me and you and you're a gang member from the streets and I, as a cartel guy, got all kind of drugs, I got guns, I got everything, and I tell you, 'You want to work for me? I'll pay you this.' You're going to see the money and all the drugs and guns, and you're going to say, 'Yeah.'

"So, I'm going to tell you, 'Okay, you start getting people to start selling for you, and it's only going to be me and you—you're going to come to me. Don't bring nobody else. As soon as you get people, come and tell me what you need, and I'll give it to you, but never introduce me to nobody.' You know what I mean? You're going to be like the shot caller, but I'm the one taking care of everything. You're going to report to me, but everybody's going to report to you."

This was the arrangement that Patricio was familiar with from the law enforcement perspective. "Prior to 2008, we had Barrio Azteca moving kilos of cocaine out of here. It wasn't the whole gang. It was just certain members who'd gotten to having the right people at the right place, having the source available for the narcotics. So, they were moving multikilo and multiton quantities of marijuana and multikilo quantities of cocaine out of the El Paso area. Once the war between the Juárez Cartel and the Sinaloa Federation started, that changed. We started seeing a lot smaller volumes of narcotics coming to El Paso in a given time. They didn't want their narcotics all popped at one time. They started reducing the quantity coming over, stockpiling it here, and then moving it out."

The El Paso and Juárez branches of Barrio Azteca might have slightly different reputations on the street, but they cooperate in transborder affairs. The two sides of the gang have distinct leadership, with two bosses in charge of each side, who have different styles that square with the different political realities of the two cities. "It's the same gang," Emiliano said, frankly. The Aztecas of both cities work together to coordinate drug shipments, kidnappings, intimidation, and backup, if necessary, for particular operations. "Once the war started, everybody was on standby," Pancho explained. "You have to be there for your family."

The war negatively affected the street retail trade as well as the wholesale trafficking undertaken by the gang. According to both police and gang members, the availability of quality product to serve local users declined because those who were in charge of transporting the wholesale loads were more interested in moving the product deeper into the United States, where they could earn better prices compared to offloading it in El Paso.

"Right here, they just leave the little scraps," Pancho said. "If they bring in like fifty keys, they just leave like two here, just to supply the people right here, and that's it. Usually, everything goes up north."

According to Patricio, the pattern of supply in El Paso is dependent on the connections that the regional boss has. "It depends who's in power and who happens to be the leader at the time. If it's somebody who's got the access to out of town, they themselves are moving ounce or kilo quantities of heroin out of here or multipound quantities of marijuana out of here. If whoever's in power doesn't have that, then they're mostly doing local distribution for your local users."

Not being part of the Aztecas, however, does not necessarily preclude a person from being a drug dealer at the street or wholesale level. Frank, for example, as a member of a Juárez-based gang, can ask members of his gang in Mexico to supply him. Gang membership is helpful but not necessary for getting a plug; it is possible for nongang members such as Armando, a middle-class man from El Paso, to get in on the action too, though such relationships are probably atypical. I met Armando through my housemate Pablo. Armando had gone to prison for dealing drugs. In prison he was with Chuco Tango, but he was never involved with the street gangs. Being a *cholo* wasn't his scene. He grew up in a middle-class family and was drawn to dealing drugs because of the money he could make. He knew that he could buy wholesale, break down the product into individual portions, and double or triple his money.

"Somebody gave me a pound of weed, and I broke it down, started getting that money, and I loved the power, I loved the money I was getting," Armando told me. "I ended up moving to cocaine and more pounds of weed."

For Armando, luck played a large part in his initial ability to get wholesale amounts. "This guy just landed on my lap. I wasn't expecting that connect. I knew people from the barrio that I grew up in, Calavera, but I used to go in there, and 'Hey I need this; I need that.' They would give me the small amounts that I was wanting. I started dealing in big amounts with this man that landed on my lap. And it lasted for about a year."

Being in that community, Armando found it easy to replace his drug connect. He knew whom he had to approach, and he had personal history and the social capital required to be in the same places where those people would be. Armando managed to avoid trouble in part because he had friends who were part of the gangs but also because he operated in a market that did not overlap with the gangs', thus bringing less attention to himself. He was operating in the margins of the drug trade. For the majority of his fifteen years of selling, he managed to avoid police scrutiny and gang threats, thereby making money hand over fist.

To understand the money at play, one needs to understand where value is added to the product. One night at the Tap, an iconic bar in downtown El Paso, a group of three men from the oil fields of West Texas were out celebrating their buddy's last night of freedom before he was to face trial for moving dope. One of them, Guillermo, a man who had spent time in prison for trafficking drugs on the other side of the state, explained the markup to me as we shared a pitcher of beer.

"When you get a kilo of coke, it comes packaged tight like a golf ball and it's wrapped up in a banana leaf. The cartel gets you started. The first time you buy one key, and you get another. It's about fifteen, sixteen thousand dollars if you get it over in Mexico. Then you have to ship it over. It's not a big deal. We train our own dogs to test the methods. Then once you've got it north, you cut it. You know the best thing to cut it with?"

"Baking soda?"

"No, not baking soda. The best thing to cut it with is baby teething aspirin. It creates an effect that makes people think that it's pure. It numbs the gums. For the people who spark it, it doesn't take too much away from the high.[11] If you slam it, it cooks up clean; no residue.[12] Once it's cut, then you turn your money over quickly. You make five times your investment back.

"With that life, you can have what you want: cars; drugs; pussy. The trick is not screwing up. It's scary, man. I have had guns pointed to my head while I pointed guns at other people who thought I was cheating them. The cartel gave me cut product and I called them on it, but they wanted the price for a pure brick. I got busted because I made bad decisions when I was high. But I was honest, and I lived. That's all in my past, though; now, I push concrete."

What Guillermo described was an operation that sought to maximize potential profit margin by engaging in two high-risk, high-reward activities that increase profit potential. First, there is value added to smuggling the contraband across the border. The $15,000 to $16,000 price he stated for a kilo of "pure" cocaine, which would be expected to be 85 percent cocaine or better, was consistent with what I had heard reported from other dealers I interviewed, though some claimed that with the right connections or bulk purchases, better prices could be had. In El Paso, the same kilo could be moved for somewhere between $22,000 and $25,000, meaning that an initial markup would be a minimum of $6,000 for a single kilo of cocaine. This price increases again once drugs are smuggled through the internal CBP checkpoints, which are stationed within one hundred miles as the crow flies on all roads that come from a border crossing. Crossing these checkpoints is less risky but represent an additional $2,000 increase in value added to a single kilo of cocaine.

Second, there is the retailing of the product on the street. The raw product can be cut with an adulterant. Guillermo used aspirin, but a large array of other substances, including benzocaine and lidocaine, are commonly used.[13] In addition, the product can be turned into crack cocaine, a preparation cooked with baking soda into smokable rocks, thus augmenting its volume. These adulterated products can be sold at volume, again with a markup, to a trafficker who will move the product to another market, to a distributor who may then supply a street-level dealer locally, or retailed directly to individual street-level clients. Each smaller quantity is more expensive, by active ingredient, than the previous larger one. It's a pattern that mirrors licit wholesale and retail markets, where bulk purchases result in per-item discounts.

The process of procuring drugs as described by Guillermo dispels the idea that drug trafficking organizations are vertically organized organizations reaching from the plantation to the street.[14] Historically, a vertical organization that encompasses producer to street retailer has rarely existed. Accordingly, three types of organizations that are participating in the drug trade can be identified. Drawing from the language of the licit world, we have drug trafficking organizations acting as firms as they operate large logistics and manufacturing enterprises; prison gangs acting as subcontractors as they operate medium security, distribution, and retail enterprises; and private citizens acting as small businesspeople as they run small retail enterprises (figure 7).

The firms' primary business includes production, transportation, wholesale, and, most fundamentally, protecting their interests. Accordingly, the firms' reach does not extend beyond those activities; further activities would subject them to comparatively greater visibility and the additional risk that comes with it. Thus, one should think of the true cartel operatives as members of a reasonably small but powerful firm that, after establishing functioning protection rackets, coordinates the logistics of achieving its business goals. The drug trafficking organization undertakes only those tasks that are the most profitable or that cannot be entrusted to anyone else, such as wholesale air shipment and providing protection.

This strategy was not unique to Mexican drug trafficking organizations; they copied it from the Colombian drug trafficking organizations they supplanted as the primary drug suppliers in America when the US war on drugs cracked down on the Caribbean-based drug routes in the 1970s.[15] The Mexican organizations improved upon the Colombians' strategy by diversifying the products offered and by minimizing their risks.[16] When the risk of holding a product and con-

Firms, Subcontractors, and Small Businesses in the Drug Trade

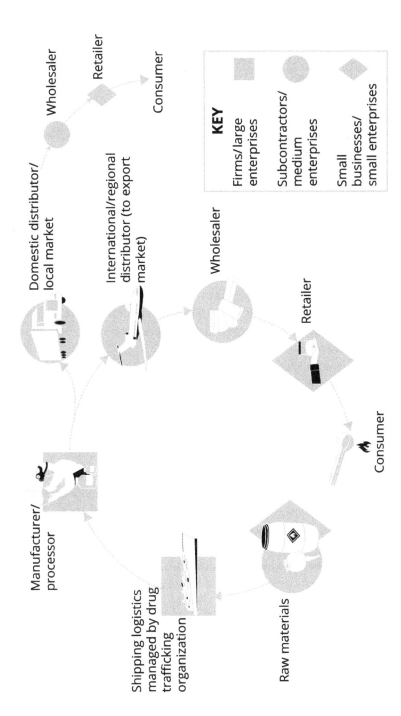

FIGURE 7. An example of a possible supply chain of illicit drugs as that pass via Mexico.

Diagram by Florence Lourme.

tinuing to protect it exceeds the opportunity to capitalize on the product by shifting it, the Mexican drug trafficking organizations disperse their high volumes of product across several distributors or wholesalers who specialize in moving the product onward into regional wholesale and retail markets.

Drug trafficking organizations engage a similar practice of offloading risk to subordinate actors as they participate in the protection market. This strategy is evident in the use of gangs to enforce protection at the street level. Although for most of the 2000s and 2010s Barrio Azteca had been clearly associated with La Línea and, by extension, the Juárez Cartel, it is not correct to conflate the two. Gangs act as subcontractors and as such can withhold their services or restructure, as the Barrio Azteca Vieja Guardia did in response to La Línea's unwelcome meddling in the gang's leadership affairs.[17]

The relationship between firm and subcontractor is forged between leaders in both organizations. The majority of the subcontractor's staff never meets anyone in the firm; the subcontractor takes orders from his or her boss, who is, in theory, operating in accordance with the wishes of the firm's leadership. Failure to promote the firm's vision can result in the subcontractor being replaced, likely after being exterminated, again exemplified by the conflict between La Línea and the Barrio Azteca Vieja Guardia.

Though long-term relationships between firms and subcontractors can and do exist, individuals do not appear to enjoy interorganizational mobility between subcontractor and firm, between a gang and a drug trafficking organization. Though the Zetas, as an organization, successfully *transformed* from being a subcontractor into being a firm, none of its members had previously successfully transitioned from the subcontractor group into the firm.

Historically, there has been little lateral movement between cartels or gangs. Intraorganization mobility typically results from internal promotion. The best, or most ruthless, operatives rise through the ranks and take charge, such as the various gang members who came to lead Barrio Azteca when their predecessors were killed or captured. One rare example of someone moving laterally is Juan José "El Azul" Esparragoza Moreno, a former Guzmán associate, who had roles variously in the Guadalajara, Juárez, and Sinaloa Cartels and reportedly could move between the Juárez and Sinaloa Cartels based on his capacity to facilitate trade outcomes that were mutually beneficial.[18] But excepting such rare cases, there is little reason to believe that individuals move between firms with any facility. More probably, individuals leave one firm to attempt to create a competitor, as when Chapo Guzmán left the Guadalajara Cartel.[19] When one firm supplants another, it either absorbs or eliminates the defeated organization's remnants. Similar patterns of behavior are seen among competing prison gangs.

Managing the highest levels of the wholesale drug market is risky enough that firms seek to narrow their risk portfolios. They do so by delegating the responsibility for the retail distribution of the product or the undertaking of dangerous actions to subcontractors. The subcontractor assumes risk in return for an arbitrage opportunity. The firm foregoes that opportunity in return for divesting itself of the associated risk. These subcontractors can be organizations, such as prison gangs, or individuals, such as Pedro and Margarito Flores, the twin brothers who developed a distribution crew that supplied several US wholesale drug markets with billions of dollars' worth of drugs from the Sinaloa Federation.[20]

Bruce, who became an *esquina* for Barrio Azteca, talked about a time during his boyhood when he accompanied his father, who worked as a transportation subcontractor for a drug trafficking organization, on a trip to Chicago to smuggle drugs. "He had set it up with a cartel in Juárez. He was a truck driver, so he had means of taking them the *lizo*.[21] Either you're lucky or you're not lucky. We passed by Sierra Blanca; we were lucky that time. We took it in an 18-wheeler. Later we dropped the 18-wheeler off, took the dope out of the trailer. There are seals [that shipping companies place on the trailers to deter tampering]; you can make seals to match their seals on the trip.[22] We put the dope on a U-Haul, and we took off heading toward Chicago."

On their journey north they were stopped by the police, and his father was arrested; the burden of the loss lay squarely on his father's shoulders. Possession, though not necessarily ownership, of the product and the risks that went with the opportunity to sell the product on had been transferred from the cartel to him.

Along the border the relationship between the firms and the subcontractors is quite close, given that El Paso and Juárez are two sides of the same coin. However, the transfer of risk associated with the drug trade does not cease with a product's first transfer; risk remains attached to the product and affects an array of businesses and individuals as it trickles down to the streets. These dynamics were not part of what I could access in El Paso.

Nonetheless, on the border, one thing's clear: Americans who live far from the border see the drug trade as a bigger threat than almost anybody who lives along the border. In El Paso, locals enjoy a safe and friendly community. While some are wary of crossing the border to go to Juárez, others continue to cross over to visit family and go to events while understanding that there are always risks. Though people fear the apparent randomness of drug violence in Juárez, they often identify the biggest and most consistent headache as the local police, who try to extort *mordidas* (bribes) for nonoffenses.

"They stop you and they always find something wrong with you," said Carla, warning me to always keep a little money on hand for the *mordida*. The cops will come up with the dumbest hustles, leveraging their badge to nip at the pocketbooks of the traveler uninterested in fighting over a handful of dollars. Carla went through some common scams. "The cops will say, 'Blow into my hand, let me smell the alcohol' like they can trap your alcohol breath in their hand or 'Let me smell your fingers. Oh! They smell like weed; we're going to take you in.' Then they always say that you can fix it with a little payment, which, of course, if you don't pay, they put you in jail. It's constant. One time, we were coming home after a gig and two *federales* stopped us not five blocks from each other. We told the second guy, 'We just got pulled over! What do you want?' And, fortunately, he let us go. It's total bullshit."

Those kinds of stories help keep the drug trade in perspective. Yes, many people are murdered in Juárez; the violence is undeniable. But keeping an eye out for corrupt police, who may well be in cahoots with La Línea, is perhaps a more immediate concern than keeping an eye out for the criminal element, particularly as one goes about daily life.[23]

The transnational connections that once bound both sides of the Paso del Norte into a single community had weakened as the ongoing violence and corruption in Juárez discouraged people from living truly transnational lives. But for people in El Paso, media and politicians' allegations of violent actors coming through town did not ring true. The rumors of MS-13 activity or incursions by drug cartels or other gangs from elsewhere in the United States into the city were routinely debunked by the police and local gang members alike. The city was quiet, and most of the criminal actors who continued to ply their trade in El Paso knew to keep it that way.

There are, of course, exceptions, usually undertaken by bit players with little to lose. One such example was Fidencio "Filo" Valdez, who was on trial for the murder of eighteen-year-old Julio Barrios. That Valdez was a Barrio Azteca was a fact advertised not only by the newspaper reports leading up to the trial but also by the image of an Aztec warrior tattooed on his throat. Valdez had attempted to rob Barrios of thirty or forty ecstasy pills valued at $300 as Barrios was selling four of the pills to him. The robbery went sour, and Valdez shot and killed Barrios. Though not part of this trial, Valdez was also accused of murdering Ralph Ed Tucker at Sal's Lounge, a strip club, during the course of another robbery a few days before the Barrios killing.

Valdez's trial underscored the importance of keeping the claims pertaining to the drug trade's volume, the number of people with access, and the size of the criminal conspiracy in perspective. The trial showed that participation in the big-money world of the drug trade was not as easy as one might imagine. A life of crime specifically in the drug trade, even close to the border with seemingly endless opportunities to make money in it, was not one that often paid well. The low-level guys in the drug trade still made peanuts, and much of what they earned went out in expenses just as quickly.

And that's what Valdez was: a relatively low-level member of a gang, albeit a notorious one, who despite any status on the street or within the gang was still struggling for his day-to-day existence. The idea that Valdez was a big or important player in the gang or the drug trade in general was shredded as the facts of the case unfolded. The evidence and testimony supported the accusations against the defendant, actions that a rational actor in a position of power or with access to sufficient money or product would never have taken. Valdez had indeed killed the teen over a handful of ecstasy pills. Barrios, despite his mother's claims that he was destined to be an astronaut, was trying to enter a world of retail drug sales. Why a member of the Barrio Azteca, the best-connected gang in the city, needed to buy a handful of ecstasy pills from Barrios, a kid barely out of high school with no proven connection to a wholesale plug, never seemed to cross Barrios's mind. It was also curious that Valdez would waste his time mugging Barrios over pills worth $300; it made no business sense. The robbery-cum-murder had a small yield, was noisy, left a lot of evidence, and brought the cops in to investigate what happened.

The trial also showed that Valdez clearly didn't have much money. As was later learned, Valdez had indeed schemed to rob Sal's Lounge for an easy payday. It was a visible activity that used guns, two elements that most gang members shunned in El Paso. Plus, Valdez's ex-wife testified that she would shoplift in order to generate money to buy drugs for them. These facts were not representative of someone turning over large volumes of cash, as is often alleged of the drug trade. Like many gang members throughout the United States, Valdez was struggling to make ends meet and was on the lookout for any hustle that would net some profit.[24]

By the end of the trial, it was apparent that Valdez, who was convicted, was very much a bit player in the El Paso criminal underground. Had he been anything else, he would have been brought to face charges of conspiracy under RICO, and the prosecution would have tried to establish a narrative of a much larger conspiracy. Instead they just sought to execute him, leaving his daughters to grow up just as he had, without a father.

Fidencio Valdez's behavior may have been an anomaly in the context of the gang, but it was a reminder that money, volume, and access to the drug trade are not assured. Moreover, his trial showed that even in a world where finding people who are closely connected to the wholesale drug trade is relatively easy, it's not a given. Even in a place as peaceful as El Paso, where the gang strives to keep its profile low on the street to keep its business healthy, there are people whose lives are linked to the drug trade who do not earn enough to keep them from the temptations that could make life for the illicit entrepreneurs in the margins more difficult.

Ultimately, the Paso del Norte revealed that those margins were broader in Ciudad Juárez than they were in El Paso. In Juárez, there was still violence on the street and a deep distrust of the police, particularly when it came to reporting drug-related crime. Criminal actors act more brazenly and compete in the protection market alongside state actors. Accordingly, criminal actors can act with a degree of impunity; there is less need to be invisible so long as one's actions emanate enough power to intimidate rivals. In Juárez life is cheap and, tragically, casualties of the drug trade continue. Nonetheless, most drug-related activity is banal and not worthy of the embellished stories portrayed on the silver screen or broadcast on television.

In El Paso there is little visible violence, the only exception being an act of terror undertaken by a White nationalist in 2019. The gangs and drug trade organizations know that El Paso, a safe community that generally trusts its law enforcement, does not afford much margin for error. In El Paso visibility brings unwanted attention, with any display of power likely met proportionately, since fear and violence are not tolerated. Corruption still has a place on the border to grease the wheels of the drug trade, but at the border the violence must halt. And for the majority living in El Paso, like the majority living in Juárez, life continues apart from the drug trade.

THE OASIS

With the big red, pickup truck packed, I bade farewell to the borderlands, my home for the past five months. I headed west through the Franklin Mountains and found myself in New Mexico. The first town I passed was Chaparral, a place that had come up in conversations during my time in El Paso. Some immigrant families prefer to settle in Chaparral because property there is less expensive than in El Paso and because it is a small community where folks know each other. There they can enjoy recognized social status more readily than in the city. From the road, Chaparral is little more than a collection of small homes and trailers scattered among the desert vegetation, but for some people that's what living the American dream looks like.

New Mexico is one of the five poorest states in the nation. Many of the towns I drove through rang of small-town America, centered around quaint local grocery stores. The drive through Deming and Silver City was characterized by a large number of trailer parks, each with a small cluster of homes. They didn't detract from the beauty of the desert, which was often featured in the meth-making capers of the characters of AMC's *Breaking Bad*, a television show that brought a fantastical representation of the meth trade to millions of viewers. A picture-perfect sky, blue with a smattering of wispy white clouds, illuminated the brown and green hues of a landscape first framed by low foothills and distant mountains and then stretching into an endless, flat plain. The colors alone broke up any threat of monotony the drive posed.

Crossing into Arizona was a welcome change of pace from the flats of southwestern New Mexico; the Sonoran Desert was gorgeous. The twisting roads passed a variety of rock formations, and saguaro cacti adorned hills as far as the eye could see. The landscape recalls the untamed frontier and its outlaws and bandits, including famed cattle rustler Billy the Kid and Pearl Hart, the only woman known to have robbed a stagecoach. It was a frontier punctuated by gun violence, such as the 1881 gunfight at the O. K. Corral in Tombstone, where famed lawmen Wyatt Earp and Doc Holliday and two others killed three members of an outlaw group called The Cowboys.[1] Even today more than a century later, gun violence remains a concern.

Over four hundred miles from El Paso I finally pulled into Greater Phoenix, which lies in a large, flat valley, an area twice as large as El Paso and home to a rapidly growing population, nearing four and a half million people.[2] The sprawling metropolis, where roughly two-thirds of the people of the Grand Canyon State live, felt like an oasis of humanity in the desolate Arizona landscape.

Phoenix proper is home to over one and a half million people, making it the sixth-largest city in the United States and about the same size as Juárez.[3] However, Phoenix is part of a larger metropolis unlike most I've visited. Greater Phoenix includes several towns, each with its own identity. South of the metro area is the country's largest public park, the South Mountain. To the north there are more mountains, including Piestewa Peak. In some ways Greater Phoenix, with its mountainous skyline, crappy drivers, and clearly disparate neighborhood incomes, reminded me of El Paso and Juárez.

The city lies just shy of two hundred miles from the border, and its residents' demographics are more diverse than El Paso's. About four out of every ten people in Phoenix are Hispanic, which was evident in the neighborhoods that felt, culturally, like El Paso; there, people spoke to each other in Spanish and did their grocery shopping at supermarkets that offered freshly made tortillas, chicharones, and salsas.[4] Other neighborhoods were typical of suburban White America, full of big houses, many owned by snowbirds who came to the city to escape the cold winters of their summertime residences.

As I drove through the city looking for a place to live, I recognized how much more aggressive the drivers in Phoenix were than in El Paso. In El Paso, it felt like a solid 80 percent of the drivers cruised under the speed limit, oblivious to their surroundings. In Phoenix more people were speeding, indifferent to the danger they posed to others as they wove through traffic. The roads were wide and fast, and getting from place to place was easy. The street signs were helpful, telling me in which town within the Phoenix metropolitan area I was.

I started the search for a room in Phoenix a couple of weeks before I left West Texas. As I flicked through room ads, I noticed three distinct ad types: normal, sober living, and questionable. The normal ads requested a roommate or someone to move in for a sublet during the summer months. Sometimes these ads were placed by rental agencies. Nonetheless, normal ads, without weird strings attached, seemed to be in short supply. I responded to any ad that had enough information to be taken seriously.

Then there were the sober living ads, which offered rooms by the week rather than the month. These ads led me to believe that Phoenix had either a lot of rehab centers or a lot of drug users seeking to get clean either by choice or by court order. Though the houses seemed nice and the price was right, those dwellings were not for me. It turned out that my second supposition was correct: one of my respondents, a recovering heroin user, lived in such a place and invited me in. The inhabitants were all in recovery. Ashtrays overflowed with heaps of cigarette butts, as nicotine and caffeine were the only drugs permitted on-site.

Finally, there were ads trying to entice renters with "free rent" in exchange for "cleaning and companionship" or other more thinly disguised requests for sexual favors. Though the vast majority of these ads were put up by men looking for women companions, some were put up by women, or so they said; perhaps they were scammers looking for marks.

As I drove around most of the city of Phoenix looking for a place to stay, it became apparent that living in Phoenix was more expensive than living in El Paso. Most of the housing I considered was located in relatively new housing developments a good distance from my downtown office. After viewing several rooms, I came to realize that I didn't want to live outside Phoenix proper in towns that felt like suburbia and that were too far—both physically and politically— from the communities that I sought to study.

I moved into a small house located just west of the city center. The signs on the neighborhood's street read "Historic Oakland." Although it was a low-income area, the businesses, such as the modest Las Palmas Inn on the edge of the neighborhood, and the houses seemed to be in pretty good condition except one home up the street that some crackheads had burned down. I saw kids playing in the street. Plus, I could afford it. That I was within reasonable walking distance to my office was a bonus.

As I walked around the neighborhood, I felt fine. People greeted me. Some even stopped to chat. The demographics were primarily Hispanic—Latinos who were mostly either Chicanos or Mexican nationals—though there was the occasional older White person who apparently had lived in the area for ages. One house's mailbox comically read "MALE BOX." Yes, there were some guys who were gang members, dressed as *cholos*, with clearly gang-related tattoos adorning their arms. They were out in the evenings, possibly selling dope, but that didn't deter kids from playing at the same time in the nearby streets. I never saw any static; the neighborhood was calm and reasonably safe.

FIGURE 8. Las Palmas Inn. The motel was situated on the edge of Oakland, the neighborhood located in downtown Phoenix where I lived.

Photo by R. V. Gundur.

It was quite the surprise when one night, perhaps around 10:00 p.m., the doorbell rang. When I opened the door, I found myself face-to-face with a bounty hunter who went by only "Aaron." The White, muscular guy in his thirties standing in front of me had the appearance of a police officer, complete with badge, a holstered gun, and a flak jacket.

"There been a red Saturn parked in front of this house?" he asked.

"No, I haven't seen a car like that around here," I said.

The bounty hunter showed me the mug shots of two White folks and asked, "Have you seen either of these people?"

"To be honest, there aren't a whole lot of White people in this neighborhood. No White people live in this house, I can promise you that. The only White person I know is the lady next door, and she is way older than those people."

"Are you sure these people don't live here?"

"Like I said, I haven't seen that car, and I haven't seen any White people."

On any given Friday night, one could see older Mexican men sitting at tables in front of their houses playing cards, drinking beer, and listening to norteño music pumping from the speakers of their beat-up pickup trucks. They usually nodded to me or greeted me as if I were a longtime neighbor, making me feel at home. All things considered, Oakland was just a normal working-class neighborhood.

The worst thing about the area was its proximity to Van Buren, a street that was frequented by people high on drugs, mostly tweakers.[5] The Circle K's parking lot was full of unwashed men and women panhandling, approaching everyone who was unfortunate enough to need to buy gas or desperate enough to buy a four pack of Steel Reserve malt liquor there. The panhandlers slept on the sidewalks unmolested. Sometimes at night, people with severe mental illnesses could be seen walking down Van Buren Street screaming in self-dialog. Barring the number of drug addicts in close proximity, Oakland felt a lot like the Sunset Heights neighborhood of El Paso where I had stayed: there were some seedy elements, but, on the whole things were ordinary. I was well situated and ready to get back to work.

As I moved through the different parts of the city, the distinctly rich and poor neighborhoods echoed the inequality of the neighborhoods of Ciudad Juárez. Perhaps that shouldn't have been so surprising. Though some in the United States like to speak of its exceptionalism and superiority, it's a place where inequality has been growing since the 1980s as wealth has become increasingly concentrated in the hands of a few.[6] The poverty that many Americans see and deride in the so-called developing world is in the United States too. The US Gini coefficient, where zero represents perfect equality and 1 represents perfect inequality, is only slightly better than Mexico's: 0.411 (United States, 2016) versus 0.454 (Mexico, 2018). There is no indication that the United States will maintain its edge, but there is every indication that the US Gini coefficient will continue to grow.[7] Phoenix appeared to embody this trend, as parts of the city offered large, expensive-looking homes populated by middle-aged or older White people who preferred to live in gated communities. The rich and the middle class disappeared behind tall protective walls, away from have-nots they'd rather not associate with. Unlike in Juárez, there was no broken glass on the top of the walls for an extra layer of protection, but the walls were there just the same.

Adorning the streets during the summer of 2014 were political ads dominated by Republican US House hopefuls who slammed their (often fellow Republican) opponents for being too liberal or for being too close to President Barack Obama. The south-side neighborhoods, which someone told me were the ones to avoid, seemed to be made up of smaller single-family homes, likely occupied by blue-collar Chicano, African American, or immigrant families. I didn't notice many election signs there, perhaps an indication of the lack of political participation expected or even demanded from the area's residents.

I soon came to realize that my perception of Phoenix's politics was not entirely accurate: Phoenix was not solidly Republican. US politics since before the twenty-first century has been characterized by large urban centers voting more Democratic and rural America voting more Republican. But with the majority of Arizona's population living in Phoenix, the urban-rural divide isn't clear; the city has both Republican and Democratic strongholds. Republican strongholds are often formed by older Americans who have moved from other parts of the country to the wealthy pockets of Greater Phoenix to retire. Their support has certainly contributed to Arizona's consistently selecting Republican presidential candidates from 1952 until 2020, when it voted for Democrat Joe Biden, and Republican senators from 1994 until 2018, when it elected Democrat Kyrsten Sinema.

However, elections have often been decided by relatively narrow margins; a consistent bedrock of Democratic support in Phoenix has long existed. Notably, in 2014 the city was home to two of the most liberal congressmen in the country: Raúl Grijalva, cochair of the Congressional Progressive Caucus, and Ruben Gallego, a vice chair of the caucus. Yet for much of the 2000s, Maricopa County and Arizona's conservative Republican governors grabbed the headlines. Maybe such coverage was just good media strategy by the Republican Party and the Maricopa County Sheriff's Office, then led by the self-proclaimed "toughest sheriff in America" Joe Arpaio, who became famous first for making inmates wear pink undies and then, in 2017, for being convicted of criminal contempt after knowingly violating a federal judge's order in 2011.[8] The judge told Arpaio that he could not detain immigrants simply because they lacked legal status; nonetheless, Arpaio's deputies carried on with the practice for eighteen months. Donald Trump later pardoned Arpaio, whom Trump celebrated as a talisman for the anti-immigrant rhetoric that was a centerpiece of Trump's political platform.[9]

Nationally visible anti-immigrant discourse long predated Trump, and Arizona was a center of gravity for it in 2010 as the state's Republican politicians advanced Arizona S.B. 1070, formally known as the "Support Our Law Enforcement and Safe Neighborhoods Act." S.B. 1070 was a nationally controversial Arizona State Senate bill that appeared to target unauthorized immigrants for the state's woes and any serious crime, particularly kidnapping, human trafficking, and drug trafficking.[10] It was signed into law by Republican governor Jan Brewer on April 23, 2010.

The law had become controversial because it appeared to *obligate* local law enforcement, such as sheriffs, police, and other policing bodies, to arrest unauthorized immigrants: "No official or agency of this state or a county, city, town or other political subdivision of this state may adopt a policy that limits or restricts the enforcement of federal immigration laws to less than the full extent permitted by federal law."[11] The emotional impetus behind the bill fed off the Latino threat narrative, placing the blame for many of the ills identified in Arizonan political rhetoric on the shoulders of unauthorized Mexican immigrants, but the bill was advertised as simply and impartially "enforcing the law." It would be a rhetorical trope that conservative lawmakers routinely harked back to: "enforcing the law to prevent crime." That the laws being enforced disproportionately targeted foreigners, who on average offend less than the native-born population, and that the purported crime epidemic had no empirical evidence were of little concern to politicians.[12] In trading in moral panic, these conservative politicians gained political capital among their base, and that was all that mattered.

However, not all law enforcement shared this view. For instance, Jack Harris, the former Phoenix chief of police, told me that he did not support the intent of the bill, given the detrimental effects that asking for and investigating immigration status would have on police-community relationships. It was a position that the evidence from El Paso and Ciudad Juárez supported.

When the community trusts the police, as it does in El Paso, community members are likely to call the police when they witness bad behavior. Thus, violent, serious, and organized crimes are forced to the margins of society and must operate outside the public view if business is to continue unabated. However, when the community distrusts the police, such as in Juárez, community members are unlikely to call police even when they witness serious crimes, including murder, because they cannot be sure the police won't use their authority to harm them.[13] Though there is no evidence to suggest that Arizona police coordinate with criminal actors, unauthorized migrants and people in the communities where these migrants live and contribute will be less likely to call the police about violent crime if doing so threatens an arrest for an immigration violation. Simply put, given the low offending rates of immigrants, the police should prioritize preventing and responding to violent crime.[14] Not enforcing immigration violations builds the trust necessary for members of those communities to not only cooperate with the police but also call upon them when serious crime is afoot. That position was frequently, though not universally, repeated in my interviews with Phoenix police and other law enforcement personnel.

Another part of the broader political rhetoric in Arizona and Phoenix specifically included claims about the risks that Phoenix faced. The rhetoric was one of many examples where anecdotal reasoning triumphed over the available data. This phenomenon of "alternative facts" that drives misinformation is detrimental to the development of good policy that correctly identifies problems and offers plausible solutions with minimal collateral damage.[15] Yet conservative politicians and talking heads spun stories demonizing unauthorized immigrants, while the authors of S.B. 1070 targeted them.

These claims captured the imagination of the public and convinced many that there was real danger present, even though there was a lack of empirical evidence to support those claims. Some alleged that unauthorized immigrants were responsible for a rash of kidnappings, a claim that made the national press.[16] These kidnappings created a Greater Phoenix area–based moral panic in which both police and journalists declared Phoenix the kidnapping capital of the United States.[17] The optics were thrust to the forefront of the public imagination. Ryan, a police commander, reflected on the coverage of the busts and how ultimately the kidnappings were a function of a failed strategy to stage drugs by drug traffickers.

"The bosses who are calling the shots were setting up stash houses in affluent parts of Phoenix," Ryan said. "We'd go in, find 4,300 pounds in a house next to a golf course, and all of a sudden there was a panic. That bust got the media attention because of the people who lived in that neighborhood. The same bust happening in a poor Latino neighborhood wouldn't get nearly as much press, in part because the press doesn't care about the safety of the people who live in poor neighborhoods that have a history of gang presence as much as they do for the people who live in rich ones."

A report commissioned by the City of Phoenix showed that while the number of claims was difficult to verify, Phoenix had a home invasion problem "closely linked to the drug trade and human smuggling."[18] Speaking with 20/20 hindsight, several police commanders indicated that while there were a lot of kidnappings, the risk to the general public was nominal; those who were victims were generally people living in stash houses.

The Arizona attorney general lists several instances of drug trafficking organization activity since 2008.[19] And while such operations indicate a lot of illicit drug traffic through Phoenix and Arizona more broadly, there is little evidence to support implications that local law enforcement has ceded control to drug trafficking organizations in the region, such as those made by Pinal County sheriff Paul Babeu and on the National Geographic–produced *Drugs, Inc.: Cartel City, Arizona*.[20] Those claims were downplayed or contradicted not only by the law enforcement people I interviewed but also by the gang members. After sorting the wheat from the chaff, I was left with a far less sensationalized understanding of the drug market in Phoenix. What awaited me, again, involved looking at life in the margins and how a few people exploited those spaces to further their illicit enterprises.

GANGS OF THE VALLEY

When I first started studying the drug trade, I thought I was going to learn about the role drug cartels play in the United States. But in my first days in El Paso, it became clear that what I needed to focus on were prison gangs. They—not the drug cartels—were the true facilitators of the drug trade along the border, especially on the US side. In Paso del Norte, prison gangs were the important facilitators for much of the wholesale trade across the border and were responsible for the lion's share of the retail trade in El Paso. They were responsible for the most quotidian facets of the drug trade, affecting the streets of local communities. Clearly, understanding prison gangs meant understanding the drug trade.

As in El Paso, my early conversations with people involved in policing or facilitating Phoenix's drug trade made it appear that claims that the Sinaloa Federation or other drug trafficking organizations controlled Phoenix's drug trade were likely false. Even if cartel operatives worked in the city, they, like their counterparts in El Paso, were probably careful not to attract any unnecessary heat; their goal was to ensure that their high-value operations continued unabated, and the operatives had no interest in interfering in the risky retail trade. In the mid-2010s the media talked about big drug-related problems in both El Paso and Phoenix, but this talk seemed to be part of a moral panic narrative that overstated or misrepresented the facts on the ground. A handful of kids with the flu in a schoolhouse doesn't constitute a pandemic. I suspected that the same could be said about the drug trade in Phoenix.

Traveling from the Nogales port of entry, Phoenix is the second major city one reaches after the college town of Tucson. Phoenix lies on the highways that lead west and north, connecting to markets in Los Angeles, Portland, Seattle, and Denver. The Phoenix metropolitan area has a fertile local market for both heroin and meth, seemingly at an order of magnitude greater than El Paso's. With money to be made in both the wholesale and retail drug trade, why anybody would do anything to jeopardize it is always a question worth asking. Violence doesn't make good business sense. But even an absence of visible violence doesn't necessarily mean that violence isn't present below the surface. The question remained, however, as to how the business model of illicit drug entrepreneurs unfolded in Phoenix. Since the Valley of the Sun had its share of street and prison gangs, understanding their role in the drug trade seemed as good a starting point as any.

The official publications produced in Arizona that address the subject of gangs identify them as an ongoing threat and cite their role in drug dealing, violence, kidnapping, trafficking, and home invasions, among a litany of other offenses.[1] Arizona law enforcement claims that over 90 percent of the crime that occurs in the state is attributable to gangs.[2] The wide and serious array of offenses attributed to "gangs" in the Arizona Criminal Justice Commission reports appears to stem from a very inclusive reading of what gangs are; the reports include, in addition to street gangs, trafficking groups and prison gangs. The difficulty of defining a gang notwithstanding, understanding the trends of "gang crime" over time from official publications is difficult. Over time the response rate of law enforcement bodies to the questionnaires that underpin the reports has plummeted, making any comparative, longitudinal analysis less accurate.

To understand the Phoenix-area gang makeup, I spoke to a wide range of people, including community workers, police officers, and current and former street and prison gang members. According to these people, street gangs are relatively small and typically do not manage large conspiracies. Kirk, a commander who had worked in Phoenix his entire career, told me that the gang makeup of Phoenix consisted of small geographically and ethnically based gangs present in various parts of the city. Natividad Mendoza, who has developed his expertise on Phoenix gangs by running the program From Gangs 2 Jobs, designed to help former gang members reintegrate into society, for nearly a decade, echoed Kirk, saying that gangs in Phoenix "have neighborhoods, a couple of blocks at a time, like right here in our little spot: we have 40th Street, we have Brown Pride, we have 48th Street, and we have 44th Street. We have four gangs right here in this little square mile."

Kirk noted that violence related to gangs still pops up from time to time but has changed a lot over the years. According to the police commanders I spoke to, street gangs are less pervasive. Moreover, the violence that featured in gang-related activities, which were particularly troublesome in the late 1980s and early 1990s, has diminished greatly, a characterization that echoed the trend my respondents recounted in El Paso.

"I think we are unique in our gang strategy," Kirk said. "We have a state gang task force [the Gang and Immigration Intelligence Team Enforcement Mission, or GIITEM] which uses sophisticated techniques to identify and go after the structure of a gang. On the prosecution side, we use Arizona's organized crime statute, particularly parts dealing with racketeering, conspiracy, and gang membership, to prosecute the higher-level targets and disrupt the gangs' organizational structure. Therefore, we've been successful in reducing gang activity. We don't have the issues of LA or Chicago; the gangs are not as controlling in communities."

Elmer, a lieutenant whose department focused specifically on gangs and drug traffickers, explained how his department had undergone a philosophical shift to focus on "syndicate investigations instead of just hitting one gang member for doing an aggravated assault and then going after another gang member. We actually started targeting the gang itself and identifying its structure and identifying what kind of illegal activity its members are involved in. Then we started being able to attack the whole gang, and as a result, I think that the city saw a decrease in gang activity. It didn't go away, but I think, right now, we are still in that kind of a lull where our gang activity isn't really that extensive here in the city of Phoenix."

From what Kirk and Elmer recounted, it was clear that the threat posed by the gangs to state authority and to the communities had diminished over time, even though drug distribution continued out of sight. The decrease in overt violence and visible drug use on Phoenix's streets, similar to the transition El Paso successfully made from the early 1990s to the 2000s, was considered to be a positive development. To that end, in addition to a shift in the way law enforcement targeted street gangs, officers spoke about the importance of community-based policing, a tactic whereby police seek to collaborate with members of the community to identify and solve community problems. Universally presented as a useful and helpful strategy, community-based policing not only reduces the incentives for youths to join gangs but also improves the relations the police have with communities that have been historically apathetic or uncooperative.[3]

"We know that the police can't arrest our way out of crime," Kirk explained. "So, we have several community-based policing practices like the G.R.E.A.T. program.[4] Before we had those programs, we would sometimes have difficulty working within communities."

Baxter, who used to be the precinct commander of a largely Latino area that was notorious for drug trafficking and gang activity and had a population that generally did not cooperate with the police, explained the multipronged strategy he employed in that community to improve police-community relations. "First of all, you remove the violence from the environment. Second of all, you have to give these kids something to do rather than associate with the gang trends that were occurring within the geographic area. We *have* to give them an alternative.

Thirdly, most of the issues related to crime are always, as you know, 60 to 70 percent of all people arrested are either high or drunk or impaired in some way. You have to deal with that to transform a community."

By several accounts, these strategies have reduced overt gang activity. Eddie, a longtime member of the Arizona Mexican Mafia, which, like elsewhere that has a prison gang with that name, was locally referred to as "the Eme," proclaimed street gangs dead. "You don't see nobody no more wearing bandanas or throwing gang signs. You don't see it. It's changed a lot." Manny, a career burglar whose relatives were members of the Eme, described the southside of Phoenix during his youth. "It used to be like shootings and stabbings all the time. Now, you might hear it once in a while, like probably a dispute or something. I don't know. They say how bad it is. It used to be worse a long time ago." The lack of activity was notable for outsiders who knew the gang life from elsewhere. Skinny, a former California gang member who had moved to Phoenix to make a clean departure from his past criminal life, noted the absence of visible gang-banging in the area when I chatted with him at a lowrider car show. "It's way different here. It's nothing like what you would see in South Central LA. There's less gangbanging, less tagging, less wearing colors, and less violence."

"What do you mean that there is less violence?" I asked.

"Look, if I was to go back to my old 'hood and wear a little red," Skinny said, pointing to a prominent red letter on his white shirt, "some idiot might shoot me."

"Why, because he thought you were a Blood?"

"Bloods and Crips are a Black thing. The [Californian] Hispanic gangs are the Nuestra Familia and the Sureños. The Nuestra Familia are the 14's, the 'N's.' They wear red. We're the Sureños, the 13's—because we're linked to the Mexican Mafia, 13's, the 'M's.' We wear blue."[5]

"So, what are you seeing here in Phoenix? Is the Eme laying it down on the street?"

"You know, I've been here for two years, and I'm still trying to figure out how the politics work. I don't know exactly how it goes here. Like I said, I've taken a step back now that I have my family. I haven't done time here in Arizona, so I don't know what exactly to expect if I were to go back to prison. I've heard that some of the things are different. The Chicanos here apparently beef with the *paisas* and the Califas, who ride together.[6] I don't know if that's still true or what. But I'm trying to figure it all out for myself in case I end up getting locked up here."

"Why is it so hard to figure it all out here?"

"I'm telling you, man, you just don't see so much out on the street like you do in California."

For the most part, Skinny's assessment of Phoenix proved to be true. I saw some gang members posting up in my own neighborhood from time to time, but for the most part there was little street activity.[7] Violence, however, did occur, albeit rarely, with petty conflicts sometimes escalating into murder.

One gang member, Fito, was shot to death in the wee hours of Labor Day Monday, apparently the result of a gang-related altercation. Fito's killing brought unwanted police attention; investigating the murder, a homicide detective, looking for Fito's sister, Calista, showed up at the carwash fundraiser the gang held for the deceased.

"Is Calista here?" the cop asked one of the people waiting for dirty cars to arrive. She wasn't. He waited in the shade until she pulled up. He had Fito's cell phone and was hoping that one of his relatives knew what the pattern was in order to unlock it. Maybe they could identify some information regarding the murderers. No one could, so he left.

I asked Calista whether she had any new information.

"There's a rumor going around that the police found the gun used to kill Fito. I don't know what to make of that."

"Is that what the detective was here for?"

"No, he was trying to unlock the phone. He didn't tell me that. I heard that from someone else."

"The cops haven't told you anything, then?"

"Nothing. We haven't been able to see the body. We don't have any information. We don't know how many times he was shot. We don't know when they'll release his body to us for the funeral. Hopefully, it will be next week sometime."

With all of the unknowns surrounding Fito's death, some of his homies were conducting an investigation of their own to determine who the killer was. Moreover, if they found out who Fito's murderer was and the police failed to make any arrests, they were going to pay the shooter back in kind for his transgression. I never found out how the conflict continued—whether, ultimately, it was all talk and no action—but it was an attitude that was distinct from any I had heard in El Paso, where upon the orders of the prison gang that controlled the streets, conflicts were handled as low-key as possible and certainly without guns.

By most accounts—those of members of the community, current and former gang members, and police—the everyday presence of street gangs in Phoenix was declining. However, the Arizona Criminal Justice Commission, in its survey of law enforcement throughout the state, reported that gang activity on the street had remained more or less constant in the 2010s. Furthermore, the report indicated that street gangs played a significant role in the retail drug trade.[8]

Likewise, by most accounts prison gangs continue to have a significant presence in the Arizona prison system. As in Texas, Arizona prison gangs generally self-segregate by race. The prison gangs certified by the Arizona Department of Corrections include the Sureños, Grandel, the Border Brothers, and the New and

Old Arizona Mexican Mafias, all of which have a primarily Latino membership; the Aryan Brotherhood, which has a White membership; the Mau Maus, with an African American membership; and the Warrior Society and Diné Pride, which feature Native American members.[9] My respondents focused on, in order of increasing importance, the Warrior Society and Diné Pride, Mau Mau, the Aryan Brotherhood, and the New Mexican Mafia, which was usually referred to simply as "the Eme." This Eme was a split-off from the Old Mexican Mafia, a gang not related to the prison gangs of California or Texas; nonetheless, its structure had been inspired by the original California iteration. In addition, respondents indicated that the *paisas*, who don't organize formally as a group—possibly due to the lack of street gang members in their ranks and the fact they will likely be deported upon discharging their sentences—stick together out of need for protection from the bigger, more established inmate groups. Other smaller groups exist as well and may or may not be present on any given prison yard; they appear to have minimal relative impact in terms of influencing the overall inmate political order.

The groups that feature in the Arizona prison system all have vertical hierarchies; nothing like the Tangos in Texas seems to exist. As in the Lone Star State, membership within a prison gang is one of choice but is generally restricted along racial lines. Doing time on one's own is likewise possible, but more privileges are to be had in being part of a family.

Current and former members of Arizona prison gangs described a process of entering a group and rising in the ranks that paralleled the vertical operation of prison gangs in Texas: potential members were recruited by their respective prison gangs upon entry and then had to "put in work" in order to progress and had to abide by specific rules to remain in good standing. For some gangs such as the Aryan Brotherhood, the New Mexican Mafia, the Warrior Society, and Diné Pride, this process is formalized in a constitution with established bylaws.[10]

"You ain't cliqued up just because you're *esquina*," explained Lil G, a former Eme member, describing the progression of status within a gang. "Just because you're *esquina*, that don't mean nothing. You got to be patched or something to be a brother. *Then* you'll be cliqued up."

Once prospects get the gang patch, they step onto a rung of a clear hierarchy that exists in each group. Although many of the top leaders are locked away in solitary confinement, each prison gang has individuals who are in charge in the yard, and in order for a member to climb the ranks, the member must earn the approval of these "big homies" to be initiated or promoted.

All of the former male inmates I spoke to said that the prison gangs' rules underwrote the social order of the prison yards. Duke summed up the generic rules, echoed by most, generally expected of and respected by "standup" inmates. "You ain't supposed to be talking to another race. You ain't supposed to be fucking no faggots, but that's bullshit; all the heads of the prison gangs be fucking faggots anyway. You ain't supposed to do drugs. Don't be talking to police more than two minutes, unless you got somebody with you. It's just commonsense stuff."

Historically, as was the case in California and Texas, prisoners formed prison gangs in Arizona to protect themselves against the prison administration and each other. Breeze, who spent more than a decade behind bars in Arizona for various drug-related crimes, said that groups formed and made a collective effort to fight against the prison administration's attempts to take away privileges, such as weights on the yard and care packages from home. Regarding interracial violence, most former inmates, irrespective of their race, reported the segregation imposed by the unwritten rules of the prison yard and spoke of a need to protect their own in the event of a prison riot or against predatory inmates. Nonetheless, these violent events and threats were seldom brought up in my conversations with former inmates, and when they were, it was clear that such events were increasingly uncommon.

In Arizona as compared to Texas, there appeared to be less intraracial conflict. One prison gang for each race dominated and, through its preeminence, attracted most of the new recruits of that race. Some smaller groups, unwelcome in the dominant gangs, banded together; likewise, they did not have significant conflict with the established gangs. For instance, Native American groups were viewed as nonplayers in the broader prison social order; as a result, they kept to themselves and avoided the politics of the prison yard.

"The Hopi and the Navajo hang out," explained Dru, an Apache who had done time in several prisons throughout the state. "They don't mess around. They stick to themselves completely."

Duke, who had served time on a murder charge, spoke about the disparate African American groups, which sometimes fought with each other but came together if a bigger problem, such as a riot, occurred. "Race mattered a lot, rest assured. I rolled with the Southside. If two Black dudes got into it, one of them from the Southside, one of them from the Westside, I was on the Southside's side. That was just mandatory, though. But African Americans were under the same umbrella, regardless, but there was circles within circles."

Bryan, a member of the Aryan Brotherhood, described an attempt by some White boys from Mesa to start their own separate branch of Aryan Brotherhood in the joint. "We used to call them a 'sisterhood.' It was like a Mesa clique that tried to come in, but we stomped them out. I mean, you got to stomp shit like that out quick. You can't let no one else have your piece of the pie." That being said, other groups were tolerated so long as they didn't challenge the existing power structure. "Hell's Angels, Dirty Diapers, Dirty Dozen—all those dudes, when they hit the penitentiary, they shut up. They don't say shit because Aryan Brotherhood is running the show for the White inmates."

The Mexican Mafia is the only group that has a history of successfully and significantly contesting the existing social order in the Arizona prison system, something that has happened twice. In the early 1980s, the original Arizona Mexican Mafia faced internal challenges that led to a schism between the "Old Eme" and the "New Eme."[11] For a time, both organizations maintained their vertically organized leadership structures to dominate the Arizona prison system's social order. Together, they ensured that other start-up organizations could not take hold, and transplants—that is, gangs that came into the system because members from other states were being incarcerated in Arizona—could not influence the prison system's social order. Over time, according to multiple respondents and the estimated numbers reported by the Arizona Department of Corrections, the New Eme came to dominate Chicano prison life.[12] The Old Eme became a small organization, populated largely by older Latino inmates serving long sentences, often in administrative segregation.

Linus, a man who chose to stay unaffiliated while serving his time in prison, described the split that happened while he was incarcerated. "The New Mexican Mafia, they put a stop to a lot of the Old Mexican Mafia ways, and no more raping and killing people in prison was one of them. And a lot of the Old Mexican Mafia used to bully the youngsters. The youngsters took over. There's more youngsters than OGs now.[13] So, these youngsters put a stop to it. There's a New Eme. They said, 'No more.' Now the youngsters are bullying the OGs, you know, but in a certain way. They don't go around beating them up or nothing, but they let them know 'This is our shit. You kick back, and you follow *our* rules.'"

That status quo was in effect for the better part of twenty years. But in the early 2000s, the New Eme faced a challenge from within, characterized by an internal power struggle to control the business on the yard.

"There's been a lot of fights and battles," said Victor, who was a soldier for the Eme. "It's not all candies and roses. It's not. You know? When it really comes down to it, it's all about money. It's all about money. I have a lot of love for them. You know, they're my brothers and we've did so much, but when it really comes down to it, it's about the money. They could give a fuck about you. Really, you're just another part. You know what I mean? That's all it really is. Gang members don't see the inside like that, but once you're in prison, it's not a pretty sight." In other words, the social order in prison is based on the ability to control the drug trade within the prison walls, which has become the New Mexican Mafia's raison d'être in recent years, marking a shift from controlling politics on the street to focusing on the politics of prison.

The prison administration in Arizona had attempted to reduce the influence of prison gangs within the prison system by placing validated prison gang members in Special Management Unit II, known among inmates as "SMU II," which is solitary confinement.[14] The use of restrictive housing to control gang activity in prison is relatively commonplace throughout the country and especially in prison systems that have large gang populations and histories of inmate violence.[15] In Arizona in an effort to stamp out potential violence before it occurs, the prison administration sometimes puts gang members directly into restrictive housing by labeling them validated members of security threat groups, apparently based on their street gang affiliation. Conrado, a member of a street gang whose members almost always associated with or became members of the Eme when they went to prison, observed that "when people from this neighborhood go to prison these days, we get labeled as STG [members of a security threat group]. I don't know what goes on, but that should tell you something."

By locking confirmed prison gang members into SMU II, the prison administration was attempting to wrest back a degree of control that it had ceded as such organizations grew within the prison system. However, unlike the inmates who formed the Tangos in Texas, the inmates in Arizona did not respond to the lockdown of the established gangs by eschewing the traditional vertically configured prison gang for a horizontal model. Instead, the prison gangs changed their overt behavior; they began to conceal their actions and visible markers of gang membership from the gaze of the corrections officers. One immediate behavioral change involved the practice of tattooing for rank and association; now, it was done clandestinely or not at all.

"All my work—my 'Pride,' my eagle, my bolts, swastika—it's all on one arm. It's all out there to see," explained Bryan as he showed me his Aryan Brotherhood-related tattoos, most of which he received some twenty or more years earlier. "Now they hide everything. Do you see how I got the American flag and the Arizona flag behind a chain link fence? Today, they might hide 'A.B.' within that somehow. You know what I'm saying? Try to disguise it. Before, like we used to put it on our chest, big ol' fucking tat. Like Aryan Barbarian's got it tattooed across his back 'Aryan Barbarian.'[16] You'd never do that now because you'd just go to the hole and stay there until you get released.[17] If you're doing ten years, twenty years, fuck that! The hole's the most horrible thing you could do to a person because it's just—your whole world is that TV. Nothing else. I mean every show, you just become a part of the show in your life because that's your reality. You don't come out of your cell. I mean, it's just a horrible existence."

Raúl, who was an *esquina* for the Eme but never tried to climb the gang's ranks, discussed how difficult it was for any gang to authorize and commit violence in prison and thus underwrite its authority.

"Now there's really no control because they're all locked down, bro. There's no movement because the big homies are all locked up behind cell doors," said Raul. "Yeah, you can say, 'Hey, I want this yard to go off over here because they're fucking up' or 'The White boys are fucking up. You know what? Let's fuck up the White boys. Let's go have a riot.' That shit happens a lot, yeah. But, as far as the Eme controlling? Nah, they're not. Not even the Aryan Brotherhood, not even the Crips or nothing. There's nobody in control no more, man. It's so tight. Locked down so tight. Only if you're getting information from somebody that's in the hole, then that's how shit's getting taken care of. As far as the guys in solitary sending words out here to the street? Nah."

As the prison administration reasserted its presence within the social order, prison gang members avoided behaving in ways that would lead to their being classified as security threat groups and placed into solitary confinement. Instead, prison gang members focused on becoming consistent and clandestine players in the illicit drug trade within the prison walls, although they simultaneously maintained the rhetoric of protection to incoming inmates. "Pretty much for every prison gang, it's about the money," explained Breeze. Bryan elaborated further. "It's all a numbers game, and it's all a money hustle game. The more dudes a boss has on his side to push stamps, to push store, dope, drugs, whatever, the more money *that* dude makes, supposedly for the dudes in lockdown."[18]

Making money certainly wasn't just the White man's hustle. Victor explained that within the segregated norms of the prison social order, it was okay to deal with other races. "If you want to go outside of your race, then it's just for money purposes. You know? And that can stop at any moment. You have to be a little bit more cautious. You bump the prices up outside of your race. Say you sell something to another race, whether it be a White, Black, or Native. If they don't pay in a certain amount of time, there's no ifs, ands, or buts; that time line, it's to be dealt with." To that end, Duke explained that "every time a conflict between prison gangs occurs, it always has to do with drugs, always comes back to drugs because most of the head guys are drug users."

Every respondent reported the presence of drugs in prison, and every respondent pointed to a prison gang—or the *paisas*—as the organization that was bringing the drugs in to varying degrees. In conducting the prison drug trade, the prisoners still rely on the old hierarchical structures to resolve disputes. Being in control of the drug trade is power; however, those in charge are no longer necessarily overt, ranking members, given the propensity for such people to be thrown into solitary confinement. Instead, those who have power are those who are able to facilitate the entry of drugs within the constraints of prison.

Despite the prison administration's focus on prison gangs, former inmates maintained that administrations still allowed a certain amount of segregation and hierarchizing to occur among the inmates as a means to maintain order. "We keep order in there by our hierarchy," explained Wrangler, a man who had served time for burglary and had associated with the Aryan Brotherhood while incarcerated. "The prison administrators allow hierarchy to a certain extent because we keep order for the prison. The prison guards can't keep order in prison. There is no way. You look at the numbers of how many criminals are in and understand that the inmates could take the prison at any given time."

In short, the prison administration has forced the existing prison gangs to change their outward appearance and behavior within the prison. They have become more clandestine and less violent; however, the hierarchical arrangements that have historically been in place have not been challenged by the prison administration to the point of destroying prison gangs, as all respondents reported their continued and healthy existence. Moreover, these prison gangs, in addition to providing protection, have a reason for existing, and that reason is to make money from the drug trade, which—by the former inmates' accounts—appears to be pervasive within the prison system. The allegation that the prison administration has reasserted control over the prison yard should be taken with caution, since the administration may have only forced a reconfiguration of the inmates' ways of instituting social order.

The amount of influence that prison gangs have on the street varies greatly among the different racial groups. Many of the non-Chicano prison gangs have a cohesive presence only in prison. For instance, Dru explained that the Warrior Society does not appear on the reservation: "That's only a prison thing." Duke told me that the Mau Maus are an umbrella organization that keeps disparate groups of Black inmates together inside prison, while, on the outside, they are nothing compared to the individual street gangs and as such have little influence on street politics. Bryan and Wrangler indicated that the lack of White street gangs was a qualitative difference for Aryan Brotherhood compared to Latino prison gangs; the primary street-level organizations for White people were outlaw motorcycle gangs, such as the Hells Angels, whose business interests lead them to eschew a lot of the White supremacist rhetoric to maintain cordial relationships with other non-White criminal groups that supply them with drugs.

Prison gangs that have a clear presence on the street are exclusively Chicano, namely the New Mexican Mafia. The Eme's behavior echoes the traditions of the Latino prison gangs of Texas. As is the case in Texas, for the Eme—and Latinos joining prison gangs generally—membership is theoretically for life, with members being obligated to provide for incarcerated members or to do their bidding in the free world. Ideally, in the view of the Mexican Mafia, members participate in and dominate the drug trade in the free world. Sometimes they use the connections they develop in prison to secure wholesale shipments for local distribution.

According to Everett, a former undercover gang officer for GIITEM, the Mexican Mafia has been trying to unite the Latino street gang sets in Arizona, forcing them to "pay tax on whatever their criminal business is." This strategy is contingent on members of the Eme returning to their old neighborhoods or establishing a presence in a new one whereby they can impose and collect the taxes. Their presence may become the linchpin of the local retail trade in which they provide the street-level dealers with product and demand a percentage in exchange for continued support as well as protection, thereby allowing the illicit enterprise to continue unimpeded.

As in Texas, prison gangs' ability to influence street politics is predicated upon the notion that eventually everyone involved in the gang will end up in prison or have someone he cares about end up there. Accordingly, prison gangs' influence on the street is a function of the ability to provide and impose protection within prison. Street gang members need to ensure that protection will be available for them within prison. This influence extends to the women's prison as well, where the Eme's wishes are enforced by a Chicana shot caller. Adelita, a woman associated with the Eme, fulfilled that role for many of the twenty-five years she served in the women's yard at Perryville prison.

"I have more juice with the inmates and the guards than the warden. With one word, I can bring everything to a halt. It's appreciated on both sides. Sometimes the guards would come to me to resolve problems. If a chick steps out of line on the outside, word gets sent to me on the inside, and I take care of it when they get sent there. I realized a long time ago that it isn't what I want to do. It goes against my own code of ethics. But I have fifteen nephews in prison right now. The deal is that I take care of business when asked and that way I know the Eme has my nephews' back when they go to the men's prisons."

In principle, the historic protection arrangement whereby the Eme establishes rules for the criminal behavior on the street and punishes violations of those rules in prison is still in force. But in practice, it appears that the Eme's ability to enforce these rules is inconsistent due to an overall weak street presence. For instance, Raúl lamented the Eme's failure to persuade young street gang members to contribute to the welfare of those who are locked up. "Right here on the street? Well, people really aren't too scared of the Eme. They're nobody out here. You know what I mean? We—the ones that been locked up—we know what's going on. We know we can come out here and tell these youngsters 'Hey, dude, you got to respect what's going on in there, man, because them dudes are fighting for you guys in there. When you guys go in there, you guys can live a comfortable life in there.'" For many, it's a message that lands on deaf ears: they don't see the Eme controlling anything because its members can't stay out of prison. Luis, a former member of the Westside street gang, summed it up. "When they would come out, they would all usually go back in."

ADELITA AND CALISTA

¹ [A Psalme of Dauid.] The Lord is my shepheard, I shall not want.
² He maketh me to lie downe in greene pastures: he leadeth mee
beside the still waters.
³ He restoreth my soule: he leadeth me in the pathes of righteousnes,
for his names sake.
⁴ Yea though I walke through the valley of the shadowe of death,
I will feare no euill: for thou art with me, thy rod and thy staffe,
they comfort me.
⁵ Thou preparest a table before me, in the presence of mine enemies:
thou anointest my head with oyle, my cuppe runneth ouer.
⁶ Surely goodnes and mercie shall followe me all the daies of my life:
and I will dwell in the house of the Lord for euer.

—Psalme 23, *King James Bible* (1611)

The Town of Guadalupe, which incorporated in 1975, sits just beyond the city limits of Phoenix. The town's Catholic priest, Father David Myers, has been there serving the community since before incorporation. He talked of various drug traffickers and dealers who had come and gone throughout the years. The early ones were Mexican men who had brought part of the wholesale trade with them and whose presence became the linchpin of the drug trade the community experienced. While drug use continues in the community—glass being the flavor of the day—Father Myers told me that "It's not common, and there's not a lot of people doing it."¹ Those who eventually end up using, dealing, or trafficking represent a minority of the community. However, that minority garners considerable attention from the press, the community, and law enforcement.

I learned from Natividad Mendoza, whose nonprofit used to operate in Guadalupe, that the town had historically produced street gang members, several of whom during their incarceration had become involved with the Arizona Mexican Mafia. One of the highest-ups in the Eme, who at the time was in prison, hailed from Guadalupe. Its street gang culture appears to belong to a particular generation whose members are in their thirties and forties. Most youths do not participate in gang culture in the same way that the older generation did. Father Myers described the current gang activity of the town. "Some kids [might be]

146

FIGURE 9.   Our Lady of Guadalupe Church, Guadalupe, Arizona.

Photo by R. V. Gundur.

walking down the street looking for a fight, and maybe they are high, although not necessarily, and they see some other kids and they say, 'Well, let's beat them up.' And then they say, 'Well, it's our gang against your gang.' That's about where it's at." His description of a small, loosely organized gang presence was supported by local gang members I interviewed.

Nevertheless, as the drug trade and different street gangs have come and gone, the core problems of Guadalupe have remained the same. According to Father Myers, during his forty-year stay, poverty, low graduation rates, and high suicide rates consistently rank as the community's biggest problems. "Of every one hundred children who enter first grade, two graduate from high school," Father Myers explained. Drugs appear to be a symptom of these prevailing problems.

To illustrate his point, Father Myers recounted a time when he taught an ethics class at the Guadalupe campus of Stone Mountain Community College. He posed the following scenario to his students: "You want to support your family, and you can't get a job and you've really, really tried. Really, you've tried. You *can't* get one. Would it be okay to sell drugs? Everybody said yes. *Everybody.* Men, women, young, old. They said yeah. And I gave them a scenario in which you have to support your spouse and your children, so it's not to get rich, just to support your family."

Julie Marquez, a lawyer who had once defended members of the Cosa Nostra, echoed this sentiment and applied it to a broader scale in referring to the motivations of the small proportion of people who become gang members, cartel operatives, or mafiosos. "The common denominator in this world of organized crime is poverty. You have to realize that the driving force of crime is economic. People choose to commit crimes because it looks like a good way to get what they want. They continue to do so because it proves to be their best option, all things considered."

The world of poverty was one that Adelita and Calista knew intimately while growing up in Guadalupe. As girls, they were childhood friends with similar lives. Both had fathers involved in the drug trade: one man facilitated the importation of cocaine, and the other facilitated its sale on the street. Their neighbors included gang members and low-level drug dealers.

As teens, Adelita and Calista began to follow in their fathers' footsteps and joined their neighborhood street gang. They did not finish high school, but they grew up fast. Calista was pregnant at fourteen and became a single parent at seventeen when the father of her baby was shot to death. At eighteen, Adelita pleaded guilty to a drug charge to protect her lover, who had prior convictions, from a prison term that would have been much longer than the six years she was sentenced to.

With Adelita's incarceration in adult prison, the women's lives diverged. For nearly twenty-four years Adelita and Calista traveled along parallel roads, even though their lives crossed through the men in their families who participated in the drug trade as members of a street gang and later, as members of the Eme. Calista, who was the epitome of Father Myers's example, developed a business that was low-profile and managed to avoid trouble.

"I never wanted to rely on selling drugs. I always had regular jobs. But whenever I would become unemployed, I would always fall back to selling. That was my biggest problem," Calista said. "I didn't like it, but it was the only way I knew how to make enough money to pay for everything. Even when I was in school, I would sell. It was easy money, and I had so many mouths to feed; it was a way for me to do that. Throughout my life, I guess I just met the right people. I would sell for the Eme and for myself. Because of that, I had little risk. I never sold the drugs on the street. I've always had people under me. I just managed the spots."

For many years, Calista enjoyed the protection of the Eme and did not have to worry about any threats to her illicit enterprise. She kept her operation low-key, dealing to known associates to avoid the risks associated with selling to strangers.

By contrast, Adelita spent most of the next two and half decades developing a presence in Perryville, the prison where she invariably returned. With no help to be had, her addictions got the better of her; the dirty urine tests resulted in one parole violation after another. Her prolonged and repeated experience of being incarcerated forced her to teach herself how prison politics worked. She became the top inmate on the women's prison yard, astutely maintaining order and adjudicating disputes among her peers.

But then Adelita's and Calista's roads crossed. Having spent three months short of twenty-four years in prison, almost her entire adult life, Adelita was ready to transition out of prison and stay out. Meanwhile, Calista was adjusting to the notion that she would be going to prison as she prepared to plead guilty to a drug charge that would send her to Perryville for four and a half years. She had gotten romantically involved with a member of the Eme, who was considered a good earner. He had set up a trap house in her home and was selling drugs. "I didn't like it, but I went along with it. He was the boss. Whatever he said, went," she told me. "I didn't know how to stop it. I guess you could say that I was intimidated." Calista feared that if she turned her back on her boyfriend, his fellow gang members might retaliate. So, she pleaded out and was sentenced to four and a half years of incarceration; she would serve every day of that sentence.

The violence and coercion Calista experienced formed a common but seldom assessed story among women who are incarcerated, and such violence and coercion may compel women to reoffend.[2] Violence and coercion also formed a strong undercurrent in Adelita's life. Her partner in the free world was constantly jealous and controlling. Although he was uninterested in returning to a life of dealing drugs, his behavior meant that Adelita, like many women who struggle to establish financial autonomy upon release from prison, could not live independently.[3] As the women transitioned into each other's domains, each helped the other to face her new reality. They found comfort in the protection of the Lord as promised in Psalm 23, but they knew that they needed to learn from one another if they were to survive.

Knowing the rules of prison is critical in serving out a first prison sentence minimally scathed, so Adelita prepared Calista for life in Perryville. First, however, Calista had to arrange for her departure from the free world, the most important matter being the well-being of her young children. Adelita's child had been raised by members of her extended family; the same was about to be true for Calista's children. Who would care for them, pay their bills, and ensure that their future would not be marred by the temptations of a life of crime? These were Calista's primary concerns.

Adelita, heading in the other direction, was also concerned and scared and rightfully so. Calista introduced Adelita to people who could employ her and help her get on her feet and teach her about life outside prison. But Adelita, now far from the heights of power she had occupied within prison, found herself worse off than a nobody. Nobodies concern no one. But Adelita was a somebody, a somebody with a criminal record, a scarlet letter that for most is a brand burned into the skin rather than a piece of felt pinned onto a dress. The law-and-order crowd repeat the old adage "If you do the crime, you do the time." However, for the vast majority of former prisoners, the time never ends.

Without resources, the stigma of a criminal record is hard to outrun. Adelita was not among those—such as television personality Martha Stewart, actor Robert Downey Jr., former New York City police commissioner Bernard Kerik, and former Maricopa County sheriff Joe Arpaio—who could have a second act, with no detrimental strings attaching them to their pasts. Adelita, like the majority of formerly incarcerated people, was not free to resume life as a restored person who had atoned for her misdeeds. And most of the times she was released from prison, she lacked the capital and support she would need to get back on her feet, make a fresh start, and avoid reincarceration.[4] The struggles that Adelita had faced upon her release were ones that Calista, later, would be destined to face upon hers.

Adelita needed help moving some furniture, so she enlisted me, the only person she knew with a truck and time. I met her with the red pickup at her mother's house at eight o'clock in the morning. Hungry for breakfast, I offered to take us to a café on the way. When we got to the café, Adelita's eyes lit up. She lagged behind the hostess, walking slowly to our table, absorbing all of the decor and ambiance of the place. We ordered coffee; that was the easy part. The menu options were a bit too much for Adelita; in prison she never had very much choice. She settled on a bagel with cream cheese. As we waited for the food to arrive, we chatted about what it was like for her to be out and about.

"This is only the third time that I've been out someplace since I got out of prison. It's really nice here. My nephew took me out one day, and another time we went to Denny's. It doesn't sound like much, I know, but I enjoyed it."

The waitress brought us our bagels, and Adelita was thrilled.

"Oh, yay! They're toasted. You know in the joint, back in the day, we used to take those old-fashioned popcorn cookers they gave us to toast the bagels in the microwave."

She spread her cream cheese evenly on the two bagel halves and bit into it cautiously, somehow doubting the flavor she had chosen.

"Wow. This is *really* good!" Adelita exclaimed after one bite. "It might be the best bagel I've ever tasted. I'm going to have to tell my sister about this place."

Enjoying her experience at the café was part of Adelita's adjustment to her new life, a life, she insisted, without further incarceration.

"Things are different now. Lots of my siblings, who I used to do drugs with, have died. I don't have them as partners in crime anymore. I miss them, but I don't have them as triggers anymore. I'm learning the value of honestly earned money. It used to be, when I was selling drugs, easy come and easy go with the money I earned. Now, I appreciate the few things that I have been able to get for me and my family. I'm trying to find a job, you know, but it's been hard. Lots of people won't hire felons."

"Didn't you tell me you got some kind of license when you were in prison?"

"Yeah. I did. But I did that more as a challenge for me, not because I *really* wanted to do that work. My big problem here is that I don't have my driver's license."

"Why can't you get it? Did it expire when you were in prison?"

"I owe something like sixteen hundred bucks on it. I have to pay that before I can apply for it again."

"What on earth did you do? You've been locked up for so much time."

"It's from something that happened in '94. I was in an accident without a license. I never paid the fines and, over those twenty years, the interest on them just accumulated."

That financial burden was just one of the many obstacles—the ongoing punishments—Adelita faced in her journey to reintegrate into society. I paid our bill, and we left to drop off the furniture. As we drove through the streets of Phoenix, Adelita discussed the frustrations she was facing in her new position. With no license and no car, she couldn't move easily through the city. With no steady work, she couldn't provide as adequately as she would like for her family. And she struggled with her relationship with her child, which had frayed during her long incarceration. As she talked to me, she had worry painted across her face as if the weight of her many new free world concerns could come crashing down on her head at a moment's notice.

We pulled up to Adelita's relative's house, located in a well-kept and decidedly middle-class neighborhood in southern Phoenix. As I backed into the driveway, I was concerned about blocking the neighbor's exit.

"Oh, don't worry about that. That *vato* got busted for selling coke or some shit. Nobody lives there anymore. Sometimes, the kids go around back and play on the trampoline that got left behind."

We collected and dropped off our cargo and continued with the day. Adelita reflected on the many things that were new to her upon her release from prison, such as the new light rail and other technological advancements that had changed everyday life.

"I have only been here once, and that was when I rode the light rail," Adelita said as I navigated the streets near the downtown campus looking for parking. "I had read about it when I was sitting in prison, and I wanted to ride it, to see what it was like.[5] I thought it would go lightning fast. It didn't, but it was all right. A lot has changed, you know, since I was out before. It's funny. I don't even know what all of the rules are out here. You see those lines there? I don't even know what they mean. And I still know all of the prison rules inside and out."

I found parking, and we went up to my office because Adelita needed to use a computer to complete an assessment for a job application she had recently filed. I showed her how to look for free things on Craigslist and how to check her email. All these skills came slowly to her. She was figuring out some of this newfangled technology, especially enjoying the marvels of Facebook on her smartphone, an older model that one of her family members had given her so she could be connected to her family in the modern way. Adelita resisted other bits, saying that she wanted to live as basic as possible. She was an anachronism. I was often surprised to learn what Adelita had never experienced. With her skill set she was a person who would have functioned well about fifteen years before her release, but as she sat in Perryville, the world had passed her by.

That evening there was a *quinceañera*, and I was invited along.[6] We rolled in a bit late; there was no beer or water left. The only beverage available was hard liquor. Since I was tired and driving, I passed. The friendly barman, who was packing up, poured out three shots of vodka for Adelita. She picked up the small white cup and smelled it.

"Whoa! What is this stuff?"

"It's Ketel One," I said.

"Ketel One? What's that?"

"It's a kind of vodka."

"Oh, okay. You'll have to forgive me. You know I've been away for a long time."

"Sure, don't worry about it. I only know that brand because I used to tend bar. I don't drink much hard liquor myself."

Adelita sipped on the chilled, clear liquid, and before I knew it, all three of the little cups were sitting stacked up within each other, empty.

"Wow, I'm already starting to feel buzzed."

"Vodka will do that to you."

"You know, I've never had it before."

"Really? I guess it's better than diesel fuel."

"What's that?"

"Grain alcohol."

"People drink that?"

"Yeah, it's stupid cheap."

"I don't know how people drink this shit," Adelita said, wincing as she sipped on another shot of vodka.

"Well, a lot of times people drink vodka with a mixer. Put it in some orange juice, and it'll go down easy."

After a short while, Adelita started to get woozy. She sat and smoked a cigarette and greeted different people she hadn't seen for years. Her drunken state accelerated quickly, and as the party came to a close, I offered to drive her home. We got into the truck and set out for her house. As she sat slumped to the side in the passenger seat, she became aware of how drunk she was.

"I'm so sorry. I didn't mean to get this drunk. You have to realize, I've never drank this stuff before. Oh my God. I can't believe how bad I feel. My head is spinning."

It was kind of funny, actually. It reminded me of the first time I got totally shit-faced drunk. I was visiting my friend in Italy and took advantage of being able to drink freely and legally before the age of twenty-one. After a splendid evening, I was sick and throwing up in the back of his car. Fortunately for me Adelita didn't puke, but I saw a glimpse of my nineteen-year-old self in her stupor.

"I'm never going to drink this shit again. Oh . . . my . . . God. It's really hot in here."

I was kind of cold, but I blasted the air anyway.

"Ha! That's what we've all said. Next time you're at a cookout, you'll be asking for those margaritas again."

"No. I *mean* it," she slurred. "This feels awful. I don't know why people drink that stuff. I don't know what I'm going to do."

"Well, how on earth did you get that drunk?" I asked. After all, she only had maybe four standard drinks. "Did you eat tonight?"

"Not really."

"Well, that's a rookie mistake. You've got to eat."

"Well, I don't think I could eat anything right now. Can you pull over somewhere?"

"Do you think you're going to throw up?"

"Maybe."

"Well, we're almost to your house. We'll be there in five minutes. Do you think you can hold out?"

Like a teenager, she didn't have keys to the house, so she pulled out her phone and called her mom to let her in. Her mom was up, waiting for her to come home. I pulled up to the house, opened the gate, and watched her go to the door, reminding her to drink plenty of water. The next day she told me how, after downing a glass of water, she passed out with her clothes on—the first time that had happened to her while on alcohol. As a kid, she skipped that experience and went straight to heroin. Free again, she was able to dial back and have a proper introduction to the age of nineteen, even if it happened twenty-five years late.

Adelita didn't manage to stay out of prison; she relapsed and violated her parole once again, but that stint would be her last. Once out, she continued to look for work, occasionally getting some. In prison, she had exhibited skills that would have made her an excellent employee. She was organized, regimented, and rule-based, but in the free world she was relegated to doing menial labor; in another life, she could have been a general manager for a successful business. In 2020 she had been out of prison for four straight years, her longest consecutive stretch of freedom since she was a girl. She had finally succeeded in avoiding the behaviors that had deprived her of her freedom for so many years. She lived her life honestly, contributing to the needs of her community and encouraging young people in her circle to avoid crime and the trouble it brought.

Just before Halloween, a group of four people went on a robbing spree throughout the Greater Phoenix area.[7] Their last stop was Guadalupe. As they attempted to rob someone, Adelita intervened, preventing the robbery. But one of the assailants shot her. Adelita was taken to the hospital, where she died six weeks later from her injuries; she was forty-nine years old. Adelita's freedom had been taken from her once again. And despite her gang affiliation, a court never took her freedom from her because of that affiliation; rather, the revocation of her freedom was a function of two pernicious plagues: addiction and gun violence. That her killers are in custody and will likely be convicted, unlike Facundo's murderers in Juárez, is only a small consolation.

For millions of former prisoners redemption is elusive, with society broadly stigmatizing them for the rest of their lives and refusing to recognize them as people who can positively contribute to society once again. Society condemns them, at worst, to a future of further incarceration, to be expressly erased through their express exclusion or, at best, to a future of toiling at the margins of society, to be forgotten in their obscurity. But Adelita had value in her community. There, she was living proof to her community that violence and a life of crime were best avoided. As an elder stateswoman she had respect, and people listened to her as she warned them off of illicit activities.

Yet outside Adelita's community, her accomplishments followed the typical script that rendered them invisible and unrecognized. Nevertheless, Adelita's last act of life was selfless, heroic, and visible. She came to the aid of a stranger on the street. She lived her ethics and refused to stand by and allow harm to come to another person while she was present. And despite that, Adelita was never named in any of the newspaper articles that covered the incident. The journalists only reported that the robbery was interrupted by a woman and that she was in critical condition but was expected to survive her wounds. When she died, there was no follow-up to the original story; no obituary appeared in any newspaper. However, an outpouring of love, stories, and admiration for her bravery, reminding us that she had intervened when too many of us would have been afraid to do so, adorned her Facebook page. And though Adelita struggled to shake off the negative labels associated with her incarceration and gang association as she tried to navigate and reintegrate into the free world, it was clear that within her community she was recognized for what she was: a hero, unbothered by anyone else's judgments.

A FEAR OF CORNERS

"Why are you focusing on gangs?" asked Eddie, a member of the New Mexican Mafia. We had been talking about street gangs for the past hour; he was confused and agitated as to why I thought they were important in terms of understanding the drug trade in the area. Eddie wasn't the first person in Phoenix—gang member or cop—to tell me that street gangs were in decline in the area, but he was the first to couch the declining role of street gangs in entrepreneurial terms. Street gangs had historically served as drug retailers, often serving low-volume customers who were intent on buying product on street corners. The Arizona Criminal Justice Commission said that street gangs held this role well beyond the time I was talking to Eddie.[1]

But Eddie claimed that relying on street gang members to stand on the corner and sell dope was a thing of the past. "Street gangs are dead, man. They're nothing. The Eme doesn't use them to sell drugs. They're not even left around to sell for us. Look at where the money is. We deliver directly to sons of doctors and lawyers or whoever has money. That's who's buying. There's a driver system now to sell drugs. I have a series of drivers who deliver for me. My drivers aren't going to know who I am. How does that happen? Let's say I know you and I trust you. Okay, I'm giving the drugs to you, and then you know your cousin and you trust him. You give him the drugs, and he delivers. He gets phone calls with directions. There are spots; they change. The directions would be 'Get the pickup at this spot and drop it off over there.' That's how it would work for longer deliveries. The driver's number would be changed every two months, maybe sooner. He gets paid depending on the weight he is moving."[2]

Luis, who continued to sell drugs despite ceasing to participate in his gang, told a similar tale, though the actors in charge were somewhat reversed in his story. According to Luis, the Eme didn't have much sway on the street; members of his gang negotiated connections with their own plugs—drug wholesalers—and would then in turn find non–gang-affiliated *paisas* to sell their product.[3] "All the drivers were *paisas*. All of them," Luis explained. "The *paisas* would buy an ounce or two of heroin from one of us, sometimes more, chop it up and balloon it—put everything in balloons [for retail sale]—and send out their drivers."

It would take some doing to sort out what was going on with the street and prison gangs, but the driver-delivery system undoubtedly featured in the contemporary drug scene; it had been present in California since at least the 1990s, so naturally it migrated to Arizona.[4] Adelita succinctly described what the chain of distribution in a typical drug crew looked like. "At the top, you got the *mero* who's running it, who's the shot caller; then you got the next one that transports it; the next one that distributes it; and the last one that delivers it, like in the car." Her description summed up what I learned from other users, dealers, and law enforcement officers. While the delivery system meant that "the street-level drug trade in Phoenix isn't what it used to be," as Jake, one longtime Phoenix police officer, indicated, the retail drug trade persisted.

From my conversations with players in the drug trade and the officers who policed it, the drug trade in Phoenix included three broad market types: specialty, retail/street level, and wholesale. The specialty markets are relatively small. They feature drugs with comparatively little demand by volume, such as crack cocaine and "wax," a product derived from cannabis resin. In Phoenix, such niche products have specific but steady client bases that allow the relatively small producers to generate enough business to stay afloat. Duke spoke about his past as a crack dealer. He had served the largely Black users who preferred crack to the other hard drugs—heroin and meth—commonly available on the street. His business had generated enough money to satisfy his needs and desires. But he wasn't big time. "I wasn't balling by no standards.[5] In a month I'd probably sell six ounces, somewhere around there."

Bryan, a member of the Aryan Brotherhood, described the success of his wax business. "My household has a monopoly on it in Tempe because we're the only ones figured out how to do it.[6] It takes a lot of weed. But the profits are staggering." He went on to describe the community of users he serves and how the market dynamics worked below him. "It's always younger people who want wax. Not necessarily kids, but younger people. Shit, you get a couple of them younger people that are hip, cool, especially in Tempe where they got a little money. They always know everybody. You start slinging it to him, he slings it to his friends, and then you just kick back and don't do shit. Make wax and kick it. There's no risk because how many potheads have ever told on anybody? No pothead's going to tell on anybody."

Nonetheless, these markets do not appear to be very big or, in the case of wax, even well known to the city's regular drug users, who tend to prefer, besides marijuana, the three main hard drugs offered for retail sale, cocaine, heroin, and methamphetamine, with the last being the most widely consumed hard drug in Greater Phoenix.[7]

Cocaine, heroin, and meth are now imported from Mexico. Most of the heroin and meth consumed in Phoenix and probably the United States is likely produced and processed in Mexico.[8] Heroin has long been produced in Mexico, and Mexican producers supply more of the US market than the large-scale Asian producers of the drug do.[9] The war on drugs made producing heroin profitable in the 1970s, thereby encouraging Mexican producers to enter a market that had been previously dominated by Turkish goods.[10]

"Black tar heroin [had been] produced by the Mexicans for a long, long time. And they realized that the black tar heroin is not as appealing to middle- and upper-class [users] because you have to shoot it, and [those consumers were concerned about] the needles, AIDS, all that kind of crap," explained Elizabeth Kempshall, who when I spoke to her was head of the Arizona HIDTA, which is part of a federal drug-prohibition enforcement program. "So, what the Mexicans did was they brought in chemists from China and Colombia and said, 'Teach us how to make this white heroin.' So, what the Mexicans do, they make a cinnamon-colored heroin that you can snort, you can smoke, makes everybody really happy, and not have to use a needle. So, the vast majority of heroin abused in the United States is coming from Mexico."

Though currently most of the meth consumed in the US market is produced in Mexico from precursor chemicals shipped in from Asia, that wasn't always the case.[11] Until the early 2000s, US meth was largely produced domestically and sold by outlaw motorcycle gangs.[12] Then, Mexican producers recognized the economic potential of meth and began producing it in wholesale amounts.[13] Moreover, the Mexican product is crafted in a laboratory setting that yields a product purer than what could be typically produced in the backroom labs that dotted Arizona and California during meth's domestic heyday.[14] Law enforcement cracked down on the smurfing operations, which sent individuals to pharmacies to purchase the cold medicine needed to make the drug, and the impromptu meth labs. These measures, coupled with the cheap influx of superior-quality product, led to the demise of the domestic meth producers in the American Southwest and to a shift in the actors involved in the local meth trade in Arizona and California.[15]

Regardless of the hard drug sold, most participants in the drug trade with whom I spoke and the police who worked that beat consistently reported that illicit entrepreneurs relied on business connections to help maximize their comparative advantages. Notably, building these business connections on the street means abandoning the race politics of prison. While the prison policy of sticking with one's own kind remains in effect for the most intimate relationships, business is business, and opportunities to expand are not to be missed. Plus, violence is to be avoided because it brings unwanted police attention, which is bad for business. Many law enforcement personnel spoke of how opposing prison groups put aside their differences when dealing with business in the free world.

"The Aryan Brotherhood will be associated with White supremacist groups in their day-to-day lives in the free world," explained Everitt, a law enforcement officer who worked for the statewide task force GIITEM. "But you'll just as readily find an Aryan Brotherhood member working in conjunction with a Hispanic because it's a dope connection. And they might hang out together and party together. Because he's White supremacist in prison, he may not necessarily hold true to those beliefs on the outside."

Bridget, a police lieutenant whose assignments exposed her to several aspects of the drug trade, described an informant she once used who progressed up the ranks. When she caught up with him ten years later, he had become a full-fledged "Mexican Mafia member who was dealing dope with a White motorcycle gang."

Baxter, a Phoenix police commander, described the Mexican Mafia as "forward-thinking" in its efforts to diversify its business partners: "They are smarter. Absolutely. Actually, they work with the Aryan Brotherhood, if you can believe that. Who would have ever saw that one coming? Or that the Mexican Mafia would actually work with [White outlaw motorcycle gangs like] the Dirty Dozen and the Hells Angels?"

Ultimately, suppliers with connections to transnational wholesalers aim to offload their product as efficiently as possible; who purchases the products is of less importance than the consistency of that business. Once wholesalers acquire the products, they resell them to people who process them into by-products such as wax or crack and sell them on or to individuals who retail them. The retail drug trade occurs via a variety of phases and locations that involve a wide array of people, including some who, despite the inherent interpersonal relationship between buyer and seller, never interact with each other when best practices are followed. However, the market does have a bottom, an entry point for those with no connections but a desire to get high: the corner. And while the role of gangs in running the corner may be declining, it is not yet completely dead.

"There still needs to be a corner where the dope is at, for the people who don't have phones, don't have cars, don't have a place where they can be," explained Natividad, himself a former member of the Bulldogs, a California prison gang.

FIGURE 10.   Central Arizona Shelter Services, Phoenix, Arizona.

Photo by R. V. Gundur.

Phoenix has many users who fit Natividad's description. Several loitered on the main street near where I lived.

Their presence was explained by my neighborhood's proximity to the Human Services Campus, home to the Central Arizona Shelter Services (CASS), located some six blocks from the state capitol. The difference between the capitol and CASS is stark. Around the capitol, clean, well-coiffed, well-dressed people who work in the government buildings walk purposefully to their jobs. Around the Human Services Campus, unwashed, disheveled, raggedly clad people loiter or mosey along with no obvious direction.

Fidget, a man who became homeless about twelve months prior to meeting me, described the chaotic lives of the vast majority of people he had met while living on the streets and hanging around CASS. "Everybody out of the fifty I have met living out on the street are on drugs. They go across the street from the shelter to a store and steal a bottle of whiskey. 'Hey, do you want to sell this?'" Fidget shook his head no, as if to respond. "'Why not? I need a bum,' So I tell them 'Like why don't you just drink it? It might do you a little better.' Drug us-

ers are always looking to scam; always, to get something to pay for that next hit."
For these drug users with chaotic lifestyles, open-air markets are the best and
perhaps only place to score their next fix.

Occasionally I went to CASS with Teddy, a young man who ran a clandestine harm reduction program. He fielded a lot of interest in his program from
people who reported that they were intravenous drug users, his target population. Unlike in Juárez, giving out clean hypodermic needles is illegal in Phoenix. "Normally, I do outreach on a bike," Teddy said. "If I see a five-0, I'd be out
of here because if they caught me with needles, I could be in big trouble.[16] Fortunately, I've never been caught. The bike helps me get a move on quick." Ordinarily, Teddy provides users with a kit similar to the one Facundo delivered to
his clients in Juárez. The kit consists of clean hypodermic needles; a cooker; cot-
ton filters; alcohol swabs; condoms; two vials of Naloxone, an antiopiate used to
pull people out of heroin overdose; the syringes needed to administer the Naloxone; and a pamphlet that explains how to use it.

Teddy's contact number is circulated by word of mouth, and he responds to
whoever calls for his help after a short vetting process over the phone. A former
intravenous drug user himself, Teddy explained that twelve-step–style desistance
programs are not for everybody. "Not everyone, for example, wants to do religion. I didn't. Sometimes people need the accountability of safe using before they
can turn the corner." For Teddy, responsible usage was a first step to reducing
the chaos that characterized these drug users' lives, the chaos that drove them
to buy from the corner.

Individuals who dealt and used drugs described a correlation between the degree of trust a dealer had in a client and the degree of access that client had to the
wider supply chain of which the dealer was a part. All users, unless vouched for
by a trusted party higher up the supply chain, have to start with the open markets
and demonstrate their reliability to the community of suppliers they wish to deal
with, a pattern that is common in various markets throughout the United States,
including Phoenix.[17] The dealers working the corner, selling individual-use quantities for five to twenty dollars, are often though not always gang members who
are looking to earn some capital.

Dealers in the drug trade attempt to manage risk; however, when they cannot,
they must often accept whatever terms they come by, balancing that risk against
the potential financial gain of moving up the ladder within the drug trade. Mike,
a Black gang member originally from California, had worked as an underling
who had no choice but to accept the risks placed on him if he wanted to be part of
the drug trade. He described the ability to sell drugs on the corner as a favor that
a midlevel retail dealer would grant a subordinate. Money was to be made in
"doubling up," that is, cutting the product: "So half cocaine, half baking soda.

The dude's not losing nothing.[18] He gained his money, but you, the homie, he want to see you eat. You know what I'm saying? So, what they do, I mean, they make rock.[19] That's how they make rock. They cut it up. Ol' boy, he already making more than his money back. So, like, 'This is the little homie. I want to see him have a little extra money in his pocket.'" The adulteration allows the corner retailer to pay back the principal and buy another batch that is then cut and resold to become net income.

Cops and gang members alike noted that hand-to-hand selling on the corner was infrequent compared to just a few years before in the early 2000s, but it still existed. Sellers understand that visibility is risky and have made efforts to reduce it. In the past neighborhoods, such as Oakland where I stayed, featured open-air markets that could accommodate relatively large requests; now anything larger than a daily-use quantity requires a visit to a supplier's house, out of public sight. As in El Paso, the open-air drug scene in Phoenix is quiet: it's unusual to see gang members posting up on the street corner. In my neighborhood, which had a few gang members, I rarely saw any groups congregating. Most of the time when I spotted a gang member, he was in transit at dusk or dawn or simply sitting on his porch, drinking beer or hanging out with his family. Being in a residential area meant that illicit businessmen kept their trade to a minimum and out of plain sight so as not to draw attention to themselves. Nonetheless, I learned from the officers who responded to a call I made after being burglarized that it was unlikely that anyone in my neighborhood would ever call the police unless something affected them personally or there was a serious incident, such as a murder.

Everitt, who was part of several undercover missions for GIITEM, which primarily targets gangs and those involved in the drug trade, attributed this shift away from the corner to successful law enforcement operations and prosecutions against street gang members. "We used to see neighborhoods where guys were posting up on corners or walking down the street, five and six deep, dressed in their colors and flying their flags and hanging their rags out of their pockets. You don't see that anymore because GIITEM has been working the gang cases on them. So, the street gangs changed the way that they do business because they try to keep their opposition, which typically is going to be law enforcement, off their backs."

Users, stable enough to buy product reliably and perhaps in slightly larger quantities, would develop their supplier's trust so they could enter the supplier's house. Developing trust is essential because suppliers want to ensure that desperate addicted users are kept at bay. They are not a clientele that many dealers want to engage with. Linus, who sold "G"—the clear, highly processed methamphetamine made in Mexico that resembles glass shards—felt that the corner was too risky. "Out of the house is different because you got people knocking on your door, and you ain't going to answer the door unless you know them or somebody brought them there."

Breeze talked about his move from buying off the corner to gaining access to suppliers shortly after he began looking for cocaine in the 1980s. His wife, who was dealing to her friends—"housewives and other women like that"—lost her connection, a White guy, whom she failed to pay one too many times. Breeze then sought to find another source of cocaine. "I started going to the inner city, in Phoenix. The 'Mexicans' approached me.[20] I was down there in the barrio looking; I knew it was rampant down there. This was the beginning of crack. So, people were walking up to people like me and saying 'Do you want something?' and they were talking about crack."

At first, Breeze bought quantities that would last him for a week or more. But then as he became more and more addicted, he returned to the neighborhood to buy smaller quantities that he would consume immediately. Though an addict, he was a reliable customer and an ex-con, two attributes which gave him "as much trust as anybody can expect to have in that community." Breeze usually brought his money. But if he didn't have money, he was willing to do some dirty work such as beating up another debtor for his dealer, which allowed Breeze to earn credibility and respect from his drug suppliers.

That trust earned Breeze invitations to enter his suppliers' homes and to hang out with them. It allowed him later on to access larger quantities, which he then provided to the motley crew of people who occasionally stayed in his house. Though he never considered himself to be a drug dealer, Breeze assumed the role of supplier to his circle of friends who traded services and errands for a taste of what was on hand. Being a supplier allowed Breeze to gain the contacts necessary to supply his demands.

Stu, a recovering meth user, recounted a similar progression. His dealer, who lived in a remote edge of the Greater Phoenix area, did not offer a delivery service. Stu described the dealer as "a nice guy" who was on friendly terms with Stu's brother. Stu's brother had introduced Stu, and that introduction enabled him to approach the dealer on his own. Stu never got too friendly with the dealer, but his brother did and after a while was introduced to "Mexicans from Mexico, and they would sell him the stuff really cheap. So, he was getting ounces of meth."

Not all the houses where drugs are sold are so chummy. Calista described the trap house she lived in when she was arrested. Her partner, a member of the Eme, ran the business from her house with her children present. According to Calista, the house was a place where clients were served but were not welcomed as guests.

Nonetheless, by most accounts such houses were places where dealers connected with reliable users and vice versa, despite the police's relatively successful efforts to find and raid them.[21] Compared to the street corner, dope houses are centers of low risk for drug dealers, who in most cases are users too and are pleased not to have to deal with the chaotic clientele the corner offers. In parallel, the houses are loci of social development for users who garner trustworthiness within the drug community they want to enter. After the initial point of contact is negotiated, either through successful, repeated street-level purchases or by being vouched for by a trusted connection to the proprietor, the house provides an entrance to that larger community, usually in the form of a driver who will make personal deliveries or, in rare cases, a bigger supplier who provides quantities that can be retailed.

Getting a telephone number of a delivery driver requires a different degree of trust than just being able to rock up at a dealer's house.[22] Sometimes that trust can be gained simply by being a certain type of client. Today, rather than going to the 'hood to find dope, a client tries to get a phone number. Anne, a harm reduction worker, reported that most of her clients were "people who meet the delivery guys in parking lots" after having called in an order. Anne's clients would be less chaotic drug users, perhaps college kids looking for some dope to party on the weekend.

For the regular user, however, trust must be earned. That trust may be earned in various ways: doing errands for the dealer, being his pal, or buying more than what the street dealer can supply. Everitt described how he worked up the drug supply chain as an undercover agent. "I got hooked up with a street gang member, and he gave me a phone number because I started to buy more than this guy could supply. That number might lead me to a *paisa*, and that *paisa* was now delivering. And the driver had a guy that he was getting from, and maybe I could work up to that guy. Maybe not. More than likely not; I would always get delivered to."

The identification of a *paisa* as the typical delivery driver came up time and time again with outreach workers, police, and gang members, who frequently recounted the image of a Mexican national, typically dressed as a campesino or a vaquero.[23] Breeze, who spoke about the driver system as existing in the late 1980s or early 1990s, described the drivers he first dealt with. "The dealers have got guys who come from Mexico, who just have arrived and have been brought by coyotes.[24] In order to work off that trip, which sometimes costs a few thousand dollars, the recent arrivals become drivers. They become like pawns: completely expendable."

Everitt corroborated Breeze's account. As an undercover buyer, Everitt found it difficult to go up that chain of distribution. "When I bought drugs from *paisas*, it was rare that they would even want to put me in touch with whoever their source of supply was, and I don't mean the trafficker; I'm talking about just a guy that's running a crew. Typically, there would be a guy that might have a crew of five or six or seven different guys—Mexican nationals—that are basically errand boys. They're just middlemen. They're mules for the dealer's drugs so that he doesn't ever have to get his hands dirty. He doesn't have to show his face and he doesn't have to present himself or put himself out there to get caught."

The delivery system benefited both consumers and the intermediaries in the supply chain. Clients who preferred to avoid the safety and legal risks of buying drugs in open-air markets could do so. Moreover, the delivery system is a service that has adapted with the times, with one police commander, Ryan, telling me that "it's even moving into cyberspace. You can go online and place an order to trigger the delivery." In addition, users reported that the delivery service was reliable. After calling in an order, the delivery driver would be "at your house in thirty minutes or less," explained Tony, a recovering heroin user. Moreover, Tony preferred dealing with the drivers rather than his friends because the *paisas* offered consistent quality and prices. "The *paisas* were suppliers, so it was a business to them."

Although the delivery system did not feature any of the glitz and glamor of Hollywood drug kingpins, it shielded the dealers and allowed them to hide in plain sight. Breeze described how the dealers managed their drivers, sending "the *paisas* out in a car that was bought expressly for delivering drugs. It was chosen for its characteristics: it was not too new; it wasn't too old; it wasn't too big. The drivers always did have a pager, and once phones came out, they always had a phone." Their instructions were to deliver the products to the customers, collect payment, and if a problem occurred destroy communications to their dispatcher. The drivers kept their phones "really close to them," Breeze recalled. "And that phone got destroyed if they got popped. That was the first thing that was going to happen if they got pulled over. That phone was not going to work." The drugs were next. The drivers "would carry McDonald's cups full of balloons in water," Luis explained. "So, if they got pulled over, they would drink it. Boom! Swallow the whole thing real quick." The drivers had a strategy to minimize the evidence they possessed and to shield whoever they were working for. Upon arrest, they had little incentive to inform on anyone, since they viewed their superiors as either trustworthy or paramount to their future success. A driver's clean record and possession of a relatively small quantity of drugs would likely result in a minimal custodial sentence, if any, followed by deportation.

Certainly the *paisa* drivers, despite their provenance, were neither members nor employees of Mexican drug trafficking organizations. They were merely parts of subcontracted drug-running crews serving consumers and operated on or just above the street level. With that clientele and pattern of service, the drivers possessed only relatively small amounts of product at any given time to minimize the legal ramifications if they were caught. Nobody I spoke to who was involved in dealing viewed drivers as people who either desired or were able to move up the ladder within the criminal enterprise they worked for. Yet the drivers, being *paisas,* created confusion among some of the client base, who thought that they were dealing with somebody who was "connected" to an ostensibly violent Mexican drug trafficking organization. This strategy creates a smoke screen, an opaque barrier of *paisa* subcontractors, that both obfuscates the identities of the actors and logistics further up the supply chain and conjures up an illusion that "the cartel" is present and ready to act. This smoke screen, which mid- to high-level drug entrepreneurs deliberately and carefully deploy, cause others—subordinates, retail customers, and even law enforcement—to misidentify the higher-ups.

As essential elements of this smoke screen, higher-level figures employ cutouts: people, such as the *paisa* drivers, who do not know who their employers are or who believe their employers are persons they are not. Such cutouts, themselves often fooled or blinded by the smoke screen they help form, represent hard breaks in the investigatory chain from user to kingpin that undercover officers such as Everitt struggle to work their way up. When an investigator such as Everitt reaches a cutout, he may find himself forced to settle for low-level busts, eliminating the cutout from the supply chain but leaving the critical machinery of the drug trade intact. When cutouts are compromised, they are replaced with others, equally ignorant of or misinformed about the supply chain above their station. The new cutouts are similarly useful in contributing to the smoke screen that allows midlevel dealers to imply that they are part of a powerful, sinister organization, perhaps the Sinaloa Federation or the Cartel Jalisco Nueva Generacíon. In this way, the midlevel dealers blunt the efforts of law enforcement while striking useful fear in intermediaries and subordinates.

Ironically, however, this smoke screening benefits law enforcement even as it frustrates them. The implicit threat of cartel violence, real or mythological, in a given community can help law enforcement mobilize public support. So long as law enforcement focuses on the operations of drug trafficking organizations, it can use the moral panic often generated by the media in response to include funding on the public agenda and to coax politicians into approving budgets that fund antidrug operations.[25] If residents believe that a notorious, internationally present criminal organization is operating in their city and contributing to violence and drug misuse, the community is more likely to voice support for expanded police funding and more invasive tactics. Accordingly, when funding is on the line, it is in law enforcement's interest to foster rather than debunk the myths that emerge from the smoke screen. This sets up a conflict between the press room and the beat, where such a strategy is obviously antithetical to the objective of outing big players. Instead, this conflict helps those who want to conceal their identity and assert control among the lower ranks of their organizations by providing additional credibility to their claims of violent prowess.

14

CONNECTIONS

Located on the major highways of I-10, which runs east and west, and I-17, which runs north, Greater Phoenix is an ideal place for "staging" wholesale quantities of drugs. Staging involves the temporary storage of shipments before routing them onward to destinations farther from the border. The prevalence of stash houses in Phoenix was responsible in part for the rash of kidnappings that plagued Phoenix in the late 2000s.[1] Unlike El Paso, where local demand is so small that little volume of quality goods remains in the city, Phoenix apparently has sufficient local demand to merit supplying the local distributors with reasonable-quality product.[2]

Phoenix's wholesale drug market, along with other factors including the kidnappings, generated sensational headlines about "Arizona's crime problem" in the US press. Some commentators, in light of the kidnappings, conflated human smuggling with the drug trade; however, it appears that while *polleros*, the people who transport smuggled migrants within the United States, may use similar routes as drug smugglers, generally speaking there is little overlap in the market actors and activities.[3] Thus, it is critically important not to mistakenly characterize the drug trade as a major component of human smuggling (or human trafficking, for that matter) or vice versa.

Developing a history from the testimony of the people involved with the wholesale drug market in Phoenix was difficult; negotiating direct access to such people was not possible. Most of my respondents who had contacts with wholesale traffickers had not asked questions during their time with them and remained consciously ignorant of their plugs' further business dealings. Being inquisitive could have blown the connection or put them at risk, since asking questions was beyond the realm of acceptable conduct in these relationships. Rubén, a man who had spent nearly his entire adult life in prison, talked about his relationship with drug traffickers in Mexico some twenty-five years before. His street gang had a relationship with a *paisa* wholesaler. An understanding of respect existed between Rubén's gang and its *paisa* suppliers, and this understanding was observed to minimize the need for violence. "I didn't fear them because, like I said, I stayed loyal and I stayed doing things. I called it doing things right and correct."

For midlevel dealers seeking suppliers, doing things "right and correct" is only a small part of developing the relationships necessary to forge a business connection with higher-level suppliers. Navigating the supply chain, moving up from the street corner and closer to midlevel and big players, is no easy task even for consistent street-level dealers. A person must develop a lot of trust to make such a connection and to get a chance to gain direct access to a wholesaler.

But gaining trust with a well-placed connection can require more than just savvy; ethnicity or social capital can play a role in permitting or barring access to suppliers. Mike, a Black gang member who spoke no Spanish, described the difficulty his gang faced to get supplied. "Everything comes from Mexico, believe it or not. So, you have to know a Mexican that knows a Mexican that knows a Mexican just to get the plug.[4] Now Black people—don't get us wrong, we gangbang and we do the other bullshit. But when it comes down to business and drugs and stuff like that, we have to go to a Mexican 'hood." Here, Mike is talking about Mexican Americans who would have a Mexican supplier, a *paisa*, whom Mike was never allowed to meet directly.

Wrangler, a White man who associated with the Aryan Brotherhood while in prison, described how the changing demographics of his neighborhood led to his being introduced to *paisas* who were moving meth in from Mexico. "The illegals started moving in, and that's when I got the illegal drug dealer. When I was probably like sixteen, I started dealing with him." Wrangler went on to describe a specific contact from his neighborhood, Carlos, who was the child of unauthorized immigrants from Mexico. Carlos had gone on to become part of a Latino street gang and later a prison gang and had a connection with a wholesaler.

Eventually Carlos was deported to Mexico, but Wrangler was able to continue to exploit the connection and get supplied because he had been introduced around. "I knew Carlos's cousins and I still know his cousins, and they all live in the same neighborhood. And I knew them individually and kind of together, but now, the guy I was working with, his best friend is Carlos's homie's cousin. That's kind of how their links work. They're all related by blood or gang-related."

Duke, an African American who dealt crack but claimed no gang affiliation whatsoever, had to rely on people he knew from the neighborhood until he went to prison and met better connections. Duke explained that his plugs were "a lot of dudes he grew up with." When asked whether they were all African Americans, Duke responded affirmatively.

Duke's main connection for drugs was a man from his neighborhood who had a relationship with the Eme, a group that he viewed, incorrectly, as being a Mexican drug cartel. Duke described how, while in prison, a member of the Eme offered to supply him with drugs upon his release. While in prison, Duke cut hair. According to Duke, it is taboo for an inmate to get his hair cut by a barber from a different race. Nonetheless, a Latino inmate, who had enough clout to ignore that prison norm, sat in Duke's chair. As in a barbershop in the free world, patron and client chatted during the haircuts, and Duke eventually learned that he and his client "knew a couple of the same people. One is a guy on the South Side, from my neighborhood. He a connect forever, but he never would tell nobody: it was this dude's uncle.[5] His name was Grandpa. You know Grandpa? Yeah, I know Grandpa; I've been knowing that dude for like fifteen years, and they'd been selling dope about that long. Come to find out, that was the connect in my neighborhood and he was trying to hook me up."

Duke's anecdote illustrates the role prison plays in connecting people who otherwise may not be connected in the outside world. Duke was considered a "stand-up" inmate, one who was trustworthy and abided by the inmate code. Otherwise, the Eme member would never have approached him. Inmates knew that Duke had dealt before and was in prison on a murder conviction, which garnered him additional respect. These elements combined to overcome the racial barrier to entry that Duke faced on the streets with Latinos who would have more direct access to wholesalers.

Latino dealers generally did not report the difficulties that Mike and Duke faced in accessing drugs to retail. For example, Linus, a member of the Wedgewood Chicanos street gang, never had a direct connection but simply used connections he developed in his gang community to gain access to supply. "I didn't have no access to *paisas*. I didn't talk to them. I didn't know any. But you got people that are, and those people usually have connects here within, among our people, and that's how I had access."

Lil G, a disgraced member of the Eme, talked about how in the past he had choices when it came to finding a plug. "There's always more people out there. If you're selling dope, I mean, you could get dope. Dope's easy to get. That's not a problem. I got connects." Lil G went on, indicating that at his purchasing and status level, he was in a buyer's market. Accordingly, he never had any issues with the supplier, who always delivered what was promised because the driver "knew who he was fucking with. He knew he could get killed. He knew we would kill anybody. He knew if he created a problem, we would end it. But he was respecting."

Many respondents identified the Eme as being the first intermediary from trafficker to street-level dealers. Nonetheless, Adelita, who had a long history with the Eme and knowledge of the area's drug trade, contrasted Lil G's braggadocio by highlighting the importance and preeminence of the Mexican suppliers. "The plug is always a *paisa* at the end of the day, no matter if the Eme want to deny it. However, they want to deny it if they're dealing with another Chicano. But, still on the top, it's a *paisa*. It's always *México*."

Victor, another member of the Eme, described how he had developed his plug over the course of several years, starting with his willingness to smuggle dope in a car over the border while he was a young man in the early to mid-1990s. "My relationship with the Mexicans started back when I was in high school. I started running it across the border and then, from there, driving it. You know, they trusted me. I'd been doing it for quite some time. I bought hundreds of pounds from them time after time. Even when I couldn't pay for it all, they would front it to me. And I gave them their money, so I gained this trust thing with them. So, when the time came—time for me to come up again, when I was down and I just got out of prison, they shot me a little bit of something."

Like Victor, Damián, who used to sell marijuana and powder cocaine, talked about the time it took to develop his relationship with a quality plug. For him, it involved slowly going up the ranks and meeting more people within the network. "My friends would take me to their connections and I'd just weed them out, you know, who were the ones that had the good stuff and better price. So, I mean, it just didn't happen overnight. This was a couple of years in the process, but then finally I started running into the *paisas* that were literally just bringing it from Mexico to over here. And at the point, because the one thing they want in Mexico is guns—and the one thing that I have is guns—I found out that I could do better trades with guns for drugs. You know? It's cheaper. It works out cheaper for me because I can get the guns cheap and I can give it to them for a higher price, and they'll give me the drugs for a cheaper price."

Paisas were consistently identified as the main connections for supply. At the lower levels, where *paisas* were hired to be delivery drivers, those who were dealing considered them to be disposable runners indebted to whomever ran them. But the *paisas* who were supplying weight were far less understood; some of my respondents viewed them as middlemen, while others viewed them as bona fide cartel operatives even though they did not have the flashy "narco junior" appearance that some members of law enforcement described as cartel operatives' calling card.[6]

The junction of Nogales, Arizona, and Heroica Nogales, Sonora, a two-and-a-half-hour drive south of Phoenix, is the closest border crossing to Phoenix. From

Tucson to the border, the posted distances are measured in kilometers, though the speed limit remains in miles. The small towns still advertise their existence by announcing the year they were founded and their elevation. Nogales reminded me of Del Rio, Texas, in some respects: a small town on the decline. Every other gas station and corner shop was vacant, and the abandoned buildings were dilapidated. Unlike Del Rio, Nogales has no US military installation to buoy the local economy, but it does have a small jail. The downtown area is in decent condition: duty-free shops line the walkway into Mexico, and parking lots offer a parking space for five or six bucks.

The Arizonan and Sonoran border towns are smaller than many of their Texan and Chihuahuan counterparts. Nogales clocks in at around 21,000 people, and Heroica Nogales has just north of 220,000 inhabitants. No river flows between the two towns, so there are no bridges to cross. The border is marked by a line on the floor of the port office through which vehicles and pedestrians cross the towering fences that separate the United States and Mexico. One crosses the line, skips pressing the revision button (as in Juárez), and presto, "¡*Bienvenidos a Heroica Nogales!* Would you like to visit a pharmacy?"[7]

To get a handle on the differences between the Arizona and Texas borders, I spent a few days in Heroica Nogales speaking with four local reporters who covered the police beat and the drug trade in the area. One of the journalists, Germán, showed me around town. Railroad tracks cut the town center into two. Abandoned storefronts stood near the tracks. According to Germán, this neighborhood is one of the most conflicted areas of the city. It isn't the poorest part of town, but it is a prime area for crossing drugs given its proximity to the fence and the underground water channels that run beneath the fence. It is also a good place for digging tunnels which can be used for smuggling goods into the United States. Ironically, Heroica Nogales's poshest restaurant is located in this neighborhood in the midst of strip clubs, some of which double as brothels, and derelict lots, where the addicted drug users live in the rotten squalor and dilapidated buildings that now characterize the once prosperous area.

"You almost never see heroin here," Germán told me. Heroin was so uncommon in Heroica Nogales that Germán wasn't even familiar with the term *tecato*, which described the pervasive heroin users in Juárez. "The users here mostly smoke methamphetamines," he informed me. We walked past the posh restaurant to the edge of the neighborhood and back to the border fence.

"We have to be careful. We can't go wherever we want," Germán cautioned. "We can't talk in earshot of other people because we don't know who they might be. I can promise you that somebody is watching us now." Even the police couldn't be trusted. "It's hard to trust the police here. Nobody really trusts them. They are all owned by the cartels. And you don't know which one they are working for, so it's better not to say anything to them."

One thing was certain: there were no gangs in plain view. In Heroica Nogales, no gangbangers run around. The buildings are not tagged up. The city's residents are more worried about the individuals they don't recognize on the streets than the possibility of being attacked by a gang member. The dangerous people keep a low profile; they prefer to be invisible. Although some people claim that everyone knows who is involved with the drug trafficking organizations, no one will disclose names or discuss drug trafficking in public. And although people are not afraid to be on the streets, there are certain conversations no one is comfortable having in the open. The same was true in Juárez, where certain questions and words would elicit fear and extreme caution, even in "safe" places.

In Heroica Nogales, people talk about cartels—cartels, not gangs, are the criminal actors of note. According to the reporters I spoke to in Heroica Nogales, regardless of what US law enforcement say, there are two cartels: the Sinaloa Federation and the Pacific Cartel (formed from the remnants of the Beltrán-Leyva Organization). They have divided the town between them, and neither can enter the other's territory without grave consequences. Germán told me that if we tried to enter a neighborhood where we didn't belong, we too might run into problems, though most likely somebody would just intimidate us into leaving.

Despite the similarities of having a contested plaza and the perceived corruption and collusion of the police, the criminal landscape of Heroica Nogales is in sharp contrast to that of Juárez, where the drug trafficking organizations work in tandem with local gangs to drive their agenda. Violence exists but is quieter than the violence in Juárez, perhaps due to the lack of foot soldiers willing to fight or a conscious strategy to minimize unwanted attention. Plus, the criminal enterprises of Arizona and Sonora do not share a relationship across the two Nogaleses comparable to that enjoyed by Barrio Azteca in Juárez and El Paso, where the gang's members often move innocuously across the border, going to and fro in their daily lives visiting family, shopping, or engaging in nefarious activities.

In short, Mexican Americans in Phoenix who have family in Mexico seem to spend less time and have relatively less contact with their families in Mexico. As a result, familial ties do not seem to be as strongly maintained as they are in the El Paso/Juárez area, where families can meet up frequently. This difference in familial ties in turn affects those who are involved in the transnational drug trade. Many members of Barrio Azteca in El Paso are likely to have a relative or a connection with a fellow gang member who lives in Juárez, meaning they are more likely to know someone who has contact with a Mexican wholesaler. Moreover, given the nature of the drug trade in the El Paso/Juárez metropolitan area, participants in the drug trade may play a larger array of roles—enforcer, transporter, and dealer—potentially working for either their gang or the drug trafficking organization that has co-opted their gang.

The ability and opportunity for Phoenix-area gang members to do the same is virtually nonexistent. Phoenix-area Chicano gang members may have family members who come from farther afield than Nogales, the closest port of entry for licit and illicit goods. Geographically, Nogales is not a short drive from Phoenix; plus, those driving north are subjected to the internal CBP checkpoint. Consequently, Phoenix-area Latino criminal groups have fewer members who have legitimate and consistent contact with wholesalers in Mexico compared to people in El Paso. Those individuals who do have contact have it for one of two reasons: they come from families who have one or more members who are directly involved with the transporting or staging of wholesale amounts of drugs into the United States, or they have cultivated a relationship with a wholesaler over time by negotiating contact and becoming a valued part of the distribution network.

The practical consequence of this relationship dynamic is that in Phoenix, compared to El Paso and Juárez, there are fewer direct connections between the people involved with wholesale trafficking activities and the people involved with retail activities. "Distance decay," a concept used by human geographers to measure how distance affects interaction over space, can be used to describe this phenomenon as well (see figure 11).[8] Furthermore, compared to El Paso, family interaction between Mexican Americans in Phoenix and their extended families in Mexico has deteriorated. Accordingly, as family interactions deteriorate, the network of actors participating in the drug trade becomes more disassociated; as the distance between each individual node increases, with fewer contacts connecting them, the development of key relationships becomes a matter of cultivating successful business arrangements rather than family and community history.

While it is important not to underestimate the opportunities that the physical proximity to the US-Mexican border and the cultural connections that link those who live in Paso del Norte to one another offer to those interested in getting involved in the drug trade, it is equally important to recognize that most people who live near or who cross the border, legally or illegally, likely have no involvement in the drug trade. As in Texas, judging by the proceedings at immigration court in Eloy, Arizona, where I was told that the worst criminal aliens are processed, I saw little that suggested that a high percentage of unauthorized immigrants, relative to

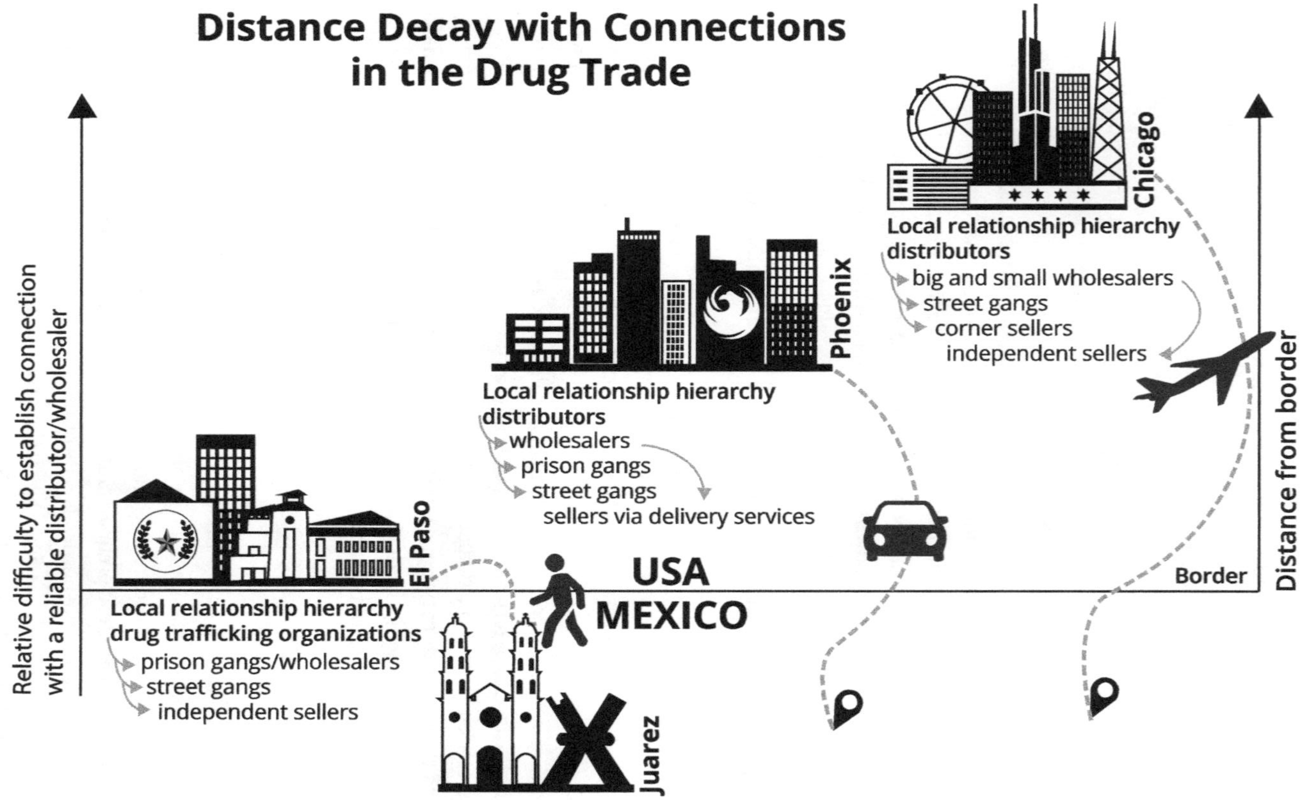

Distance Decay with Connections
in the Drug Trade

FIGURE 11. It becomes more difficult, all things being equal, to establish high-level connections with drug wholesalers and traffickers the farther away from the border one is.

Diagram by Florence Lourme.

the number who immigrated, were engaging in the drug trade at any level. One of the immigration judges with whom I spoke at the Eloy detention facility noted that several of the people who appeared in her court were indeed traffickers. While that may have been the case, I seldom observed "reason-to-believe" trafficker cases in the Arizona courts, which I observed just as frequently as the Texas courts, making it difficult for me to assess just how many "several" could be. Reason-to-believe trafficker cases are those in which the government believes that it has reasonable, substantial, and probative evidence—which is not necessarily a criminal conviction—that a person participated in drug trafficking.[9]

Although some unauthorized immigrants are part of the drug trade at its various levels, it is difficult to judge the proportion of unauthorized immigrants who are involved and what their roles most likely are. Based on what I saw in court, the proportion would be relatively small. Moreover, determining the legal status or the relative position of any given *paisa* within the drug trade is difficult.

As with the retail market, the higher-ups in the wholesale market create smoke screens of underlings, who are either ignorant or misinformed of their superiors' status, to deflect investigation and to suggest that their bosses are the most dangerous or the best-connected people in the trade.[10] Smoke screening also signals the presence and perhaps the dominance of soft power within the US wholesale drug market. As within prison, there are managerial tactics and organizational politics within the wholesale drug trade: "upper management" or a criminal organization imparts upon its direct subordinates and contractors the desire to maintain an enterprise that runs with minimal friction. Ultimately, the US side of the trade must attract willing subordinates who share the core management group's goals and who are determined to behave in a manner that is beneficial to the enterprise. Soft power's "ability to get what you want through attraction rather than coercion" comes into play when those in control forgo violence and resort to blacklisting subordinates who steal or disobey.[11] Business is good, and connections are scarce; for most subordinates, these facts—not a threat of violence—keep them in line.

But smoke screening is not the only tool mid- to upper-level dealers employ. Those who run the wholesale drug trade successfully run it like a game of three-card monte: they want those who are watching the game they are playing—law enforcement and enemy crews—to bite on what they consider to be important while the drug traffickers execute a sleight of hand that leaves the watchers bewildered. Julie Marquez, a lawyer whose defense of members of the Cosa Nostra gave her an unusual insight into the everyday world of organized crime, summed up the underlying philosophy and presence of the most successful criminals succinctly: "Smart criminals are *invisible*. They have a presence everywhere, but they understand that they do not need any attention."

Like most modern businesses, the drug trade relies on division of labor to reduce risk of internal fraud and external information leaks. This segmentation of jobs and roles in the wholesale trade is the basis of what is called "blind compartmentalization," a strategy that the actors higher up the drug supply chain use to conceal their identities from retail clients and anyone else who might be able to identify them to police.[12] Like smoke screening, which occurs at all levels, blind compartmentalization achieves the separation of knowledge by creating a cutout that limits physical contact between dealer and buyer by interposing one or more human or technological intermediaries—such as a cell phone—between both parties.[13] By reducing the number of people within the network who possess knowledge of its structure and nodes, blind compartmentalization reduces risks inherent to the illicit business, such as being cheated by clients, robbed by enemies, or cut out by others in the drug trade or the supply chain. It also reduces the risk of arrest by law enforcement, and in the event that one link of the supply chain is compromised, blind compartmentalization reduces the risk that law enforcement is able to take the entire network down.[14] Instead, upon compromise, a link higher up in the chain finds a replacement and moves on.

Charles Loftus, who was then the assistant chief in the Arizona Attorney General's Office, described the trafficking networks by comparing them to licit businesses that use independent contractors. Such businesses have centralized administration, but the contractors are not employees of those businesses. Contractors effectively operate their own enterprises and, accordingly, assume their own risks without much recourse to the business that has contracted them. Drug trafficking networks work similarly. As Loftus explained, most of the contractors run at "a little bit of arm's reach distance, whereas the central organization would be [the one who has] direct cartel links, but those [connections] are tight. So, everybody has a role. [The drug trafficking organizations] compartmentalize very well."

Elizabeth Kempshall, director of the Arizona HIDTA, described the wholesale trafficking structure as a "command-and-control" system that manages movements through Arizona, which, according to her, is the Sinaloa Cartel's "primary corridor to bring their illegal product into the United States. So, you have a distribution center here, where the command-and-control elements in primarily Phoenix talk directly to the Tier 1 or Tier 2 targets in Mexico, and they get their instructions on where to move the drugs and how much to move it and all of that kind of stuff."

The relationship is pyramidal whereby tasks are delegated via a chain of command, much in the same way Al Capone ran his criminal enterprise in Chicago.[15] "You've got your organizational leaders," explained Kempshall. "Then you have the Tier 1, which talks directly to the organizational leader. The Tier 2 is the one that talks to that Tier 1."

Elmer, a lieutenant with the Drug Enforcement Bureau in the Investigations Unit of the Phoenix Police Department, listed the broad array of jobs that a Tier 2 contact could have subordinates perform. These jobs included receiving back-packers or other traffickers across the border, transporting people or products within Arizona, manning the staging location, picking up the money and trans-porting it back to the bosses, and providing muscle for the rare instances when violence was deemed necessary. Elmer went on to note that whatever the job, "that may be that person's responsibility and that may be his only responsibil-ity, and understand that if he's doing that job, he's probably one of dozens that do that job. He just gets the phone call from the boss."

In other words, any given actor involved in large transactions has only one specific job to perform at any given point in time to minimize the risk of loss. Elmer explained the division of labor. "So, this guy is handling dope, but he doesn't handle money. If he gets popped with dope, that's fine. The organization can afford to get rid of him, but the organization doesn't lose its money at the same time. The coordinator has another group that handles money, that trans-ports money back, whether they're doing deposits in banks or whether they're doing boat carrying across the border, however they're getting the money across. Sometimes people will be used to do both things, but they're not doing it simulta-neously. I'm not taking you a load of dope and getting the money from you. That's typically not the process because there is too much to lose when you do that."

The segregation of duties is practiced throughout the trafficker's hierarchy, from the trafficker to just a step above the driver or street dealer, in an effort to diffuse risk by preventing any given person from knowing too much. It is a tactic used within licit business practices in order to safeguard assets by limiting fraud, opportunities for embezzlement, or data exfiltration. In accounting, for example, when handling inventory orders, "one person orders goods from suppliers, and another person logs in the received goods in the accounting system. This keeps the purchasing person from diverting incoming goods for his own use."[16]

To illustrate the segregation of duties in a high-level criminal context, Eliza-beth Kempshall referenced the financial practices of the wholesale drug trade. Drug trafficking organizations receive significant proceeds from their wholesale deals; the cash flows need to be returned across the US border to the drug traffick-ing organizations in Mexico. Accordingly, traffickers run two separate command-and-control systems. There is "drug element command-and-control and financial command-and-control, and, usually, in most cases, the cartel tries to keep these two things separate because . . . [law enforcement] hurts the cartels more because [if we take out a centralized command-and-control structure, we are] not only able to take out their drugs, but [we're] able to take out their money. So, they've adapted to law enforcement techniques over the years, so they try to keep it separate. So, [there are] two different corridors that are running through Arizona." With drugs coming in and money going out and both being transported by separate and often revolving entities, it becomes difficult for outsiders to know where to look within the drug trafficking networks and how to identify the parties—gangs, cartels, or other operators—involved.

Nonetheless, hard power's ability to get what is desired, through coercion via violence, remains important on the street, where those lower in the supply chain face a higher relative risk. At each level of the drug trade, an actor assumes a risk balance that involves two inversely related components: the quantity held and the visibility to consumers, competitors, and law enforcement. Opportunities to diversify risk as well as a corresponding loss tolerance that exist higher in the supply chain are less available further down it.

Licit and illicit retailers alike face risk as a function of the quantity of product held and per-unit value: wholesalers seek to move large volumes to generate their income, while retailers operate off large margins to generate theirs. Thus, between any link within a supply chain, when sellers sell a product, the risk associated with that product is transferred to buyers. Moreover, the per-unit value becomes higher not only in absolute terms but also to the buyer. Furthermore, because buyers, such as retailers, have comparatively less product and less capacity to diversify their portfolio, each unit lost represents a higher financial hit compared to unit losses sustained by those above them in the supply chain. In short, as products progress further down the supply chain, the holder of those products is more invested in protecting each unit by any means necessary.[17]

Links further up the supply chain may be able to cope with loss by diversifying their strategies and calculating acceptable tolerances for loss. For instance, if a delivery driver experiences arrest, robbery, refusal to pay, or any other event that results in the loss of product, the amount lost in proportion to the whole amount being sold at a given point in time is more likely to be tolerated by his superiors, who have not charged him with a significant proportion of their overall business. If the driver is lost he is replaced, and business continues.

However, links further down the supply chain may not have the capital reserves to enjoy such a luxury. This dynamic means that the higher up one is in the supply chain, the more likely it is that the seller can set the terms and conditions for the buyer immediately below, including amounts to be paid and precautions to be observed. In this regard, the illicit drug industry works similar to licit wholesaling: a person buying in bulk makes payments usually significant in magnitude, thereby garnering a favorable cost for volume.

Conversely, when one is moving small quantities, the street market offers parallels to the problems encountered by licit retailers whereby demand, availability of disposable income, and competitors' or rivals' behaviors affect the retailers' ability to offload the product. Street-level drug dealers may be faced with consumers who may be less reliable. Accordingly, if street-level dealers are to maintain a client base, particularly when clients are short of income, they may have to allow for a degree of loss due to nonpayment or offer delayed payment schemes, comparable to selling on credit in the licit economy, or be prepared to violently collect for that loss should those debts default. Moreover, should a rival interrupt business through theft or violence, then hard power must be used to reestablish one's position on the street corner; failure to do so would result in banishment from the market. Thus, there is an asymmetric willingness to use violence in the drug trade, with high-level actors eschewing it and low-level actors, such as street and prison gang members, embracing it when their business is threatened. In short, those who do not control supply must ensure that the supply they have maintains its value and that payment is received.

Links higher in the supply chain do not want to be associated with this type of visible violence, which is more likely to occur in the retail drug sector; consequently, compartmentalization occurs. Higher-ups understand that low-level dealers face relatively high risks: they are more likely to be arrested and offered a deal by police and prosecutors to cooperate in exchange for better treatment. Blind compartmentalization helps to manage this risk by instituting degrees of separation between each node and each tier of nodes in the network, thereby preserving network integrity while insulating higher-level wholesalers and traffickers who hold larger quantities of product from the risk of exposure associated with low-level dealers. As Everitt, the GIITEM officer, explained, at the street delivery level, should a driver get arrested, "he may know who his source is, but he may not know where that supply is kept." Drivers, who are merely links between nodes, cannot inform on their coconspirators should they be arrested or captured by rivals.

To that end, by limiting subordinates' knowledge of the network's nodes and overall structure, those better positioned in the drug trade limit the capacity for law enforcement to map entire distribution networks, even if links beneath them are successfully pressed for information. Plus, upper-level bosses understand that having many nodes in the trade beneath them guarantees that if one component sours, the rest are resilient enough to compensate for the loss.[18] Through blind compartmentalization, subordinates are forced into a pattern of behavior that requires tasks to be done singularly and disjointedly. This tactic ensures that any given participant below the core management group remains ignorant of the broader structure of the network. That compartmentalization strategy enables the members of the core management group to protect themselves and maintain operational longevity, in part by finding participants, often gang members, willing to do the riskiest work.

With money in the balance, it appears that most of the people involved in the drug trade prefer to keep a low profile and to avoid intergroup violence or violence that results in innocent victims. Phoenix police precinct commander Baxter noted that over his career in law enforcement, criminal groups had undertaken measures to reduce violence and minimize attention by punishing those in the areas they control for behaving in ways that attract police attention. "It's a business decision. If the police are taking out all of the connections and the lieutenants, the hierarchy and all the people who make you money because they keep getting arrested, then those people are giving the organization no value. So, at that point, those people are subject to discipline."

"I think we've done a good job discouraging those guys to be in Phoenix." Ryan, another police commander, added, talking about violent actors of the drug trade. "I think that they are avoiding us. Phoenix will always be a transit point given its geographic location, but I think it's less of a point than it used to be. Focusing on the drops in crime and the good things, however, doesn't win you elections. It's hard to show that in pictures."

Thus, as in El Paso, violent acts such as drive-by shootings are almost unheard of in Phoenix. But irresponsible and heavy drug use remains a problem in the city; if the number of people wandering the downtown streets in search of drugs is any indication (along with the official reports), then the drug trade remains a lucrative business. To that end, most people who fall victim to crime in Phoenix experience nonviolent crimes such as home invasions, which my respondents—police and gang members alike—said were often undertaken by those who are desperate for the funds necessary to support their drug habits.

Nonetheless, despite relatively low violence for a city of its size, the media generated its panicked narrative, which conveniently forgot the city's history.[19] According to police and gang members alike, Phoenix's relative calm, like El Paso's, was in contrast to the modus operandi for street gangs during their heyday of the late 1980s and early 1990s. As business becomes the focus of street and prison gangs, violence appears to be discouraged in day-to-day activities. Phoenix, however, experienced a notable exception: rip crews, groups that target traffickers and their stash houses. These actions underwrote the panic about kidnapping, which proved to be overblown: ordinary citizens only fell victim in the extremely rare cases of mistaken identity.

Occasionally, gang-related violence still occurs. Some respondents said that intragang violence, designed to keep members in line, did occur. Lil G, who worked as muscle for the Eme, spoke of an attempt by a rival faction of the Mexican Mafia to extort him as he ran a drug house, something that his seniority should have allowed him to do without disturbance. Breeze and Duke, mid- to lower-level dealers, both spoke of violence being contracted out to rival factions to control rogue members, who might be out of reach, for intragang discipline.

There remains the question of who sets the terms of engagement within Phoenix's illicit drug trade. Some members of the Eme maintained that they held the balance of power against the wholesalers, given their superior firepower and manpower, and refuted any notion that the drug trafficking organizations "ran the street" beyond supplying it with drugs. In other words, the Mexican drug trafficking organizations' presence in wholesale networks in the United States is transactional rather than territorial. Transactional organizations focus on trafficking; that is, they engage in behaviors that keep their illicit activity at low visibility to ensure that their business can continue undetected. On the other hand, territorial organizations attempt to establish territorial control—as prison gangs often do—by establishing violent protection rackets to contest competitors and tax underlings.[20]

By contrast, the gangs that facilitate trafficking may retain territorial goals. Eddie and Victor claimed that the Eme was able to tax not only underlings but also the drug trafficking organizations that moved dope through the gang's turf. "You know what, the cartels are paying a percentage, maybe 15 percent, to bring the large loads of heroin, weed, coke. I bet you didn't know that," Eddie told me bluntly. "The Mexican Mafia controls the traffic. Nothing happens without them knowing, taking a cut. And I can tell you that if somebody tries to move anything through here, they're not moving anything unless they're paying the Eme. Why don't we bring it? Why take the risk? The traffickers want money. They're still going to move it."

"This cartel guy says, 'I'm going to bring x amount of weed.' And the Eme says, 'Okay, if you're going to bring this much into *my* state, I want this much money to allow you to distribute it here,'" Victor explained, as he went on to note that the traffickers pay because they have the money and want to avoid the conflict that would negatively impact their bottom line. Avoiding violence was worth the money paid. Consequently, Damián said he never feared that those with whom he dealt would act against him "because, honestly, we had more guns than they did."

Certainly, drug markets are dynamic; players involved, particularly down the supply chain, are often easily interchangeable. That reality helps to explain why both street gang members and law enforcement questioned the extent to which the Eme controls not only the local retail markets but also the wholesale market. While some gang members and police are adamant that the Eme does exert control over the street, others suggest that its control was fading. This contrast was apparent when talking to Máximo and Rosa, a born-again Christian couple who used to be with the Eme.

"As far as taxation, the Eme does run the street," Máximo explained. "But they aren't going to tax what doesn't hit the street. So, if somebody has a dope house or is running drivers in a neighborhood controlled by the Eme, for sure they're going to get taxed. If they are just stashing the drugs to sell onward, the Eme isn't going to touch that if those people have nothing to do with the Eme. They can't touch what they don't own. And if the dope is stashed and no one knows about it, then they aren't collecting tax. It's only when dope hits the street or if somebody who is moving something is clicked up, then something will get kicked back, but that's the only way."[21]

Rosa felt that Máximo's characterization was correct when taxation efforts were working. However, she now believed that taxation was no longer prominent, since the police had successfully arrested gang members who were then convicted for various crimes and sentenced to long prison terms, which diminished the gang's territorial control. "People in the neighborhoods aren't being taxed because there isn't anyone there who has come out of prison yet to tax that neighborhood," Rosa said. Precinct commander Baxter supported Rosa's analysis, explaining that the Eme had control in the early 1990s. "We had gangs killing gangs because enemy gangs were in the Eme's turf. They were committing crimes in their area. There were shootings where they were trying to sell drugs in their area, and that was typical of all around the nation. Again, Phoenix PD put an enormous amount of people in prison. Since that time, they're there, but they're not attempting to control as much as they have in the past."

Jake, who had been a Phoenix cop for several years, described the contemporary Eme presence on the street. "We have a unit that only focuses on the Eme, and that's because they do have a presence. It is a group that is very violent and ruthless. They influence street gangs, but to what extent they manage them— they don't manage them; they intimidate them into doing what they want, sometimes. I don't give them much credit. There might be certain individuals who have pull, but as a group they're not that organized."

The lack of organization was a problem that others, especially people who had been associated with the Eme, also recognized. Victor noted that in some neighborhoods, prison gang contact had been lost, and taxation no longer occurred. Elmer, the lieutenant with the Drug Enforcement Bureau, believed that part of the problem was geographical. "There are so many different entities that are bringing dope into the Valley that it would be difficult for anybody to be able to say, 'Okay, once this dope crosses the threshold of the city of Phoenix, we control it.' It's just really difficult to do that. Geographically, our city is so spread out that you can't even maintain a grip on a particular portion of the city."

Nonetheless, even if the Eme is taxing some actors, given the structure of the drug trade in Phoenix, the Mexican drug trafficking organizations are not likely being directly taxed. Those who are being taxed are likely to be groups that are subcontracting for the drug trafficking organizations' stateside distribution; therefore, the claim that the Eme is taxing traffickers but not the Mexican drug trafficking organizations per se seems plausible, at least in some cases.

But no prison-based organization appears to have clear dominance over either the street market or the wholesale market in Greater Phoenix, which is in sharp contrast to the market dynamics of El Paso. While certain neighborhoods may be influenced by the Mexican Mafia, the whole of Greater Phoenix is certainly not. Accordingly, the protection market that exists within the criminal underworld in Arizona is less consolidated than the one in West Texas. Unlike El Paso, Phoenix-based prison gangs cannot consistently impose their will on street gangs. Plus, the reduction of visibility in the drug trade even at the street level, with many drug transactions moving from the street corner to private houses, seemingly offers a layer of protection against incarceration. The reduction in visibility, coupled with the apparent decline of street gangs, undermines the idea that prison is inevitable for those who are involved in the criminal underworld, particularly when those activities are centered on the drug trade. In sum, these characteristics of the Phoenix underworld result in a reduction of the Mexican Mafia's ability to influence, much less control, the street's politics.

Ultimately, the idea of "criminal control" appears to refer to the degree of monopolization that exists in a particular market in a particular place, such as the wholesale market in Phoenix. It is language used by the police and the press; however, once the term is picked up by the public, it carries with it the connotation that the whole neighborhood has gone to hell. I came to this realization when I fell victim to a home invasion. Our landlord had put National Rifle Association stickers up everywhere, despite nary a bullet between me and my Jordanian housemate. Someone, probably searching for guns, broke into our house and took most things of value. The officer who responded to the scene told me, "You know what, I don't think you know what kind of neighborhood you live in. This neighborhood is *controlled* by a street gang. The gang in this area is Barrio Trece Cuatro. If I had to guess, I bet this is one of their jobs."

The notion of control in the way the cop meant it—as if the gang were running protection in the neighborhood—seemed strange to me. I had been living in the neighborhood for a few months, and my housemate had been living there for over a year. At no point did anyone ever threaten us, tell us to watch ourselves. There was never any ruckus, and there were no fights. My most uncomfortable experiences included the bounty hunter knocking at the door and the people loitering in the Circle K parking lot, but even these experiences were not distressing. And more to the point, I had never heard of the gang, and none of my neighbors—even the old crusty ones who sat on their porches, watching all the neighborhood activities—had any concern about gangs. There was no indication that there was an authority to answer to in the neighborhood. At a certain point, one has to wonder if we can be under the control of an entity if we are unaware of its existence. That's just not how protection rackets work.

Nonetheless, a local street gang may be aware of the crime that happens in its territory. Adelita certainly felt that way. When Adelita learned that my home had been burglarized, she noted that she didn't have any pull on the street, being fresh out of prison; she still lacked the connections necessary to call for any response. Plus, the neighborhood gang had no relationship with anyone she knew; the Eme didn't control my neighborhood. She wanted to know why I hadn't tried to rent a place in her neighborhood, where nobody would dare mess with me: I was her friend, and as a friend in her community, she wouldn't let anything happen to me. I believed her; it was the way she lived.

"If you lived in our neighborhood, that wouldn't have happened to you," Adelita said. "But if it did, I would have made sure those idiots brought all of your stuff back. And if it wasn't your stuff, they would have replaced it with things that were just as nice."

For Adelita, control meant that the Eme was aware of the activities undertaken in its own neighborhood and that a portion of the proceeds generated by those activities would be paid in tax to the Eme. She felt that it would be unusual for a gang that controlled the neighborhood to rob from one of its residents because, quite simply, you do not shit where you eat. When asked, some people in the neighborhood thought that my things might surface in the contraband markets run by the local gang, but others were skeptical, attributing home invasions in the neighborhood to "lerpers," meth addicts who steal to pay for their next hit.

Whatever "control" may be in the criminal context vis-à-vis a place, it meant little in the day-to-day life of my neighborhood. Nobody ever dropped by to intimidate me or to let me know the rules of play. None of the neighbors spoke of any underlying threat. None behaved strangely. Kids played in the street until dinnertime, and people hung out on their porches in the cool of the evenings. Though the neighborhood's appearance was blighted by a shell of a burned-down house, there were no bullet holes, much less sounds of gunshots to be heard, in the streets of Historic Oakland. As to my home invasion, nobody in the community expected the police to find anything or follow up on their investigation; it was just part of life in an otherwise unremarkable working-class community.

As the summer came to an end, so did my time in Phoenix. What was clear was that nobody truly controlled the drug trade in any meaningful way in Greater Phoenix. The area's combination of being a fertile local market and a good staging ground meant that the drug trade had an economic incentive to thrive in the city. Business interest, as in El Paso, drove violence down. The drug trade operated because it offered an income for some willing to sell a product in demand. With those lessons reinforced, I packed up the red pickup and drove northeast, passing by Monument Valley, a scene—like the margins of society—that is as American as any.

THE CITY BY THE LAKE

As I drove back to Chicago, I crossed over the Rocky Mountains of Colorado and then through the utter flatness and endless cornfields of the Great Plains of Nebraska. There, I pulled into a small town outside Omaha where José "Raulio" Fierro Rivera lived.

José came out to greet me with a great big welcoming smile. There, standing in his pajamas and wearing a knit hat to keep warm from the chilly evening, was the man who had founded Barrio Azteca almost thirty years before. If I didn't know, it would have been hard to believe that this man, standing five foot six with a cherubic face, was the guy who started one of the most notorious prison gangs in Texas. But in Nebraska, José was a world away from El Paso—at least, the El Paso where he had grown up. He had been transplanted from one time and place to another: his location, livelihood, name, friends, and nuclear family had all changed. He, like many people who left gang life, sought a place where all his past criminal connections and identities would mean nothing to anybody.

José spent his first days in Omaha living in a homeless shelter, trying out religion. A roofing job gave him a foothold in an ordinary working-class existence. In time, he remarried and had a daughter. He even got a mortgage on a house, a converted rail car on a little plot of land. But despite achieving these milestones, he still found himself squarely within the margins of society. Jobs were never steady, and his criminal past haunted him, preventing him from getting the reliable work he desperately craved to become a stand-up member of society. And although José knew that even in small-town America there were opportunities to sell drugs or engage in other illicit activity, he never engaged in such activities to assuage his financial struggles.

With his past life—a chaos of crime and drug abuse—long behind him, José focused on being a family man, working whatever jobs he could find, and making sure prison remained firmly in his past. And for him, prison remained in his past: he never went back. Though reformed and contributing to his community as best he could for the decade he lived in Nebraska, José was never able to escape the poverty that kept him firmly in the margins. He lived and died like millions of blue-collar Americans: no health insurance, escalating bills, and growing concern over how to make ends meet.

I have always enjoyed driving into Chicago at night and seeing its sparkling, big-city skyline. The dark silhouettes of towering skyscrapers and high-rise condominiums, with their windows illuminated haphazardly, are backlit by the dull glow of streetlights. With some of the tallest buildings in the world, including the Sears Tower and the John Hancock Building, the Chicago skyline is an impressive scene particularly when juxtaposed with the darkness of Lake Michigan, especially for a kid who grew up downstate amid corn and soybean fields that extend as far as the eye can see.[1]

Chicago is big in every way imaginable. The Greater Chicago area, sometimes referred to as Chicagoland, is expansive, covering over seven thousand square miles, and spreads beyond the northeastern corner of Illinois into parts of two other states: Indiana and Wisconsin.[2] The metro area has a population of about 9.5 million people, with the city proper accounting for 2.7 million of that total. For the time being, given that its population is stagnating, Chicago is the third-largest city in the country.[3] Chicago has it all: restaurants, shopping, entertainment, and museums. The city is so large that every time I visit there is something new or different to see, do, or experience, and it is so vast that it feels as if each new thing is at least a half-hour drive away.

Ethnic enclaves appear throughout the city, a testament to the numerous migrants who have come from various parts of Europe, Asia, Latin America, and sub-Saharan Africa to make Chicago their home.[4] In the late nineteenth and early twentieth centuries, Chicago provided opportunity to migrants who lacked English-language and advanced labor skills in the form of employment in the city's stockyards and steel mills. Into the twenty-first century, Chicago has the largest industrial labor force of any American city, an element that would attract an ever-expanding diversity of new residents from abroad whose cultures enrich the city's offerings.[5]

FIGURE 12. The Sears Tower. One of the tallest buildings in North America, the Sears Tower is an iconic Chicago landmark. It was renamed the Willis Tower in 2009.

Photo by R. V. Gundur.

One can pass through the ornate Chinatown Gate on Wentworth Avenue and Cermak Road for excellent Chinese food or bubble tea; visit Taylor Street, home to the city's Little Italy—one of the Outfit's old haunts—to eat at one of the many Italian restaurants; stop by Bridgeport, a traditionally Irish neighborhood on the city's south side, home to five of Chicago's mayors; or drop by one of the Indian, Polish, or Mexican neighborhoods whose populations, in ascending order, are the three most significant foreign-born populations in the city.[6]

I chose to live in the old Polish downtown area during my stay. It was a far cry from the areas in which I had lived during my stays in El Paso and Phoenix. I carefully deliberated on my choice of neighborhood. After having been burglarized in Phoenix, I was left rattled. Plus, having grown up in Illinois, I had heard nothing but negative stories about the rough parts of Chicago, and recently there had been an uptick in violence. Unlike in the Southwest, drive-by shootings still occur in Chicago. While living outside the rough ends affected my ability to network, by living with my college buddy, Neema, a lifelong Chicago resident, I was able to access social capital that I didn't have in the other sites.

My neighborhood was clean and safe, filled with four-story apartment buildings that were once single-family houses. Neema explained that about ten years earlier, the neighborhood was rough and violent. A few relics from that time, graffiti markings at the bus stop and a gang symbol carved into the cement as it dried, remain. Today, the neighborhood is home to a mix of people and is one of the areas in Chicago that appears truly cosmopolitan. Our block was home to families of all ethnicities and several nationalities. The area continues to be gentrified; its middle-class families worry that soon they won't be able to afford to live there anymore: as property values increase, so too does their rent.

In contrast to the old Polish parts of Chicago, the Mexican parts of town retain a decidedly Mexican identity, given that the Hispanic population has been growing annually and has contributed to the maintenance of the city's food and cultural traditions.[7] Pilsen, in spite of its Czech name, is a Mexican/Mexican American neighborhood where tacos, gorditas, carnitas, and other Mexican foods, comparable in taste and quality to those in Juárez, can be had. Like Pilsen, Little Village is another growing, heavily Mexican and Mexican American neighborhood that was once home to eastern Europeans. Unlike the old Polish parts of Chicago, parts of these neighborhoods are known for a continued gang presence, which I was able to observe when Mateo invited me to join him.[8] Mateo serves as a violence interrupter, a former gang member whose job involves mitigating situations where, historically, violence has been used to respond to conflict. Mateo invited me to explore the neighborhood and meet various members of the Two Six clique he was assigned to.

Chicago as a "Social Laboratory"

The European migrants who populated the slums of early twentieth-century Chicago were the focus of the studies published by groundbreaking sociologists including W. I. Thomas, Florian Znaniecki, Ernest Burgess, and Robert Park, all based at the University of Chicago.[9] The success of these scholars and those who followed in their footsteps brought attention to the ethnographical methods and interpretations that underpin what has become known as the "Chicago School" of sociology. In addition, the success and influence of these Chicago School studies promoted the city's status as an important "social laboratory" where complex social interactions could be readily observed.[10] Accordingly, Chicago has been the site of numerous studies regarding issues of poverty, community, crime, and responses to crime, making it perhaps the most studied city in the United States.[11]

Though "the Chicago School highlighted the importance of structure and ecology in the making of the modern American city," whether Chicago is representative of "the modern American city" and the criminological problems that characterize it should be questioned.[12] While Chicago has been used time and again as a sociological laboratory, the many lessons that have been learned are not necessarily applicable to other big-city contexts. As Paulina, an agent who worked for the Chicago HIDTA and was previously stationed in the Atlanta office, quipped, "Chicago is a whole different animal" in terms of identifying problems and solutions vis-à-vis the drug trade. In other words, while most large cities experience general problems that are applicable to all large cities, each city faces problems that are distinctly its own.

Chicago stands apart from El Paso and Phoenix not only in magnitude but also in terms of geography, history, demographics, and crime. Its sheer size made it a difficult place to study with the modest resources available to me. Consequently, with one exception, a trip to the suburbs to meet a high-up member of the Black P. Stone Nation, I focused my efforts on the city proper. Given the vast amount of research that has been undertaken in this social laboratory, much scholarship already exists detailing the context and depth of Chicago gang life. Simply put, being a place where crime, particularly that which relates to gangs and organized crime, has been studied intensively for many decades, Chicago is an important point of comparison in any study of gangs, the retail and wholesale drug trade, and international drug trafficking. Though negotiating access in Chicago proved to be difficult, it was still a place where law enforcement's historical priorities vis-à-vis the drug trade—getting drug pushers off street corners and getting drug lords off their perches—and the consequences of those priorities were on full display.

GANGLAND

Chicago's complex and intertwining histories of migration, discrimination, machine politics, and crime inform the drug trade in the city and the people and organizations involved in it. These histories serve as the basis upon which gangs were formed within the city during the early twentieth century and continue to affect the evolution of Chicago's gangs and criminal entrepreneurs. In his classic study of gangs in the city, *The Gang: A Study of 1,313 Gangs in Chicago*, University of Chicago sociologist Frederic Thrasher deemed Chicago "Gangland." However, like most of the University of Chicago sociologists of the era, Thrasher minimized the role of race and focused on the disputes among the Italian, Irish, Jewish, and Polish youth groups throughout the city.[1] Nonetheless, perhaps the histories most critical to understanding the development of Chicago's gangs and, to a lesser extent, organized crime are the intertwined histories of migration and discrimination that have existed in Chicago in one form or another for much of the city's existence.[2]

Chicago has a long-standing history of migration. Less than seventy years after Jean Baptiste Pointe du Sable, a Black Haitian frontiersman, first settled the area in 1779, Chicago became an important transportation hub and a significant receptor city of immigrants.[3] By 1870, nearly half of the city's denizens were foreign-born.[4] The employment opportunities, including the infamous meatpacking plants described in Upton Sinclair's *The Jungle*, the rural areas with the farmland that the "old country" lacked, and the different communities that foreigners could and still can plug into directly, along with the promise of upward mobility, have attracted millions of migrants, both nationally and internationally, for nearly two centuries.[5]

In the 1800s and early 1900s, European immigrants flowed into Chicago to work in the city's emerging legitimate industries.[6] But Chicago, being the crossroads of America, was also a magnet for illicit enterprise. "Armies of gamblers and prostitutes and the burgeoning ranks of concert saloons, massage parlors, and other illicit entertainments" sprung up to cater to the men traversing the city in its early days.[7] Historian Mark Haller noted that in 1930 when the Chicago underworld was already robust, not a single leader of Chicago-area criminal organizations, despite being White, was recorded as being "of native born stock."[8]

The new European arrivals of the late 1800s and early 1900s formed the initial underclass of Chicago's society and were often viewed as flawed. Even Jane Addams, who famously took immigrants in at Hull House to integrate them into American society, was critical of Italians and other immigrant communities she considered inferior.[9] The outbreak of World War I slowed European migration to Chicago. Then, between 1915 and 1950 the Great Migration brought African Americans to the city, making them the city's new whipping boys.[10] Though a significant proportion of the "six million African Americans [who] left their homes in the South and moved to states in the North and West" during the Great Migration came to Chicago, the primary receptor communities consisted of only three neighborhoods: Douglas, Grand Boulevard, and Washington Park.[11] These three neighborhoods were in the heart of the area known as the Black Belt, an area where the Black population of Chicago was concentrated due to restrictive covenants, bolstered by measures undertaken by White gangs, to prevent African Americans from moving into White neighborhoods.[12]

After World War II, the courts struck down the restrictive covenants that had prohibited African Americans from living in most neighborhoods in Chicago, paving the way for "diversification."[13] Nonetheless, overt violence directed toward African Americans, discrimination, and de facto segregation, often through discriminatory Chicago Housing Authority policies, remained.[14] When African Americans finally moved to other parts of the city, White families abandoned these neighborhoods, meaning that little integration occurred and the city remained largely segregated.[15] This White flight is a clear example of what criminologist Robert Sampson describes as "spatial separation reinforced by homophily, or the tendency of people to choose to live near like others on valued characteristics, and distant from those disvalued."[16] Consequently, despite African Americans' attempts to move to "better neighborhoods," White flight, which siphoned resources away from those neighborhoods as White people departed, kept African Americans in lower socioeconomic positions.

The de facto segregation was so significant that in January 1966 Reverend Martin Luther King Jr. and Coretta Scott King moved into a dingy apartment located in a violent West Side neighborhood, not far from where the Vice Lords street gang had gotten its start.[17] The Kings moved there to protest housing discrimination and to shine a spotlight on the dismal living conditions of the poor. Reverend King participated in dramatic marches through all-White neighborhoods, appealing to Mayor Richard J. Daley to reform the discriminatory housing practices across Chicago."[18]

In the latter half of the twentieth century after the Hart-Celler Act of 1965 outlawed the preference for White immigrants that had been in effect since 1790, non-White immigrants began to come to the city.[19] Asian and Latino communities grew. The continued growth of the Mexican communities in Chicago is one of the city's few sources of population growth.[20] Nonetheless, although people of different European roots now live together, the city has failed to achieve any significant level of integration. Despite being home to an increasing array of ethnic populations and having an equitable split of major ethnic groups, with non-White Latino, Black, and White populations each making up about one-third of the city's population in the late 2010s, Chicago remains one of the most segregated cities in the United States.[21]

Moreover, despite the diversification of the city's residents, political scientist Wesley Skogan notes that there are "three distinct Chicagos," with Latino, Black, and White people often living apart with little intermingling.[22] This degree of segregation led the Chicago police to stop me as I walked down the road in a primarily Black western Chicago neighborhood. I was "too White" for the neighborhood. For the cops who stopped me, my presence could be explained only by a desire to buy drugs. It was a unique experience for me; never before or since has my being not dark enough been a problem.

The imagery of Chicago tells two tales. There is the Chicago of the towering, ritzy buildings that house *Fortune* 500 companies or wealthy socialites' apartments; fancy, Michelin-starred restaurants; hipster donut stalls; gentrifying neighborhoods; and the expensive wares of glitzy stores on the Magnificent Mile of Michigan Avenue. Standing in stark contrast to the Chicago of wealth is the city's underbelly, some of which is literally underground in the access tunnels below the street level of Michigan Avenue, where homeless people and drug users take shelter from the bitter wind and cold of winter. The underbelly once included the now-demolished notorious high-rise housing projects famed for their poverty and violence.[23] Those high-density projects, which housed thousands of poor, mostly Black people in areas of Chicago that historically had been slums, no longer exist. In 1998, nearly nineteen thousand of the underfunded and poorly maintained buildings failed viability inspection; under federal law,

FIGURE 13. Underneath Chicago. Downtown Chicago is built on a series of passages and tunnels, which homeless people sometimes use as an area of refuge.

Photo by R. V. Gundur.

the Chicago Housing Authority had to demolish the units within five years.[24] The 2000s saw the demolition of these buildings, the last of which, the Cabrini-Green housing project, was brought down in 2012.[25] The people who once lived in those cramped conditions were displaced throughout the city.[26]

Today, the underbelly is characterized by the crumbling neighborhoods in the South and West Sides where some of Chicago's poorest inhabitants live. Here, neighborhoods include boarded-up brick buildings, houses in various states of disrepair, and walls marred by graffiti and bullet holes, reminders of the continued violence that scars those areas despite the statistics showing a relative decrease in violence since the 1990s.[27] There is a clear division between the areas of the haves and the have-nots, which is typically—though not always—split along neighborhoods' dominant ethnic identities.

Chicago's continued segregation is an important backdrop for studying competing narratives of the city's protracted struggle with violence.[28] In Chicago, violence has not decreased at the same overall rate as crime, with drive-by shootings continuing to be a problem, in stark contrast to their decreases in cities such as El Paso and Phoenix.[29] One narrative links Chicago's ongoing violence with particular racial and ethnic groups. This public narrative attributes the visible violence to Latino and Black street gangs and the scourge of the drug trade, which occurs openly on some of the city's corners. Similarly, the narrative pushed by law enforcement organizations, including the Chicago DEA and the Chicago Crime Commission, maintains that the city's drug trade is one in which street gangs work for Mexican drug cartels, most notably the Sinaloa Federation.[30] Toward the end of the 2010s the narrative of the Sinaloa Federation's preeminence softened, with law enforcement reports noting that there are several drug trafficking organizations that compete to supply the market.[31]

A competing narrative focuses on inequity in Chicago's policing. Since the city's ills are often considered along racial lines, aggressive policing solutions, rather than community solutions, are often favored. This leaves communities of color to feel unjustly overpoliced.[32] The sense of injustice in Chicago is particularly present today. Tensions between minority communities and the police remain high following a number of prominent incidents in which police have killed unarmed Black men throughout the United States. And these tensions are especially salient in Chicago. From 2004 to 2016, the city paid over half a billion dollars to settle police brutality claims, which disproportionally affect Black and Latino communities, and the international press has exposed the presence of a secret "black site" detention center at Homan Square where police reportedly beat and tortured suspects.[33] These communities' neighborhoods are marginalized by not only heavy-handed policing but also disenfranchisement from the political system. The Democratic political machine, historically, has not tolerated political competition; through gerrymandering, it has ensured that independent competitors were kept out of political contention so that the Democratic Party alone runs the city and oversees Chicago's police force.[34]

A Brief History of Gangs and Organized Crime in Chicago

Street gangs and organized criminal organizations have a long history of existing—surviving—and being studied in Chicago.[35] As noted above, Thrasher's pioneering work on gangs focused on White gangs in marginalized immigrant communities who were considered to be the biggest players in the criminal underworld for much of the twentieth century, an unsurprising focus given the predominately White European–rooted demographics of the city.[36]

While most of the Chicago School operated during the rise and fall of Al Capone, only sociologist John Landesco studied organized crime in the city during this period.[37] Landesco outlined what he deemed to be the kernel of a "gangster's psychology," saying that "usually the gangster is brought up in neighborhoods where the gang tradition is old. He grows up into it from early childhood in a world where pilfering, vandalism, sex delinquency and brutality are an inseparable part of his play life. His earliest relation with the law is with the policeman on the beat, who always has something on the little gang, and 'copper hating' is the normal attitude."[38] This statement indicates that like his colleagues of the Chicago School, Landesco viewed the ecology of the city as the chief contributing factor to the fostering of criminal careers. He argued that contrary to the "alien conspiracy" stereotypes that label migrants as prone to crime, criminal entrepreneurs came up from the slums of the city.[39] Homegrown poverty, not immigration, was the factor that needed to be addressed.

That insight—that crime is best fostered within the margins of society—is fundamental to understanding not only the history of organized crime but also the history of gangs in Chicago. As White people of European stock moved out of the marginal neighborhoods and up in the ranks of society, a new underclass arrived, creating an "ethnic succession" within the criminal underworld, which in Chicago would eventually include African Americans and Mexican Americans.[40] Some within those newly arrived groups would replace the previous generation's fading gangs and criminal entrepreneurs.[41] Nonetheless, the attempts of new groups to fully take over the old rackets and obtain the same degree of influence their predecessors held were not always successful.

In the early twentieth century, gangs were a function of Chicago's machine politics. Early examples include the Irish gangs, which beyond engaging in street scraps played a role in ensuring that their political candidates—in this case of the Democratic Party—were elected in exchange for social mobility in the form of jobs as city employees, including being police or firemen.[42] During the same period, similar politically charged White gangs—organized as athletic and social clubs—representing other groups of national origin formed.[43] While there was little tension between the White gangs, they violently targeted the nascent Black communities in the 1919 race riots.[44] White violence directed toward African Americans would occur periodically over the next fifty years and would encourage collective action in the Black community that would contribute to the development of internal protection rackets, in the form of street gangs, to defend against and respond to the abuse.[45]

The rise of the Italians and the African Americans in the illicit marketplace, replacing the Irish and Jewish gangsters who had faded from a life of crime into societal respectability, was a development that was buoyed by politics.[46] Both groups supported the Republican machine—which in the early twentieth century was still the party of Abraham Lincoln and was heavily supported by Black voters—and vice versa, which helped to facilitate the illicit enterprises that each group wanted to undertake.[47] The Italians, led by Capone's syndicate, specialized in bootlegging during Prohibition (1920–1933). The African Americans ran the "Policy" numbers racket, an illegal lottery.[48] Capone, intent on maximizing their profits in the lucrative illicit liquor market, struck a deal with the African Americans in which the Italians promised not to interfere with the Policy. In the predominately Black communities of Chicago, sophisticated illicit enterprises existed beyond the Policy, with vice rackets becoming commonplace.[49]

As the African American population in the city grew, White gangs resumed their original roles of intimidation and violence. In the 1940s and 1950s, White gangs engaged in White supremacist terrorism to prevent African Americans from leaving the Black Belt for other parts of Chicago.[50] The effective containment of African Americans to the Black Belt during these decades led to the rise of Black gangs that developed within the context of their segregated existence. Unable to properly contest White gangs outside the Black Belt, these Black gangs emulated the behaviors that Thrasher described in White gangs some thirty-five years before, fighting among each other for prime territory.[51]

However, the established Black illicit entrepreneurs did not give these youth gangs access to the upper echelons of criminal opportunity—the vice rackets and especially the Policy—in the Black community.[52] Without a deep organizational structure, Black criminal entrepreneurs, collectively, were eventually overpowered by the Outfit, the Italian/Italian American mafia presence in Chicago. In time, the Outfit reneged on Capone's promise to leave the Policy alone. In an effort to consolidate control over the illicit enterprises of Chicago, the Outfit took over the Policy circa 1950.[53] In the racial politics of the era, the Italians enjoyed a competitive advantage over the African Americans in political connections. This advantage proved decisive, and the Italians moved on the Policy without interference from the existing political order.[54]

Outmaneuvered politically, Black gangs in the late 1950s and 1960s began cultivating a political presence. The era saw an "explosion" of Black gangs, with gang membership tallying "more than 50,000."[55] Notable and influential Black gangs and gang leaders who came to prominence in this era included Jeff Fort's Blackstone Rangers, which later became the Black P. Stone Nation; David Barksdale's Devil Disciples, which later became the Black Disciples; Jerome "King Shorty" Freeman's Black King Cobras; Larry Hoover's Supreme Gangsters; and Bobby Gore's Conservative Vice Lords.[56] The period also saw the development of some of the most significant Latino gangs still in existence, such as the Latin Kings, Two Six, and the Satan Disciples.[57] Initially, many of these organizations— particularly the Black ones—emulated the model followed by the successful White gangs of old: enter politics and engage in crime.

At first, some of these groups were successful in accessing the city's political landscape. Some Black gangs adopted some elements of the Black Power movement and sought to carve out a political space for their constituents that had previously been denied to them.[58] In some cases, gang leadership met with civil rights leaders; the Vice Lords and the Black P. Stones met with Martin Luther King, Jr. Moreover, the Vice Lords and the Black P. Stones were able to secure federal financing for political action committees and other social organizations.[59]

One man I interviewed, Tyrell, who as a little boy in the early 1990s had become a Gangster Disciple, reflected on what gangs were like prior to his involvement. "Gangs weren't initially formed to terrorize the neighborhoods. Like the BGDN [referring to the original Black Gangster Disciple Nation]: gangs were formed to preserve the neighborhood and all those that lived in it. What society calls 'gangs' weren't really gangs when they first started in the '60s, under David Barksdale and Shorty Freeman. They weren't gangs per se, you know, how the media portrays gangs to be. They weren't that. They were preservers of the neighborhood. They used to have clothing drives and soup kitchens and book drives for the kids. But that started dying out, especially with the inception of crack cocaine."

However, the Black gangs had to contend with more than media portrayals. Politicians and police—unlike their treatment of White gangs of the early twentieth century that allowed those gangs to be subsumed into political structure and later into legitimate society—cast Black gangs as nothing more than criminal entrepreneurs. This labeling stripped any legitimate political agency from these organizations, at least within the public narrative.[60] Moreover, the labeling was an easy sell to the public as leaders and members of these groups were arrested and convicted for crimes, such as drug dealing, murder, and terrorism.[61] Violence in Chicago escalated as these emerging gang coalitions formed and expanded throughout the city in the late 1970s and more opportunities for conflict developed, particularly as the lucrative drug crack cocaine began to hit the Chicago streets.[62]

The increased violence on the Chicago streets led to a rapidly increasing number of Black and Latino men going to prison in the 1960s and 1970s (and beyond).[63] Criminologist James B. Jacobs, who wrote about Illinois's maximum-security Stateville Prison, located in Crest Hill just north of the city of Joliet, described an evolution of prisoner order that echoed what John Irwin had described in California. In an era of increasing minority prisoners, minority prisoners organized to contest the dominant White status quo, creating a system of prison organizations that split mostly along racial lines in order to provide protection for one another.[64] At the time—the late 1960s and early 1970s—most Latino inmates joined the Latin Kings organization; Black inmates joined one of the three significant gangs, the Black P. Stone Nation, the Devil's Disciples, or the Conservative Vice Lords; and White inmates, except for those connected to the Outfit, were left to fend for themselves.[65]

Illinois differed somewhat from the prison order of Arizona, Texas, and California, where inmate organizations were founded and developed membership from within the prison walls. From early on, the Chicago gangs within prison had their roots firmly in the streets; leaders from the outside remained leaders on the inside. As such, these leaders remained preoccupied with outside activity and enjoyed outside support, something that had been nonexistent prior to the 1970s.[66] Chicago gangs' interest in the illicit affairs of the streets at that time foreshadowed what was to come three years later within the prison system.

In 1978, Illinois prisons saw the formation of two "nations"—consortia—of gangs, known as the Folks and the People. The Folks developed from the efforts of Larry Hoover in Stateville to unite several street gangs from different parts of the city and represent various ethnicities under one umbrella for protection.[67] The People, an alliance between the Black P. Stones, the Vice Lords, the Latin Kings, and other smaller street gangs, formed in response. These nations were and still are unusual in the gang landscape of the United States in that they are not racially exclusive. Historically, Black, Latino, and White gangs have been part of either coalition within prison and, at least in name, on the street.[68] These consortia sought to unite gangs with like philosophical and entrepreneurial outlooks.[69] To that end, each consortium served an "enterprise syndicate" that sought in the free world to centralize illicit enterprise by minimizing competition among member gangs.[70] In prison, these consortia also attempted to maximize the potential benefits of collective action.

Though Larry Hoover was sentenced to 150 to 200 years for ordering the murder of William "Pookie" Young in 1973, his ascent to leadership of the Gangster Disciples occurred while incarcerated after the 1974 death of David Barksdale.[71] Functionally illiterate upon his entry into the penal system, Hoover earned his GED and began to read profusely.[72] He was especially taken with *Boss*, Mike Royko's 1971 biography of Richard J. Daley, the mayor of Chicago during Hoover's youth. "'It was very motivating, because it showed you can make a transition from a street gang to a socially acceptable gang,' [Hoover said], referring to the Irish and other white immigrant gangs in Chicago in the early 1900s."[73] It was a history that inspired Hoover to develop his "New Concept" whereby he renamed the Gangster Disciples "Growth and Development" and reorganized the gang into "a corporate-style business and social organization."[74] Despite these changes, the Gangster Disciples remained one of the most prolific drug distributers in the city. A similar trajectory was undertaken by the Black P. Stones. Notwithstanding its outward presence as a community organization inspired in part by the teachings of the Nation of Islam, the Black P. Stones also sold drugs (but initially resisted selling crack).[75]

The Folks and the People competed against each other for a share of the market. A high rate of violence accompanied the resulting crack wars that occurred in Chicago—as in other major US cities—during the 1980s and 1990s.[76] However, the Black gangs never matured as Larry Hoover had envisioned. Black gang members never transitioned en masse into the legitimate economy as the White immigrant gang members before them had done. They never competed with the Outfit and its dominance of the majority of the criminal rackets in the city with the notable exception of the wholesale drug trade. And Black gangs never became independent operators of the drug trade; they required someone—usually a Latino gang member—to connect them to a wholesale supplier.[77]

Moreover, the postracial world created by the People and Folks nations was one that functioned due to the need for protection rather than from any absence of racism. In fact, criminologist John Hagedorn chronicled how in the 1990s the Latin Folks attempted (though ultimately failed) to develop their own independent consortium of gangs, in part with the blessing of the fading Outfit, with the goal to emulate the success in illicit enterprise that the Italians had enjoyed for the better part of the twentieth century.[78] One of the advantages the Latino gangs had compared to the Black gangs was that they had closer access to the wholesalers. Although not every Latino gang had a direct connection to wholesalers, Latino gangs prioritized each other over gangs of other races, so most Latino gangs were able to obtain heroin and cocaine with relative ease.[79] In the 1990s the gang that supplied the rest of the Folks was the Maniac Latin Disciples, whose membership overlapped with the Herrera Family of Little Village.[80]

For a time, the Herrera Family drug trafficking organization—an organization that was united chiefly by the kinship ties of the six families involved—was perhaps the biggest and most resilient player in the wholesale drug market in Chicago.[81] The earliest members of the family emigrated from Durango, Mexico, to Chicago in the 1950s.[82] They moved mostly heroin through a supply chain that they almost entirely controlled. They farmed opium poppies in Durango, processed the opium into heroin, transported the heroin to the marketplace, and supplied it to distributors, making it (almost) a farm-to-arm provider, which is unusual in the wholesale drug trade.[83] Later when US interdiction efforts shut down the Colombians' Caribbean routes, the Herrera Family started moving cocaine and established a small stake in marijuana and methamphetamines.[84] By the late 1970s, some estimates placed the Herrera Family's collective earnings at $60 million as its distribution network expanded past Chicago, its principal distribution hub, to several other major US cities, including Denver, Los Angeles, Miami, and Pittsburgh.[85]

The Herrera Family's success in introducing its brown heroin to the Chicago market made the organization a target for law enforcement.[86] By the mid-1980s, the Herreras were suffering significant losses at the hands of the justice system, which had managed to identify, arrest, and convict dozens of the family's operatives.[87] While the Herrera Family's distribution was initially left reeling from these arrests, by 1988 it had replaced its key operatives, allowing them to return to wholesaling.[88] In the early 1990s the Herrera Family distributed much of its product to street retailers via Hugo "Juice" Herrera, a member of both the Herrera Family and the Folk Nation's Maniac Latin Disciples.[89] However, the Herrera Family—like the drug trafficking organizations that have followed it—did not exclusively operate among Latinos or the Folk Nation, for that matter. Instead, the Herrera Family sought profitable ventures wherever available.

Biggs, a general for the Black P. Stone Nation in a Chicago suburb, described his plug from the 1990s when he used to move significant amounts of cocaine—a handful of kilos at a time—as being a "cartel from Durango" that stamped its product with a scorpion, likely the Herrera Family or one of its subordinates. Biggs said he "inherited" his connection from an older man who was interested in slowing down his own illegal activities. Mutual friends had introduced the two. "When I got out here, I was running cocaine, but just small shit, like an ounce or two a day; then I found out dude was plugged with the weight."[90]

Biggs went on to explain that his connection was not affiliated with any particular street gang. This lack of affiliation allowed him to be recruited into the fold of the suburban cocaine crew. "The people in the crew were getting robbed by gangs out here, you know. Latin Kings—that stuff come up a few times—the Kings stuck them over a few times.[91] And Gangster Disciples didn't stick them up, but they wouldn't pay them back. The crew would front the GDs work; they wouldn't pay it back.[92] So, the crew came to me because they knew I was already plugged in the streets and nobody would fuck with me, so they wouldn't have no problems like that anymore. So, that's what it ended up being. And my connect inherited the plug from his uncle, so he passed it down to us. When he stopped, we took over with the cartel and started distributing for them."

In short, although the actors have changed from time to time, the Herrera Family's relationship with the gangs reflects the relationship between drug trafficking organizations and gangs that exists today in Chicago. In the mid-2010s, the foremost law enforcement view vis-à-vis the wholesale drug market in the city, as related to me by the agents working at the Chicago HIDTA, was that "Sinaloa is dominant and established in Chicago. They have relationships with gangs and distributors." But as in El Paso and Phoenix, it would soon become clear that while there are indeed relationships between high-level players, for the ordinary people participating in the retail drug trade, the hurdles to develop the capital necessary to be part of those wholesaling conversations are too high.

CATCHING CASES

When I was a little boy growing up under spacious skies that illuminated amber waves of grain (and emerald waves of soy), my teachers taught me to believe in the American dream. The idea was so simple that I could understand it as a child: in the United States, if someone puts in enough effort no matter who they are or where they come from, they can become whatever they want to be. The American dream was what made our country and our people exceptional.

Unfortunately, that idealism always has been just a dream for the vast majority of people who live in the United States. For most, the American dream is a far more constrained concept underwritten by the reality that while it is possible to work toward improving one's station in life, hard work does not unequivocally translate into success. For most, there are clear ceilings partway up the social ladder; indeed, social mobility has declined in the United States since 1975.[1] And though our lives are not predetermined, there are factors that make certain outcomes more likely. For instance, take wealth: the factor that best predicts whether a person becomes wealthy is whether that person has a parent who was wealthy.[2] Or take incarceration: a significant factor that predicts whether a person becomes incarcerated is whether that person has a parent who was incarcerated.[3]

As for being exceptional, the United States certainly is exceptional where incarceration is concerned. With over two million people on remand or in prison, the United States incarcerates more people than any other country in terms of both absolute numbers and as a percentage of population.[4] When I was a kid, my friend Ricky's father was one of those Americans in prison. Shortly after he released, when we were twelve years old, Ricky's dad was murdered. It was the first of a sequence of events that led Ricky to catch his first case. He was convicted and sentenced to juvenile detention before I learned how to drive; he was sentenced to prison before I graduated from high school, becoming one of the 20 percent of Black men who are incarcerated by the time they are thirty years old.[5]

Two hundred miles north of us in Chicago, imprisonment was an outcome that Alyssa feared for her son, Michael, whose father, like Ricky's, was murdered when Michael was twelve. Alyssa knew that she needed to stack the deck to give her son a fighting chance to stay out of trouble. She knew that in her lifetime, which saw the 1980s panic regarding crack cocaine on the streets of Chicago, the rates of Black men sent to prison for drug offenses had skyrocketed.[6] She also knew that if her son had a college degree, the risk of his going to prison would decrease.[7] Most importantly, she knew that her son's opportunities started with her.

Before Michael's father was murdered, Alyssa looked to the military for opportunity, since the local job market offered her jobs with low ceilings. She wanted to earn a living that could provide the best opportunities for her son. In the military she thrived, and for a time so did Michael, making good grades at school and staying out of trouble. With the money she earned, Alyssa invested in a little house in the working-class neighborhood of South Shore, where she thought she could insulate Michael from the temptations of the street. Despite Alyssa's efforts, her partner's death shook the foundation of her son's existence. While Alyssa offered a life of normalcy, routine, and opportunity, Michael looked to the men in his extended family—former gang members, some of whom had served time—as role models for being a man. For those men, the boundless opportunities of the American dream weren't even a consideration; their American dream was far more parochial.

"They don't think life is bigger than the block. It's like a neighborhood full of people with PTSD.[8] They're shell-shocked. They don't think they can go anywhere. They don't think they can do anything. I mean, other than a little nickel-and-dime job, scratching and surviving for every single dollar," Alyssa explained. "They're not comfortable when sometimes it's not a constant state of struggle. If the guy next to you has ambitions to be something bigger and better, on the surface you say, 'Oh wow! That's good!' But crabs in a barrel: 'I don't really want you to go further than I can go.'"[9]

With her support network crumbling—her grandparents, who were her foundation, died—and Michael's straight A's giving way to skipping class to hang out with gang members on the street corner, Alyssa was at a loss. "I actually committed him into a hospital—a mental hospital. I didn't know what else to do. People don't understand. I didn't know what the hell was going on within my son."

At the mental hospital, Michael was diagnosed with bipolar disorder. Alyssa, despite being educated, tenacious, drug-free, and all-American, struggled to keep her son from joining a gang and becoming part of the drug trade. Michael continued to look up to the local gang members. They groomed his ego so that he would be willing to take on the risks of hand-to-hand drug dealing they no longer wanted to undertake. And Michael, despite his mother's support, was tempted by the seemingly easy money of the street and its promise of independence. Michael dreamed of being big-time, but like the American dream for most Americans, Michael's dream was never a likelihood. Instead, the police raided a trap house he was in. There were drugs and guns, and Michael was held responsible. Michael, like Ricky, was in prison by the time he was twenty.

In Little Village, twelve miles from Alyssa's South Shore home, a mother watched four of her seven children follow her husband's footsteps into the drug trade. Her husband was Margarito Flores Sr., a Mexican immigrant who by all appearances was living his American dream. Margarito Sr. had permanent residency and held down a good job at the massive Brach's candy factory, apparently earning enough to support his five children and afford the new Chevrolet station wagon parked in front of his house.[10] But Margarito Sr. had a secondary source of income: smuggling. At first he smuggled people into the United States; later he shifted to heroin, driving as much as thirty-five kilos of the drug from El Paso to Chicago each month to wholesale for the Herrera Family, the dominant Mexican drug trafficking organization serving Chicago at the time.[11] An informant told on him, and law enforcement set Margarito Sr. up to sell to an undercover federal agent. Margarito's wife was pregnant with twin boys when he was arrested.

When the twins, Pedro and Margarito Jr., were born in June 1981, Margarito Sr. was beginning a ten-year sentence in an Illinois state prison. Before their dad was paroled, two of their older siblings, Hector and Armando, became members of the Latin Kings, the most prominent gang in Little Village.[12] And like their father, Hector and Armando dabbled in the drug trade. Both caught charges when Peter and Junior—as the twins were known to their family and friends—were in middle school.[13]

When the twins were seven, Margarito Sr. was released from prison early; he immediately began teaching his young sons how to conceal drugs in vehicles. He took Peter and Junior on trips where he would jump marijuana across the US-Mexican border. But when Peter and Junior turned twelve their father returned to Mexico, where he started another family.[14] Their brother, Armando, took over not only their father's duties as patriarch of the family but also the wholesale marijuana business Margarito Sr. had developed upon his release from prison.[15]

Armando made an effort to keep his younger brothers out of the gang life and out of the drug trade, paying them to avoid the temptations of the street. The twins worked at McDonald's and went to Farragut Career Academy, the public high school that served the Little Village area.[16] But Armando caught another case in 1998 when the twins were in high school. Like his father, Armando was convicted for drug conspiracy. Unlike his father, Armando was deported to Mexico after serving his sentence.[17]

The twins' wives, Vivianna Lopez and Valerie Gaytan, writing pseudonymously as Mia and Olivia Flores in their book *Cartel Wives*, claim that the twins took over Armando's business to raise money for their large nuclear family.[18] With Margarito Sr. absent, an urgent need to generate capital likely did arise, but undoubtedly the twins also saw a golden business opportunity. Peter and Junior quietly took over Armando's logistics and wholesaling business and rapidly expanded it. Even as seventeen-year-olds they made sound business decisions, drawing on the lessons received from their brothers, their father, and—of all things—their employment at McDonald's, where they learned that if everyone has only one job to do, then mistakes seldom occur.[19] The twins' strategies not only kept them out of trouble—at least for the short term—but also made them wealthy very quickly.

The twins had a decidedly unusual foray into the illicit drug business: unlike most who had to work their way up the drug trade by first taking risks on the street corner and then progressing step-by-step up the ladder, Peter and Junior walked into a wholesaling job—something akin to walking straight into middle management with no experience. That move was possible because as it turns out, when the Flores twins took over Armando's business, they also inherited key assets, just as if they had taken over a licit business.

In the drug trade, those assets were respect and connections. The twins were able to survive as newcomers to the wholesale marketplace because they were accorded the respect that their gang-connected brother had earned as a Latin King. They also maintained strategic friendships with key players such as Rudy "Kato" Rangel Jr., who was a leader within the gang.[20] This respect afforded Peter and Junior the protection necessary to avoid being robbed or deposed when they first entered the drug trade. And as time went on, the twins were able to maintain their respect due to their excellent connections.

Peter and Junior's connections linked them to two key sets of people. On one hand, they were connected to brokers in Mexico who had worked with their father and brother such as Tomas Arevalo-Renteria, whom the twins knew since childhood and who was their first supplier, and Guadalupe "Lupe" Ledesma, "an old family friend and associate of the Sinaloa Cartel who for many years served as [the twins' primary] supplier."[21] On the other, they were connected to the Latin Kings, whose corporatized gang model—which drove the gang to "accumulate revenues in underground economies"—made the gang's leaders reliable wholesale purchasers.[22] These connections, coupled with Chicago's geographic advantages of being "halfway to everywhere" and a historically important distribution hub for other midwestern cities, were the foundation of the twins' logistics business.[23] While it would become the most successful single drug trafficking operation in the history of Chicago and perhaps the United States, the twins were just a continuation of a line of people who ran similar organizations facilitating the arrival of drugs into the United States.

There is a lot of confusion as to what a "drug cartel" is. Lawmen like to create an image of vertically organized organizations that control everything from the production of drugs, transportation, wholesaling and retailing, and transporting proceeds of their sales to laundering that money. Few organizations, however, take on that much responsibility internally; the risk is too large. Instead, the drug trade is made up of several organizations working in concert with one another.[24] Some named "cartels" have organizations, with independent leadership, operating under their banner.[25] At times, several Mexican drug trafficking organizations have formed federations and cooperated, maximizing their individual strategic advantages.[26]

The notion that the Sinaloa Federation or another Mexican drug trafficking organization controls or has controlled the streets of Chicago or of other American cities is one that has surprising political currency. The links between the Flores twins and the Sinaloa Federation were sufficient for the Chicago Crime Commission to declare Joaquín Guzmán, a man who has never set foot in Chicago, to be "Public Enemy No. 1," the city's first since Al Capone.[27] But that image of a dominant cartel calling the shots in Chicago was misleading; the Flores twins didn't have allegiance to one supplier: they trafficked product obtained from both the Sinaloa Federation and the Beltrán Leyva Organization. Nonetheless, the image of a cartel evokes violence, and violence gets law enforcement resources. Commentators, popularizing the cartel narrative, ignored that the Flores twins' organization, like others in the drug trade throughout the United States, acknowledged that business is business and that violence is bad for business.

By following that maxim, Peter and Junior's business boomed. By 2008, the twins had one hundred employees across ten cities throughout the United States and were trafficking tons of heroin, cocaine, and methamphetamines to all of them.[28] And they were living a life of luxury in Mexico, having moved there in 2004 to flee a federal indictment for trafficking drugs to Milwaukee, the first city they expanded to from Chicago.[29] But when the alliance of the Sinaloa Federation, the Beltran Leyva Organization, and the Vicente Carillo Fuentes Organization (aka the Juárez Cartel) fractured in early 2008, the twins were caught in the middle of looming threats of violence.[30] Both of their Mexican suppliers gave them an ultimatum: buy from the other, and you die.[31] Peter and Junior decided that the risk of being killed by one of their two former business partners was too high. By all accounts, the twins had never used violence in their business practice, so they had no muscle to protect them.[32] Moreover, they couldn't simply leave the drug trade unseen; once one reaches the heights that Peter and Junior had reached, being invisible triggers suspicion among one's allies, and in the world of drugs, suspicion is a death sentence. The twins realized that they had only one viable option: call their brother Armando's lawyer in Chicago to facilitate contact with the DEA and cut a deal.[33] Though the twins had long since been fugitives in the United States, they had never caught a case. Now, they were handing themselves in.

In exchange for the possibility of leniency in their sentences—they knew that the charges against them could land them in prison for the rest of their lives— the Flores twins gathered evidence over the course of 2008 to help prosecutors build cases against various participants in the drug trade. Later that year the twins surrendered to DEA agents in Mexico and were flown to the United States, where they were taken into formal custody. Their father would never forgive them for becoming informants.

In 2009, Peter entered a statement in court that described in broad terms the component elements of the organization.[34] That statement was heavily redacted when released to the public, but it made clear that Peter and his brother engaged in the large-scale wholesale transportation of heroin, cocaine, and methamphetamines from Mexico to the United States and wholesale distribution of those drugs within various cities in the United States.[35] The twins coordinated the transnational and intrastate carriage of the drugs, which occurred via a variety of transportation methods including freight containers that move by land and sea, semitrucks that haul trailers cross-country, and air freight shipments. They repackaged the product in stash houses and supplied around thirty large local wholesale distributers in Chicago. The twins replicated this model in other cities.

Pedro Flores's statement was the first public information regarding the drug trade credited to him. During hours of interviews with DEA agents, the twins shared their knowledge of the high-level drug trade in Mexico and the United States, particularly as it pertained to the mechanics of their logistics and wholesaling operations.[36] Later they provided evidence to grand juries that was used to extradite and convict a vast array of people, including employees of their own operation; associates such as Tomas Arevalo-Renteria; rivals such as Saul Rodriguez, who once kidnapped Peter; and key members of the Sinaloa Federation, including Vicente "El Mayito" Zambada Niebla and Joaquín "El Chapo" Guzmán Loera.[37]

With the 2008 fracture of the alliance among the Sinaloa Federation, the Beltran Leyva Organization, and Vicente Carillo Fuentes Organization came violence, just as Peter and Junior foresaw, resulting in thousands of drug-related murders per month in Mexico over the next decade.[38] And with that violence, arresting the heads of these organizations became a priority for both US and Mexican law enforcement.[39] One of the first notable arrests was the March 2009 capture of Vicente Zambada Niebla, the son of Ismael "El Mayo" Zambada García, one of the men who ran the Sinaloa Federation along with Vicente's father-in-law, Joaquín Guzmán.[40]

Upon Vincent's arrest, Mexican officials said that he "had been designated by his father to oversee operations, logistics and security" for the Sinaloa Federation.[41] Being the son of El Mayo, Vicente had grown up in the high-level drug trade, becoming a "narco junior." While some of the children of Mexico's drug lords lived lives outside the drug trade, starting their own licit businesses, earning college degrees, and making honest lives, the narco juniors were the children of established drug traffickers who chose to pursue wealth by participating in the drug trade.[42]

Unlike their fathers, most of whom grew up in abject poverty and had to fight their way to the upper echelons of the drug trade, narco juniors grew up in sublime luxury and were elevated into the upper echelons of the drug trade on the capital and authority their fathers possessed. Moreover, unlike their predecessors, who kept low profiles, narco juniors were ostentatious, driving luxury sports cars and flaunting their wealth on social media.[43] Vicente, for instance, was living in the affluent Mexico City neighborhood Jardines de Pedregal, with fancy cars parked in his driveway and designer clothes in his closet when he was arrested by Mexican soldiers.[44]

Vicente, who was extradited to the United States in February 2010, sat in custody for almost two years before cooperating with the US government. He faced a life sentence, and the Flores twins were prepared to give evidence against him. Even so, the circumstances in which one turns informant matter. Unlike the Flores twins, whose US citizenship afforded them the relative security of participating in the witness protection program upon their release from prison, Vicente had to angle for an S-5 visa for witnesses and informants, which would allow him and his family to remain in the United States for three years with the possibility of receiving permanent residency afterward.[45] Receiving an S-5 visa was crucial for Vicente. Those who cooperate with law enforcement are typically marked men in Mexico. Vicente's bodyguard, José Rodrigo "El Chino Ántrax" Aréchiga Gamboa, cooperated with the US government. Aréchiga Gamboa, after fleeing his US house arrest to return to Mexico, was soon found murdered in Sinaloa, most likely by members of his own organization for his betrayal.[46]

A two-minute phone call from Ismael Zambada García, who gave his son permission to cooperate with the US authorities, marked a change in Vicente Zambada Niebla's level of cooperation.[47] The delay was necessary for Zambada García to change his tactics, insulating him and his colleagues from capture. But Vicente, in an effort to avoid life imprisonment and with his father's tacit permission, secretly accepted a plea deal in 2013 whereby, like the Flores twins, he admitted to his role in trafficking drugs and agreed to provide evidence and testify against Guzmán and over a hundred other associates.[48]

As the Flores twins and Zambada Niebla began to give evidence against Joaquín Guzmán, Guzmán remained on the lam, as he had been since his 2001 escape from a high-security Mexican prison in a laundry basket.[49] For his part, Guzmán had many made-for-TV escapes, avoiding capture time and again over the course of more than a decade. He drilled escape plans and built hydraulic doors that accessed escape tunnels in the residences where he stayed for protracted periods.[50]

In 2014, Guzmán's luck finally seemed to run out. A team of DEA and Homeland Security Investigations agents tracked communications between Guzmán and his subordinates, intercepted his unsecured BlackBerry text messages, and pinpointed his location.[51] In 2015 Guzmán made yet another brazen escape from Mexico's supermax Altiplano prison, where his engineers tunneled into his cell to break him out. However, his affinity for using BlackBerrys proved to be ruinous; once more, law enforcement tracked his unencrypted communications and captured him yet again in January 2016. There would be no further escape; he was extradited to the United States in January 2017. In 2018 in New York, Joaquín Archivaldo Guzmán Loera finally stood trial for his crimes. As they had promised Federal prosecutors years before, Pedro Flores and Vicente Zambada Niebla testified against Guzmán.

LOGISTICS

In a federal courtroom in Chicago, US District Court chief judge Ruben Castillo sentenced twins Pedro Flores and Margarito Flores Jr. to fourteen years in federal prison. The modest sentence was in recognition of the information the twins had provided. Once they chose to cooperate with the US government, the twins were destined to serve their sentences under a shroud of secrecy, which obscured the federal prisons in which they served their time, and to spend their postrelease lives in witness protection.[1] Vicente Zambada Niebla was sentenced by the same judge to a similarly modest fifteen years in light of his cooperation.[2] Vicente's future is uncertain; his S-5 visa allows him to remain in the United States for only three years upon completing his sentence. By contrast, in New York, Joaquín Archivaldo Guzmán Lorea, spared a death sentence as part of the terms of his extradition from Mexico, was sentenced by Chicago-born US District Court judge Brian Cogan to life in prison plus thirty years; Guzmán will die in a supermax facility in Florence, Colorado.[3]

When sentencing the Flores twins Judge Castillo said, "You and your family will always have to look over your shoulder. Any time you start your car, you're going to be wondering, 'Is that car going to start or is it going to explode?'"[4] Such statements reflect the violent reputation that drug trafficking organizations such as the Sinaloa Federation possess not only in Mexico but also in the American public consciousness. Nonetheless, from the Flores twins' and Zambada Niebla's plea agreements and sentencing memoranda, the Guzmán trial, the public record, and my conversations with people who are part of the drug trade on the streets of Chicago, five lessons emerge that dispel some of the sensational attributes that the public often associates with drug trafficking organizations. These lessons illustrate the processes and opportunities that link the people and businesses of the drug trade.

First, drug trafficking organizations are specialist bulk logistics providers that respond to and compensate for stresses in the market. Second, most of the organizations, transporting bulk shipments of illicit drugs into and within the United States, are best described as "contractors" rather than "subsidiaries" of Mexican drug trafficking organizations. Third, the arrests of kingpins do not significantly curb drug supply in the medium to long term. Fourth, there is little evidence to suggest that a significant proportion of the violence in Chicago is underwritten by Mexican drug trafficking organizations or their US counterparts. Fifth, the money generated by the drug trade may be voluminous, but only a few actors deal in big revenue.

Lesson 1: Drug Trafficking Organizations Are, Principally, Specialist Bulk Logistics Providers, Built to Withstand Market Fluctuations

Popular notions of "drug cartels" evoke images of groups that are pyramidal in their organizational structure. Moreover, they have an essential capo at the top, engage in violence, and, most importantly, traffic illicit drugs. Of these three elements, only the final one is consistently present across different types of drug trafficking organizations, which variously may focus on transporting drugs within international, regional, or domestic contexts. Indeed, large-scale drug trafficking organizations are often considerably broader at the top than many would imagine. As novelist Don Winslow correctly observed,

> The critical thing to understand is that Guzmán wasn't—and never would be—the sole "boss" of the Sinaloa Cartel. We tend to think of cartels as pyramids, with a single head at the top, but in fact they're more like wedding cakes with several tiers.
>
> Guzmán was on the top tier, with others, the most important being Juan [José "El Azul"] Esparragoza Moreno, the late Renzo Coronel Villarreal, and a man named Ismael "El Mayo" Zambada, who has been prominently featured, albeit in absentia, in [Guzmán's] trial.[5]

In short, the Sinaloa Federation was not a product of Guzmán's sole efforts, nor was it governed by Guzmán's decisions alone. Rather, it was cogoverned by many others, including his last wife, the daughter of former collaborator Renzo Coronel

Villarreal, Emma Coronel Aispuro, who pleaded guilty to helping her husband run his business.[6] As when Guzmán was previously incarcerated, the Sinaloa Federation persists despite his absence, though its capacity may be diminished.

Nevertheless, drug traffic volume cannot be permanently reduced by taking out or diminishing a single organization. Guzmán was hunted not because his capture would impact drug trafficking—it didn't. Other drug barons and their firms, such as Nemesio "El Mencho" Oseguera Cervantes and his Cártel de Jalisco Nueva Generación, were ready and able to fill any gap in the wholesale drug market that might appear with a disruption in Guzmán's organization.[7] Guzmán was hunted because his capture would be a boon for politicians and law enforcement in both the United States and Mexico; it would prove that they were serious about winning the war on drugs. Capturing Guzmán, who had become a cultural touchstone, immortalized in television and song, and whose name had become as ubiquitous as Pablo Escobar's was in the 1980s, meant huge political currency.

Mexican drug trafficking organizations were initially couriers for their Colombian suppliers, but in the late 1980s people such as Guzmán's mentor, Miguel Ángel Félix Gallardo, head of the Guadalajara Cartel and the most important Mexican drug trafficker of his time, began requesting payment not in cash but rather in the drugs they trafficked.[8] This strategy allowed the Mexican cartels to supplant their Colombian suppliers as the primary suppliers to the US distributors. Plus, the liberalization of the political sector created opportunities to use violence to dispose of the old and usher in new leadership. Thus, Guzmán gained access to the upper echelon of the drug trade: he was an effective assassin for his boss, Félix Gallardo.[9] Once Félix Gallardo was imprisoned in 1989, Guzmán assumed control of the trafficking operations through Sinaloa and developed his own offshoot organization.[10] By all accounts, he was successful in improving smuggling routes, corrupting officials, and using violence to buoy his position. Guzmán's success earned him the social and financial capital needed to develop and expand his connections with Colombian suppliers.[11] He was far from alone in engaging in those activities.[12]

The preeminent Mexican illicit firm type operating in the drug trade facilitates the transport of illicit drugs and their precursors from their countries of origin to Mexico. These firms compete for the ability to conduct "transit crime," moving wholesale volumes of product through Mexico and to partners on the US border, who then transport the products farther north to supply other distributors, wholesalers, or large retailers.[13] Other Mexican firms participate in the cultivation of drug crops, such as opium poppy, or the manufacture of methamphetamines. Some Mexican cities have retail markets, run by gangs and other street-level criminals.[14]

The relationships between the organizations that underpin the drug trade vary; however, there are large-scale drug logistics firms that employ specialists to procure precursor materials, manufacture products, transport those products, launder money, and engage in targeted violence.[15] These firms are built to withstand a degree of loss of product, money, and personnel. Concerted strategies maximize the resilience and flexibility of their supply chains in the event that any link is compromised or weakened or fails. These strategies include shipping drugs in smaller quantities to defend against improved interdiction efforts and developing networks of key actors to allow organizations to substitute services when needed.[16]

Mexican drug trafficking organizations typically transfer their product to distributors, like the Flores twins, who specialize in distributing processed products within the countries where they will be retailed. The relationship between drug trafficking organizations and distributors may be close and consistent, but once goods and money are exchanged, the drug trafficking organization does not dictate what the distributor should do with the product. In turn, distributors transfer their product to wholesalers. Once wholesalers acquire the product, their responsibility is to pay the distributor and to move the product onward, independently of any oversight from the distributor. Wholesalers supply smaller-scale wholesale customers, who likely sell to those involved in breaking the product down for retail sale.

Like Guzmán, the Flores twins' rise to the upper strata of the wholesale drug world had much to do with their early success, which garnered the attention of higher-level contacts. The Flores Crew was a multifaceted enterprise that differentiated and compartmentalized tasks (albeit not blindly), starting with the twins themselves. Junior connected smugglers and/or transporters to the product in Mexico, while Peter coordinated the distribution to local wholesalers, first in Chicago and then in other cities including Cincinnati, Columbus, Detroit, Milwaukee, Philadelphia, Washington, D.C., and Vancouver.[17] Just as in McDonald's, the twins' employees had specific jobs to perform. However, instead of being line cooks, cashiers, runners, or cleaners, the twins' employees were purchasers, *fleteros* (couriers), repackagers, wholesalers, money counters, or transporters.[18]

The twins also differentiated stash houses by function. Each stash house had only one purpose: to handle drugs or to handle money but never both. While the Flores twins ensured that the people who staffed these houses were unaware of other members of the organization and their roles, they maintained personal relationships with many of their employees so as to build trust and consistency in the operation, eschewing the best practices of complete blind compartmentalization and smoke screening.[19] That choice placed the twins in the crosshairs of federal law enforcement, who uncovered the twins' identities while chasing drug leads in Milwaukee in 2003; individuals picked up in drug sweeps revealed their names. That practice also allowed the twins to identify dozens of their employees when prosecutors asked.

Unlike Guzmán, the Flores twins did not have elaborate escape plans in the event the police came knocking on their doors. They didn't have redundancies built into their organization in the event of their demise. They depended on luck. They were away from their residences when the police came searching for them. Facing arrest, they fled to Mexico.[20]

Despite being off the ground in Chicago, being in Mexico afforded Peter and Junior opportunities that allowed them to grow their business in Chicago and expand to other cities. It was relatively easy to make connections with key actors in the drug trade to diversify supply and shore up business positions, even without meeting players at the top tier of the drug trafficking wedding cake. When Lupe Ledesma, the twins' longtime supplier, kidnapped Peter for ransom, Junior, out of desperation, sought to meet with top-tier players to save his brother. Junior was able to meet Guzmán in person, secure the release of his brother, and establish a business connection that would see the twins become one of Guzmán's preferred US distributors, given their reliability in paying their bills and coping with large amounts of product.[21]

In Mexico, the twins also found it possible to bribe officials to ensure that they wouldn't be subject to arrest. However, the lack of rule of law also meant that the Wild West rules of settling debts were in play; the only way the twins could leave that world was through a physical exit. The twins were such key players in the distribution of Guzmán's product that once they stopped distributing his cocaine, Guzmán never found a single point man to replace their distribution capacity in the United States; instead, Guzmán had to rely on a variety of less prolific and less reliable distributors.[22]

Lesson 2: The Flores Crew Operated as a Contractor

The process of drug procurement, transportation, and distribution, as described by Pedro Flores, indicates that the Flores Crew operated with its own risks in the United States, and these risks were not mitigated in any way by the actions or guarantees of their Mexican suppliers.[23] When drugs were transferred for money, the associated risks inherent in the handling of the product were transferred as well. Simply put, once the Flores Crew took the drugs from its suppliers at the Sinaloa Federation or the Beltrán Leyva Organization, the Flores Crew assumed the risks associated with the product, including the risk of losing the drug shipments or being unable to move the product.[24]

Therefore, the Flores Crew's ability to generate income depended on its ability to ensure the products' safe transportation, delivery, and sale to wholesale customers in the United States. The mechanics of this process were the sole responsibility of the Flores Crew and did not involve the Sinaloa Federation in stateside operations, meaning that no Sinaloa protection for the product was offered after it was transferred to the Flores Crew. Pedro Flores's statements in court debunk the notion that the wholesale drug trade in Chicago is an enterprise that is directly controlled and managed by bosses in Mexico. Consequently, we must reconsider the domestic characterization of the drug trade, how it ought to be policed, and how policy should respond to the drug trade since the specter of the Sinaloan bogeyman is more lore than reality.

Although the Flores twins were born and bred in Chicago, albeit to Mexican parents and specifically to a father who was involved in the wholesale drug trade, there is little indication that significant operations of the Sinaloa Federation, either to oversee the Flores Crew or to replace its operational capability once it was dismantled, existed in Chicago.[25] The Sinaloa Federation has not migrated or expanded organizationally to Chicago beyond its relationship with the Flores twins. Instead, the Sinaloa Federation maintains its Mexican base and relies on an array of subcontractors, always replaceable, to operate the stateside command-and-control structure that transports and distributes its illicit wares to domestic markets.[26] This arrangement maximizes income while minimizing operational risk over time in the US market. When the Flores Crew ceased operations, this provided an opportunity for other suppliers to enter that market. No single distributor appears to have filled the void, and law enforcement now maintains that several Mexican drug trafficking organizations supply Chicago with drugs via a "loosely associated network of profit-driven intermediaries."[27]

Lesson 3: Typical Wholesaling Arrangements Are in Flux and Numerous

Despite the arrests of high-ranking members in Mexico associated with the Sinaloa Federation and the fall of the Flores twins, the retail illicit drug market in Chicago and indeed across the United States has proven quite resilient.[28] The Flores Crew was a significant but not irreplaceable cog in the machinery of the Chicago wholesale drug trade that included several wholesalers, some of whom, seemingly independent from one another, contracted with the Sinaloa Federation and other Mexican drug trafficking organizations.[29] While some dealers reported a drop in the quality of product available and an increase in price upon the Flores twins' arrest, depending on one's connections cocaine and heroin in

the Greater Chicago area remained available. The Flores Crew was an organizational anomaly that grew quickly and dominated the market by offering
best value for quality product. Its demise meant that the Sinaloa Federation and
the remnants of the Beltrán Leyva Organization, seeking to supply the markets
that the twins distributed to, were forced into arrangements with smaller distributors. These arrangements continue to prosper as evidenced by the enduring large-scale supply of illicit drugs available in Chicago.

That drugs still flow into Chicago is of little surprise: demand has remained
robust since at least the 1970s. Previously, the market remained resilient and well
stocked despite the decline of the Herrera Family; other market players met demand relatively easily when the Herreras could no longer do so. Like resilient
licit markets, the illicit drug market comprises a variety of links among the component parts of its network that are not easily severed or if severed are quickly
reforged, even following severe or complete disruption of the operations of firms
with extraordinary capacity, as was the case in the Flores twins' arrest.[30]

It appears that the Flores Crew was atypical in its capacity; there was no indication in Guzmán's trial that there were similar large-scale US based organizations. Undoubtedly, given the tendencies of drug trafficking organizations to
structure risk within their supply chains so that if one component fails the whole
chain does not entirely collapse, an array of transportation networks existed parallel to the Flores operation, which allowed the Mexican drug trafficking organizations to continue servicing Chicago. Little information exists as to who the
current key large-scale distributors are; current groups are likely engaging in
smoke screening to keep their identities and origins under wraps.

While the HIDTA agents told me that in 2014 the wholesale supply was the
responsibility of Mexican drug trafficking organizations, primarily groups that
were part of the Sinaloa Federation, they noted that unlike other cities such as El
Paso and Phoenix where Hispanic gangs monopolize the retail sale, both African
American and Hispanic gangs engage in widespread retail sale in Chicago. This
assertion was consistent with reports that the Flores twins had multiple distributors from their childhood circles as well as from African American neighborhoods.[31] Nonetheless, it's probable that some of the current distributors and
wholesalers maintain firm links to specific cartels and eliminate the middleman,
though it's difficult to determine whether this practice is a norm or just a possibility in the city.[32] Whatever the organizational presence in Chicago may be, business, not violence, drives entrepreneurial relationships.

Getting connected is not always a straightforward process. The Flores twins'
success was the best-case scenario for a young person dreaming to make it big
in the drug trade.[33] For most not born into the drug trade, luck, persistence, and
sometimes a combination of both are needed to establish connections. Despite

the claims of the HIDTA agents at the time, the street didn't indicate one monopolizing supplier. One Chicago police officer, Liam, who worked plainclothes and dealt with drug and gang issues, described the smoke screening process he observed on the beat. "We know the cartels provide the drugs to the gangs. But at the street level, most of their influence is evaporated. They are increasingly using runners and cutouts to move their products."

"What is a 'cutout'?" I asked.

"Cutouts are people who are not in direct contact with the drug cartels," Liam explained. "They receive orders and payments via third-party facilitators. This allows the cartels to stand back and minimize their risk. Through this system, the cartels have no problems supplying rival gangs. At the street level, it's all about business. It doesn't matter who is paying for the drugs to get here."

Liam explained that there is an "even mix" of cartel-supplied distributors delivering the products to gang members and gang members traveling outside Chicago to pick up their supply. According to Liam, gang members often venture into the southern suburbs where there are stash houses to pick up drugs even though there are stash houses in Chicago proper. Liam felt that locating stash houses is somewhat of a crapshoot; however, by his estimation, they could be more common in working-class Hispanic neighborhoods not known for any sort of gang presence. The Flores twins, as was the case with people who set up stash houses in Phoenix and El Paso, targeted middle-class or sometimes affluent neighborhoods close to airports and freeways.[34]

Broadly speaking, when I asked about the origin of their product, most who had dealt drugs could provide only vague answers, though the ethnic origins reported varied past the stereotypical "Mexican" plug, indicating the possibility that drug trafficking organizations originating from other countries had at least a partial market share. Nonetheless, a few respondents had direct experience with wholesalers.

June, a woman who now worked as a secretary but had been convicted of selling drugs in the 1980s, described the wholesale market of the 1980s as one that included the Colombians, a plausible claim given that the decade was their heyday in supplying cocaine to the United States. She had stumbled into trafficking when a high school friend, Lisa, invited her to participate in an interstate drive from Miami to Chicago. Lisa was a first-generation Colombian girl whose family—like the Flores family—was involved in drug trafficking. One day when they were nineteen, Lisa asked June if she wanted to go on a trip to Miami.

"We were sitting around, talking," June said. "We were young and didn't really think about going to college or anything like that. We were always hustling, you know, doing jobs—TJ Maxx, Marshall's, whatever—nothing illegal, trying to figure out how to make money. Lisa then asked me if I wanted to go on this trip to

Miami. She was up front about it. We were going there to pick up some drugs and drive them back. They would be hidden in compartments that she would know how to access. We would each get seven thousand dollars. I said yes." June didn't really think much about it. For her, though she didn't use, drugs were a normal part of life in the community where she grew up. Plus, there was nothing scary about the job. It didn't feel like a risk. June trusted Lisa and wasn't scared at the prospect of going to Miami.

The car was unremarkable except for the mechanism hidden in the cigarette lighter that released hidden panels behind which the cocaine was to be hidden. June guessed that it was one of the modifications made at the auto body shop run by Lisa's relatives. The drive took two days. June described it as if it were a road trip undertaken by two friends. "We would stop along the way to eat, switch drivers. It wasn't anything special."

The young women spent two days in a suburb of Miami visiting with Lisa's family and having a good time. At some point, the car was taken and loaded. "I wasn't there when it happened," June said. "One of Lisa's family members loaded it up for us, and eventually it was just time to go back to Chicago. I don't even know how much we brought back with us. It was the first trip for both of us, and it could have been as little as the two keys I saw afterwards."

As June tried to offload the product, she was eventually caught. The arrest stigmatized her within the trafficking network, so she was not invited to participate in the trafficking activities any further. Eventually she faded out of that circle of people and knew nothing more about them.

Biggs, a general for the Black P. Stone Nation, whom I interviewed in a public library in the Chicago suburb he was responsible for, described his relationship with the wholesalers as one that allowed him access to a product that had been already smuggled to the Chicagoland area. Like June, Biggs merely picked up a preloaded car and took it to its final destination. Over the years he was given more and more quantity to move, though the total amount never exceeded fifteen kilos a week, an amount that occurred only once. Eventually in the early 1990s, Biggs was arrested for possession with the intent to distribute and decided to stop taking the risk of moving large quantities that could put him behind bars for a decade or more. He described how connections are passed on between wholesalers and gang members.

"When I quit—when I semiretired—I plugged the cartel with one of my other guys that was working through this time because—I don't know if you know—but the cartel don't want to see that money stop. I made a lot of money for them. And 'it just stopped' is unheard of. You don't just quit without going to the joint or dying. They'll understand and respect the fact that you ain't doing it no more because you went to the penitentiary or you've been killed behind it. So, for me to just up and quit, I had to basically show them I'd have somebody else that's going to get the slot. I had to ensure the cartel guys that 'you ain't going to lose money; these are guys you can trust; he's been working with me already in the past couple of years,' which he was. So, he basically took over. Took over the business for me so there was no stopping their money. You know, my guy works good; they like him, and they've been going ever since."

Renzo, a midlevel drug dealer who supplied wholesale quantities of drugs to street dealers in his own clique and dealt from his house, indicated that while introductions were still a critical part of getting a wholesaler, there was also a series of norms that had to be adhered to, which meant that a lower-ranking gang member could not circumvent a higher-ranking one to get that introduction. This practice ensured that lower-ranking dealers did not know who their ultimate suppliers were.

"Do you think the people who are buying wholesale from the gang know which cartel they're doing business with?" I asked Renzo.

"No, they don't know nothing. They don't. You're not supposed to tell them. That's what our code of silence means. We're not going to give up our connect to somebody. You know?"

"So, you [as a customer from the gang's main supplier] don't even care who the connect is? Like you don't care whether he's from Gulfo, whether he's from Sinaloa, or whatever," I asked.

"Yeah, we don't care. We don't care obviously. We don't 'set clique' with [the wholesalers] like that."[35]

The clique functions as an enterprise that runs independently of the wholesaler. Ted, a gang member whose responsibility was to show the new recruits the ropes, outlined some of the principal roles undertaken by members of his gang. There is the main boss for the neighborhood, who deals with connecting the gang to its wholesale source, and there are a few other higher-ups who provide guidance. "They're the business type. They're kind of like Al Capone and focus on the money," explained Ted. "They never tell anybody who doesn't need to know what they're doing. They won't even tell their girlfriends. Their job is mostly to buy and sell the drugs at a wholesale level. They don't really gangbang anymore unless they get drunk and get wild after a night out or something.

"When violence is to happen, the big homies encourage us [the younger guys] to make a blueprint before doing a drive-by. We need to know what clothes we're going to change into, the route we're going to take, the location we're going to hit, and the possible cuts. You need to have a reason and ask permission before you shoot. Then, if it's good, you'll get a gun and go handle your business. So now some of the younger guys will be asking me for that permission."

A tier below are the enforcers. "We're all about territory and you need guys who can handle that," Renzo said. Then there are the senders. "We have guys who we send to move a bag. Sometimes they are moving weight; they don't always know. We know the cops are watching him, so we let him get halfway to where he needs to go and then send him back. We create decoys so it's hard for the cops to know what we are doing. Some guys don't gangbang on the street, but they're still part of the gang. Take my cousin. He drives a truck for the city. It's perfect cover for him to make deliveries."

Finally, at the bottom of the totem pole are the shorties—preteens and young teenagers—who only gangbang. Their job is to post up on the street corner, intimidate rivals, and sell dope. They also serve as the first line of defense in the neighborhood, as they are supposed to yell out when a stranger enters the area.

What is clear, however, is that once an individual becomes a member of a clique, he remains a member forever. In Chicago, there is no progressing to a larger gang; doing so is seen as an act of treachery. The fundamental unit of trust is the clique to which a gang member belongs. That relationship dynamic appears to be a primary reason why violence has been a constant factor in street-level gang interactions: block-level cliques vie for power in their neighborhoods, and power is often manifested by controlling the drug sales on the corners of neighboring blocks.[36] This relationship dynamic also means that gangs are not concerned about the source of their drugs so long as the quality is good enough to keep their customers coming back; accordingly, gangs pursue the wholesalers who give them the best deal.

Returning to the street view, the threat of violence means that navigating the underworld to get connected is risky though not impossible. Wilfred, who had attended a large public university downstate and traveled to Chicago to buy the drugs he dealt to the college students there, noted that although he sometimes had dealings with Mexican wholesalers, he found that his Jamaican suppliers had better, albeit inconsistent, product.

"The crazy thing is Jamaicans had a better-quality product," Wilfred explained, "because every time those Latinos passed it off, man, it got stepped on again, or got shorter: it didn't weigh what it was supposed to.[37] But with the Jamaicans, they never had the same kind of heroin all the time either. They had some China White, some Mexican Brown, some Beige, or some Concrete."

In sum, the accounts by June, Biggs, Renzo, and Wilfred show that maintaining a connection may be dependent on family or legacy ties. By relying on a vouching system and by threatening violence should that system be violated, gangs, rather than the wholesalers, impose the layers of separation that ultimately protect the wholesalers. As a result, large-scale distributors and wholesalers, such as the Flores twins, prefer to work with known purchasers who will endeavor to

Common Relationships between Illicit Drug Enterprises

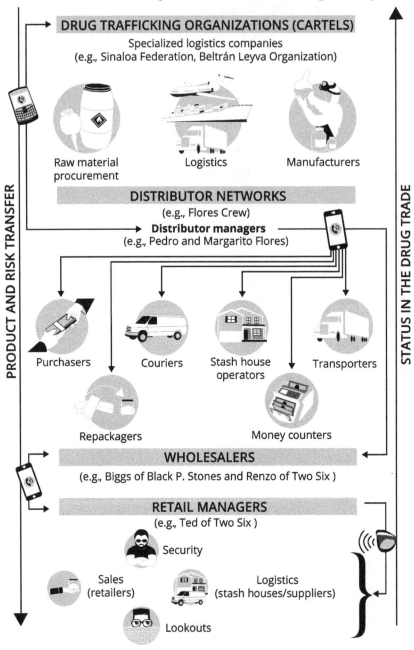

FIGURE 14. Relationships within drug trade enterprises that serve Chicago's customer base.

Diagram by Florence Lourme.

protect their source, because such parties will make for less risky transactions (at least in theory) and will limit unwanted advances from unknown, inexperienced, or untrusted parties.

Generally, the people I met who were active in the lower levels of the drug trade reported that the people who were the most reliably connected were almost always Hispanic. Nevertheless, not all Hispanic gangs have good access and may rely, just as their White and African American counterparts do, on developing a connection with a better-positioned person to plug them with a good-quality supply to sell. Though product was undoubtedly available, many respondents reported difficulties in finding good, consistent suppliers who could provide high-quality goods. Danny, a member of one of the Two Six cliques who currently sold drugs, described the intense competition among street dealers and the difficulty in finding a good plug. "Everybody wants to be some type of boss. Everyone wants their own connection. So right now, shit's fucked up. There ain't one guy with a big plug. There's lots of plugs. You can't trust people; not even your own. Sometimes guys in the mob don't have the right connects, so sometimes you have to leave the neighborhood to get the good shit.[38] I used to have to go to Harlem to get hooked up.[39] There's too much competition to be dealing garbage."

It was that very competition for the open-air markets, afforded by any given street corner, that was a significant driver of the drug-related violence in Chicago.

Lesson 4: Protection and Violence in Chicago Is (Mostly) a Function of Gangs, Not the Cartel-Connected Drug Distributors

Given that most of the wholesaling arrangements in Chicago are undertaken by subcontractors, there are few professionally executed drug-related hits in Chicago. Wholesalers, subcontracting work from the Mexican drug trafficking organizations such as the Flores twins, do not put themselves in positions where violence is necessary. They achieve insulation by minimizing the transactions in which they engage and ensuring that those with whom they do business are interested in long-term business relationships. The need for violence and enforcers was notably absent from Peter's account of his business. Likewise, the government did not find evidence to indicate that the twins or people under their command ordered or participated in violent activities.[40]

Moreover, as in El Paso and Phoenix where drug trafficking organizations do not have publicly visible operations, it appears that if the Mexican drug trafficking organizations do operate muscle in Chicago, they are careful not to leave

FIGURE 15.   Chicago street corner. This street corner, with its history of violence, has been outfitted with a police camera (just above the street sign). The laundromat that Mateo, a member of the Violence Interrupters, is walking toward has bullet holes in it.

Photo by R. V. Gundur.

evidence that implicates them. Mick Dumke, a reporter who had covered drug rings in Chicago for several years, noted that, while professional hits are not unheard of, they are rare and hard to follow up on. He gave me a recent example of an unsolved killing in which the victim, a twenty-five-year-old man named Xavier Tripp, was shot and killed. His assailants approached him in a van, executed him, and drove off in West Garfield Park.[41] Little information was published by the press, but Dumke told me that the victim was wearing body armor and was carrying an AK-47, which made him not just an ordinary victim in the ongoing Chicago gang violence and possibly the victim of an organized killing.

Even wholesale stash houses, which can house thousands of dollars' worth of product, are not staffed with armed guards. Liam described his observations while on the job. "The cartels take a very low-key approach. These 'guards' aren't armed. It wouldn't surprise me at all that most of these guys who are in the houses are picked up and told that they will be paid to sit in a house and make sure nothing happens to it. They probably are told not to go into the garage and just sit there and watch TV all day. They do it because they get paid more than they could by standing outside of a hardware store looking for work every day. Probably the guy in the house has no fucking clue about what's going on, and it's someone else who comes in to handle the product. These guards are not cartel members; it's like they are contracted by the cartel to do that one job."

The presence of cartel members is muted, because unlike in Mexico and like almost anywhere else in the United States, there is no tolerance for visible actions that leave a trail of bodies on the street. Visible violence in the United States is undoubtedly bad for business because it attracts law enforcement. Wholesale loads are valuable, and losing the ability to traffic them is too expensive to respond to problems violently.

In Chicago the power struggles between different gangs at the street level are visible, meaning that it is unlikely that wholesalers would get involved in these struggles. One gang member named Evil $ told me that the cartels "don't have no significance here besides the fact of bringing wholesale and dropping it off to wherever they got to drop it off to. The cartels—just like [gangs from outside of Chicago such as] the Mexican Mafia, just like the Crips, Bloods, MS-13—all them motherfuckers do not carry no weight in Chicago, period.[42] If they were ever to come and try to flex or try to come and set up shop or anything like that, they're going to get fucking blown out of the water because every square inch of Chicago is occupied by some type of fucking gang, and they take that shit serious."

Several facets of gang life were clear from the stories of those involved. First, gang life is still very much alive and well in Chicago, though its nature has evolved significantly since the 1980s. Unlike the El Paso and Phoenix gangs, Chicago gangs can still sustain their numbers and engage in traditional activities, such as hanging out on the street corner to sell dope or fighting with a rival group. The retail drug business in Chicago is still by and large a "street-corner conspiracy," and controlling that corner means controlling its profits.[43] Notwithstanding, as in El Paso and Phoenix, drug cartels care little about the world of the street corner in Chicago outside the demand it produces for their products. The competition among gangs over the local retail market results in the violence that has been an ongoing problem in the city since the 1970s.[44]

Second, compared to El Paso and Phoenix, Chicago gang units tend to be smaller and more focused on the block that the clique is from rather than the gang that the clique belongs to. While the block is important in El Paso and Phoenix, it has become less so over time. Moreover, the street gang cliques of the American Southwest are responsive to the commands and whims of the prison gangs that supersede them in ultimate authority on the street. But on Chicago streets, disputes may emerge even between cliques that are in theory part of a larger gang. This intragang conflict is qualitatively different from what I observed in both El Paso and Phoenix.

Third, taking control of a block in Chicago is not an arduous process, nor does it require a lot of resources. "A 'bad neighborhood' is often the result of a handful of people, maybe one or two houses that are running an illicit enterprise," explained investigative journalist Mick Dumke. "These criminal actors take advantage of . . . areas that have a culture against snitching, and the residents lose confidence in a neighborhood and the police's ability to police it adequately." Alyssa added to Dumke's description, characterizing the South Shore neighborhood she lived in as one that had a very mixed community where blocks that appeared to have the safety afforded to middle-class America were next to blocks that were blighted by gang violence. Nonetheless, on the whole, she still considered her community as the "'hood," a place where "you don't have an option not to know how to fight or you'll be easily devoured."

Finally, the fractionalization of the gangs on the streets of Chicago indicates that unlike El Paso and Phoenix, control does not appear to be exerted from prison, despite the ongoing loose affiliations that occur within jail and prison. This lack of control means that prison gangs—unlike in the southwestern context—cannot effectively curb the ongoing violence that has come to publicly characterize Chicago over the past decades as smaller cliques fight over the open-air markets on which they depend to sell their product.

Chicago's violence is often grounded in conflict among cliques seeking to control territory and to gain benefit from that control, which would allow them to sell or warehouse drugs.[45] Over the years, the nature of the competition among cliques has changed significantly. As previously noted, historically, gangs have been organized under the People and Folks.

Individuals who had served time in county jail or state prison described a system inside similar to what I had heard described in the Southwest. Several layers of control exist, from a board of directors to securities to gallery coordinators. However, these individuals don't appear to have the same kind of control that their counterparts in southwestern prisons enjoy, particularly when it pertains to maintaining status upon their release, requesting favors from gang members living free on the outside, or exerting their will on the street. CB, a Gangster Disciple who had served time in various Illinois state prisons, explained that membership in the federation is "about living, trying to live there as comfortable as possible; you got certain areas you can go in and a certain space."

Historically, those alliances also mitigated acrimony on the street. However, by 2008 and perhaps before, those alliances broke down, with the younger generation having a new outlook, one driven by money. The fast-money culture prioritizes the ability to make a buck over the relative protection afforded by being part of a bigger consortium of gangs. One high-ranking corrections official, who had much experience in high-security settings in Illinois prisons, noted that the disintegration of the alliances under the People and the Folks at the street level might be traced to the successful arrest and incarceration of the higher leadership of these gangs, which disrupted the hierarchy necessary to impose a vertical control structure. Some of the biggest names who weren't already dead in 2020, such as Larry Hoover, Jeff Fort, and Gino Colón, were serving life sentences. According to the corrections official and nearly all of my gang-affiliated respondents, nobody had stepped into those leadership roles, so the organizations were fractured, particularly among African American gangs.

Miles, a police officer whose work focused on gangs in the northwestern part of the city, described the current situation. "We've seen leaders in different segments in more of a district-type level that may have a little bit of weight, but nothing resembling that [historical, overarching] leadership role, mainly because of the big time that's been handed out to those big-time leaders. It goes hand in hand with what we were seeing with this kind of breakdown in this leadership, this whole hierarchy. Gang enforcement used to be real big on every three to six months going down the hierarchies, and it was just getting more and more difficult trying to establish who was who because everything got so small. And it became a warlord like. We got different factions that don't talk to other factions, and they're in the same gang. Years ago, there was always a bridge with different factions."

Liam explained a similar phenomenon in his southern beat. "Today, the Hispanic gangs are more committed to hierarchy; they are much more organized and committed to their history. The Black gangs are more disorganized. With us having incarcerated so many of the older members we now see very, very young kids—I'm talking about thirteen, fourteen, or fifteen years old—who create their own little gangs inside the more established gangs. Some end up growing and exerting influence. They gain status by engaging in shootings. The vast majority of drive-bys and most of the violence is carried out by young guys between thirteen and eighteen years old, trying to make a name for themselves. With the Black gangs, there is often no reason for aligning with one of the established gangs or another. Now affiliation can be based on a whim that is influenced by whatever music is popular. Say Chief Keef is popular; then, a lot of the kids want to become Black Disciples.[46]

"A lot of what we see today is a departure from what we saw historically. There used to be something like a board of directors for the Black gangs. But the Black gangs are becoming increasingly flat organizations. It's a function of how small the gangs are becoming. Yes, there are historic animosities between groups such as the BDs and the GDs.[47] But that's not how conflicts are necessarily drawn today. The paper might report that there are 30,000 GDs, and the reader presumes that there are 30,000 unified members. But the truth is that some of these gang members are friends with one another, but many are not. There are 600-plus gang factions of 50 to 250 individuals, and they mostly beef with each other at a neighborhood level.

"But, in the end, money trumps everything. Some guys grow out of the gang life. A lot of guys get to their midtwenties or early thirties and begin to filter out. Some get jobs. Others get incarcerated. And those who don't get jobs or get incarcerated for too long mature into the senior leadership. These guys tend to be the smarter ones. They're harder to detect because they work as if they were running a business. They are responsible for the criminal enterprise part of the gang."

Older gang members described a pattern of splintering and creating competing groups that stemmed from greed. Renzo corroborated Liam's description of the fractionalization of Chicago gangs by describing a fracturing in his gang, Two Six. "Back in the days, you could be Chi-Town, you could be Kart, you could be K-Town, and, you know, when we were together, we wasn't showing animosity among ourselves. But things are changing now. People are changing. It's the money. Either the money's changing gangs or something's changing us that we're not as united as we used to be. Now we're setting. Now we're block cliquing. If you're not from our block, it's like, you know, 'Man, if you come at us, we're going to go at you.'" Likewise, one African American gang member, Doc, evoked the religious metaphor of the fall of Lucifer to describe the balkanization of the gangs in Chicago. "Folks and Peoples: it all started off as one. There was always one. Then you had one person that wanted more than what he was given. He wasn't satisfied. Just like God and the devil."

Underpinning this fractionalization is the inability of prison gangs to exercise their authority on the street. From the descriptions of gang life in prison I received, it became clear that in Illinois, the existing People and Folks federations—which both started as street gangs—used to exercise enough vertical control to have a say in what happened both on the street and in prison. However, once their leadership was destroyed by the state, the gang structures flattened out and focused on prison solidarity, much like the emergence of the Tangos in Texas. On the street, the street gang identity, down to the block, is the primary organizational unit. Accordingly, by the 2010s, membership in a federation appeared to be primarily a function of being incarcerated and the need for protection while incarcerated; it held little importance on the street.

Just as in Texas and Arizona, protection is important for Illinois inmates. Many former inmates felt that they had no choice but to join an inmate group, given the severe disadvantages of attempting to do one's time unaffiliated. "If you're a neutron, you got treated like crap. You got stolen from. People took your food, took your clothes. You didn't have no protection. You was on your own," Jay, a former Gangster Disciple from Chicago who was a member of the Folks when incarcerated, explained. "If me and my group of friends decided to push you around today, then we could push you around today because ain't no one going to help you and stop us."

In other words, as in other large prison systems, joining a group meant joining a "survival unit," a group that is able to attack enemies and defend against them.[48] However, unlike in California, Texas, and Arizona in previous decades, in Illinois, membership within these units does not involve a larger hierarchy that subsumes street gangs. Accordingly, there are few standing orders that come from the prisons to dictate the terms of a given faction's activities on the street. In fact, many warring groups may even be part of the same nominal gang but only reliably cooperate while incarcerated. The social control that vertical groups can exert on the streets is not a typical characteristic of horizontally organized prison gangs, meaning that while prison authorities may have more relative control in prisons, policing bodies may have to deal with more fractionalized criminal groups competing in the free world.

In Chicago, when someone is absent from the block for any protracted period of time, he is simply replaced. Tyrone, a longtime Vice Lord, described being incarcerated and being free as being distinct in terms of one's gang life and identity. "When you come to the streets like I said, it's two different worlds. N—as in the streets get money; they aren't trying to hit that shit in the jail; you're free now. It's all about survival out here." Turnover is high in Chicago gangs, and those who go to prison are often soon forgotten. When a gang member is unable to work, his standing in the gang's hierarchy is lost. When a gang member goes to prison, he likely becomes a member of a prison gang; however, that membership does not seem to result in connections and respect that endure past the point of incarceration. When released, most inmates return to their neighborhoods. If they are fortunate a spot is available for them, and they can resume their activities; unlike gang members in Texas and Arizona, they do not return to a position of greater authority on the street based on time served and status gained in prison. If no spot is available, they have to start over at the bottom of the drug trade or fade out of importance in the context of the gang.

With gangs still on the streets, the open-air markets in Chicago are alive and well. Risk is an inherent part of the job. Retailers risk getting caught by the police, getting shot by an enemy, or getting stiffed by a client. Plus, according to police and gang members alike, the retail drug trade in Chicago is highly competitive, so retailers risk losing clients if the product is not good.[49]

As a result of the risks faced, an inverse relationship develops between sellers' willingness to use violence and the value of their individual transactions. While this phenomenon was the same in El Paso and Phoenix, it was underscored in Chicago, which has more retail transactions and heavier retail competition. Although transactions are small, they represent a large part of a retail seller's earnings over the short to medium term. Retail sellers face the highest overall risk and defend their positions against potential loss, particularly loss to competitors, with proportional force. As one moves up the hierarchy, perhaps becoming a low-level wholesaler, the overall risk burden lessens, as does visibility. Given that violence is visible and that the goal for successful drug dealers, distributors, and wholesalers is to be invisible, the likelihood that violence will be deployed as a tool of conflict resolution decreases as one moves up the dealing and gang hierarchy.

The high risk of entry into the world of narcotics dealing discourages some recruits. Matteo, a violence interrupter, introduced me to a clique, which included recruits who were both young and new. Matteo remarked that should I return to the same house in four or five months, half of the kids I met that day would no longer be there; they would have returned to their prior lives, having discovered that gang life was truly not for them.

Lesson 5: The Money Generated by the Drug Trade May Be Voluminous, but Only a Few Actors Deal in Big Revenue

Gangs trade on the age-old recruitment tactic that recognizes that young boys without direction are always looking for guidance, acceptance, and status. The high risk of entry to the drug trade is acceptable to youths who consider the potential reward of status via the capital they could earn. The few successful members, invariably present in any long-lasting clique, tantalize youngsters. These youths view the drug trade as an opportunity to earn unlimited amounts of money. That very few rise through the ranks to earn big bucks is not a deterrent. Fresh recruits tend to be quite young and immature; they romanticize the drug trade and do not yet understand the gravity of the crimes they must commit to rise within it.[50] Tyrone, a Traveling Vice Lord, joined the gang when he was in the eighth grade, some twenty-five years ago. "When I joined the organization, I got a chance to get money. I got a chance to get a car, something I never really—I used to dream about cars when I was a little kid."

"How was this chance provided to you?" I asked.

"A job. I was offered a great job," Tyrone said.

"What was that job?"

"Selling narcotics."

Tyrone succinctly described the struggle to "make it," a struggle that many young people across the country face. The idea of accessing capital that would otherwise be unattainable—in addition to solidarity and comradery—is a theme that most of the current and former gang members I spoke to cited. But one does not need to be a gang member to want more than what is available: the desire to earn more money than her current ceiling motivated June to accept Lisa's offer.

Some of the young gang members I spoke to dreamed of becoming big-time pushers. Danny was a low-level gang member who had been in and out of prison several times in his young life. In Chicago, going to prison frequently made it difficult for him to move up in the street gang's hierarchy. He dreams of meeting a cartel member and possibly working for a trafficking organization so he can become rich. Nonetheless, he concedes that it is a difficult road. "I don't have the money. I've got to build my empire before I can have enough money to approach a big connect. There are a lot of middlemen, and it's hard to get around them. The middlemen are easy to find, and they could be anybody: Blacks, neutrons, Two Six, regular White guys."

The mid- and upper-level positions in a gang or distribution crew are difficult to achieve. Only the lucky few who survive or overcome the risks they face can climb from the bottom to these levels. Most gang members earn barely enough to survive, and their proceeds go directly to goods and services or to re-up their supply of product to sell.[51] The older gang members who gained those positions had measured expectations. They recognized the ceilings of realistic attainment and their good fortune not to be in prison or dead. Midlevel players such as Biggs and Renzo seemed to describe a sweet spot, a point where one is above the street level and its quotidian risk of hand-to-hand sales in open-air markets but below the gaze of law enforcement. This point involves handling middling quantities of product, decidedly less than the amounts handled by their suppliers. It was enough to earn a good living but not enough to afford a sexy or ostentatious existence that the young gang members often dream of. Just as Biggs had left the heavy traffic behind him, Renzo had no aspirations to move up from his current life. "Once you get older, it gets less appealing. You know, you start becoming slower." Renzo is trying to transition away from illicit enterprise. "I started working now. It's okay, but I guess the streets bring me more money."

Although some of the successful mid- to high-level gang members don't earn enough to need to launder their money before they can spend it, a few lucky ones make so much money that they do. Those who need to launder their money develop clear and consistent methods. Often these individuals are associated with the gangs that have the best connections, such as the Latin Kings. According to Georgina, one of the agents at the Chicago HIDTA, Hispanic gangs, generally speaking, are more likely to have the institutional knowledge required to get rid of excess funds. "The Latin Kings are business-oriented. They engage in activities like money laundering. Some of them own money services. They are married with kids but still fulfill a role for the gangs. Such individuals evolve. They go from being gang members to illicit entrepreneurs engaging in behaviors which mirror traditional organized crime. Some of these entrepreneurs who operate at the fringes of the formal economy turn legitimate over time." According to the agents, a couple of Chicago's favorite Mexican restaurants were originally fronts for the Herrera Family's network for which Margarito Flores Sr. trafficked; over time, the restaurants went straight.

Court documents show that those in the drug trade use a variety of strategies to launder money. Setting up a licit business as a front, like Georgina described, has been a long-standing, common strategy. Many of these businesses, which include barbershops, restaurants, and currency exchanges, have large cash turnovers, allowing dirty money from the street to be laundered through their registers.[52] Moreover, the veneer of legitimacy that these businesses possess allows the businesses to be leveraged for legitimate acquisition of property. For instance, the Flores twins used their barbershop and reported earnings from it as collateral for bank loans for their stash houses.[53]

Other businesses, such as meat export companies, furniture companies, and money exchangers, offer ancillary advantages. A beef export company owned by a Mexican drug trafficking organization accepted payment for more beef than was provided to restaurants that were fronts for dirty money, facilitating the bulk transfer of the proceeds of crime via trade-based money laundering.[54] The furniture company the Flores twins owned allowed them to smuggle and transport drugs in the same vehicles used to transport furniture.[55] Currency exchanges, such as those operated by Cesar Hernandez-Martinez, a man associated with the Sinaloa Federation, facilitated the changing of dirty money into clean money in other currencies; other currency exchange schemes facilitated direct payments to suppliers abroad, who preferred to be paid in their local currency.[56]

Even those whose world included only Chicago and the surrounding areas learned to diversify their interests and criminal activities. "They've gotten better at ID theft and credit card theft," explained Georgina. "They've gotten organized to commit mortgage fraud and invest in real estate, generally.[57] They've gotten better at fencing stolen products; their schemes are more sophisticated. By sophisticated, that doesn't necessarily mean that they are more technologically advanced; it's more likely the case that the criminals engage in ever more complicated behaviors. They may innovate new communication techniques that are more difficult to trace."

Indeed, the volume of sales and the bulk cash that these sales generate create specific needs in Chicago. Georgina described some of the strategies she had seen. "Being that Chicago is a cash consolidation point, those involved in the drug trade might develop complex financial transactions, such as setting up and engaging in a hawala-type system of underground money exchange. A hawala system circumvents the need to move money physically across international borders by using a system of [reciprocally acknowledged debts among] brokers to settle accounts.[58] Though this system was used by the Colombian drug trafficking organizations, where it was known as the 'Black Market Peso Exchange,' it marks a departure from the 'money smurfs' where transactions are structured, that is, broken up into small amounts [and transported physically across the border]. The hawala system eliminates the need for [and cost of] such a work-around since the money doesn't actually need to move. It results in trade-based money laundering."

Certainly, laundering via the transfer of bulk cash has been a long-standing concern of the US government; the Patriot Act criminalized bulk cash smuggling into or out of the United States in 2001.[59] Bulk cash transfer, along with wire transfers and the issuance of traveler's checks, underwrote the money laundering processes that Wachovia and HSBC facilitated in the 2000s.[60] Other reports regarding bulk cash smuggling showed that bulk cash was smuggled into Mexico and then returned to the United States in armored vehicles, avoiding declaration requirements because of a regulatory loophole for armored vehicles.[61] Notably, the Flores twins' wives, Vivianna Lopez and Valerie Gaytan, reported having rooms in their homes with millions of dollars of cash, which they would use to purchase whatever they desired, including jewelry, luxury homes, and high-end cars.[62] Court documents, however, showed that purchases were done using strawmen, indicating concerted laundering processes; Lopez and Gaytan were indicted for money laundering a few months after their husbands' release.[63]

Other schemes circumvented the need to move physical cash. The Guzmán court proceedings showed how the use of prepaid debit cards, with cash at levels beneath the mandatory reporting thresholds, allowed individuals to transport a large amount of value across the border and through ports of entry without bulk or an explicit need to report the money.[64] Another scheme included purchasing scrap gold, melting it down, and reselling it, while yet another scheme used money mules to create several bank accounts to structure electronic and physical cash transfers.[65]

Chicago's successful criminal entrepreneurs certainly used modifications of several of the strategies described by the HIDTA agents and the court documents. Journalist Mick Dumke told me that as he investigated drug rings in Chicago, he saw drug dealers reinvest their proceeds into different ventures, such as real estate, in order to launder their money and ensure that their windfalls were not squandered. Miles, the longtime Chicago police officer, noted this trend as well. "I've followed gang members now for twenty years, and I've seen them move from house to house to house, and they're getting stopped by suburban departments for some traffic violation, and I'm thinking what's bringing them out there? Real estate. They invest like any other gang; they invest their stuff in car washes, laundry mats, strip clubs. A lot of our Black gangs put money into recording studios. The investments are in businesses that help them launder their money. You never know how many cars you're washing in a car wash."

Clancy, a former commander of narcotics in the Chicago Police Department, had seen other ways of disposing funds in his time working the beat. "Some of the upper-level guys try and legitimize their money. The simplest way is, for example, I know that one guy on the street, if you had a winning lottery ticket, like the quick pick or whatever, you'd go to him, he'd pay a 10 percent more on it. So, you won $500, he'd give you $550, and then he would cash it out—'I'm the luckiest motherfucker on the planet; I keep winning these lotteries'—or they go to the casino. Some guys have legitimate businesses, tow trucking business, cash businesses, hot dog stands, restaurants."

The consistent reporting of laundering strategies by law enforcement indicates that it is an entrenched and important facet of the drug trade in Chicago. What is less clear is the capacity for local law enforcement to respond to their hunches. While the HIDTA's job is to run up the chain and follow up leads on big-time players and their large-scale laundering strategies, local police appear to be overburdened with their day-to-day affairs targeting street-level dealing and small-scale laundering activities.

Although Chicago has been used to describe sociological phenomena for the better part of the past century, what happens in Chicago in the modern drug trade is a departure from what can be seen elsewhere. The convergence of a unique street gang and prison gang development in the city, a history of immigration that has facilitated the rise of a few uncharacteristically effective traffickers over the years, a qualitatively different taste for drugs, and an evolution of violence distinct from that of El Paso and Phoenix have made Chicago, as Paulina, one of the HIDTA agents I spoke to, remarked, "its own animal."

Nonetheless, some of the lessons from Chicago are universal. What criminologist Robert K. Merton observed of the impoverished people of the Great Depression holds true: poverty breeds a will to make it by whatever means necessary.[66] The struggle to survive and succeed underpins many of the choices that individuals make, and these choices sometimes result in entry into and protracted participation in the drug trade. The stories that tell why youths join street gangs vary little across each of the cities I visited: a lack of family structure and opportunity at home, contrasted with the apparent acceptance, nurture, and economic opportunity that the streets proffer, are the fundamental basis of a gang's allure.

RESPONDING TO THE DRUG TRADE

At the heart of the drug trade are people: those who demand illicit substances and, the focus of this book, those who meet those demands. Most of the people who are involved in the drug trade are regular folks who live banal lives.[1] Many, though certainly not all, of the individuals who form the enterprises that largely buttress the drug trade are people who come from the margins of society. They are people like José, Adelita, Calista, Biggs, Renzo, and the more than sixty others whose firsthand experiences informed these pages. These individuals, like many others, failed to see a way out of their circumstances and accepted the lure of riches that the drug trade, often falsely, promised them.

Leaving the drug trade doesn't guarantee a clean exit from the struggles of the margins of society, despite one's best efforts. Some, like the harm reductionists in Juárez, manage not only to leave their chaotic lifestyles firmly in their past but also to guide others away from the dangers of diseases transmitted by sex or by needles. Others, such as Emiliano, find a niche in the licit economy. Emiliano installs air-conditioning units. It isn't the work he had trained for in prison, but it pays consistent wages. Others, such as Breeze, relapse into drug use. Breeze turned to smoking meth once again to ease the pain of his many ailments. And yet others, such as Facundo and Adelita, are gunned down in random acts of violence as they try to make the best of their second acts in life, contributing to their communities and living honestly.

But the images that emerge from media depictions and narratives spun by law enforcement do not capture the humanity and nuance of the people involved in the drug trade. Instead they demonize these people, casting them as opaque, larger-than-life villains hell-bent on destroying society in a drug horror story. Such rhetorical fearmongering—the implicit threat that Mexican drug trafficking organizations are taking over American cities—has no basis in evidence. No Mexican drug trafficking organization or street or prison gang controls any American city or even a majority of the illicit drug supply chain. Nor are hordes of unauthorized immigrants flooding the country for the sole or primary purpose of pushing dope on innocent Americans, as the seemingly infinite iterations of the alien conspiracy theory suggest.

While overdoses claim people's lives well before their time and violence occurs more often than should be tolerable, the people who are part of and touched by the drug trade are, for lack of a better word, ordinary, bound together by a struggle to survive and escape the margins of society. Thus, to respond to the most terrible outcomes of the drug trade, we, as members of the public, must understand how the business of the drug trade works, particularly within those margins. In doing so, we can demand that policymakers take the drug trade's architecture into consideration to create solutions that positively impact society.

The accounts that inform this book illustrate the humanity of the people who are and have been involved in the drug trade. The drug trade continues not because there are evil people hellbent on corrupting America but instead because American consumers consistently demand mind-altering substances.[2] The drug trade adeptly adapts to market desire, supplying demand wherever it presents. International and domestic traffickers have long supplied the American illicit drug markets as they have emerged, including those for smokable heroin, methamphetamines, and fentanyl. One certainty remains: As the demand for illicit drugs changes in the future, illicit entrepreneurs will always meet it. Pursuing the best opportunities available, illicit entrepreneurs will carve out their niches in the illicit drug supply chain of producers, international traffickers, wholesalers, distributors, and retailers or in the revenue remittance chain of collectors, transporters, and specialized money launderers, thereby ensuring that supply and payment never wane.

Accordingly, to mitigate the worst outcomes of the drug trade, those that are routinely seared into the public consciousness, we must consider the following. First, we must recognize that across the country and within both immigrant and native-born communities, the conflicts that underwrite participation in the drug trade are the same: poverty, coupled with a lack of economic opportunity; strained families; community distrust in the police; and policymakers' insistence on scapegoating and severely punishing those in the margins of society. Second, we must accept that demand—for the products sold on the part of the buyers and for better economic opportunities on the part of the sellers—drives the drug trade's market dynamics. Third, we must understand how those people drawn into the drug trade and its organizations contribute to the drug trade, navigate risk, and stay in business in the settings in which they operate.

The unique features of a given market's physical and cultural setting will often favor one group of actors or specific tactics. Consequently, while we can and should study the mechanics of supply chain and remittance chains in specific markets, we must accept that those mechanics cannot always be generalized to all markets in all settings. Further, a specific setting can also dictate an individual's ability to move up in the ranks of the drug trade and engage in different endeavors: notably, the ease of upward mobility decreases significantly as distance from the border grows. Finally, settings also influence the unfolding of activities associated with the drug trade, shaping the societies through which illegal drugs pass.

Across Paso del Norte, Phoenix, and Chicago, the drug trade functioned primarily in the margins of society, spaces that are often in flux. These places exhibit many general similarities. Each has been shaped by local context, including geography, community, governance, and availability of opportunity. These local contexts partly dictated the forces driving people to participate in the drug trade, how those people forged associations with one another, and how they prioritized certain activities over others. Notably, each city featured in these pages—Juárez, El Paso, Phoenix, and Chicago—had two purposes in the context of the drug trade: that of a staging ground for wholesale transshipment and that of a retail market. In these generalities, all four cities can be compared. However, the specific outcomes of these common generalities and the importance of these two common purposes changed markedly across the four sites, and those differences influenced business operations in each.

In Mexico, the most significant drug activity is trafficking wholesale quantities of illicit drugs. This business has made a few people extremely rich, selling a dream to many more that unimaginable riches are within reach, but the financial opportunity in local Mexican drug markets pales in comparison to the lucrative markets north of the border.

Underwriting that trafficking is protection. In the marketplace, protection is fundamental to any action, licit or illicit. In the spaces where drugs are trafficked and dealt, communities that the government cannot or does not protect are marginalized accordingly. But the need for protection remains. Thus, in Mexico and elsewhere where governance is weak, when the state fails to provide protection, criminal entrepreneurs fill the void.

Large Mexican border cities such as Juárez are valuable as points of entry to the United States that Mexican drug trafficking organizations have used gruesome violence to squeeze out their competitors and impose a protection monopoly. Since the turn of the twenty-first century, drug trafficking organizations have outsourced such violence to paramilitary-inspired groups, such as the Zetas, or gangs, such as Barrio Azteca and the Artistas Asesinos. These violent protection subcontractors, and especially gangs, formed and grew as the marginalized chased opportunity and advancement they perceived as unavailable or inaccessible in their local licit labor marketplaces.

Individuals who want to participate in the drug trade join organizations that are accessible through their social networks. In Mexico, to become a member of drug trafficking organizations, their armed branches, or affiliated gangs, an individual typically needs to be from a community where such organizations already exist or have an existing connection to a current member. Of these three organizations, gangs appear to be the easiest to enter. The only consistent requisite for street gang membership is a desire to join and some connection to the neighborhood; no special skills are required. To join a group higher up the drug trade's hierarchy requires established connections to those already involved in these groups or specific skills, such as being a trained soldier or a capable money launderer. For the notable few who join the ranks of these gangs and drug trafficking organizations in Mexico, the risk of a violent death is not enough to dissuade them from pursuing the financial opportunities these illicit enterprises appear to offer.

In Mexico, the state fails to sufficiently check or adequately respond to the criminal violence that competing drug trafficking organizations carry out. Drug trafficking organizations and the groups that act on their behalf perpetrate violence such as the massacre at the Villas de Salvárcar and everyday shootings in the proxy war in Juárez. Such violence, coupled with the state's inability to effectively confront it, generates fear and despondency among the people living in the margins. They come to understand that no matter their response, they lose. If community members report crime, they may be killed. If they keep their mouths shut they may survive, but they must live in a community blighted by the drug trade's violence. As a result, members of the affected communities feel discouraged from engaging with the police.

In addition, the police have a long history of corruption in Mexico and continue to fail to investigate and deter the violence that has come to characterize the worst of Mexico's crime. That history and ongoing failure make improving the public trust in police a difficult, long-term project. Some marginalized communities have responded by forming *autodefensas*, armed civilian organizations that claim to contest drug trafficking organizations but are also often labeled criminal actors by the state. As violence finds new theaters in Mexico, the state continues to struggle to fulfill its obligation to protect its citizens. Yet so far, the US-Mexican border has proven to be a barrier that visible large-scale violence, so frequent in Mexico, has not crossed.

Despite differences in opportunity, resources, safety, and government, border towns are bound together by their transnational populations, which develop cultural touchstones, families, and commercial interests that span the divide. These relationships are repeated within the social structures of the drug trade. As in Juárez, the few people who get into the illicit drug business in El Paso seek opportunities, such as smuggling, staging, or retailing drugs, that promise to provide wealth otherwise viewed as beyond their reach.

Though relatively few people engage in the drug trade, in El Paso no local drug dealer is far removed from a reasonably good supplier. Should a drug connection break, many local dealers can dip into their social networks, built over their lifetimes or via membership in a street or prison gang, and find a replacement with little effort. People, like Pancho, who try to go straight but fear a return to a life in the drug trade, know that such connections will always be available to them and can provide economic opportunity should the income from working legal jobs prove insufficient or unavailable. Transplants and people without the social ties that bridge the border, such as Bradley and his Gangster Disciples, face greater difficulty in replacing lost connections. People, like José, who successfully leave the drug trade, use this knowledge to their advantage, moving to places where those social ties are far away, thereby reducing the temptation to return to a life in the drug trade.

In Juárez and El Paso, retail markets are modest in terms of size and potential profit margins. Thus, most of the illicit drugs that pass through the Paso del Norte are staged only briefly before they continue onward. As the Flores twins' accounts and testimony in Joaquín Guzmán's trial indicated, as is the case across many ports of entry, the smuggling operations between Juárez and El Paso focus primarily on moving wholesale volumes of drugs from Mexico to the United States and remitting the proceeds of sales, in the form of bulk cash or other monetary instruments, from the United States to Mexico. The most visible El Paso—and Juárez-based organization, Barrio Azteca, fulfills a dual role when it sometimes smuggles wholesale quantities of heroin from Juárez into El Paso to supply its virtual monopoly of the city's retail trade. Although it remains to be seen what the impact on the retail market will be as Barrio Azteca's star dims and the Tangos gain prominence throughout Texas, the emergence of violence on El Paso's streets seems unlikely. Given the city's economic importance as a staging ground, any conflict between El Paso's prison gangs over the wholesale and retail drug trade will likely be settled largely in prison.

Successful smugglers operating in the Paso del Norte corridor will undoubtedly continue to ply their trade, albeit as quietly as possible. They will minimize their risk of capture or conflict by improving how they structure their drug shipments and stage their goods and by avoiding violence at all costs so they are less likely to be detected by law enforcement.[3] After all, the United States generally responds to large-scale violence more effectively than Mexico does. The low profiles that smugglers maintain in the United States to maximize the success of their illicit enterprises render fear of spillover violence, or the emergence of similar homegrown drug-related violence, fundamentally unfounded. In considering the threats of violence, one must remember the value that gets added to an illicit product when it passes through a check point. The biggest immediate jump in the value of illegal drugs occurs the moment they cross the US-Mexican border. Smuggling organizations prefer to maintain a steady flow of product with as little disturbance to that flow as possible. Accordingly, given the sensitivity to violent acts on the border, violence, when it must be committed on the US side of the border, occurs out of sight and with as little collateral damage as possible.

The late journalist and chronicler of border issues Charles Bowden once told me that experience had taught him that the farther a person gets from the US-Mexican border, the more difficult it becomes to find people who can assess the dangers associated with the border appropriately. Despite what vigilantes who patrol the US border, such as the groups that splintered from the defunct Minutemen Project, might claim, law enforcement responds quickly, particularly when violence is involved.[4] Charles's conclusion rang true in my experience. In El Paso, I never met locals who were afraid of encountering violence on their side of the border despite expressing concerns of being harmed while in Juárez; people in El Paso felt inherently safe and trusted the police to protect them.

Farther from the border, how the drug trade unfolds in Phoenix is affected by the city's equally important roles as transshipment point and retail market. Unlike the borderlands, where roles in the drug trade often merge, Phoenix clearly has those who attend to distribution, wholesale, and transshipment and others who attend to retail. This specialization is due in part to the decay of potential connections with wholesalers that retailers experience over space. In other words, a decreasing number of well-positioned people facilitate the wholesale trade the farther one moves from the US-Mexican border. Phoenix illustrates this phenomenon: although Phoenix is less than two hundred miles from the border, an average retailer in Phoenix finds it more difficult to find a connection to a wholesaler than does an average retailer in El Paso.

Positioned on the intersection of Interstate 10 and Interstate 17, Phoenix is an excellent transshipment point. The city's geography means that product can be easily shifted to markets east, west, and north of the city. Accordingly, Phoenix's location is a prime setting for events related to the wholesale trade, such as staging and transferring drugs to other distributors who move the product on to more lucrative markets farther away. Additionally, the prevalence of staging in Phoenix has created "rip crews," whose goal is to steal wholesale amounts of illicit drugs. Nonetheless, a significant amount of these products remains in Phoenix to feed the city's robust retail market for methamphetamines and heroin. Wholesalers supply local distributors, such as the Arizona Mexican Mafia and the Aryan Brotherhood, who in turn supply retailers who sell to retail clients. Sometimes these unlikely bedfellows work together to improve their business prospects, underscoring the truth that, for those intent on making real money in the drug trade, business is business and conflict is bad for business.

The Greater Phoenix area also demonstrates an unfortunate truth in America: the United States has many communities at the margins of its society. People within these communities not only face poverty but often have contentious relationships with the police, which undermine their trust in law enforcement. A negative relationship between community and the police deters those who live in the community from reporting crime. In my working-class, mainly Latino neighborhood in Phoenix, the police who responded to my call when I was burglarized said that my neighbors would more than likely say nothing; there was little point for the police to continue investigating.

That sentiment was common in lower-income Latino communities, such as Adelita's Guadalupe neighborhood, whose residents felt targeted by Joe Arpaio's rhetoric and aggressive policing strategies when he was Maricopa County's sheriff. Many in Guadalupe viewed the Maricopa County Sheriff's Department as overbearing and illegitimate. When communities feel that law enforcement is antithetical to their interests—or, simply, does not keep them safe—their members are less likely to call the police to resolve neighborhood crime problems. Instead, in some cases members of such communities may be more familiar with the protection offered by a street or prison gang, which might not only protect members of the community from crime committed by outsiders but also punish community members for calling law enforcement, thus widening the rift between community and law enforcement.

In addition, for many young men, such as José when he was a boy and Alyssa's son Michael, and sometimes for women such as Adelita and Calista, gangs provide a sense of community that they crave; the notion of venturing out alone is unpalatable. Ultimately, the gang helps facilitate the retail drug trade by providing both a structure for serving a market and a semblance of protection for the sellers; higher membership in the gang may distance a member from the risk that low-ranking individuals face but rising to those heights is far from certain. Nonetheless, that structure encourages those who remain in gangs to try to work their way up the hierarchy of the drug trade by any and every means available.

A community's rejection of the state's efforts to police its streets often helps trap that community in the margins of society. Such developments reflect a state that has not only failed to provide adequate and effective protection but has also allowed illicit enterprise to continue to function with lower costs of business. Guadalupe, for instance, had a long history of drug trafficking, facilitated since the 1970s by people such as Adelita's and Calista's fathers, and gang activity, such as the presence of the Arizona Mexican Mafia, within its small territory. Overcoming these feelings of distrust in marginalized communities is a struggle that law enforcement must undertake to police effectively; most police with whom I spoke clearly stated that developing good community relationships was critical to their job, which fundamentally involves protecting communities from the negative effects of illicit enterprises.

When social control, via effective policing or via the rules established by prison gangs, reduces overt, visible violence as a means to protect retail market share, criminal entrepreneurs are forced to innovate to stay in business. In many parts of Phoenix, as in El Paso, the hand-to-hand drug trade that once dominated drug sales had given way to a delivery system. Throughout the city, drivers served customers, from teenagers to college students to employed people from all walks of life. The delivery transactions diminished the need for explicit protection arrangements, since protection was built into the transaction via smoke screening and blind compartmentalization.

Through smoke screening, criminal actors protect their organizations, activities, and customer base from police and competition with implicit but largely illusive threats of violence, rather than with explicit displays of force. Smoke screening becomes even more effective when coupled with the blind compartmentalization that midlevel actors employ to ensure that their customers, if caught by the police, cannot identify them. This practice is a direct response to the past success of law enforcement agencies, such as GIITEM and the DEA, that ran up the supply chain and harvested the low-hanging fruit. Low-level players in the drug trade, once arrested, would provide information that allowed law enforcement to pursue larger players in exchange for more lenient sentences. Furthermore, smoke screening can create the illusion that a violent group is behind the transaction. Such an illusion encourages compliance with the norms of the transaction, such as how to pay and how to interact with couriers. And such an illusion ensures that the drug trade mostly continues without the need for violence, which in Phoenix, as in El Paso, is bad for business and discouraged by the prison gangs.

Violence has not been eradicated from the streets of El Paso and Phoenix and remains a threat primarily to those involved in illicit business; however, it is employed judiciously. Retaliation remains the primary reason for much of the violence that occurs on the street, be it an attack by one organization on another or an attack on thieves, such as rip crews. The role of social control, whether implemented by the state or by criminal organizations, underscores the importance of protection in determining how business in the illicit marketplace gets conducted. Simply put, violence threatens large-scale business activities, such as the staging, distribution, and wholesaling of drugs, so most illicit entrepreneurs, act-ing rationally, seek to minimize it.

In Chicago, the city's importance as a retail market dwarfs its importance as a staging ground, despite being a hub that connects product to cities farther afield. While regional small-market retailers go to Chicago to buy product from wholesalers, the demand for cocaine and heroin on the Chicago streets gener-ates significant aggregate profits for retailers. Chicago's retail market provides an organizational response that often consists of several small-scale gang cliques competing to serve customers. Unlike large-scale illicit entrepreneurs, like the Flores twins, who could use their economic clout to retaliate against bad actors and eliminate competitors, these cliques often use violence to establish primacy in a territory.

The wholesalers of Chicago are elusive to most retailers; big suppliers only do business with a small number of trusted partners, who then sell on to smaller wholesalers. Compared to their counterparts in Phoenix and El Paso, most re-tailers in Chicago receive relatively small, more adulterated quantities of drugs to resell. As is the case throughout America, while some of Chicago's small-time gang members dream of climbing the ranks and becoming kingpins, those dreams are largely abandoned by the old heads. The veterans have survived gru-eling lives making money primarily from the drug trade, and they understand that the risks of their position often outweigh the benefits. Those who have suc-cessfully climbed within the drug trade appreciate their luck in escaping the two most likely endgames: death or a long-term prison sentence.

Incarceration has clear consequences inside and outside the prison walls. In the prison setting, historically, the state has engaged in two strategies of man-aging inmates. In one strategy, common in Arizona and Texas since the 1980s, the state relinquishes control and allows inmate solidarity organizations to self-police to an extent; the state asserts only the minimum control necessary to keep prisoners within the walls and responds to only the most serious grievances. This strategy causes prisoners to feel that protection from other prisoners is neces-sary and results in the formation of solidarity groups, some of which later blos-som into prison gangs. These resulting protection rackets lead to the development of gangs that can build further criminal enterprises, such as trafficking drugs or other contraband within the prison walls and running illegal stores that sell goods to other inmates.

Moreover, as seen in the American Southwest, the protection that prisoners establish in prison can extend onto the street, which is a more dynamic setting. While the state is supposed to monopolize violence as a function of its sovereignty, in the margins of society such a monopoly does not exist. As prison gang mem-bers return to their communities, such as with Barrio Azteca in El Paso and the

Mexican Mafia in Phoenix, a new code of practice becomes normalized, and the prison gang imposes social control on the underground actors of the streets who run in the same circles. The protection that prison gangs provide comes with clearly established rules that must be followed on the street so long as those prison gangs maintain standing within the jail and the prison system. When a member of the criminal underworld violates those rules and then when that person or someone close to that person is incarcerated, prison gangs mete out punishment. The informal social control that prison gangs can impose onto street gangs has decreased violence in the streets of the American Southwest.

In the other strategy of managing inmates, common in the Illinois prison system, the state asserts control by cracking down on prisoner solidarity organizations. When the state controls the inside of prison by providing a regimented structure that does not tolerate even relatively benign prisoner solidarity organizations, much less prison gangs, whatever illicit enterprise still manages to survive within prison tends to be of the mom-and-pop variety, with only well-connected individuals fulfilling underground market demand. Plus, as seen in Chicago, the lack of informal social control imposed by prison gangs appears to have allowed the balkanization of street gangs. As the ongoing conflict among Chicago street gangs goes unchecked, violence continues to be visible in many of Chicago's poorest neighborhoods. With that violence comes police attention.

Just as in the overpoliced neighborhoods of Phoenix, members of communities with a gang presence in Chicago seemed torn in their support of the police. As Chicago's Police Accountability Task Force's final report indicated, the department has a reputation for being violent and unaccountable and for responding in ways that are against the wishes of the community. Unsurprisingly, people who live in such communities are often reluctant to report crime in their neighborhoods.[5] Thus, the state fails to provide protection and allows street gangs to compete to establish it.

Some of Chicago's street gangs aspire to become increasingly businesslike and to develop market share in the retail drug economy. They understand, just as do Mexican illicit entrepreneurs who operate within a context of ineffective policing, that by establishing protection, their illicit enterprise can build and expand. In the United States, although not always in Mexico, competitors seeking to build and expand market share often establish more violent protection schemes in markets or settings where individual drug transactions are small.

At the bottom of the supply chain, petty disputes can result in high-violence resolutions. For many of Chicago's gang members who sell from the corner, the need to defend the block is critical; losing that position means an end to—or at least an intolerable interruption of—their ability to sell product and generate their meager incomes. Street-level dealers are the least protected people in the entire supply chain. They are the most visible, making them vulnerable to arrest and rivals' attacks. They are also the most replaceable, meaning that so long as the demand to work the corner and the illusion of future wealth remain high, an organization can afford to lose any given street-level dealer, and anyone can be substituted into that unskilled role. So long as demand for illicit drugs continues, some will accept the risk that those roles pose for an opportunity to make it.

By contrast, higher up in the supply chain at the strata occupied by preeminent distributors such as the Flores twins, violence is not welcome. For most who have any significant money in the drug trade, conflict avoidance is critical. Protracted conflict provides openings to competing groups. In short, conflict equates to money lost and the potential for the enterprise to go bust or to be overtaken by competitors. If a distribution or wholesale operation were to resort to highly visible displays of violence in the United States, the resulting law enforcement attention would increase its probability of losing a large shipment or even being partly compromised.

Many drug smugglers in the United States appear to be subcontractors for the Mexican drug trafficking organizations; they pick up the product in Mexico and transport it into the United States. Consequently, these smuggling organizations depend on low profiles to avoid losing their product through contact with law enforcement.[6] Moreover, these smuggling organizations don't appear to have developed security apparatuses like the cartels of Mexico. Instead, they manage the risk of having their protection breached by limiting direct contacts, especially direct business contacts, and by keeping valuables in neighborhoods without a gang presence.[7] In the event of an unresolvable dispute, rather than retaliate with violence, well-placed illicit entrepreneurs ensure that their assailants are simply blackballed in the future.

During the five years following my fieldwork, I monitored antidrug rhetoric in the United States. I found it to be replete with claims that increasing violence was caused by foreign criminal actors—claims that run counter to almost all evidence.[8] In times when rhetoric, rather than reason, sways public opinion, we, as members of the public, must reject the persistent but unsubstantiated narrative that defines America's problem with drugs as a patriotic battle against foreign cartels and their imported gang lackeys. The war on drugs narrative argues that ruthless drug cartels and gangs associated with them are corrupting Americans with drugs. We must consider a new narrative, one that examines the marginalization, poverty, and policing failures and above all the ongoing demand for mind-altering substances that make the drug trade commercially viable. We must challenge discussions that focus on organized crime and its dangers by refocusing on the problems and societal circumstances that encourage people to take up illicit entrepreneurship.

Father Myers, the priest in Guadalupe, Arizona, is right: when studying these phenomena, we should not lose a sense of perspective. Despite the massive criminal proceeds attributed to the drug trade, the number of people involved in any given community, and particularly as a percentage of any given society at large, is quite small. Nonetheless, the actions of a few can have a disproportionate impact on a community, particularly when rhetoric amplifies the threat. So long as the problem remains misdefined, antidrug crusaders at the highest level of government will continue to promote failed war on drugs strategies that focus on curbing supply through drug crop eradication and border security.[9] These strategies fail to recognize and respond to the demand that drives the drug trade and underwrites its worst outcomes, including the ongoing tragedy of synthetic opioids, such as fentanyl, that at the end of the 2010s drove a wave of opioid overdose deaths four times higher than that of nearly twenty years earlier.

Ignoring demand and attempting to stop the drug trade via enforcement alone is a failed tactic. Occasional law enforcement successes occur: stash houses are uncovered in El Paso; gang members are arrested in Chicago; national distribution networks, such as the Flores Crew, are disbanded; and Mexican-based drug trafficking organization heads such as Guzmán are captured, extradited, and convicted. However, law enforcement is staring at an evolving business machine that learns from its past errors and strives to improve its design to better protect itself and its business interests; arrests and seizures do not impact demand. And so, the drug trade plods on; while the people who partake in it may change, their histories are eerily similar across place and time.

Meanwhile, in many countries around the world, the thinking about drug consumption and the responses to the business of illicit drugs are slowly changing. Harm reduction, which focuses on reducing the harms of drug use, is becoming more commonplace. In the places where it has been deployed, harm reduction has been shown to return good value for money, as it improves public health outcomes related to drug use and reduces drug-related street crime.[10] Decriminalized drug possession for personal use—making possession a civil rather than a criminal matter—is also gaining traction. In Portugal, decriminalization in 2001 led to "reductions in problematic use, drug-related harms and criminal justice overcrowding."[11] In Mexico, however, decriminalization in 2009 had little impact; arbitrary policing remains a significant barrier to treatment among drug users, who continue to be targets of police extortion.[12] In 2020 Oregon voters approved Measure 110 to decriminalize the possession of all drugs, becoming the first US state to do so.

Though decriminalization efforts continue to materialize slowly, marijuana legalization initiatives have been successful in a few US states, including Illinois and Arizona, and an increasing number of countries.[13] These legalization efforts have had mixed returns; some studies report outcomes similar to the efforts of harm reduction and broad decriminalization, while others report increases in crime and problematic use.[14] Moreover, how to legalize marijuana has been open to debate; the United States appears to prefer the commercialization and taxation of marijuana as a vice product like alcohol, an approach that prioritizes commercial viability over control of negative public health outcomes.[15] Though the public health and crime-related outcomes of legalization of marijuana are still matters of contention, legalization is changing the marijuana business, bringing what was once illicit trade into the folds of licit enterprise.

This transition, however, has largely missed the opportunities to involve formerly illicit entrepreneurs into the emerging licit marijuana economy. Many cannabis business licensing requirements require a clean criminal record, leaving many people convicted of crimes that were once illegal to languish at the margins of society rather than affording them the opportunity to go into a business they already know.[16] In the past, the integration of criminal actors into the formal economy reduced the presence of criminal organizations. The early twentieth-century integration of European-based gangs in Chicago and elsewhere should be revisited so that the state can better integrate people with criminal records into the licit economy. The emerging cannabis economies represent an opportunity to help the marginalized into the mainstream. But those opportunities are passing by as regulatory policies exclude those very people. Instead, even as public attitudes towards drugs soften, hard-line, zero-tolerance policing and punitive criminal sanctions, promoted in law-and-order rhetoric and criminal justice policy, continue to push those in the margins further away from mainstream society and, in so doing, afford illicit enterprises additional space in which to form and grow.

TRAINSPOTTING

I had visited my mother in Springfield, Illinois, one last time before heading out again. The train from Springfield to Chicago was crowded; I squeezed on with my bags. There were no seat assignments, so I had to sit wherever there was a free spot. Most people gave me a look that plainly said "Don't you *dare* sit next to me." Since no friendly faces appeared in the front of the car, I tried my luck farther back.

A young man was sitting next to a window, listening to his tunes. He saw me looking for a place and emphatically patted the empty seat next to him, moving his stuff to let me know it was fine to sit there. I put my bags on the overhead rack and sat down. I thanked him and made small talk. He was a laborer from St. Louis, Missouri, headed to North Dakota to work on a construction site in the oil patch. It was good money, and it could mean a better life. He had a long trip ahead of him; he would be arriving at his destination sometime the following afternoon.

After a few minutes, our conversation trailed off. He put his head next to the window to doze; I pulled my computer out to work. An hour or two went by. Suddenly I realized he was reading over my shoulder, so I glanced over.

"What is it that you're working on?" he asked me.

"Well, I study the drug trade," I told him.

His eyes perked up, and he seemed to be quite interested. He had never met someone who was working on a doctorate before, and he found it fascinating that someone could spend so much time just thinking about one subject.

"So, why did you even start working on this stuff?"

"I was frustrated about how much nonsense seems to get said in the news. I mean, what does the public actually know about how it all works? For instance, what comes into your head when I ask you about the drug cartels?"

"Heroin. Because that's what I use," my fellow traveler said, taking me on an unexpected turn. I would never have guessed, though I should have known better: the drug trade was part of ordinary life, and ordinary people form a large part of the user base. Unlike the emaciated heroin users that I had met in the shooting gallery of Juárez or seen on the streets of Phoenix, the guy seated next to me looked an ordinary laborer, big and strong. Until that point, I hadn't noticed the trail of puncture marks on his arms.

"Yeah, man, I've got some medicine. I'm trying to give it up, but it's hard. You know. You've met some junkies before, I'm sure."

I nodded.

"So, if you don't mind me asking, what kind of heroin do you do?" I asked.

"Tar."

"You never see powder?"

"Nah, man. Just the tar. That's all I ever see anymore."

"Is it hard to get?"

"No, not really. I just go to my guy, you know, and I get a fix."

"Is he a gang member?"

"Sometimes you have to go to them, but nah. I've got a guy I trust. Another White guy."

"Wow. Is it expensive? Some folks have been telling me the dope comes from Chicago and then goes back down south. I hear it's more expensive in St. Louis than up here."

"I'd say you've been told right. It's more expensive down there. Maybe two or three times as much as what I could get in Chicago. Plus, it's not as pure. I can get better stuff in Chicago."

"You get stuff in Chicago sometimes?"

"Yeah, man. I've got two hours between my trains. I can tell you right now that I've got twenty bucks in my pocket, and in that two hours I'll get some heroin and I'll be back on the train. It'll be one last time, you know, before I start the medicine. It's really hard to get stuff in North Dakota. I mean *really* hard, man. In a way, it's good that I'm going. I might finally get off this shit."

"You're not afraid to go to the 'hood to get some dope? How do they know you're not a cop?"

"I look the part, man. They know. They deal with junkies every day. And that's what I am: a junkie. They take one look at me and they know I'm no cop. I mean, look at me. I've got the marks on my arm. What cop would go through that effort?"

Our conversation moved on. We talked about other rather ordinary things for the last half hour of the journey—music, sports, Mount Rushmore—chatting away until the train pulled into Union Station.

Notes

1. HOME

1. A *handle* is typically a 1.75-liter bottle of alcohol.

2. Smith, "Paragons, Pariahs, and Pirates."

3. *Oxy* refers to oxycodone, sold, inter alia, under the brand name OxyContin, is an opioid medication used for treatment of moderate to severe pain.

4. Wilson et al., "Drug and Opioid-Involved Overdose Deaths." From 1999 to 2018, prescription and illicit opioids were involved in 446,032 deaths in the United States.

5. Linnemann, *Meth Wars*.

6. Hamilton, "Methology 101." Farmers use anhydrous ammonia to fertilize their fields. The ammonia helps restore nitrogen levels in the soil. Methamphetamine producers used anhydrous ammonia to aid in the extraction and conversion of pseudoephedrine into methamphetamine. Spilde, "Chemical Makes Anhydrous Ammonia Useless in Making Meth." The theft of anhydrous ammonia has declined in recent years due to two phenomena. First, producers learned to chemically treat the ammonia, rendering it useless in methamphetamine production. Second, there was a shift to the shake-and-bake method of methamphetamine production, which creates anhydrous ammonia via a chemical reaction.

7. Garriott, *Policing Methamphetamine*.

8. Gleicher and Reichert, *Illinois Drug Threat Assessment*, 1–27.

9. Moser, "Illinois Is in the Middle of America's Meth Belt"; Dighton, "The Festering Problem of Methamphetamine in Illinois."

10. The D.A.R.E program began in 1983 as a partnership between the Los Angeles Police Department and the Los Angeles Unified School District. D.A.R.E.'s objective is to keep kids off drugs and away from violence. The program spread to several school districts throughout the United States in the 1990s.

11. Ritalin is a trade name for methylphenidate.

12. Kinder and Walker, "Stable Force in a Storm"; Anslinger and Cooper, *Marijuana*.

13. National Public Radio, "Thirty Years of America's Drug War"; Alexander, *The New Jim Crow*.

14. Carey, *Women Drug Traffickers*; Miller, *Drug Warriors and Their Prey*.

15. Associated Press, "AP IMPACT."

16. McCoy, *The Politics of Heroin*.

17. Webb, *Dark Alliance*.

18. Scott and Marshall, *Cocaine Politics*, 66–72.

19. Webb, *Dark Alliance*; Schou, *Kill the Messenger*; Bowden, *Down by the River*; Bowden, *Murder City*.

20. Woodiwiss and Hobbs, "Organized Evil and the Atlantic Alliance Moral Panics"; Miller, *Drug Warriors and Their Prey*.

21. Alexander, *The New Jim Crow*; Blumstein and Beck, "Population Growth in US Prisons, 1980–1996."

22. Durán Martínez, *The Politics of Drug Violence*.

23. Popovich, "A Deadly Crisis"; Szalavitz, "Commentary"; Cherney, "Mexican Cartels Are Putting Mom and Pop Meth Cooks Out of Business"; Drug Enforcement

Administration, *United States*; Lippert, Cattan, and Parker, "Heroin Pushed on Chicago by Cartel Fueling Gang Murders"; Aguilar, "Central American Gang's Tentacles Reach Deep into Texas"; McKinley, "Mexican Cartels Lure American Teens as Killers."

24. Forbes, "The World's Billionaires."

25. Vulliamy, "How Will El Chapo's Recapture Affect Mexico and Narco-Trafficking?"; Ahmed, "El Chapo, Mexican Drug Kingpin, Is Extradited to U.S."; Dumke, "The Drug Warrior."

26. Heinle, Molzahn, and Shirk, *Drug Violence in Mexico*; Correa-Cabrera, *Los Zetas Inc.*; Jones, *Mexico's Illicit Drug Networks and the State Reaction*; Kan, *Cartels at War*; Calderón, Rodríguez Ferreira, and Shirk, *Drug Violence in Mexico*; Molzahn, Ríos, and Shirk, *Drug Violence in Mexico*.

27. Drug Enforcement Administration, *United States*; Drug Enforcement Administration, *2015 National Drug Threat Assessment Summary*.

28. Campbell, *Drug War Zone*; Bowden, *Murder City*; Jusidman de Bialostozky et al., "La realidad social de Ciudad Juárez"; Martínez, *The Politics of Drug Violence*.

29. Aguilar and Ura, "Border Communities Have Lower Crime Rates"; Montoya, "Cuellar."

30. Thompson, "History from Below"; Decker and Chapman, *Drug Smugglers on Drug Smuggling*; Cromwell and Olson, *Breaking and Entering*.

31. Campbell, "The Road to S.B. 1070."

32. Bourgois, *In Search of Respect*; Adler, *Wheeling and Dealing*.

33. Gundur, "Using the Internet to Recruit Respondents for Offline Interviews in Criminological Studies."

34. Shooting galleries are places where intravenous drug users can purchase and use their drugs. Often, they rely on a "doctor" to inject the drugs into their veins. The doctor is usually another drug user but one who is considered to have a steady hand, thus reducing the risk of missing the vein, a possibility that is high when a person is "dope sick," that is, feeling the effects of withdrawal.

35. Bourgois, *In Search of Respect*, 46.

36. Gang intelligence officers, known as GIs, typically work in prisons within a gang intelligence unit and seek to identify gang members and gather information on gangs and their plans.

37. Goffman, *The Presentation of Self in Everyday Life*.

38. Trammell, *Enforcing the Convict Code*.

39. Innes, *Signal Crimes*, 155.

2. THE SOUTHERN BORDER

1. Jamieson, *A Survey History of Fort Bliss, 1890–1940*.

2. Jamieson, *A Survey History of Fort Bliss*, 17.

3. US Department of Commerce, "QuickFacts Beta," 2019 data.

4. McDonald, "Why Follow the Rio Grande." In Mexico, the Rio Grande is called the Río Bravo. The river was channelized after the Convention of February 1st was signed in 1933 by both the United States and Mexico. The channeling of the river has placed the original Border Patrol station on the Mexican side of the international border and in the present day has left the river nearly dry, rendering it neither grand nor bravo.

5. Castro, *Chicano Folklore*, 177.

6. *Total Recall* (1990) is a sci-fi movie directed by Paul Verhoeven and starring Arnold Schwarzenegger, Rachel Ticotin, and Sharon Stone.

7. United Nations Statistics Division, "City Population by Sex, City and City Type," 2020 data.

8. Young et al., *The Social Ecology and Economic Development of Ciudad Juárez*, chap. 1.

9. Neumayer, "Unequal Access to Foreign Spaces."

3. IMMIGRATION COURT

1. Cohen, *Folk Devils and Moral Panics*.

2. Hatjoullis, "Schrödinger's Immigrant."

3. Smith, *The Mafia Mystique*.

4. Lacy and Odem, "Popular Attitudes and Public Policies," 143–44.

5. Combs and Nicholas, "The Effect of Arizona Language Policies on Arizona Indigenous Students"; Macedo, "The Colonialism of the English Only Movement"; Chin et al., "A Legal Labyrinth"; Stumpf, "Crimmigation, Surveillance and Security Threats."

6. Tinessa, "Marginados, minorías e inmigrantes"; Welch, *Detained*; Harris and Gruenewald, "News Media Trends in the Framing of Immigration and Crime, 1990–2013."

7. Kanstroom, "Criminalizing the Undocumented"; Smith, *Illegal Immigration*.

8. Addady, "Donald Trump's Immigration Reform May Be Less Severe Than We Thought"; Geisler, "Accumulating Insecurity among Illegal Immigrants"; Hickman and Suttorp, "Are Deportable Aliens a Unique Threat to Public Safety?"

9. McNevin, *Contesting Citizenship*, 56–57.

10. Chicken Little, also known as Henny Penny, is a character in folk tale that warns against mass hysteria. The protagonist warns those around him that "the sky is falling," thinking that the world is coming to an end. He is wrong.

11. The relevant regulation is Public Access to Hearings, 8 C.F.R. § 1003.27 (2021); this regulation appears not to have been updated since 2002. See also Executive Office for Immigration Review, *The Immigration Court Practice Manual*.

12. United States Courts, "Visit a Federal Court."

13. Respondents in immigration cases are sometimes detained, depending on how they were apprehended or what prior offenses their records contain. Often, they are held in custody until they appear before an immigration court also appear on a different docket, and security associated with these detained respondents is heightened, making it difficult for the public to access and report on immigration proceedings in such detained settings.

14. I observed sixteen judges in six different courts: El Paso, Texas (detained and nondetained); San Antonio, Texas; Phoenix, Arizona; Eloy, Arizona; and Denver, Colorado. I spent over one hundred hours observing across all the courts and observed as many of the judges as possible; some were on leave during the times that I visited. Most of the hearings I observed were master calendar hearings and bond hearings. I did observe a few special dockets: one that involved people who were remotely detained, another that involved men who were about to finish their criminal sentences, one that featured unaccompanied minors, and a docket that involved women and their children. In total, I observed hundreds of master calendar hearings, dozens of bond hearings, and three asylum hearings; however, I was not privy to the final decisions. I managed to have a few informal chats with the judges after the dockets were over, since they could not talk to me in the context of a formal interview. Occasionally I chatted with government attorneys, who would offer some brief insight concerning their work. I met and talked with several immigration attorneys but only interviewed four of them formally, since they lacked knowledge about the kinds of criminal actors I was interested in.

15. Goldstein and Eggen, "Immigration Judges Often Picked Based on GOP Ties." Prior to 2008, immigration judges were generally appointed without public competition for the position. Appointments were often based on political ties, without regard to past immigration law experience. Guadalupe Gonzalez, who was the top government immigration attorney in El Paso, was appointed to the bench in 2010. However, she had been

passed over on several occasions for lesser-qualified candidates. She sued the US attorney general, and a US District Court judge, Emmet G. Sullivan, determined that Gonzalez had demonstrated that there had been a pattern of discrimination. Both men appointed to the bench before her, Robert Hough and Thomas Roepke, had less experience than Gonzalez at the time of their appointments in 2006. As a result of the ruling, "immigration judges are considered civil service employees who may not be chosen based on political factors, unlike judges in federal criminal courts."

Notably, when immigration attorneys expressed disdain for any particular judge, Roepke was the usual target, as he seldom granted asylum and was seen as a political appointee. In my conversations with immigration attorneys, judges were deemed "good" if they had better asylum approval rates. Nonetheless, from what I observed, due process was taken seriously by all judges; no judge wants his or her cases to be overturned with any degree of frequency. Moreover, Roepke's high rejection rate can be explained in part by his handling of a docket of convicted felons, who have little relief available to them.

16. Villazor and Johnson, "The Trump Administration and the War on Immigration Diversity"; Pierce, Bolter, and Selee, "US Immigration Policy under Trump."

17. Keith, Holmes, and Miller, "Explaining the Divergence in Asylum Grant Rates among Immigration Judges."

18. Family, "The Future Relief of Immigration Law," 393.

19. Schmidt, "An Overview and Critique of US Immigration and Asylum Policies in the Trump Era."

20. Miroff and Van Houten, "The Border Is Tougher to Cross Than Ever."

21. Dudley, *MS-13*, 238–41.

22. Hernández, *Los señores del narco*; Ravelo, *El narco en México*.

23. Applicants' claims must be made on specific grounds and evidence; claimants must establish that they face assured harm based on someone hating their race, religion, political opinion (defined broadly as anything to do with governance), nationality, or membership to a specific social group. While all of these requirements seem straightforward, in the eyes of the law proving these cases is not.

24. US Department of Homeland Security, *Independent Review of U.S. Customs and Border Protection's Reporting of FY 2013 Drug Control Performance Summary Report*. "'Turnbacks' are defined as, 'A subject who, after making an illegal entry into the US, returns to the country from which he/she entered, not resulting in an apprehension or gotaway [an escape].'"

25. Within the immigration court if a government attorney can show that there is reason to believe that a respondent is either a drug trafficker or a money launderer, the respondent can be denied relief. According to one judge in the El Paso court, the "reason to believe money laundering" charge is never pursued by Homeland Security attorneys.

26. Shoichet, "Mexico's 'Queen of the Pacific' Pleads Guilty in U.S. Drug Case"; Franklin, "Queen of Cartels." Sandra Ávila Beltrán pleaded guilty to being an accessory after the fact in aiding cocaine traffickers in the United States and was convicted on money laundering charges in Mexico.

27. Ávila Beltrán would have been fifty-three at that time.

28. ICE Newsroom, "ICE Deports Sandra Avila Beltran."

29. Shoichet, "Mexico's 'Queen of the Pacific' Pleads Guilty in U.S. Drug Case."

30. Schmidt, "An Overview and Critique of US Immigration and Asylum Policies in the Trump Era," 96. The legal grounds for withholding of removal are the same as for political asylum; however, it is harder to qualify for withholding of removal because applicants must show a clear probability of future persecution if they were to be returned to their country of origin. The test is objective and requires very convincing evidence including country reports, suggesting that it is more likely than not that the applicant

would be persecuted. The Trump administration narrowed the scope for persecution claims, making it increasingly difficult to have asylum, withholding of removal, and CAT claims granted in immigration courts.

31. *Ramirez-Peyro v. Holder*, 574 F.3d 893, 900-01 (8th Cir. 2009).

32. Olate et al., "Evidence-Based Community Interventions for Tackling the Problems of Youth Gang Violence and Delinquency in Central America." Barrio 18 is also referred to as the 18th Street Gang, Calle 18, Mara 18, and La 18. Barrio 18 is the name most commonly used in a Hispanophone context, whereas 18th Street Gang is the most commonly used in an Anglophone context.

33. Manwaring, *A Contemporary Challenge to State Sovereignty*; Manwaring, "Security, Stability and Sovereignty Challenges of Politicized Gangs and Insurgents in the Americas"; Wolf, "Mara Salvatrucha"; Fontes, "Beyond the Maras"; Fontes, *Mortal Doubt*.

34. Barak, León, and Maguire, "Conceptual and Empirical Obstacles in Defining MS-13."

35. Barak, León, and Maguire, "Conceptual and Empirical Obstacles in Defining MS-13."

36. Stumpf, "Crimmigation, Surveillance and Security Threats"; Provine et al., *Policing Immigrants*.

37. Van Koppen et al., "Criminal Trajectories in Organized Crime"; Van Koppen, de Poot, and Blokland, "Comparing Criminal Careers of Organized Crime Offenders and General Offenders."

38. Street, Zepeda-Millán, and Jones-Correa, "Mass Deportations and the Future of Latino Partisanship"; Kretsedemas and Brotherton, *Immigration Policy in the Age of Punishment*.

39. Diaz-Cayeros and Magaloni, "Party Dominance and the Logic of Electoral Design in Mexico's Transition to Democracy."

40. Ainslie, *The Fight to Save Juárez*, 180–195.

41. US Department of State, "Mexico Travel Warning."

4. THE SANTA FE STREET BRIDGE

1. Crowley, "The Committee to Save Mexico."

2. Moreno, "Enrique Peña Nieto's TIME Cover Sparks Outrage in Mexico"; Hernández, "Las autodefensas contra el narcotráfico en México"; Phillips, "Inequality and the Emergence of Vigilante Organizations."

3. Gagne, "'El Mayo,' the Unsung Leader of Mexico's Sinaloa Cartel"; Phillips, "Inequality and the Emergence of Vigilante Organizations."

4. This question has persisted. In 2019, former Mexican secretary of public security Genaro García Luna, who served under President Felipe Calderón from 2006 to 2012, was arrested and charged in the United States for assisting the Sinaloa Federation in its efforts to smuggle drugs into the United States in exchange for millions of dollars in cash.

5. Ahmed and Archibold, "Mexican Drug Kingpin, El Chapo, Escapes Prison through Tunnel."

6. Vulliamy, *Amexica*.

7. Shirk, *Drug Violence in Mexico*; Calderón, Rodríguez Ferreira, and Shirk, *Drug Violence in Mexico*.

8. Aguilar, "El Paso Ranked Safest City in U.S. for 3rd Straight Year."

9. Lawrence Karson, *American Smuggling as White Collar Crime*; Campbell, *Drug War Zone*. The Paso del Norte is the El Paso/Juárez metropolitan area.

10. Gorbea, "Mexico's Tiny Minimum Wage is about to Increase—by Almost Nothing."

11. Cepeda and Nowotny, "A Border Context of Violence."

12. Staff and Agencies in Washington, "US Supreme Court Upholds Policy of Making Asylum Seekers Wait in Mexico."

5. BUSINESS AS USUAL

1. Shirk, Wood, and Olson, eds., *Building Resilient Communities in Mexico.*

2. Henderson, *In the Absence of Don Porfirio*; Branch and Rowe, "The Mexican Constitution of 1917 Compared with the Constitution of 1857"; Yllanes Ramos, "Social Rights Enshrined in the Mexican Constitution of 1917."

3. Bailey, "Revisionism and the Recent Historiography of the Mexican Revolution."

4. Diaz-Cayeros and Magaloni, "Party Dominance and the Logic of Electoral Design in Mexico's Transition to Democracy."

5. Magaloni, "The Demise of Mexico's One-Party Dominant Regime."

6. Celaya Pacheco, "Narcofearance"; Weber, *The Theory of Social and Economic Organization.*

7. Frye and Zhuravskaya, "Rackets, Regulation, and the Rule of Law."

8. Tilly, "War Making and State Making as Organized Crime"; Black, "Crime as Social Control"; Varese, "How Mafias Migrate."

9. Varese, "How Mafias Migrate," 412.

10. Krasner, *Sovereignty.*

11. Ruggie, *Constructing the World Polity*, 47.

12. Tilly, "War Making and State Making as Organized Crime," 169.

13. Snyder and Durán Martínez, "Drugs, Violence, and State-Sponsored Protection Rackets in Mexico and Colombia."

14. Tilly, "War Making and State Making as Organized Crime," 170.

15. Magaloni, "The Demise of Mexico's One-Party Dominant Regime."

16. Snyder and Durán Martínez, "Drugs, Violence, and State-Sponsored Protection Rackets in Mexico and Colombia"; O'Neil, "The Real War in Mexico"; Durán Martínez, *The Politics of Drug Violence.*

17. Lupsha, "Drug Lords and Narco-Corruption."

18. Velasco, "Drogas, seguridad y cambio político en México."

19. Thomson, "State Sovereignty in International Relations."

20. Snyder and Durán Martínez, "Drugs, Violence, and State-Sponsored Protection Rackets in Mexico and Colombia"; Patenostro, "Mexico as a Narco-Democracy."

21. Jones, *Mexico's Illicit Drug Networks and the State Reaction*; Reuter, "Systemic Violence in Drug Markets."

22. Lupsha, "Drug Lords and Narco-Corruption," 47.

23. Grayson, *Mexico.*

24. Durán Martínez, *The Politics of Drug Violence*, 65–110.

25. Martínez, *The Politics of Drug Violence*; Ainslie, *The Fight to Save Juárez.*

26. Fukuyama, "What Is Governance?"

27. Krozer and Moreno-Brid, "Inequality in Mexico"; Chabat, "Mexico's War on Drugs."

28. Klesner, "Review: An Electoral Route to Democracy?"

29. Snyder and Durán Martínez, "Drugs, Violence, and State-Sponsored Protection Rackets in Mexico and Colombia."

30. Gambetta, *The Sicilian Mafia*; Reuter, *Disorganized Crime*, chap. 7.

31. Hernández, *Los señores del narco.*

32. Jones, *Mexico's Illicit Drug Networks and the State Reaction*; Shortland and Varese, "State-Building, Informal Governance and Organised Crime"; Astorga, *El siglo de las drogas.*

33. Tilly, "War Making and State Making as Organized Crime," 170.

34. Fukuyama, "What Is Governance?," 3.

35. Kan, *Cartels at War.*

36. Correa-Cabrera, *Los Zetas Inc.*

37. Grillo, *El Narco.*

38. Sabet, "Corruption or Insecurity?"; Lupsha, "Drug Lords and Narco-Corruption"; Nagle, "Corruption of Politicians, Law Enforcement, and the Judiciary in Mexico and Complicity across the Border."

39. Lupsha, "Drug Lords and Narco-Corruption."

40. Poppa, *Drug Lord.*

41. See Comas, "Detenido el 'zar del narcotráfico' del norte de México." Gilberto "El Greñas" Ontiveros Lucero earned his nickname for his disheveled hair. Like Rafael Caro Quintero, another well-known Juárez-based drug kingpin, and late Colombian kingpin Pablo Escobar, El Greñas was known for his opulent yet philanthropic spending. In 1986 he was arrested and convicted for the kidnapping and torture of Al Gutiérrez, who worked for the now-defunct *El Paso Herald-Post* newspaper.

42. A *casa de cambio* is a money exchange, common in Mexican border towns where there is a lot of demand to exchange dollars for pesos and vice versa.

43. A *gabacho* is a white American.

44. *Cuota* is a tax to be paid to the individuals who controlled the territory in order to conduct illicit business within it.

45. Poppa, *Drug Lord.*

46. Ravelo, *El narco en México.*

47. Miller, "Suspected Drug Lord Shot to Death at Mexican Resort."

48. Ravelo, *El narco en México*; Hernández, *Los señores del narco.*

49. Hernández, *Los señores del narco.*

50. Poppa, *Drug Lord,* 306.

51. Durán Martínez, *The Politics of Drug Violence.*

52. Rodríguez Castañeda, *El México narco.*

53. Hernández, *Los señores del narco*; Campbell, *Drug War Zone.*

54. Astorga, *El siglo de las drogas.*

55. Campbell, *Drug War Zone.*

56. Black, "The Geometry of Terrorism," 15.

57. Kan, *Cartels at War.*

58. Hernández, *Los señores del narco*; Ravelo, *El narco en México.*

59. Correa-Cabrera, *Los Zetas Inc.*

60. Gambetta, *Codes of the Underworld.*

61. Kan, *Cartels at War*; Hernández, *Los señores del narco.*

62. Andreas, "The Political Economy of Narco-Corruption in Mexico."

63. Hernández, "Las autodefensas contra el narcotráfico en México."

64. José Armando Rodríguez Carreón was murdered on November 13, 2008, at his house in front of his daughter. His murder went unsolved for many years. The chief federal investigator looking into Rodríguez's death was also murdered, as was his replacement. Some officials have indicated that the man responsible for the killing was José Antonio "El Diego" Acosta Hernández, who was the leader of La Línea, the enforcement arm of the Juárez Cartel, at the time of the killings. Acosta Hernández is now serving life in prison in the United States. The only man convicted in the case is Juan Alfredo "El Arnold" Soto Arias, who was a leader of Los Linces, a hit squad that operated for the Juárez Cartel.

65. México Evalúa, "Índice de inseguridad ciudadana y violencia."

66. Witte, *Undeniable Atrocities.*

67. INEGI, *Encuesta nacional de seguridad pública urbana*; INEGI, *Encuesta nacional de victimización y percepción sobre seguridad pública*.

68. Innes, *Signal Crimes*.

69. Dresser, "Mexico after the July 6 Election."

70. Black, "Crime as Social Control."

6. FATHER AND SON

1. Substance Abuse and Mental Health Services Administration, *Key Substance Use and Mental Health Indicators in the United States*. In 2019, according to the National Center for Drug Abuse Statistics, 20.4 million people in the United States age twelve or older had a substance abuse disorder: 12.1 million people had an alcohol use disorder. 5.9 million had an illegal drug disorder, and 2.4 million people suffered from both.

2. I was introduced to José "Raulio" Rivera Fierro (1959–2017) by the late Charles "Chuck" Bowden (1945–2014), or, rather, Chuck gave José my phone number, and José called me one day out of the blue. I volunteered to work on a memoir manuscript that José (the name that he preferred at the time) had written and sent to Chuck after hearing him on National Public Radio speaking about the violence in Juárez. The content of this section is largely based on the manuscript José has written and the three interviews I conducted with him in person, which were undertaken to flesh out the creation story of Barrio Azteca.

The origins of Barrio Azteca, like the origins of many gangs, are murky. Limited information is available in various corners of the Internet; some printed resources echo what is available online. The history that is commonly rehearsed has some elements, such as dates, that seem reasonable. José is credited in these accounts as one of a handful of Barrio Azteca's founders; however, his nickname "Raulio" is always misidentified as "Rabillo."

Shortly before Chuck died in the fall of 2014, he told me that he had looked into José's prison records and that José was as billed. José's account of prison life is consistent with the few articles that have been published regarding the events that occurred while he was in prison that led to the development of Barrio Azteca, with dates being very close to the published accounts though often differing by one or two years. Consequently, the dates in this section should be considered approximate.

3. Hampton and Ontiveros, *Copper Stain*.

4. Robins, "A Follow-Up Study of Vietnam Veterans' Drug Use."

5. Kirk, *A Historical Review of Gangs and Gang Violence in El Paso, Texas*.

6. Güero was José's friend and fellow street gang member. Together, they committed several crimes.

7. The H. H. Coffield Unit, established in 1965, is the largest Texas Department of Criminal Justice prison for men. It houses prisoners classified at all prison custody levels and has an administrative segregation unit and an outside trusty program.

8. Gundur, "Negotiating Violence and Protection in Prison and on the Outside."

9. *La malia*, or dope sickness, refers to the withdrawal symptoms from suddenly stopping the use of heroin.

10. Emiliano is a pseudonym.

11. Pager, *Marked*.

7. LA CARRUCHA

1. Selby, "Rick Perry Says Violence from Mexico Reaching El Paso, with Bullets Flying and Bombs Exploding"; O'Rourke, "Cornyn Says Spillover Violence in Texas Is Real and Escalating."

2. The HIDTA is a law enforcement organizational unit created by the Anti-Drug Abuse Act of 1988.

3. Grillo, *El Narco*; Borunda, "Birthday Party Attack Directed by Cartel, Gang."

4. Lacey and Thompson, "Two Drug Slayings in Mexico Rock U.S. Consulate."

5. Federal Bureau of Investigation, "Barrio Azteca Lieutenant Who Ordered the Consulate Murders in Ciudad Juarez Sentenced to Life in Prison."

6. Rodríguez Nieto, *The Story of Vicente, Who Murdered His Mother, His Father, and His Sister*.

7. Ralph and Marquart, "Gang Violence in Texas Prisons"; DiIulio, *Governing Prisons*; Campbell, "Politics, Prisons, and Law Enforcement."

8. Horton, and Nielsen, *Walking George*; Alpert, Crouch, and Huff, "Prison Reform by Judicial Decree."

9. Horton and Nielsen, *Walking George*; DiIulio, *Governing Prisons*.

10. DiIulio, *Governing Prisons*.

11. Reavis, "How They Ruined Our Prisons"; Ralph and Marquart, "Gang Violence in Texas Prisons"; Marquart and Crouch, "Judicial Reform and Prisoner Control."

12. Campbell, "Politics, Prisons, and Law Enforcement"; Horton and Nielsen, *Walking George*; Ekland-Olson, "Crowding, Social Control, and Prison Violence."

13. Marquart and Crouch, "Coopting the Kept."

14. Fong, "The Organizational Structure of Prison Gangs."

15. Ralph and Marquart, "Gang Violence in Texas Prisons"; Reavis, "How They Ruined Our Prisons."

16. DiIulio, *Governing Prisons*, 53.

17. Alpert, Crouch, and Huff, "Prison Reform by Judicial Decree," 297.

18. Fong, "The Organizational Structure of Prison Gangs"; Pelz, Marquart, and Pelz, "Right-Wing Extremism in the Texas Prisons"; Ekland-Olson, "Crowding, Social Control, and Prison Violence."

19. Ralph and Marquart, "Gang Violence in Texas Prisons"; Fong and Buentello, "The Detection of Prison Gang Development."

20. "Ike and Mike" rhymes with "spike" and indicates an attempt to convince a person to have sex.

21. Alpert, Crouch, and Huff, "Prison Reform by Judicial Decree," 292.

22. *Ruiz v. Estelle, 503 F. Supp. 1265* (S.D. Tex. 1980); DiIulio, *Governing Prisons*.

23. Alpert, Crouch, and Huff, "Prison Reform by Judicial Decree," 295.

24. Marquart and Crouch, "Judicial Reform and Prisoner Control"; Justice, "Consent Decree in the Matter of Ruiz v. Estelle, Jr."; Ekland-Olson, "Crowding, Social Control, and Prison Violence."

25. Ekland-Olson, "Crowding, Social Control, and Prison Violence."

26. Alpert, Crouch, and Huff, "Prison Reform by Judicial Decree"; Ekland-Olson, "Crowding, Social Control, and Prison Violence."

27. DiIulio, *Governing Prisons*; Horton and Nielsen, *Walking George*; Pelz et al., "Right-Wing Extremism in the Texas Prisons."

28. Ekland-Olson, "Crowding, Social Control, and Prison Violence," 392.

29. Burman, "Resocializing and Repairing Homies within the Texas Prison System."

30. Fong, "The Organizational Structure of Prison Gangs," 37.

31. Fong, "The Organizational Structure of Prison Gangs," 38.

32. Irwin, *Prisons in Turmoil*, 74.

33. Fong, "The Organizational Structure of Prison Gangs," 36.

34. Fleisher and Decker, "An Overview of the Challenge of Prison Gangs."

35. Texas Department of Public Safety, *Texas Gangs*; Weide, "The Invisible Hand of the State"; Fischer, *Arizona Department of Corrections*.

36. Marquart and Crouch, "Coopting the Kept," 579.

37. Ralph and Marquart, "Gang Violence in Texas Prisons"; Fong and Buentello, "The Detection of Prison Gang Development."

38. The Darrington Unit, established in 1917, is a Texas Department of Criminal Justice prison for men located in unincorporated Brazoria County, Texas, just south of Houston. Like the Coffield Unit, Darrington houses inmates classified at all prison custody levels.

39. Fleisher and Decker, "An Overview of the Challenge of Prison Gangs."

40. Fong, "The Organizational Structure of Prison Gangs."

41. "Let's start our own ride [gang]. What do you think? Everyone is there."

42. "It wouldn't be bad, Raulio. Let's have a meeting in the yard this evening with our people and talk it over."

43. Nye, *Soft Power*.

44. Pyrooz and Decker, *Competing for Control*; Lopez-Aguado, *Stick Together and Come Back Home*.

45. *Paisa* is a bastardization of the Spanish term *paisano*, meaning "countryman." Though it is often used to mean Mexican national, it can refer to any native Spanish-speaking, non-US born Latino.

46. Calderón, Rodríguez Ferreira, and Shirk, *Drug Violence in Mexico*; Heinle, Molzahn, and Shirk, *Drug Violence in Mexico*.

47. Newcomb, "Immigration Law and the Criminal Alien"; Texas Department of Public Safety, *Texas Gangs*; Texas Department of Public Safety, *Texas Gang Threat Assessment, 2015*.

48. "Put the word out that there are not going to be anymore drive-bys. The next guy who goes down for a drive-by, kick his ass."

49. Ortiz Uribe, "Barrio Azteca Gang Shows How Crime Transcends Borders."

50. *Jacketing* is a concept that the gang members adopted from the prison administrators whereby an inmate would be jacketed if he were to have a negative history recorded in his official file. Fleisher and Decker, "An Overview of the Challenge of Prison Gangs"; Hunt et al., "Changes in Prison Culture."

51. *Kite* is the general term for this means of communication, with *wila* (also spelled *huila* and *güila*) being the term used specifically by Latino gangs. A kite takes its name from its original physical form. It was a note that had a string attached to it. An inmate would try to land the note within reach of his target, but the string was there so that in the event the initial placement failed, he could pull the note back and try again. This strategy ensured that information communicated would not easily fall in the hands of the guards should the note fail to reach its intended destination. Both terms have come to mean a form of communication between gang members in prison or between prison and the free world.

52. Ortiz Uribe, "Barrio Azteca Gang Shows How Crime Transcends Borders"; O'Neill, "The Reckless Will."

53. Gundur, "The Changing Social Organization of Prison Protection Markets."

54. Pyrooz and Decker, *Competing for Control*.

55. Skarbek, "Prison Gangs, Norms, and Organizations"; Pyrooz and Decker, *Competing for Control*.

56. Skarbek, *The Social Order of the Underworld*; Jacobs, "Race Relations and the Prisoner Subculture."

57. Skarbek, *The Social Order of the Underworld*; Tapia, Sparks, and Miller, "Texas Latino Prison Gangs"; Wacquant, *Las cárceles de la miseria*; Marquart and Crouch, "Coopting the Kept"; Lopez-Aguado, *Stick Together and Come Back Home*.

58. Pyrooz and Decker, *Competing for Control*.

59. Skarbek, *The Social Order of the Underworld*.

60. To have someone's *esquina* means to have someone's back. It comes from the idea that you cannot be easily attacked from behind if you are fighting in a corner.

61. Intermediate Sanction Facility. The facility is "an in-custody treatment alternative for medium to high-risk felony offenders in Texas who are facing probation or parole revocations." Varghese, "ISF."

62. Brendel, "Who Is 'West Texas?'"

63. Gundur, "The Changing Social Organization of Prison Protection Markets."

64. Lauderdale and Burman, "Contemporary Patterns of Female Gangs in Correctional Settings."

65. Brownsville is in southern Texas, right on the border. "West Texas" is a clique that rolls any town that fails to associate with one of the other cliques. Most of these towns are in West Texas, however, hence the name.

66. Pyrooz and Decker, *Competing for Control*.

67. Texas Department of Public Safety, *Texas Gang Threat Assessment, 2018*; Gundur, "Negotiating Violence and Protection in Prison and on the Outside."

68. Tapia, "Texas Latino Gangs and Large Urban Jails"; Tapia, Sparks, and Miller, "Texas Latino Prison Gangs"; Pyrooz and Decker, *Competing for Control*.

69. Texas Department of Public Safety, *Threat Assessment 2018*; Vijayan, "Monterey County Charges Northern Riders as a Gang for the First Time in State." An analogue to the Tangos called the Northern Riders exists in the California prison system. It's a gang that initially was formed by former gang members of the Norteño coalition who did not wish to abide by obligations imposed by the Nuestra Familia prison gang.

70. Texas Department of Public Safety, *Threat Assessment 2018*.

71. Simon, "The 'Society of Captives' in the Era of Hyper-Incarceration," 301.

72. Texas Department of Public Safety, *Threat Assessment 2018*.

73. Hunt et al., "Changes in Prison Culture."

74. *Cora*, short for *corazón* (heart) is a term that means "prospect" and is used by several Latino prison gangs including Barrio Azteca. The phrase translates to "Do you want to be a prospect?"

75. The numerals 2 and 1 represent the letters B and A, respectively, indicating the wearer's membership in Barrio Azteca.

76. Skarbek, *The Social Order of the Underworld*.

77. Texas Department of Public Safety, *Threat Assessment 2015*; Texas Department of Public Safety, *Texas Gangs*.

78. Texas Department of Public Safety, *Threat Assessment 2018*.

79. Texas Department of Criminal Justice, *Statistical Report*.

80. Gundur, "Negotiating Violence and Protection in Prison and on the Outside."

81. Campbell, *Drug War Zone*; Campbell, "Drug Trafficking Stories."

82. Felson, *The Ecosystem for Organized Crime*.

83. Wolf, "Maras transnacionales"; Ward, *Gangsters without Borders*; Zilberg, *Space of Detention*; Fontes, *Mortal Doubt*; Barak, León, and Maguire, "Conceptual and Empirical Obstacles in Defining MS-13."

84. Sullivan, "The Barrio Azteca, Los Aztecas Network"; Gundur, "Negotiating Violence and Protection in Prison and on the Outside."

85. Wolff, "Violence and Criminal Order"; Rodríguez Nieto, *The Story of Vicente*.

86. Human Rights Watch, *World Report*.

87. Wolff, "Violence and Criminal Order"; Rodríguez Nieto, *The Story of Vicente*; Ortiz Uribe, "Eating Ice Cream with a Gangster in Jail."

88. Martínez Ahrens, "El narco impone su ley en la mitad de las cárceles mexicanas"; Wolff, "Violence and Criminal Order"; Ortiz Uribe, "Eating Ice Cream with a Gangster in Jail"; Grillo, *El Narco*.

89. Rodríguez Nieto, *The Story of Vicente*; Grillo, *El Narco*; Borunda, "Prison Violence Kills 20 in Juárez."

90. Ortiz Uribe, "Eating Ice Cream with a Gangster in Jail"; Rodríguez Nieto, *The Story of Vicente*; Ainslie, *The Fight to Save Juárez*.

91. Ortiz Uribe, "Eating Ice Cream with a Gangster in Jail"; Texas Department of Public Safety, *Threat Assessment 2018*.

8. VIOLENCE

1. Correa-Cabrera, *Los Zetas Inc.*; Jones, *Mexico's Illicit Drug Networks and the State Reaction*, 21.

2. Ainslie, *The Fight to Save Juárez*.

3. Correa-Cabrera, *Los Zetas Inc.*

4. Grayson and Logan, *The Executioner's Men*.

5. Jones, *Mexico's Illicit Drug Networks and the State Reaction*.

6. Klein and Maxson, *Street Gang Patterns and Policies*, 176–77.

7. Hazen and Rodgers, *Global Gangs*; Jones, "Understanding and Addressing Youth in 'Gangs' in Mexico," 8.

8. Gundur, "Negotiating Violence and Protection in Prison and on the Outside."

9. Klein and Maxson, *Street Gang Patterns and Policies*, 177.

10. Klein and Maxson, *Street Gang Patterns and Policies*, 178.

11. Durán Martínez, "Drugs around the Corner."

12. Manwaring, "Security, Stability and Sovereignty Challenges of Politicized Gangs and Insurgents in the Americas"; Manwaring, *A Contemporary Challenge to State Sovereignty*.

13. "Soldiers" are gang members.

14. Calderón, Rodríguez Ferreira, and Shirk, *Drug Violence in Mexico*; Heinle, Molzahn, and Shirk, *Drug Violence in Mexico*.

15. Transparency International, "Mexico, Corruption by Country/Territory."

16. Witte, *Undeniable Atrocities*.

17. For example, in Italy, the anti-Mafia proceedings led to the murders of many antimafia actors, including Judges Giovanni Falcone and Paolo Borsellino. The actions were an attempt to halt the anti-Mafia efforts by intimidating any survivors. Nonetheless, the violence ultimately resulted in the promulgation of various antimafia measures. Paoli, *Mafia Brotherhoods*.

18. Daugherty, "Explaining Mexico's Decision to Extradite Alleged Drug Lords."

19. Doing something "underwater" means to act in a manner that does not draw attention.

20. "Heat" is law enforcement attention.

21. Durán Martínez, "Drugs around the Corner"; Magaloni et al., "Living in Fear."

22. Castillo, "Should Drug Policy be Aimed against Cartel Leaders?"

23. Texas Department of Public Safety, *Texas Gang Threat Assessment, 2014*.

24. Varandani, "Who Is Jesus Salas Aguayo?"

25. Martinez, "Barrio Azteca Member Sentenced in RICO Case"; Department of Justice, "Final Barrio Azteca Member in El Paso Sentenced to Federal Prison on RICO, Drug Trafficking and Money Laundering Charges."

26. Martinez, "Barrio Azteca Member Sentenced in RICO Case."

27. Grayson, *Mexico's Struggle with "Drugs And Thugs"*; Ríos, "Why Did Mexico Become So Violent?"; Friman, "Drug Markets and the Selective Use of Violence"; Kan, *Cartels at War*.

28. Mosso, "Cae en Michoacán 'El Tablas,' uno de los 10 más buscados por FBI."

29. Borunda, "Mexico Federal Police Arrest Reputed Barrio Azteca Gang Leader 'El 300' in Chihuahua City."

30. Borunda, "Mexico Federal Police Arrest Reputed Barrio Azteca Gang Leader 'El 300' in Chihuahua City."

31. Borunda, "Mexico Federal Police Arrest Reputed Barrio Azteca Gang Leader 'El 300' in Chihuahua City."

32. Campbell, "Narco-Propaganda in the Mexican 'Drug War.'"

33. In 2016, Jean received a suspended one-year jail sentence along with two years of probation for the vandalism. Martinez, "Man Gets Probation in 'Plata o Plomo' Case"; Valdez, "Las Vegas Man Arrested in Connection with Threatening Billboard Graffiti."

34. Solomon, "The FBI's List of the Most Dangerous Cities in Texas"; Wilson, "Crime Data and Spillover Violence along the Southwest Border."

35. Dube, Dube, and García-Ponce, "Cross-Border Spillover"; Pérez Esparza and Weigend, "The Illegal Flow of Firearms from the United States into Mexico."

36. The Border Patrol agent's view was consistent with a reported uptick of corruption to a level that alarmed officials at the time but said little about the history or status of corruption within CBP previously. Archibold and Becker, "Border Agents, Lured by the Other Side."

37. Devereaux, "An Unchecked Union."

38. Schatz, "The Border Patrol Is Setting Itself Up to Hire Some Bad Hombres."

39. Archibold and Becker, "Border Agents, Lured by the Other Side"; Steinle, "13 CBP Employees Arrested for Corruption This Administration"; Schatz, "New Report Details Dozens of Corrupt Border Patrol Agents—Just As Trump Wants to Hire More."

9. THE STREET

1. To jump is to beat up.

2. Segundo Barrio, the second ward of El Paso, located next to the border with Juárez, is historically a low-income area.

3. Mad-dogging is staring down another person in a menacing way as if to attempt to trigger a conflict.

4. The Stash House Unit is an initiative started in 1989 by the El Paso HIDTA with the goal to disrupt wholesale drug traffickers' distribution networks by identifying the places where they store large quantities of drugs to be transported for sale in other parts of the United States.

5. Gundur, "Prison Gangs."

6. Texas Department of Public Safety, *Texas Gang Threat Assessment, 2015*.

7. Skarbek, *The Social Order of the Underworld*. This echoes economist David Skarbek's findings on the governance mechanisms of prison gangs.

8. Here, "family members" refers to fellow gang members.

9. Something that is spoken for is something that has been approved by the gang's higher-ups.

10. Becker, "Crime and Punishment," 180–85.

11. "Spark" means to smoke.

12. "Slam" means to inject.

13. Carter, Brewer, and Angel, "Raman Spectroscopy for the In Situ Identification of Cocaine and Selected Adulterants," 1876.

14. Campbell, *Drug War Zone*.

15. Cook, *Mexico's Drug Cartels*; Beittel, *Mexico's Drug Trafficking Organizations*; Wainwright, *Narconomics*.

16. Celaya Pacheco, "Narcofearance."

17. Borunda, "Mexico Federal Police Arrest Reputed Barrio Azteca Gang Leader 'El 300' in Chihuahua City."

18. Beith, *The Last Narco*.

19. Beith, *The Last Narco*.

20. Meisner, "14 Years for Chicago Brothers Turned Informants in Takedown of Cocaine Cartel."

21. *Lizo* is payload.

22. Shipping seals are placed on trailers to show recipients that the load has not been tampered with during transportation.

23. Ainslie, *The Fight to Save Juárez*.

24. Levitt and Venkatesh, *An Economic Analysis of a Drug-Selling Gang's Finances*; Naylor, *Wages of Crime*.

10. THE OASIS

1. Marks, *And Die in the West*.

2. Toll, "Maricopa County Population Growth No. 2 in Nation, but Far Short of Area's Historic Numbers."

3. US Department of Commerce, "QuickFacts Beta," 2019 data.

4. US Department of Commerce, "QuickFacts Beta," 2019 data.

5. Tweakers are methamphetamine users.

6. Liu, Wei, and Simon, "Social Capital, Race, and Income inequality in the United States."

7. Sutch, "The One Percent across Two Centuries"; Wolff, "Wealth Trends in the United States during the Great Recession and Recovery, 2001–2016."

8. Dwyer, "Ex-Sheriff Joe Arpaio Convicted of Criminal Contempt."

9. Moore and Flaherty, "The Friday Surprise."

10. Campbell, "The Road to S.B. 1070."

11. Arizona Support Our Law Enforcement and Safe Neighborhoods Act, S.B. 1070, 49th Legislature, 2nd Regular Session (AZ 2010).

12. Bersani et al., "Investigating the Offending Histories of Undocumented Immigrants"; Reid et al., "The Immigration-Crime Relationship."

13. Ainslie, *The Fight to Save Juárez*.

14. O'Brien, Collingwood, and El-Khatib, "The Politics of Refuge"; Adelman et al., "Editorial: New Directions in Research on Immigration, Crime, Law, and Justice."

15. Bennett and Edelman, "Toward a New Political Narrative"; Edelman, *The Politics of Misinformation*.

16. Sanchez, *Human Smuggling and Border Crossings*.

17. US Department of Justice, Office of the Inspector General, *Review of the Phoenix Police Department's 2008 Kidnapping Statistic Reported in Department of Justice Grant Applications*.

18. Thoreson et al., *City of Phoenix Kidnapping Statistics Review Panel*, 5.

19. Arizona Attorney General, "Drug Cartel Operations."

20. Key, "AZ Sherriff Paul Babeu"; Hewes and Carter, "Cartel City, Arizona."

11. GANGS OF THE VALLEY

1. Arizona Criminal Justice Commission, *2006 Gangs in Arizona*; Arizona Criminal Justice Commission, *2013 Arizona Gang Threat Assessment*; Arizona Criminal Justice Commission, *2014 Arizona Gang Threat Assessment*; Hawkins, Zibell, and Vidale, *Enhanced Drug and Gang Enforcement (EDGE) Report*; Zibell et al., *Enhanced Drug and*

Gang Enforcement (EDGE) Report; Arizona Criminal Justice Commission, *2018 Arizona Gang Threat Assessment.*

2. Federal Bureau of Investigation, *National Gang Threat Assessment.*

3. Schaefer Morabito, "Understanding Community Policing as an Innovation."

4. Gang Resistance Education and Training, "What Is G.R.E.A.T." According to the program's official website, "Gang Resistance Education And Training (G.R.E.A.T.) is an evidence-based and effective gang and violence prevention program built around school-based, law enforcement officer–instructed classroom curricula. The program is intended as an immunization against delinquency, youth violence, and gang membership for children in the years immediately before the prime ages for introduction into gangs and delinquent behavior."

5. In this instance Skinny is speaking of the original Mexican Mafia, founded in San Quinten Prison in California in the 1960s. Irwin, *Prisons in Turmoil*; Weide, "The Invisible Hand of the State."

6. *Califas* are gang members of Californian provenance.

7. Posting up means to establish a physical presence in an area, often the corner of a block, to indicate control of that area.

8. Arizona Criminal Justice Commission, *2018 Arizona Gang Threat Assessment.*

9. Arizona Department of Corrections, "Certified and Monitored STGs."

10. Arizona Department of Corrections, "Certified and Monitored STGs."

11. Fischer, *Arizona Department of Corrections.*

12. Arizona Department of Corrections, "Certified and Monitored STGs."

13. An OG is an "original gangster," a term used to describe older veteran gang members.

14. Fischer, *Arizona Department of Corrections.*

15. Pyrooz and Mitchell, "The Use of Restrictive Housing on Gang and Non-Gang Affiliated Inmates in US Prisons."

16. Erich Josef Gliebe, former chairman of the National Alliance, a White supremist group, boxed under the name the Aryan Barbarian.

17. The hole is solitary confinement.

18. At the time of Bryan's incarceration, stamps were used as currency among inmates. "Store" refers to reselling commissary goods from one's cell; inmates who could afford to do so would often buy products from the prison commissary and keep them on hand, selling them on credit to their peers who may not have had enough money to purchase such items when the prison commissary was open.

12. ADELITA AND CALISTA

1. "Glass" is methamphetamine.

2. Zust, "Assessing and Addressing Domestic Violence Experienced by Incarcerated Women"; Blair-Lawton, Mordoch, and Chernomas, "Putting on the Same Shoes."

3. Sanders, "Promoting Financial Capability of Incarcerated Women for Community Reentry."

4. Halsey, Armstrong, and Wright, "'F*ck It!'"

5. The Phoenix Metro Light Rail began operation in late 2008.

6. A *quinceañera* is the celebration of a girl's fifteenth birthday. The girl is dressed up in a formal evening dress, usually a ball gown.

7. Lollman, "4 Arrested in Connection to Deadly Armed Robbery in Mesa."

13. A FEAR OF CORNERS

1. Arizona Criminal Justice Commission, *2014 Arizona Gang Threat Assessment*; Arizona Criminal Justice Commission, *2018 Arizona Gang Threat Assessment*.

2. "Weight" is an amount of an illicit drug.

3. My respondents in Arizona would most often use the term *paisa* to refer to a Mexican and *Mexican* to refer to a Mexican American. I have maintained this convention in this chapter to maintain congruence with the quotes used.

4. Quinones, *Dreamland*.

5. Here Duke is saying that he was not turning over large amounts of money or spending ostentatiously.

6. Tempe is an inner suburb of the Phoenix Metropolitan Area, located between Phoenix and the rest of the East Valley. The main campus of Arizona State University is located there.

7. Cunningham, "Drug Trends in Phoenix and Arizona."

8. Brouwer et al., "Trends in Production, Trafficking, and Consumption of Methamphetamine and Cocaine in Mexico"; Shukla, Crump, and Chrisco, "An Evolving Problem."

9. Ciccarone, "Heroin in Brown, Black and White"; Paoli, Greenfield, and Reuter, *The World Heroin Market*.

10. McCoy, *The Politics of Heroin*.

11. Shukla et al., "An Evolving Problem."

12. Haislip, *Methamphetamine Precursor Chemical Control in the 1990s*.

13. National Drug Intelligence Center, "Arizona Drug Threat Assessment."

14. Scott and Dedel, *Clandestine Methamphetamine Labs*; Cherney, "Mexican Cartels Are Putting Mom and Pop Meth Cooks Out of Business."

15. Cunningham, Liu, and Callaghan, "Impact of US and Canadian Precursor Regulation on Methamphetamine Purity in the United States"; Cherney, "Mexican Cartels Are Putting Mom and Pop Meth Cooks Out of Business." Midwestern states such as Indiana, Illinois, and Missouri and rural southeastern states such as Kentucky and Tennessee still have large numbers of meth labs producing homemade products for the local markets. Moser, "Illinois Is in the Middle of America's Meth Belt."

16. Five-0 are the police, a term popularized by the television show *Hawaii Five-0*.

17. Brownstein and Taylor, "Measuring the Stability of Illicit Drug Markets."

18. The "dude" is the wholesaler who is supplying the retailer.

19. Rock is crack cocaine.

20. Here Breeze is referring to Chicanos, that is, Mexican Americans.

21. Buerger, "Defensive Strategies of the Street-Level Drug Trade."

22. Søgaard et al., "Ring and Bring Drug Services."

23. Campesinos are farmers, and vaqueros are cowboys.

24. A coyote is someone who smuggles unauthorized migrants into the United States.

25. Mazis and Staelin, "Using Information-Processing Principles in Public Policymaking"; Baumgartner and Jones, "Agenda Dynamics and Policy Subsystems."

14. CONNECTIONS

1. Thoreson et al., *City of Phoenix Kidnapping Statistics Review Panel*.

2. National Drug Intelligence Center, "Arizona Drug Threat Assessment."

3. Sanchez, *Human Smuggling and Border Crossings*.

4. A plug is a wholesale supplier.

5. In other words, the Eme member's uncle was wholesaling. Given the fact that there was a familial relationship between the Eme member and his uncle, Duke could piggy-back off that relationship without having to worry about being ratted out.

6. Hogan and Century, *Hunting El Chapo*; Riley, *Drug Warrior*.

7. Not only are the prescription medications cheaper in Mexico than in the United States, but some drugs that are heavily regulated and controlled in the United States are less regulated and more readily available in Mexico.

8. Taylor, "Distance Transformation and Distance Decay Functions."

9. *Cuevas v. Holder*, 737 F.3d 972, 975 (5th Cir. 2013).

10. Decker and Chapman, *Drug Smugglers on Drug Smuggling*.

11. Nye, *Soft Power*, x.

12. Shelley and Picarelli, "Methods Not Motives"; Jones, "Pangas, Trickery, Intimidation, and Drug Trafficking in California."

13. Berry, "Technology and Organised Crime in the Smart City."

14. Jones, *Mexico's Illicit Drug Networks and the State Reaction*; Reuter, "Systemic Violence in Drug Markets."

15. Papachristos and Smith, "The Embedded and Multiplex Nature of Al Capone."

16. Bragg, "What Is Separation of Duties?"

17. Gundur, "Finding the Sweet Spot."

18. Phippen, "Inside an Arizona Drug Smuggling Gang."

19. Federal Bureau of Investigation, "Table 6: Crime in the United States by Metropolitan Statistical Area, 2019."

20. Jones, *Mexico's Illicit Drug Networks and the State Reaction*; Gundur, "Prison Gangs."

21. "Clicked up" refers to being a member of a gang.

15. THE CITY BY THE LAKE

1. The Sears Tower was renamed the Willis Tower in 2009. Many people who grew up with the building as the "Sears Tower" continue to refer to it as such.

2. US Census Bureau, "Chicago-Naperville-Elgin, IL-IN-WI Metro Area."

3. US Department of Commerce, "QuickFacts Beta," 2019 data.

4. Franklin, "Immigrant Chicago."

5. Koval et al., eds., *The New Chicago*.

6. Lombardo, *Organized Crime in Chicago*; LockZero.org, "Political History of Bridgeport." The Chicago Outfit is Chicago's iteration of the Italian Mafia. It was initially based in Chicago's south side and rose to power in the prohibition era of the 1920s under the leadership of Johnny Torrio and Al Capone. Paral, "Chicago's Immigrants Break Old Patterns." Admittedly, the Polish presence of the city is fading as the Poles are increasingly moving to the suburbs, resulting in the closure of several of the stores and markets that used to dot the traditionally Polish neighborhoods.

7. US Department of Commerce, "QuickFacts Beta," 2019 data; Lee, "A Crumbling, Dangerous South Side Creates Exodus of Black Chicagoans."

8. Vargas, *Wounded City*; Spergel, *Reducing Youth Gang Violence*; Spergel and Grossman, "The Little Village Project."

9. Burgess, "Residential Segregation in American Cities"; Park and Burgess, *Introduction to the Science of Sociology*; Thomas and Znaniecki, *The Polish Peasant in Europe and America*.

10. Sánchez-Jankowski, "Gangs and Social Change"; Skogan, *Police and Community in Chicago*.

11. For poverty, see Zorbaugh, *The Gold Coast and the Slum*; Abbott, *The Tenements of Chicago*. For community, see Horowitz, *Honor and the American Dream*; Suttles, *The*

Social Order of the Slum; Layson and Warren, "Chicago and the Great Migration, 1915–1950"; Seligman, *Block by Block*; Sampson, *Great American City*; Drake and Cayton, *Black Metropolis*; Vargas, *Wounded City*; Koval et al., eds., *The New Chicago*. For crime and crime responses, see Hagedorn, *The In$ane Chicago Way*; Hagedorn, "Race Not Space"; Lombardo, *Organized Crime in Chicago*; Haller, "Urban Crime and Criminal Justice"; Vargas, *Wounded City*; Thrasher, *The Gang*; Landesco, "Crime and the Failure of Institutions in Chicago's Immigrant Areas"; Venkatesh, *Gang Leader for a Day*; Skogan, *Police and Community in Chicago*; Vargas, "Criminal Group Embeddedness and the Adverse Effects of Arresting a Gang's Leader"; Spergel, *Reducing Youth Gang Violence*; Smith, *Syndicate Women*.

    12. Sánchez-Jankowski, *Cracks in the Pavement*, 3.

16. GANGLAND

    1. Thrasher, *The Gang*; Pew Research Center, "What Census Calls Us." Though Americans could not choose their own race in census measurements until 1960, several racial categories were available during Thrasher's study period, including White, Black, Mulatto, Indian, Chinese, Japanese, Filipino, Korean, and Hindu. Thrasher focused purely on White people, despite the noted and tracked presence of non-White people.

    2. Hagedorn, "Race Not Space."

    3. Asbury, *The Gangs of Chicago*.

    4. Paral, "Chicago's Immigrants Break Old Patterns."

    5. Sinclair, *The Jungle*.

    6. Paral, "Chicago's Immigrants Break Old Patterns."

    7. Asbury, *The Gangs of Chicago*, xvi.

    8. Haller, "Urban Crime and Criminal Justice."

    9. Addams, "Pioneer Labor Legislation in Illinois," 183. In *Twenty Years at Hull-House*, Jane Addams wrote:

> A South Italian peasant who has picked olives and packed oranges from his toddling babyhood cannot see at once the difference between the outdoor healthy work which he had performed in the varying seasons, and the long hours of monotonous factory life which his child encounters when he goes to work in Chicago. An Italian father came to us in great grief over the death of his eldest child, a little girl of twelve, who had brought the largest wages into the family fund. In the midst of his genuine sorrow he said: "She was the oldest kid I had. Now I shall have to go back to work again until the next one is able to take care of me." The man was only thirty-three and had hoped to retire from work at least during the winters. No foreman cared to have him in a factory, untrained and unintelligent as he was. It was much easier for his bright, English-speaking little girl to get a chance to paste labels on a box than for him to secure an opportunity to carry pig iron. The effect on the child was what no one concerned thought about, in the abnormal effort she made thus prematurely to bear the weight of life. Another little girl of thirteen, a Russian-Jewish child employed in a laundry at a heavy task beyond her strength, committed suicide, because she had borrowed three dollars from a companion which she could not repay unless she confided the story to her parents and gave up an entire week's wages—but what could the family live upon that week in case she did! (183–84).

This passage belies the fact that Italian men were brought from Italy to work in highly dangerous construction projects where men died on a daily basis because it was cheaper to replace them than to enact safety measures. Addams attacks other ethnic groups as well, especially those who are not "White" enough for her. In these examples, one must wonder why Addams does not question why children were being exploited by the industrialists of the day and why adult men were being denied the right to work.

10. Lombardo, *Organized Crime in Chicago*; Hagedorn, "Race Not Space."

11. Layson and Warren, "Chicago and the Great Migration, 1915–1950"; Gosnell, "The Chicago 'Black Belt' as a Political Battleground."

12. Drake and Cayton, *Black Metropolis*; McClelland, "White Flight, by the Numbers"; Massey and Denton, *American Apartheid*.

13. McClelland, "White Flight, by the Numbers."

14. Seligman, *Block by Block*.

15. Skogan, *Police and Community in Chicago*.

16. Sampson, *Great American City*, 374.

17. Bernstein, "Martin Luther King Jr.'s 1966 Chicago Campaign."

18. Pearce, "When Martin Luther King Jr. Took His Fight into the North, and Saw a New Level of Hatred." Richard J. Daley (1902–1976) was mayor of Chicago from 1955 until his death. His son, Richard M. Daley (b. 1942), was mayor of Chicago from 1989 until 2011.

19. Chin, "The Civil Rights Revolution Comes to Immigration Law," Immigration and Nationality Act of 1965 [Hart-Celler Act] (H.R. 2580; Pub.L. 89-236, 79 Stat. 911, enacted June 30, 1968).

20. Lee, "A Crumbling, Dangerous South Side Creates Exodus of Black Chicagoans."

21. US Department of Commerce, "QuickFacts Beta," 2019 data; McClelland, "White Flight, by the Numbers"; Fessenden and Park, "Chicago's Murder Problem."

22. Skogan, *Police and Community in Chicago*, 21.

23. Venkatesh, *Gang Leader for a Day*.

24. Popkin and Cunningham, *CHA Relocation Counseling Assessment—Final Report*.

25. Austen, "The Last Tower."

26. Sampson, *Great American City*; Eads, Salinas, and Evans, "Demolished." About 56 percent of the at least 53,900 remained in the system and were displaced within the Chicago Housing Authority; the other 44 percent lost contact with the system.

27. Sampson, *Great American City*; US Department of Commerce, "QuickFacts Beta," 2019 data.

28. Fessenden and Park, "Chicago's Murder Problem"; Lee, "A Crumbling, Dangerous South Side Creates Exodus of Black Chicagoans."

29. "Crime in Chicago by Month, 2001 to Present."

30. Riley, *Drug Warrior*.

31. Elgas, "Crime Commission"; Dumke, "The Drug Warrior"; Lippert, Cattan, and Parker, "Heroin Pushed on Chicago by Cartel Fueling Gang Murders"; DEA Chicago Field Division, Federal Bureau of Investigation, and the Chicago Police Department, *Cartels and Gangs in Chicago*; DEA Chicago Field Division, *The Drug Situation in the Chicago Field Division*.

32. Skogan, *A Tale of Three Cities*.

33. Sloan and Strong, "Chicago Has Spent Half a Billion Dollars on Police Brutality Cases—and It's Impoverishing the Victims' Communities"; Ackerman, "The Disappeared."

34. Vargas, *Wounded City*.

35. Asbury, *The Gangs of Chicago*; Block and Block, *Street Gang Crime in Chicago*; Hagedorn and Rauch, "Housing, Gangs, and Homicide"; Hagedorn, "Race Not Space"; Hagedorn, *The In$ane Chicago Way*; Haller, "Urban Crime and Criminal Justice"; Lombardo, *Organized Crime in Chicago*; Zorbaugh, *The Gold Coast and the Slum*; Skogan, *A Tale of Three Cities*; Thrasher, *The Gang*.

36. Lombardo, *Organized Crime in Chicago*; Hagedorn, "Race Not Space"; Thrasher, *The Gang*; Curry, "The Logic of Defining Gangs Revisited." Though there have been many gangs in Chicago since the turn of the twentieth century, this number is not one that was ever counted by Thrasher or anyone else; in fact, it was part of a betting pool to be included in the title. Nonetheless, there were undoubtedly several dozen such organizations.

37. Lombardo, *Organized Crime in Chicago*; Landesco, "The Gangster's Apologia Pro Vita Sua"; Landesco, "Crime and the Failure of Institutions in Chicago's Immigrant Areas."

38. Landesco, "The Gangster's Apologia Pro Vita Sua," 1043.

39. Landesco, "Crime and the Failure of Institutions in Chicago's Immigrant Areas"; Smith, *The Mafia Mystique*.

40. Ianni, *Black Mafia*.

41. Lombardo, *Organized Crime in Chicago*.

42. Abu-Lughod, *Race, Space, and Riots in Chicago, New York, and Los Angeles*, 58; Hagedorn, "Race Not Space."

43. Thrasher, *The Gang*.

44. Hagedorn, "Race Not Space."

45. Alonso, "Racialized Identities and the Formation of Black Gangs in Los Angeles.".

46. Thrasher, *The Gang*; Lombardo, *Organized Crime in Chicago*.

47. Lombardo, *Organized Crime in Chicago*; Abu-Lughod, *Race, Space, and Riots in Chicago, New York, and Los Angeles*; Haller, "Urban Crime and Criminal Justice."

48. Asbury, *The Gangs of Chicago*.

49. Lombardo, *Organized Crime in Chicago*.

50. Seligman, *Block by Block*.

51. Hagedorn, "Race Not Space."

52. Hagedorn, "Race Not Space."

53. Moore and Williams, *The Almighty Black P Stone Nation*; Lombardo, *Organized Crime in Chicago*.

54. Lombardo, *Organized Crime in Chicago*.

55. Hagedorn, "Race Not Space," 202.

56. Dawley, *A Nation of Lords*; Moore and Williams, *The Almighty Black P Stone Nation*; Blakemore and Blakemore, "African American Street Gangs"; Safer and Crowl, "Substantial Assistance Departures"; Jacobs, *Stateville*; Hagedorn, "Race Not Space"; De-Vito, *The Encyclopedia of International Organized Crime*; Abadinsky, *Organized Crime*.

57. Blakemore and Blakemore, "African American Street Gangs"; Hagedorn, *The In$ane Chicago Way*; Rey, "The Latin Kings Speak."

58. Moore and Williams, *The Almighty Black P Stone Nation*.

59. Moore and Williams, *The Almighty Black P Stone Nation*; Knox, "The Vice Lords"; Pasternak, "U.S. Moves to Crack Powerful Chicago Gang."

60. Hubbard, Wyman, and Domma, *The Chicago Crime Commission Gang Book*; Haller, "Urban Crime and Criminal Justice"; Bernstein and Isackson, "Gangs and Politicians in Chicago." There are reports that gangs still influence elections in Chicago. While I doubt that the influence is as significant as it was during the early part of the twentieth century, there is undoubtedly a lot of corruption in the City of Chicago and the State of Illinois. Since 2005 several notable politicians have been incarcerated, including former aldermen Arenda Troutman, William Beavers, and Isaac "Ike" Sims Carothers; former US representative Jesse Jackson Jr.; and former governors Rod Blagojevich and George Ryan. Most were convicted of fraud, bribery, or corruption.

61. Pollack, "The Gang That Could Go Straight"; Possley and Crawford, "El Rukns Indicted in Libya Scheme." Jeff Fort's El Rukns attempted to acquire weapons from Libya and attack government buildings in Chicago.

62. Hagedorn, *The In$ane Chicago Way*; Safer and Crowl, "Substantial Assistance Departures"; Moore and Williams, *The Almighty Black P Stone Nation*; Venkatesh and Levitt, "Are We a Family or a Business?"

63. Hagedorn, "Race Not Space."

64. Jacobs, *Stateville*; Jacobs, "Race Relations and the Prisoner Subculture"; Irwin, *Prisons in Turmoil*.

65. Jacobs, *Stateville*; Jacobs, "Race Relations and the Prisoner Subculture."

66. Jacobs, *Stateville*.

67. Hagedorn, *The In$ane Chicago Way*; Moore and Williams, *The Almighty Black P Stone Nation*.

68. Hubbard, Wyman, and Domma, *The Chicago Crime Commission Gang Book*, 2.

69. Moore and Williams, *The Almighty Black P Stone Nation*.

70. Hagedorn, *The In$ane Chicago Way*; Block, *East Side, West Side*.

71. Tyson, "Journey of Chicago's Ultimate Street Tough"; Safer and Crowl, "Substantial Assistance Departures."

72. The GED is a high school equivalency diploma.

73. Tyson, "Journey of Chicago's Ultimate Street Tough."

74. Hagedorn, "Race Not Space," 204.

75. Moore and Williams, *The Almighty Black P Stone Nation*.

76. Tyson, "Journey of Chicago's Ultimate Street Tough."; Hagedorn, "Race Not Space."

77. Hagedorn, *The In$ane Chicago Way*.

78. Hagedorn, *In$ane Chicago Way*.

79. Hagedorn, *In$ane Chicago Way*.

80. Hagedorn, *In$ane Chicago Way*.

81. Paoli, Greenfield, and Reuter, *The World Heroin Market*.

82. Lupsha and Schlegel, *The Political Economy of Drug Trafficking*.

83. DeVito, *The Encyclopedia of International Organized Crime*; Grayson, *Mexico*; Giommoni, Gundur, and Cheekes, "International Drug Trafficking"; Purvis and Gundur, "The Drug Trade at a Glance."

84. Paoli et al., *The World Heroin Market*.

85. Paoli, Greenfield, and Reuter, *World Heroin Market*; Abadinsky, *Organized Crime*; DeVito, *The Encyclopedia of International Organized Crime*.

86. Lupsha and Schlegel, *The Political Economy of Drug Trafficking*.

87. DeVito, *The Encyclopedia of International Organized Crime*.

88. Abadinsky, *Organized Crime*.

89. Hagedorn, *The In$ane Chicago Way*.

90. "Dude" refers to the man Biggs was buying his supply from. "Weight" in this context means a regular large amount.

91. "Stuck over" means to rob.

92. "Work" refers to illicit drugs to retail.

17. CATCHING CASES

1. Beller and Hout, "Intergenerational Social Mobility."

2. Piketty, *Capital in the Twenty-First Century*; Black et al., *Poor Little Rich Kids?*

3. Martin, "Hidden Consequences." Children whose parents are incarcerated are six times more likely to be incarcerated in their lifetimes than children whose parents never went to prison.

4. Institute for Crime and Justice Policy Research, "The World Prison Brief."

5. Pettit and Western, "Mass Imprisonment and the Life Course."

6. Alexander, *The New Jim Crow*.

7. Pettit and Western, "Mass Imprisonment and the Life Course."

8. Post-traumatic stress disorder.

9. Here Alyssa is referring to "crab mentality," a way of thinking that can be best described by the phrase "if I can't have it, neither can you."

10. Sweeney and Meisner, "A Dad's Influence."

11. Sweeney and Meisner, "A Dad's Influence"; Lupsha and Schlegel, *The Political Economy of Drug Trafficking*.

12. Vargas, *Wounded City*.

13. Sweeney and Meisner, "A Dad's Influence"; Flores and Flores, *Cartel Wives*.

14. Riley, *Drug Warrior*; Flores and Flores, *Cartel Wives*.

15. Riley, *Drug Warrior*.

16. Riley, *Drug Warrior*.

17. Flores and Flores, *Cartel Wives*.

18. Flores and Flores, *Cartel Wives*.

19. Flores and Flores, *Cartel Wives*.

20. Charles, "Killing 'Kato.'"

21. Flores and Flores, *Cartel Wives*, xii.

22. Venkatesh, "The Social Organization of Street Gang Activity in an Urban Ghetto," 82; Vargas, *Wounded City*.

23. Feuer, "The Meeting in the Mountains That Led to $800 Million in Cash for El Chapo."

24. Government's Evidentiary Proffer Supporting the Admissibility of Co-Conspirator Statements, *United States v. Zambada Niebla*, No. 1:09-CR-383 (N.D. Ill. 2011).

25. Hogan and Century, *Hunting El Chapo*.

26. Beittel, *Mexico*.

27. Elgas, "Crime Commission." Though the FBI has named various outlaws in its "Ten Most Wanted" list throughout the twentieth and twenty-first centuries, the Chicago Crime Commission had not named anyone as "Public Enemy No. 1" since Al Capone, the first person to bear the label.

28. Flores, "Statement of Pedro Flores"; Meisner, "14 years for Chicago Brothers Turned Informants in Takedown of Cocaine Cartel"; Flores and Flores, *Cartel Wives*, 205.

29. Flores and Flores, *Cartel Wives*.

30. Beittel, *Mexico*.

31. Riley, *Drug Warrior*; Flores and Flores, *Cartel Wives*.

32. *United States vs. Flores*, No. 1:09-CR-383-11 (N.D. Ill. Aug. 23, 2012). See also *U.S. vs. Flores*, No. 09-CR-383-10 (N.D. Ill. 2012).

33. Flores and Flores, *Cartel Wives*.

34. Flores, "Statement of Pedro Flores."

35. Flores, "Statement of Pedro Flores"; Flores and Flores, *Cartel Wives*.

36. Flores and Flores, *Cartel Wives*.

37. Flores, "Statement of Pedro Flores"; Flores and Flores, *Cartel Wives*.

38. Beittel, *Mexico*; Beittel, *Mexico's Drug-Related Violence*; Calderón, Rodríguez Ferreira, and Shirk, *Drug Violence in Mexico*; Molzahn, Ríos, and Shirk, *Drug Violence in Mexico*; Shirk, *Drug Violence in Mexico*.

39. Bonner, "The Cartel Crackdown."

40. Ellingwood, "Mexican Drug Figure's Son Is Arrested"; de Cordoba, "Mexico Arrests the Son of an Alleged Drug-Cartel Leader"; Montenegro, "Californian, Businesswoman, 'Narco Junior.'"

41. Ellingwood, "Mexican Drug Figure's Son Is Arrested."

42. The term "narco junior" is also sometimes used as a catchall to refer to people in the drug trade who are young entrants and present ostentatiously.

43. Hogan and Century, *Hunting El Chapo*; Davis, "Ex-Cartel Assassin 'Chino Antrax' Confirmed Dead after Fleeing from San Diego."

44. Main, "'El Vincentillo,' El Chapo's Ex-Logistics Guru, Was a Cartel Big Shot since Teens"; de Cordoba, "Mexico Arrests the Son of an Alleged Drug-Cartel Leader."

45. Winslow, "The Dirty Secret of El Chapo's Downfall."

46. Davis, "Ex-Cartel Assassin 'Chino Antrax' Confirmed Dead."

47. Riley, *Drug Warrior*.

48. Hurowitz, "Vicente Zambada Niebla, Son of El Chapo Cartel Partner El Mayo, Sentenced to 15 Years in Prison"; McGahan, "Mexican Drug Lord's Insider Notes May Set Him Free after 10 Years"; Government's Sentencing Memorandum and Motion to Depart from the Applicable Guideline Range, *United States v. Zambada Niebla*, No. 1:09-CR-383, No. 1:18-CR-484 (N.D. Ill. May 20, 2019).

49. Mitchell, "Colorado's Supermax Prison Now Occupied by El Chapo Is 'Worse Than Death,' Ex-Warden Says."

50. Riley, *Drug Warrior*; Hogan and Century, *Hunting El Chapo*.

51. Hogan and Century, *Hunting El Chapo*.

18. LOGISTICS

1. Meisner, "14 Years for Chicago Brothers Turned Informants in Takedown of Cocaine Cartel."

2. Hurowitz, "Vicente Zambada Niebla, Son of El Chapo Cartel Partner El Mayo, Sentenced to 15 Years in Prison."

3. Feuer, "El Chapo Sentenced to Life in Prison, Ending Notorious Criminal Career."

4. Meisner, "14 Years for Chicago Brothers Turned Informants in Takedown of Cocaine Cartel."

5. Winslow, "The Dirty Secret of El Chapo's Downfall."

6. Feuer, "El Chapo's Wife Set to Plead Guilty to Helping Run Drug Empire."

7. Woody, "The US Sanctioned a 'Smooth as Butter' Cartel Operator and a Mexican Soccer Star Allegedly Working with Him."

8. Jones, *Mexico's Illicit Drug Networks and the State Reaction*, 48.

9. Saviano, "El Chapo's Rise to Power and His First Prison Break."

10. Saviano, "El Chapo's Rise to Power and His First Prison Break"; Saldaña and Payan, "The Evolution of Cartels in Mexico, 1980–2015."

11. Beith, *The Last Narco*.

12. Grillo, *El Narco*; Kan, *Cartels at War*.

13. Kleemans, "Organized Crime, Transit Crime, and Racketeering."

14. Gundur, "Settings Matter"; Durán Martínez, "Drugs around the Corner."

15. Plea Agreement, *United States v. Zambada Niebla*, No. 1:09-CR-383, (N.D. Ill. 2013); Flores's Testimony, Sentencing Letter, *United States v. Guzman Loera*, No. 1:09-CR-466 (E.D.N.Y. Sep. 26, 2019, July 10, 2019); Plea Agreement, *United States v. Fernandez Valencia*, No. 1:09-CR-383-19 (N.D. Ill. June 26, 2019).

16. Hogan and Century, *Hunting El Chapo*.

17. Plea Agreement, *United States v. Flores*, No. 1:09-CR-383-10 (N.D. Ill. Aug. 22, 2012). The Flores twins both pled guilty; though Pedro Flores's plea agreement is cited here, the contents of Margarito Flores's is similar.

18. Flores and Flores, *Cartel Wives*.

19. Flores and Flores, *Cartel Wives*.

20. Flores and Flores, *Cartel Wives*.

21. Flores and Flores, *Cartel Wives*.

22. Hogan and Century, *Hunting El Chapo*.

23. Flores, "Statement of Pedro Flores."

24. Woody, "The US Sanctioned a 'Smooth as Butter' Cartel Operator and a Mexican Soccer Star Allegedly Working with Him." A similar relationship between an independent distributor/cartel with established Mexican drug cartels was documented in the Raúl Flores Hernández organization. Flores Hernández (no relation to the Flores twins) had maintained links with various drug barons since the 1970s. When he was arrested in 2017, he reportedly had links with the Sinaloa Federation and the Cártel de Jalisco Nueva Generación.

25. Sweeney and Meisner, "A Dad's Influence."

26. Dumke, "Anatomy of a Heroin Ring."

27. DEA Chicago Field Division, Federal Bureau of Investigation, and the Chicago Police Department, *Cartels and Gangs in Chicago*, 2.

28. McGahan, "Why Mexico's Sinaloa Cartel Loves Selling Drugs in Chicago."

29. Dumke, "Anatomy of a Heroin Ring."

30. Peron, da Fontoura Costa, and Rodrigues, "The Structure and Resilience of Financial Market Networks."

31. Flores and Flores, *Cartel Wives*.

32. DEA Chicago Field Division, *The Drug Situation in the Chicago Field Division*.

33. Plea Agreement, *United States v. Flores*, No. 1:09-CR-383-10 (N.D. Ill. Aug. 22, 2012).

34. Plea Agreement, *United States v. Flores*, No. 1:09-CR-383-10 (N.D. Ill. Aug. 22, 2012).

35. Here Renzo is describing the process of becoming a group that is affiliated with another as if to be a subsidiary. His clique was one of many in the area that pertained to a larger gang that had sets and cliques throughout the city's south side.

36. Vargas, *Wounded City*.

37. The product had been adulterated.

38. "Mob" is often used synonymously with "gang" in Chicago street parlance.

39. Harlem would have been about a forty- to fifty-minute drive from where Danny normally stayed in the city.

40. Plea Agreement, *United States v. Flores*, No. 1:09-CR-383-10 (N.D. Ill. Aug. 22, 2012).

41. Lansu, "Xavier Tripp Fatally Shot in West Garfield Park."

42. Evil $ is pronounced "Evil Money." Crips, Bloods, and MS-13 are well-known gangs in other parts of the United States. However, as Evil $ noted, they have a small, arguably insignificant, presence in Chicago. Though Evil $ was not the only one to refer to the Mexican Mafia, it is unclear which branch of the gang he was referring to.

43. Rosenbaum and Stephens, *Reducing Public Violence and Homicide in Chicago*, 23.

44. Dumke, "Anatomy of a Heroin Ring"; Hagedorn, *The In$ane Chicago Way*.

45. Papachristos, Braga, and Hureau, "Social Networks and the Risk of Gunshot Injury."

46. Keith Cozart (b. 1995) is a recording artist from Chicago who is affiliated with the Black Disciples street gang. He performs drill music, a style of rap based on trap music, a genre of urban music characterized by its bleak and gritty lyrical content, often about life in the retail drug trade. Cozart's lyrics often glorify violence.

47. BDs refers to the Black Disciples.

48. Elias, *What Is Sociology?*

49. Levitt and Venkatesh, *An Economic Analysis of a Drug-Selling Gang's Finances*.

50. A district commander noted that the youth and inexperience of new gang members who are often behind shootings is one of the reasons that while shootings had been going up, fatalities had not. A year after this observation was made, 2016 saw an enormous homicide spike in Chicago. Saul, "Why 2016 Has Been Chicago's Bloodiest Year in Almost Two Decades."

51. Naylor, *Wages of Crime*; Levitt and Venkatesh, *An Economic Analysis of a Drug-Selling Gang's Finances.*

52. Dinkins and Vincent, "Money-Laundering Methods of Drug Cartels and the Capture of El Chapo."

53. Plea Agreement, *United States v. Flores*, No. 1:09-CR-383-10 (N.D. Ill. Aug. 22, 2012).

54. Mitchell, "Two Denver-Area Mexican Restaurants Tied to Drug Lord Joaquin 'El Chapo' Guzman's Money-Laundering Enterprise, Federal Suit Says."

55. Flores and Flores, *Cartel Wives.*

56. Special 2013 Grand Jury Charges and Allegations, *United States v. Anguiano Hernandez*, 14-CR-669 (N.D. Ill. 2013); "Mexico Arrests 'Money Launderer' for Drug Lord Guzman"; McAllister, "Tijuana Money Launderer for Sinaloa Drug Cartel Pleads Guilty in San Diego."

57. Georgina opined that the "Cash for Houses" billboards that are now commonplace might sometimes be underwritten by individuals who have surplus money from the drug trade and need to dump it somewhere.

58. Jost and Sandhu, *The Hawala Alternative Remittance System and Its Role in Money Laundering*, 5. "Hawala is an alternative or parallel remittance system. It exists and operates outside of, or parallel to 'traditional' banking or financial channels. It was developed in India, before the introduction of Western banking practices, and is currently a major remittance system used around the world. . . . The components of hawala that distinguish it from other remittance systems are trust and the extensive use of connections such as family relationships or regional affiliations. Unlike traditional banking . . . , hawala makes minimal (often no) use of any sort of negotiable instrument. Transfers of money take place based on communications between members of a network of hawaladars, or hawala dealers" (5).

59. 31 USC 5332: Bulk Cash Smuggling into or out of the United States, March 11, 2021, http://archive.today/2021.03.12-230728/https://uscode.house.gov/view.xhtml?req=(title:31%20section:5332%20edition:prelim).

60. Vulliamy, "How a Big US Bank Laundered Billions from Mexico's Murderous Drug Gangs."

61. Farah, "Money Laundering and Bulk Cash Smuggling"; Dinkins and Vincent, "Money-Laundering Methods of Drug Cartels."

62. Meisner and Sweeney, "Wives of Chicago Twins who Cooperated against El Chapo Arrested on Money Laundering Charges."

63. Plea Agreement, *United States v. Flores*, No. 1:09-CR-383-10 (N.D. Ill. Aug. 22, 2012); Meisner and Sweeney, "Wives of Chicago Twins who Cooperated against El Chapo Arrested on Money Laundering Charges."

64. Wolf, "El Chapo Renews US Law Enforcement Concerns about Money Laundering via Prepaid Cards."

65. Dinkins and Vincent, "Money-Laundering Methods of Drug Cartels"; Indictment, *United States v. Reynoso Garcia*, No. 3:17-CR-2203-WQH (S.D. Cal. Jan. 25, 2018); Katz, "A Cartel and a Briefcase."

66. Merton, *Social Theory and Social Structure.*

19. RESPONDING TO THE DRUG TRADE

1. Miller, *Drug Warriors and Their Prey*; Duck, *No Way Out.*

2. Miller, *Drug Warriors and Their Prey*; Hart, *Drug Use for Grown-Ups.*

3. Riley, *Drug Warrior.*

4. Hoffman, "Whatever Happened to Arizona's Minutemen?"

5. Desmond, Papachristos, and Kirk, "Police Violence and Citizen Crime Reporting in the Black Community"; Police Accountability Task Force, *Recommendations for Reform*.

6. DEA Chicago Field Division, *The Drug Situation in the Chicago Field Division*.

7. Plea Agreement, *United States v. Flores*, No. 1:09-CR-383-10 (N. D. Ill. Aug. 22, 2012).

8. Mosher and Akins, *In the Weeds*.

9. Centers for Disease Control and Prevention, "Understanding the Epidemic."

10. Vearrier, "The Value of Harm Reduction for Injection Drug Use"; Wilson et al., "The Cost-Effectiveness of Harm Reduction."

11. Hughes and Stevens, "What Can We Learn from the Portuguese Decriminalization of Illicit Drugs?," 999; Arredondo et al., "The Law on the Streets."

12. Arredondo et al., "The Law on the Streets"; Werb et al., "Police Bribery and Access to Methadone Maintenance Therapy within the Context of Drug Policy Reform in Tijuana, Mexico."

13. Benfer et al., "The Impact of Drug Policy Liberalisation on Willingness to Seek Help for Problem Drug Use"; Greenfield and Paoli, "If Supply-Oriented Drug Policy Is Broken, Can Harm Reduction Help Fix It?"; Purvis and Gundur, "The Drug Trade at a Glance."

14. Dills et al., "The Effect of State Marijuana Legalizations."

15. Caulkins, Kilmer, and Kleiman, *Marijuana Legalization*.

16. Kamin, "Medical Marijuana in Colorado and the Future of Marijuana Regulation in the United States"; Bender, "The Colors of Cannabis."

Bibliography

Abadinsky, Howard. *Organized Crime.* 9th ed. Belmont, CA: Wadsworth, 2010.

Abbott, Edith. *The Tenements of Chicago.* Chicago: University of Chicago Press, 1936.

Abu-Lughod, Janet L. *Race, Space, and Riots in Chicago, New York, and Los Angeles.* Oxford: Oxford University Press, 2007.

Ackerman, Spencer. "The Disappeared: Chicago Police Detain Americans at Abuse-Laden 'Black Site.'" *The Guardian*, February 24, 2015. https://web.archive.org/web/20210109024951/https://www.theguardian.com/us-news/2015/feb/24/chicago-police-detain-americans-black-site.

Addady, Michael. "Donald Trump's Immigration Reform May Be Less Severe Than We Thought." *Fortune*, August 21, 2016. http://fortune.com/2016/08/21/donald-trump-immigration/.

Addams, Jane. "Pioneer Labor Legislation in Illinois." In *Twenty Years at Hull-House with Autobiographical Notes*, 182–212. New York: Macmillan, 1923.

Adelman, Robert M., Charis E. Kubrin, Graham C. Ousey, and Lesley W. Reid. "Editorial: New Directions in Research on Immigration, Crime, Law, and Justice." *Migration Letters* 15, no. 2 (2018): 139–46.

Adler, Patricia A. *Wheeling and Dealing: An Ethnography of an Upper-Level Drug Dealing and Smuggling Community.* New York: Columbia University Press, 1993.

Aguilar, Julián. "Central American Gang's Tentacles Reach Deep into Texas." *Texas Tribune*, October 19, 2016. https://web.archive.org/web/20170314042534/https://www.texastribune.org/2016/10/19/ms-13-gang-houston/.

——. "El Paso Ranked Safest City in U.S. for 3rd Straight Year." *Texas Tribune*, February 5, 2013. https://web.archive.org/web/20210104064215/https://www.texastribune.org/2013/02/05/el-paso-again-ranked-countrys-safest-city/.

Aguilar, Julián, and Alexa Ura. "Border Communities Have Lower Crime Rates." *Texas Tribune*, February 23, 2016. https://web.archive.org/web/20180310155427/https://www.texastribune.org/2016/02/23/border-communities-have-lower-crime-rates/.

Ahmed, Azam. "El Chapo, Mexican Drug Kingpin, Is Extradited to U.S." *New York Times*, January 19, 2017. https://web.archive.org/web/20200222011815/https://www.nytimes.com/2017/01/19/world/el-chapo-extradited-mexico.html.

Ahmed, Azam, and Randal C. Archibold. "Mexican Drug Kingpin, El Chapo, Escapes Prison through Tunnel." *New York Times*, July 13, 2015.

Ainslie, Ricardo C. *The Fight to Save Juárez: Life in the Heart of Mexico's Drug War.* Austin: University of Texas Press, 2013.

Alexander, Michelle. *The New Jim Crow: Mass Incarceration in the Age of Colorblindness.* New York: New Press, 2010.

Alonso, Alejandro A. "Racialized Identities and the Formation of Black Gangs in Los Angeles." *Urban Geography* 25, no. 7 (2004): 658–74.

Alpert, Geoffrey P., Ben M. Crouch, and C. Ronald Huff. "Prison Reform by Judicial Decree: The Unintended Consequences of Ruiz V. Estelle." *Justice System Journal* 9, no. 3 (1984): 291–305.

Andreas, Peter. "The Political Economy of Narco-Corruption in Mexico." *Current History* 97, no. 618 (1998): 160–65.

Anslinger, Harry Jacob, and Courtney Ryley Cooper. *Marijuana: Assassin of Youth.* Springfield, OH: Crowell, 1937.

Archibold, Randal C., and Andrew Becker. "Border Agents, Lured by the Other Side." *New York Times,* May 27, 2008. https://web.archive.org/web/20210111215328 /https://www.nytimes.com/2008/05/27/us/27border.html.

Arizona Attorney General. "Drug Cartel Operations." May 15, 2016. https://web.archive .org/web/20170828191927/https://www.azag.gov/dco.

Arizona Criminal Justice Commission. *2006 Gangs in Arizona.* Phoenix, AZ: Statistical Analysis Center, 2007.

——. *2013 Arizona Gang Threat Assessment.* Phoenix, AZ: Statistical Analysis Center, 2015.

——. *2014 Arizona Gang Threat Assessment.* Phoenix, AZ: Statistical Analysis Center, 2016.

——. *2018 Arizona Gang Threat Assessment.* Phoenix, AZ: Arizona Criminal Justice Commission, 2018.

Arizona Department of Corrections. "Certified and Monitored STGs." n.d. https://web .archive.org/web/20201128082241/https://corrections.az.gov/public-resources /inspector-general/security-threat-group-unit/certified-and-monitored-stgs.

Arredondo, J., T. Gaines, S. Manian, C. Vilalta, A. Bañuelos, S. A. Strathdee, and L. Beletsky. "The Law on the Streets: Evaluating the Impact of Mexico's Drug Decriminalization Reform on Drug Possession Arrests in Tijuana, Mexico." *International Journal of Drug Policy* 54 (January 4, 2018): 1–8.

Asbury, Herbert. *The Gangs of Chicago: An Informal History of the Chicago Underworld.* New York: Thunder's Mouth, 2003.

Associated Press. "AP IMPACT: After 40 Years, $1 Trillion, US War on Drugs Has Failed to Meet Any of Its Goals." *Fox News,* May 13, 2010. http://web.archive.org/web /20180927122112/http://www.foxnews.com/world/2010/05/13/ap-impact-years -trillion-war-drugs-failed-meet-goals.html.

Astorga, Luis. *El siglo de las drogas: el narcotráfico, del Porfiriato al nuevo milenio.* Mexico City: Plaza y Janés, 2005.

Austen, Ben. "The Last Tower: The Decline and Fall of Public Housing." *Harper's Magazine,* May 2012.

Bailey, David C. "Revisionism and the Recent Historiography of the Mexican Revolution." *Hispanic American Historical Review* 58, no. 1 (1978): 62–79.

Barak, Maya P., Kenneth Sebastian León, and Edward R. Maguire. "Conceptual and Empirical Obstacles in Defining MS-13: Law-Enforcement Perspectives." *Criminology & Public Policy* 19, no. 2 (2020): 563–89.

Baumgartner, Frank R., and Bryan D. Jones. "Agenda Dynamics and Policy Subsystems." *Journal of Politics* 53, no. 4 (1991): 1044–74.

Becker, Gary S. "Crime and Punishment: An Economic Approach." *Journal of Political Economy* 76, no. 2 (1968): 169–217.

Beith, Malcolm. *The Last Narco: Inside the Hunt for El Chapo, the World's Most Wanted Drug Lord.* New York: Grove, 2010.

Beittel, June S. *Mexico: Organized Crime and Drug Trafficking Organizations.* Washington, DC: Congressional Research Service. 2015.

——. *Mexico's Drug-Related Violence.* Washington. DC: Congressional Research Service. 2009.

——. *Mexico's Drug Trafficking Organizations: Source and Scope of the Violence.* Washington, DC: Congressional Research Service, 2013.

Beller, Emily, and Michael Hout. "Intergenerational Social Mobility: The United States in Comparative Perspective." *Future of Children* 16, no. 2 (2006): 19–36.

Bender, Steven W. "The Colors of Cannabis: Race and Marijuana." *UC Davis Law Review* 50 (2016): 689–706.

Benfer, Isabella, Renee Zahnow, Monica J. Barratt, Larissa Maier, Adam Winstock, and Jason Ferris. "The Impact of Drug Policy Liberalisation on Willingness to Seek Help for Problem Drug Use: A Comparison of 20 Countries." *International Journal of Drug Policy* 56 (June 1, 2018): 162–75.

Bennett, W. Lance, and Murray Edelman. "Toward a New Political Narrative." *Journal of Communication* 35, no. 4 (2006): 156–71.

Bentle, Kyle, Jonathon Berlin, Ryan Marx, and Kori Rumore. "40,000 Homicides: Retracing 63 Years of Murder in Chicago." *Chicago Tribune*, April 27 2021. https://web.archive.org/web/20210929105500/https://www.chicagotribune.com/news/breaking/ct-history-of-chicago-homicides-htmlstory.html.

Bernstein, David. "Martin Luther King Jr.'s 1966 Chicago Campaign." *Chicago*, July 25, 2016. https://web.archive.org/web/20210825125241/https://www.chicagomag.com/Chicago-Magazine/August-2016/Martin-Luther-King-Chicago-Freedom-Movement/.

Bernstein, David, and Noah Isackson. "Gangs and Politicians in Chicago: An Unholy Alliance." *Chicago*, December 13, 2011. https://web.archive.org/web/20201225071636/https://www.chicagomag.com/Chicago-Magazine/January-2012/Gangs-and-Politicians-An-Unholy-Alliance/.

Berry, Mark. "Technology and Organised Crime in the Smart City: An Ethnographic Study of the Illicit Drug Trade." *City, Territory and Architecture* 5, no. 1 (2018): 5–16.

Bersani, Bianca E., Adam D. Fine, Alex R. Piquero, Laurence Steinberg, Paul J. Frick, and Elizabeth Cauffman. "Investigating the Offending Histories of Undocumented Immigrants." *Migration Letters* 15, no. 2 (2018): 147–66.

Black, Donald. "Crime as Social Control." *American Sociological Review* 48, no. 1 (1983): 34–45.

———. "The Geometry of Terrorism." *Sociological Theory* 22, no. 1 (2004): 14–25.

Black, Sandra E., Paul J. Devereux, Petter Lundborg, and Kaveh Majlesi. *Poor Little Rich Kids? The Determinants of the Intergenerational Transmission of Wealth.* Cambridge, MA: National Bureau of Economic Research. 2015.

Blair-Lawton, Donna, Elaine Mordoch, and Wanda Chernomas. "Putting on the Same Shoes: Lived Experiences of Women Who Are Reincarcerated." *Journal of Forensic Nursing* 16, no. 2 (2020): 99–107.

Blakemore, Jerome L., and Glenda M. Blakemore. "African American Street Gangs: A Quest for Identity." *Journal of Human Behavior in the Social Environment* 1, no. 2–3 (1998): 203–23.

Block, Alan A. *East Side, West Side: Organizing Crime in New York, 1930–1950.* New Brunswick, NJ: Transaction, 1980.

Block, Carolyn R., and Richard Block. *Street Gang Crime in Chicago.* Washington, DC: US Department of Justice, 1993.

Blumstein, Alfred, and Allen J. Beck. "Population Growth in US Prisons, 1980–1996." *Crime and Justice* 26 (1999): 17–61.

Bonner, Robert C. "The Cartel Crackdown: Winning the Drug War and Rebuilding Mexico in the Process." *Foreign Affairs* 91 (2012): 12.

Borunda, Daniel. "Birthday Party Attack Directed by Cartel, Gang." *El Paso Times*, February 11, 2010. http://archive.today/2021.01.14-041022/https://eu.elpasotimes.com/story/archives/2016/02/10/birthday-party-attack-directed-cartel-gang/80207464/.

——. "Mexico Federal Police Arrest Reputed Barrio Azteca Gang Leader 'El 300' in Chihuahua City." *El Paso Times*, November 9, 2018. http://archive.today/2021.01.12-235738/https://www.elpasotimes.com/story/news/crime/2018/11/09/mexico-federal-police-arrest-barrio-azteca-gang-leader-el-300-juarez-chihuahua/1932483002/.

——. "Prison Violence Kills 20 in Juárez." *El Paso Times*, March 5, 2009.

Bourgois, Philippe. *In Search of Respect: Selling Crack in El Barrio.* 2nd ed. Cambridge: Cambridge University Press, 2003.

Bowden, Charles. *Down by the River: Drugs, Money, Murder, and Family.* New York: Simon and Schuster, 2002.

——. *Murder City: Ciudad Juárez and the Global Economy's New Killing Fields.* New York: Nation Books, 2010.

Bragg, Steven. "What Is Separation of Duties?" AccountingTools, May 5, 2016. https://web.archive.org/web/20200612183653/https://www.accountingtools.com/articles/what-is-separation-of-duties.html.

Branch, Hilarion Noel, and Leo S. Rowe. "The Mexican Constitution of 1917 Compared with the Constitution of 1857." *Annals of the American Academy of Political and Social Science* 71 (1917): 1–116.

Brendel, Patrick. "Who Is 'West Texas?'" *Odessa American*, January 7, 2008. https://web.archive.org/web/20201207023250/https://www.oaoa.com/news/article_64efa683-e2c8-548b-af0c-52fb69ea7bdc.html.

Brouwer, Kimberly C., Patricia Case, Rebeca Ramos, Carlos Magis-Rodríguez, Jesus Bucardo, Thomas L. Patterson, and Steffanie A. Strathdee. "Trends in Production, Trafficking, and Consumption of Methamphetamine and Cocaine in Mexico." *Substance Use & Misuse* 41, no. 5 (2006): 707–27.

Brownstein, Henry H., and Bruce G. Taylor. "Measuring the Stability of Illicit Drug Markets: Why Does It Matter?" *Drug and Alcohol Dependence* 90S (2007): S52–S60.

Buerger, Michael E. "Defensive Strategies of the Street-Level Drug Trade." *Journal of Crime and Justice* 15, no. 2 (1992): 31–51.

Burgess, Ernest W. "Residential Segregation in American Cities." *Annals of the American Academy of Political and Social Science* 140 (1928): 105–15.

Burman, Michelle Lynn. "Resocializing and Repairing Homies within the Texas Prison System: A Case Study on Security Threat Group Management, Administrative Segregation, Prison Gang Renunciation and Safety for All." PhD diss., University of Texas, 2012.

Calderón, Laura, Octavio Rodríguez Ferreira, and David A. Shirk. *Drug Violence in Mexico: Data and Analysis through 2017.* San Diego: University of San Diego, Department of Political Science and International Relations, 2018.

Campbell, Howard. "Drug Trafficking Stories: Everyday Forms of Narco-Folklore on the US–Mexico Border." *International Journal of Drug Policy* 16, no. 5 (2005): 326–33.

——. *Drug War Zone: Frontline Dispatches from the Streets of El Paso and Juárez.* Austin: University of Texas Press, 2009.

——. "Narco-Propaganda in the Mexican 'Drug War': An Anthropological Perspective." *Latin American Perspectives* 41, no. 2 (2014): 60–77.

Campbell, Kristina M. "The Road to S.B. 1070: How Arizona Became Ground Zero for the Immigrants' Rights Movement and the Continuing Struggle for Latino Civil Rights in America." *Harvard Latino Law Review* 14 (2011): 1–22.

Campbell, Michael C. "Politics, Prisons, and Law Enforcement: An Examination of the Emergence of 'Law and Order' Politics in Texas." *Law & Society Review* 45, no. 3 (2011): 63–65.

Carey, Elaine. *Women Drug Traffickers: Mules, Bosses, and Organized Crime.* Albuquerque: University of New Mexico Press, 2014.

Carter, J. Chance, William E. Brewer, and S. Michael Angel. "Raman Spectroscopy for the In Situ Identification of Cocaine and Selected Adulterants." *Applied Spectroscopy* 54, no. 12 (2000): 1876–81.

Castillo, Juan Camilo. "Should Drug Policy Be Aimed against Cartel Leaders? Breaking Down a Peaceful Equilibrium," Master's thesis, Universidad de los Andes, 2013.

Castro, Rafaela. *Chicano Folklore: A Guide to the Folktales, Traditions, Rituals and Religious Practices of Mexican Americans*. Oxford: Oxford University Press, 2000.

Caulkins, Jonathan P., Beau Kilmer, and Mark A. R. Kleiman. *Marijuana Legalization: What Everyone Needs to Know*®. New York: Oxford University Press, 2016.

Celaya Pacheco, Fernando. "Narcofearance: How Has Narcoterrorism Settled in Mexico?" *Studies in Conflict & Terrorism* 32, no. 12 (2009): 1021–48.

Centers for Disease Control and Prevention. "Understanding the Epidemic." National Center for Injury Prevention and Control, last reviewed March 21, 2021. https://www.cdc.gov/opioids/basics/epidemic.html.

Cepeda, Alice, and Kathryn M. Nowotny. "A Border Context of Violence: Mexican Female Sex Workers on the U.S.-Mexico Border." *Violence Against Women* 20, no. 12 (December 2014): 1506–31.

Chabat, Jorge. "Mexico's War on Drugs: No Margin for Maneuver." *Annals of the American Academy of Political and Social Science* 582 (2002): 134–48.

Charles, Sam. "Killing 'Kato': The Story of Latin Kings Boss Rudy Rangel Jr.'s Murder." *Chicago Sun Times*, July 20, 2018. https://web.archive.org/web/20201219094855/https:/chicago.suntimes.com/2018/7/20/18371447/killing-kato-rudy-rangel-latin-kings-four-corner-hustlers.

Cherney, Max. "Mexican Cartels Are Putting Mom and Pop Meth Cooks Out of Business." *Vice*, November 15, 2014. https://web.archive.org/web/20141117225216/https://news.vice.com/article/mexican-cartels-are-putting-mom-and-pop-meth-cooks-out-of-business.

Chin, Gabriel J. "The Civil Rights Revolution Comes to Immigration Law: A New Look at the Immigration and Nationality Act of 1965." *North Carolina Law Review* 75 (1996): 273–345.

Chin, Gabriel J., Carissa Byrne Hessick, Toni Massaro, and Marc L. Miller. "A Legal Labyrinth: Issues Raised by Arizona Senate Bill 1070." *Georgetown Immigration Law Journal* 25 (2010): 47–92.

Ciccarone, Daniel. "Heroin in Brown, Black and White: Structural Factors and Medical Consequences in the US Heroin Market." *International Journal of Drug Policy* 20, no. 3 (2009): 277–82.

Cohen, Stanley. *Folk Devils and Moral Panics: The Creation of the Mods and Rockers*. London: Routledge, 2002.

Comas, José. "Detenido el 'zar del narcotráfico' del norte de México." *El País*, April 30 1986. https://web.archive.org/web/20190901023741/https://elpais.com/diario/1986/04/30/internacional/515196027_850215.html.

Combs, Mary Carol, and Sheilah E. Nicholas. "The Effect of Arizona Language Policies on Arizona Indigenous Students." *Language Policy* 11, no. 1 (2012): 101–18.

Cook, Colleen W. *Mexico's Drug Cartels*. Washington, DC: Congressional Research Service, 2007.

Correa-Cabrera, Guadalupe. *Los Zetas Inc.: Criminal Corporations, Energy, and Civil War in Mexico*. Austin: University of Texas Press, 2017.

Cromwell, Paul F., and James N. Olson. *Breaking and Entering: An Ethnographic Analysis of Burglary*. Newbury Park, CA: Sage, 1991.

Crowley, Michael. "The Committee to Save Mexico." *Time*, February 13, 2014. https://web.archive.org/web/20201031165525/https://time.com/magazine/south-pacific

/7314/february-24th-2014-vol-183-no-7-asia-europe-middle-east-and-africa
-south-pacific/.

Cunningham, James K. "Drug Trends in Phoenix and Arizona, 2013." Paper presented at the Community Epidemiology Work Group, 2014.

Cunningham, James K., Lon-Mu Liu, and Russell Callaghan. "Impact of US and Canadian Precursor Regulation on Methamphetamine Purity in the United States." *Addiction* 104, no. 3 (2009): 441–53.

Curry, G. David. "The Logic of Defining Gangs Revisited." In *The Handbook of Gangs*, ed. Scott Decker and David Pyrooz, 7–27. Oxford, UK: Wiley, 2015.

Daugherty, Arron. "Explaining Mexico's Decision to Extradite Alleged Drug Lords." InSight Crime, October 1, 2015. https://web.archive.org/web/20200919022955/https:// www.insightcrime.org/news/analysis/mexico-extraditions-drug-traffickers/.

Davis, Kristina. "Ex-Cartel Assassin 'Chino Antrax' Confirmed Dead after Fleeing from San Diego." *Los Angeles Times*, May 18, 2020. http://archive.today/2020.05.19 -074333/https://www.latimes.com/world-nation/story/2020-05-18/chino-antrax -confirmed-dead.

Dawley, David. *A Nation of Lords: The Autobiography of the Vice Lords*. Long Grove, IL: Waveland, 1992.

DEA Chicago Field Division. *The Drug Situation in the Chicago Field Division*. Chicago: Drug Enforcement Administration, 2019.

DEA Chicago Field Division, Federal Bureau of Investigation, and the Chicago Police Department. *Cartels and Gangs in Chicago*. Chicago: US Department of Justice, 2017.

Decker, Scott H., and Margaret Townsend Chapman. *Drug Smugglers on Drug Smuggling*. Philadelphia: Temple University Press, 2008.

de Cordoba, Jose. "Mexico Arrests the Son of an Alleged Drug-Cartel Leader." *Wall Street Journal*, March 20, 2009. http://archive.today/2021.03.06-204638/https://www.wsj .com/articles/SB123751471088791545.

Department of Justice. "Final Barrio Azteca Member in El Paso Sentenced to Federal Prison on Rico, Drug Trafficking and Money Laundering Charges." March 3, 2016. https://web.archive.org/web/20170710010659/https://www.justice.gov/usao -wdtx/pr/final-barrio-azteca-member-el-paso-sentenced-federal-prison-rico -drug-trafficking-and.

Desmond, Matthew, Andrew V. Papachristos, and David S. Kirk. "Police Violence and Citizen Crime Reporting in the Black Community." *American Sociological Review* 81, no. 5 (2016): 857–76.

Devereaux, Ryan. "An Unchecked Union." *The Intercept*, December 27, 2020. https://web .archive.org/web/20210108082119if_/https://theintercept.com/2020/12/27 /border-patrol-trump-biden-politics/.

DeVito, Carlo. *The Encyclopedia of International Organized Crime*. New York: Checkmark, 2005.

Diaz-Cayeros, Alberto, and Beatriz Magaloni. "Party Dominance and the Logic of Electoral Design in Mexico's Transition to Democracy." *Journal of Theoretical Politics* 13, no. 3 (2001): 271–93.

Dighton, Daniel. "The Festering Problem of Methamphetamine in Illinois." *The Compiler* (2004): 1–8.

Dilulio, John J. *Governing Prisons*. New York: Simon and Schuster, 1990.

Dills, Angela K., Sietse Goffard, Jeffrey Miron, and Erin Partin. "The Effect of State Marijuana Legalizations: 2021 Update." *Policy Analysis*, no. 908 (February 2, 2021). Cato Institute, 2021. https://www.cato.org/sites/cato.org/files/2021-01/PA908 .pdf.

Dinkins, Jim, and Peter Vincent. "Money-Laundering Methods of Drug Cartels and the Capture of El Chapo." Thomson Reuters, white paper, September 14, 2016. https://web.archive.org/web/20210127054116/https://legal.thomsonreuters.com/en/insights/white-papers/money-laundering-methods-of-drug-cartels-and-the-capture-of-el-chapo.

Drake, St. Clair, and Horace Cayton. *Black Metropolis: A Study of Negro Life in a Northern City.* Vol. 1. Chicago: University of Chicago Press, 1970.

Dresser, Denise. "Mexico after the July 6 Election: Neither Heaven nor Hell." *Current History* 97, no. 616 (1998): 55–66.

Drug Enforcement Administration. *2015 National Drug Threat Assessment Summary.* Washington, DC: Drug Enforcement Administration, 2015.

——. *United States: Areas of Influence of Major Mexican Transnational Criminal Organizations.* Washington, DC: Drug Enforcement Administration, 2015.

Dube, Arindrajit, Oeindrila Dube, and Omar García-Ponce. "Cross-Border Spillover: US Gun Laws and Violence in Mexico." *American Political Science Review* 107, no. 3 (2013): 397–417.

Duck, Waverly. *No Way Out: Precarious Living in the Shadow of Poverty and Drug Dealing.* Chicago: University of Chicago Press, 2015.

Dudley, Steven. *MS-13: The Making of America's Most Notorious Gang.* Toronto: Hanover Square Press, 2020.

Dumke, Mick. "Anatomy of a Heroin Ring." *Chicago Reader,* February 14, 2013. https://web.archive.org/web/20181230185016/https://www.chicagoreader.com/chicago/gang-violence-heroin-new-breeds-vice-lords/Content?oid=8761736.

——. "The Drug Warrior." Chicago Reader, May 27, 2014. https://web.archive.org/web/20190107141352/https://www.chicagoreader.com/chicago/division-dea-jack-riley-fights-cartels-heroin/Content?oid=13657554.

Durán Martínez, Angélica. "Drugs around the Corner: Domestic Drug Markets and Violence in Colombia and Mexico." *Latin American Politics and Society* 57, no. 3 (2015): 122–46.

——. *The Politics of Drug Violence: Criminals, Cops and Politicians in Colombia and Mexico.* Oxford: Oxford University Press, 2018.

Dwyer, Colin. "Ex-Sheriff Joe Arpaio Convicted of Criminal Contempt." National Public Radio. January 16, 2017. https://web.archive.org/web/20210104085414/https://www.npr.org/sections/thetwo-way/2017/07/31/540629884/ex-sheriff-joe-arpaio-convicted-of-criminal-contempt.

Eads, David, Helga Salinas, and Patricia Evans. "Demolished: The End of Chicago's Public Housing." National Public Radio, 2014. https://web.archive.org/web/20210104060825/https://apps.npr.org/lookatthis/posts/publichousing/.

Edelman, Murray. *The Politics of Misinformation.* Cambridge: Cambridge University Press, 2001.

Ekland-Olson, Sheldon. "Crowding, Social Control, and Prison Violence: Evidence from the Post-Ruiz Years in Texas." *Law and Society Review* 20, no.3 (1986): 389–421.

Elgas, Rob. "Crime Commission: El Chapo Is Public Enemy No. 1, Again." *ABC Eyewitness News,* 2015. https://web.archive.org/web/20180709223735/http://abc7chicago.com/news/crime-commission-el-chapo-is-public-enemy-no-1-again/851303/.

Elias, Norbert. *What Is Sociology?* Translated by Stephen Mennell and Grace Morrissey. New York: Columbia University Press, 1978.

Ellingwood, Ken. "Mexican Drug Figure's Son Is Arrested." *Los Angeles Times,* March 20, 2009. http://archive.today/2016.01.17-175732/http://touch.latimes.com/%23section/-1/article/p2p-45669701/.

Executive Office for Immigration Review. *The Immigration Court Practice Manual*. Falls Church, VA: US Department of Justice, 2009.

Family, Jill E. "The Future Relief of Immigration Law." *Drexel Law Review* 9 (2016): 393–418.

Farah, Douglas. "Money Laundering and Bulk Cash Smuggling: Challenges for the Merida Initiative." Woodrow Wilson International Center for Scholars, Working Paper Series on U.S.-Mexico Security Cooperation, May, 2010. http://www.wilsoncenter.org/topics/pubs/Farah.pdf.

Federal Bureau of Investigation. "Barrio Azteca Lieutenant Who Ordered the Consulate Murders in Ciudad Juarez Sentenced to Life in Prison." News release, April 24, 2014. https://web.archive.org/web/20191102190913/https://www.fbi.gov/contact-us/field-offices/elpaso/news/press-releases/barrio-azteca-lieutenant-who-ordered-the-consulate-murders-in-ciudad-juarez-sentenced-to-life-in-prison.

——. *National Gang Threat Assessment: Emerging Trends*. Washington, DC: National Gang Intelligence Center, 2011.

——. "Table 6: Crime in the United States by Metropolitan Statistical Area, 2019." 2019. https://web.archive.org/web/20210122013204/https://ucr.fbi.gov/crime-in-the-u.s/2019/crime-in-the-u.s.-2019/topic-pages/tables/table-6.

Felson, Marcus. *The Ecosystem for Organized Crime*. Helsinki: European Institute for Crime Prevention and Control, affiliated with the United Nations Helsinki, 2006.

Fessenden, Ford, and Haeyoun Park. "Chicago's Murder Problem." *New York Times*, May 27, 2016. https://web.archive.org/web/20211019132900/https://www.nytimes.com/interactive/2016/05/18/us/chicago-murder-problem.html.

Feuer, Alan. "El Chapo Sentenced to Life in Prison, Ending Notorious Criminal Career." *New York Times*, July 17, 2019. http://archive.today/2019.07.17-143300/https://www.nytimes.com/2019/07/17/nyregion/el-chapo-sentencing.html.

——. "El Chapo's Wife Set to Plead Guilty to Helping Run Drug Empire." *New York Times*, June 8, 2021. http://archive.today/2021.06.08-222857/https://www.nytimes.com/2021/06/08/us/politics/el-chapos-wife-guilty-plea.html.

——. "The Meeting in the Mountains That Led to $800 Million in Cash for El Chapo." *New York Times*, December 19, 2018. https://web.archive.org/web/20201108140401/https:/www.nytimes.com/2018/12/19/nyregion/el-chapo-trial.html.

Fischer, Daryl R. *Arizona Department of Corrections: Security Threat Group (STG) Program Evaluation, Final Report*. National Institute of Justice. December 2001. https://nij.ojp.gov/library/publications/arizona-department-corrections-security-threat-group-stg-program-evaluation.

Fleisher, Mark S., and Scott H. Decker. "An Overview of the Challenge of Prison Gangs." *Corrections Management Quarterly* 5 (2001): 1–9.

Flores, Mia, and Olivia Flores. *Cartel Wives: A True Story of Deadly Decisions, Steadfast Love, and Bringing Down El Chapo*. New York: Grand Central, 2017.

Flores, Pedro. "Statement of Pedro Flores—June 4, 2009." United States District Court for the Northern District of Illinois, Chicago, 2009.

Fong, Robert S. "The Organizational Structure of Prison Gangs: A Texas Case Study." *Federal Probation* 54 (1990): 36–43.

Fong, Robert S., and Salvador Buentello. "The Detection of Prison Gang Development: An Empirical Assessment." *Federal Probation* 55 (1991): 66–69.

Fontes, Anthony W. "Beyond the Maras: Violence and Survival in Urban Central America." Panel discussion, "Is There Hope for Central American Youth?," September 18, 2014, Latin American Program. Woodrow Wilson International Center for Scholars Working Paper Series.

———. *Mortal Doubt: Transnational Gangs and Social Order in Guatemala City*. Oakland: University of California Press, 2018.

Forbes. "The World's Billionaires: #701 Joaquin Guzman Loera." *Forbes*, March 11, 2009. https://web.archive.org/web/20160310160704/https://www.forbes.com/lists /2009/10/billionaires-2009-richest-people_Joaquin-Guzman-Loera_FS0Y.html.

Franklin, Jonathan. "Queen of Cartels: Most Famous Female Leader of Mexico's Under-world Speaks Out." *The Guardian*, May 16, 2016. https://web.archive.org/web/2020 1222004801/https://www.theguardian.com/society/2016/may/16/mexico-drug -cartels-famous-female-leader-sandra-avila.

Franklin, Steve. "Immigrant Chicago." Chicago Stories, 2012. https://web.archive.org /web/20201210104156/http://chicagostories.org/immigrant-chicago/.

Friman, H. Richard. "Drug Markets and the Selective Use of Violence." *Crime, Law and Social Change* 52, no. 3 (2009): 285–95.

Frye, Timothy, and Ekaterina Zhuravskaya. "Rackets, Regulation, and the Rule of Law." *Journal of Law, Economics, and Organization* 16, no. 2 (2000): 478–502.

Fukuyama, Francis. "What Is Governance?" *Governance* 26, no. 3 (2013): 347–48.

Gagne, David. "'El Mayo,' the Unsung Leader of Mexico's Sinaloa Cartel." InSight Crime, August 7, 2015. http://www.insightcrime.org/news-briefs/el-mayo-unsung-leader -mexico-sinaloa-cartel.

Gambetta, Diego. *Codes of the Underworld: How Criminals Communicate*. Princeton, NJ: Princeton University Press, 2009.

———. *The Sicilian Mafia: The Business of Private Protection*. Cambridge, MA: Harvard University Press, 1993.

Gang Resistance Education and Training. "What Is G.R.E.A.T." n.d. https://web.archive .org/web/20201112022349/https://www.great-online.org/GREAT-Home.

Garriott, William. *Policing Methamphetamine: Narcopolitics in Rural America*. New York: New York University Press, 2011.

Geisler, Charles. "Accumulating Insecurity among Illegal Immigrants." In *Accumulating Insecurity: Violence and Dispossession in the Making of Everyday Life*, ed. Shel-ley Feldman, Charles Geisler, and Gayatri A. Menon, 240–60. Athens: University of Georgia Press, 2011.

Giommoni, Luca, R. V. Gundur, and Erik Cheekes. "International Drug Trafficking: Past, Present, and Prospective Trends." In *Oxford Research Encyclopedia of Criminol-ogy and Criminal Justice*, ed. Henry N. Pontell. Oxford: Oxford University Press, 2020.

Gleicher, Lily, and Jessica Reichert. *Illinois Drug Threat Assessment: A Survey of Police Chiefs and County Sheriffs*. Chicago: Illinois Criminal Justice Information Author-ity, 2017.

Goffman, Erving. *The Presentation of Self in Everyday Life*. Edinburgh, UK: University of Edinburgh, 1956.

Goldstein, Amy, and Dan Eggen. "Immigration Judges Often Picked Based on GOP Ties." *Washington Post*, June 11, 2007. https://web.archive.org/web/20150317193411 /http://www.washingtonpost.com/wp-dyn/content/article/2007/06/10 /AR2007061001229.html.

Gorbea, Gabriela. "Mexico's Tiny Minimum Wage Is about to Increase—by Almost Noth-ing." VICE News. December 14, 2015. https://web.archive.org/web/20210104063449 /https://www.vice.com/en/article/bjk79m/mexicos-tiny-minimum-wage-is-about -to-increase-by-almost-nothing.

Gosnell, Harold F. "The Chicago 'Black Belt' as a Political Battleground." *American Jour-nal of Sociology* 39, no. 3 (1933): 329–41.

Grayson, George W. *Mexico: Narco-Violence and a Failed State?* New Brunswick, NJ: Transaction, 2010.

——. *Mexico's Struggle with "Drugs and Thugs."* New York: Foreign Policy Association, 2009.

Grayson, George W., and Samuel Logan. *The Executioner's Men: Los Zetas, Rogue Soldiers, Criminal Entrepreneurs, and the Shadow State They Created.* New Brunswick, NJ: Transaction, 2012.

Greenfield, Victoria A., and Letizia Paoli. "If Supply-Oriented Drug Policy Is Broken, Can Harm Reduction Help Fix It? Melding Disciplines and Methods to Advance International Drug-Control Policy." *International Journal of Drug Policy* 23, no. 1 (January 1, 2012): 6–15.

Grillo, Ioan. *El Narco: The Bloody Rise of Mexican Drug Cartels.* New York: Bloomsbury, 2011.

Gundur, R. V. "The Changing Social Organization of Prison Protection Markets: When Prisoners Choose to Organize Horizontally Rather Than Vertically." *Trends in Organized Crime*, February 28, 2018. https://doi.org/10.1007/s12117-018-9332-0.

——. "Finding the Sweet Spot: Optimizing Criminal Careers within the Context of Illicit Enterprise." *Deviant Behavior* 41, no. 3 (2020): 378–97.

——. "Negotiating Violence and Protection in Prison and on the Outside: The Organizational Evolution of the Transnational Prison Gang Barrio Azteca." *International Criminal Justice Review* 30, no. 1 (2020): 30–60.

——. "Prison Gangs." In *Oxford Research Encyclopedia of Criminology and Criminal Justice*, ed. Henry N. Pontell. Oxford: Oxford University Press, 2020.

——. "Settings Matter: Examining Protection's Influence on the Illicit Drug Trade in Convergence Settings in the Paso Del Norte Metropolitan Area." *Crime, Law and Social Change* 72 (2019): 229–360.

——. "Using the Internet to Recruit Respondents for Offline Interviews in Criminological Studies." *Urban Affairs Review* 55, no. 6 (2019): 1731–56.

Hagedorn, John M. *The In$ane Chicago Way: The Daring Plan by Chicago Gangs to Create a Spanish Mafia.* Chicago: University of Chicago Press, 2015.

——. "Race Not Space: A Revisionist History of Gangs in Chicago." *Journal of African American History* 91, no. 2 (2006): 194–208.

Hagedorn, John M., and Brigid Rauch. "Housing, Gangs, and Homicide: What We Can Learn from Chicago." *Urban Affairs Review* 42, no. 4 (2007): 435–56.

Haislip, Gene R. *Methamphetamine Precursor Chemical Control in the 1990s.* Drug Enforcement Administration. January 1996. https://web.archive.org/web/201704180 02517/http://druglibrary.net/schaffer/dea/programs/diverson/divpub/substance /methamph.htm.

Haller, Mark H. "Urban Crime and Criminal Justice: The Chicago Case." *Journal of American History* 57, no. 3 (1970): 619–35.

Halsey, Mark, Ruth Armstrong, and Serena Wright. "'F*ck It!': Matza and the Mood of Fatalism in the Desistance Process." *British Journal of Criminology* 57, no. 5 (2017): 1041–60.

Hamilton, Keegan. "Methology 101: Old-School Meth Labs Give Way to 'Shake and Bake'" *Riverfront Times*, May 19, 2010. https://web.archive.org/web/20151023001500 /https://www.riverfronttimes.com/stlouis/methology-101-old-school-meth-labs -give-way-to-shake-and-bake/Content?oid=2483461.

Hampton, Elaine, and Cynthia C. Ontiveros. *Copper Stain: Asarco's Legacy in El Paso.* Norman: University of Oklahoma Press, 2019.

Harris, Casey T., and Jeff Gruenewald. "News Media Trends in the Framing of Immigration and Crime, 1990–2013." *Social Problems* 67, no. 3 (2020): 452–70.

Hart, Carl L. *Drug Use for Grown-Ups: Chasing Liberty in the Land of Fear.* New York: Penguin, 2021.

Hatjoullis, George. "Schrödinger's Immigrant." Gestaltz. n.d., https://web.archive.org /web/20201222004512/https://gestaltz.wordpress.com/2015/09/03/schrodingers -immigrant/.

Hawkins, Jennifer, Amanda Zibell, and Tony Vidale. *Enhanced Drug and Gang Enforcement (EDGE) Report.* Phoenix: Arizona Criminal Justice Commission, 2013.

Hazen, Jennifer M., and Dennis Rodgers. *Global Gangs: Street Violence across the World.* Minneapolis: University of Minnesota Press, 2014.

Heinle, Kimberly, Cory Molzahn, and David A. Shirk. *Drug Violence in Mexico: Data and Analysis through 2014.* San Diego: University of San Diego, Department of Political Science and International Relations, 2015.

Henderson, Peter V. N. *In the Absence of Don Porfirio: Francisco León de la Barra and the Mexican Revolution.* Wilmington, DE: Scholarly Resources, 2000.

Hernández, Anabel. *Los señores del narco.* Mexico City: Grijalbo, 2012.

Hernández, María. "Las autodefensas contra el narcotráfico en México." El Orden Mundial, April 2, 2015. https://web.archive.org/web/20170303145439/http://elordenmu ndial.com/2015/04/02/las-autodefensas-contra-el-narcotrafico-en-mexico/.

Hewes, Jonathan, and Madeleine Carter. "Cartel City, Arizona." *Drugs, Inc.*, season 4, episode 9, National Geographic Channel, October 13, 2013.

Hickman, Laura J., and Marika J. Suttorp. "Are Deportable Aliens a Unique Threat to Public Safety? Comparing the Recidivism of Deportable and Nondeportable Aliens." *Criminology & Public Policy* 7, no. 1 (2008): 59–82.

Hoffman, Meredith. "Whatever Happened to Arizona's Minutemen?" Vice, March 22, 2016. https://web.archive.org/web/20200801090537/https://www.vice.com/en_us /article/xd7jmn/what-happened-to-arizonas-minutemen.

Hogan, Andrew, and Douglas Century. *Hunting El Chapo: Taking Down the World's Most Wanted Drug Lord.* London: HarperCollins, 2018.

Horowitz, Ruth. *Honor and the American Dream: Culture and Identity in a Chicano Community.* New Brunswick, NJ: Rutgers University Press, 1983.

Horton, David M., and George R. Nielsen. *Walking George: The Life of George John Beto and the Rise of the Modern Texas Prison System.* Denton: University of North Texas Press, 2005.

Hubbard, James D., Katherine Wyman, and Franco Domma. *The Chicago Crime Commission Gang Book.* Vol. 2, Chicago: Chicago Crime Commission, 2011.

Hughes, Caitlin, and Alex Stevens. "What Can We Learn from the Portuguese Decriminalization of Illicit Drugs?" *British Journal of Criminology* 50, no. 6 (2010): 999–1022.

Human Rights Watch. *World Report: Events of 2013.* New York: Seven Stories, 2014.

Hunt, Geoffrey, Stephanie Riegel, Tomas Morales, and Dan Waldorf. "Changes in Prison Culture: Prison Gangs and the Case of the 'Pepsi Generation.'" *Social Problems* 40, no. 3 (1993): 398–409.

Hurowitz, Noah. "Vicente Zambada Niebla, Son of El Chapo Cartel Partner El Mayo, Sentenced to 15 Years in Prison." *Rolling Stone*, May 30, 2019. https://web.archive .org/web/20201125194315if_/https://www.rollingstone.com/culture/culture -features/vicente-zambada-niebla-el-mayo-el-chapo-sentence-chicago-drugs -842245/.

Ianni, Francis A. J. *Black Mafia: Ethnic Succession in Organized Crime.* New York: Simon and Schuster, 1974.

ICE Newsroom. "ICE Deports Sandra Avila Beltran." News release, August 20, 2013. https://web.archive.org/web/20201222005032/https://www.ice.gov/news/releases /ice-deports-sandra-avila-beltran.

INEGI. *Encuesta nacional de seguridad pública urbana.* Aguascalientes: Instituto Nacional de Estadística y Geografía, 2015.

——. *Encuesta nacional de victimización y percepción sobre seguridad pública.* Aguascalientes: Instituto Nacional de Estadística y Geografía, 2015.

Innes, Martin. *Signal Crimes.* Oxford: Oxford University Press, 2014.

Institute for Crime and Justice Policy Research. "The World Prison Brief." School of Law, Birkbeck, University of London, 2020. http://archive.today/2021.03.03-215117/https://www.prisonstudies.org/highest-to-lowest/prison-population-total.

Irwin, John. *Prisons in Turmoil.* Boston: Little, Brown, 1980.

Jacobs, James B. "Race Relations and the Prisoner Subculture." *Crime and Justice* 1 (1979): 1–27.

——. *Stateville: The Penitentiary in Mass Society.* Chicago: University of Chicago Press, 1977.

Jamieson, Perry D. *A Survey History of Fort Bliss, 1890–1940.* El Paso, TX: United States Army Air Defense Artillery Center, 1993.

Jones, Nathan P. *Mexico's Illicit Drug Networks and the State Reaction.* Washington, DC: Georgetown University Press, 2016.

——. "Pangas, Trickery, Intimidation, and Drug Trafficking in California." *Small Wars Journal* 15, no. 12 (2016). https://web.archive.org/web/20201108102141/https://smallwarsjournal.com/jrnl/art/pangas-trickery-intimidation-and-drug-trafficking-in-california.

——. "Understanding and Addressing Youth in 'Gangs' in Mexico." In *Building Resilient Communities in Mexico: Civic Responses to Crime and Violence,* ed. David A. Shirk, Duncan Wood and Eric L. Olson, 89–118. Washington, DC: Woodrow Wilson International Center for Scholars, 2014.

Jost, Patrick M., and Harjit Singh Sandhu. *The Hawala Alternative Remittance System and Its Role in Money Laundering.* Lyon, France: Interpol, 2003.

Jusidman, Clara, and Hugo Almada Mireles. *La realidad social de Ciudad Juárez: Tomo 1, Análisis Social.* Ciudad Juárez, Mexico: Universidad Autónoma de Ciudad Juárez, 2007.

Justice, William Wayne. "Consent Decree in the Matter of Ruiz V. Estelle, Jr." US District Court, Southern District of Texas, 1981.

Kamin, Sam. "Medical Marijuana in Colorado and the Future of Marijuana Regulation in the United States." *McGeorge Law Review* 43 (2012): 147–67.

Kan, Paul Rexton. *Cartels At War: Mexico's Drug-Fueled Violence and the Threat to US National Security.* Dulles, VA: Potomac, 2012.

Kanstroom, Daniel. "Criminalizing the Undocumented: Ironic Boundaries of the Post–September 11th 'Pale of Law.'" *North Carolina Journal of International Law and Commercial Regulation* 29 (2004): 639–70.

Karson, Lawrence. *American Smuggling as White Collar Crime.* New York: Routledge, 2014.

Katz, Alan. "A Cartel and a Briefcase: How Drug Cash Moves on a River of Gold," Bloomberg, May 5, 2016. http://archive.today/2016.08.09-154231/http://www.bloomberg.com/news/articles/2016-05-05/a-cartel-and-a-briefcase-how-drug-cash-moves-on-a-river-of-gold.

Keith, Linda Camp, Jennifer S. Holmes, and Banks P. Miller. "Explaining the Divergence in Asylum Grant Rates among Immigration Judges: An Attitudinal and Cognitive Approach." *Law & Policy* 35, no. 4 (2013): 261–89.

Key, Pam. "AZ Sheriff Paul Babeu: Drug Cartels with AK-47s Control American Soil 30 Miles from Phoenix," Breitbart, May 15, 2015. https://web.archive.org/web

/20201210043924/https://www.breitbart.com/clips/2015/08/20/az-sheriff-paul
-babeu-drug-cartels-with-ak-47s-control-american-soil-30-miles-from-phoenix/.

Kinder, Douglas Clark, and William O. Walker. "Stable Force in a Storm: Harry J. Anslinger and United States Narcotic Foreign Policy, 1930–1962." *Journal of American
History* 72, no. 4 (1986): 908–27.

Kirk, Harry. *A Historical Review of Gangs and Gang Violence in El Paso, Texas.* Law Enforcement Management Institute report, Sam Houston State University, 1993.

Kleemans, Edward R. "Organized Crime, Transit Crime, and Racketeering." *Crime and
Justice* 35, no. 1 (2007): 163–215.

Klein, Malcolm W., and Cheryl L. Maxson. *Street Gang Patterns and Policies.* Oxford:
Oxford University Press, 2010.

Klesner, Joseph L. "Review: An Electoral Route to Democracy? Mexico's Transition in
Comparative Perspective." *Comparative Politics* 30, no. 4 (1998): 477–97.

Knox, George W. "The Vice Lords: Aspects of Formal and Informal Social Organizational
Life in a Gang." National Gang Crime Research Center, 2008. https://web.archive
.org/web/20200717113917/https://ngcrc.com/ngcrc/viceprof.htm.

Koval, John P., Larry Bennett, Michael I. J. Bennett, Fassil Demissie, Roberta Garner, and
Kiljoong Kim, eds. *The New Chicago: A Social and Cultural Analysis.* Philadelphia:
Temple University Press, 2006.

Krasner, Stephen D. *Sovereignty: Organized Hypocrisy.* Princeton, NJ: Princeton University Press, 1999.

Kretsedemas, Philip, and David C. Brotherton. *Immigration Policy in the Age of Punishment: Detention, Deportation, and Border Control.* New York: Columbia University
Press, 2018.

Krozer, Alice, and Juan Carlos Moreno-Brid. "Inequality in Mexico." *World Economics
Association* 4, no. 5 (2014): 4–6.

Lacey, Marc, and Ginger Thompson. "Two Drug Slayings in Mexico Rock U.S. Consulate." *New York Times.* March 15, 2010. https://www.nytimes.com/2010/03/15/world
/americas/15juarez.html?auth=link-dismiss-google1tap.

Lacy, Elaine, and Mary E. Odem. "Popular Attitudes and Public Policies." In *Latino Immigrants and the Transformation of the U.S. South,* ed. Elaine Lacy and Mary E.
Odem, 143–64. Athens, GA: University of Georgia Press, 2009.

Landesco, John. "Crime and the Failure of Institutions in Chicago's Immigrant Areas."
Journal of the American Institute of Criminal Law and Criminology 23 (1932):
238–48.

——. "The Gangster's Apologia Pro Vita Sua." In *Organized Crime in Chicago,* 1043–57.
Chicago: Illinois Association for Criminal Justice, 1929.

Lansu, Michael. "Xavier Tripp Fatally Shot in West Garfield Park." *Chicago Sun-Times,*
May 11, 2014. https://web.archive.org/web/20141021153735/http://homicides.sunti
mes.com/2014/05/11/xavier-tripp-fatally-shot-in-west-garfield-park/.

Lauderdale, Michael, and Michelle Burman. "Contemporary Patterns of Female Gangs
in Correctional Settings." *Journal of Human Behavior in the Social Environment*
19, no. 3 (2009): 258–80.

Layson, Hana, and Kenneth Warren. "Chicago and the Great Migration, 1915–1950."
Digital Collection, Newberry Library, Chicago, March 14, 2013. https://dcc
.newberry.org/?p=14436.

Lee, William. "A Crumbling, Dangerous South Side Creates Exodus of Black Chicagoans."
Chicago Tribune, March 18, 2016. https://web.archive.org/web/20201121115402
/https://www.chicagotribune.com/opinion/commentary/ct-black-exodus-chicago
-20160318-story.html.

Levitt, Steven D., and Sudhir Alladi Venkatesh. *An Economic Analysis of a Drug-Selling Gang's Finances.* Cambridge, MA: National Bureau of Economic Research. 1998.

Linnemann, Travis. *Meth Wars: Police, Media, Power.* New York: New York University Press, 2016.

Lippert, John, Nacha Cattan, and Mario Parker. "Heroin Pushed on Chicago by Cartel Fueling Gang Murders." *Bloomberg Markets,* September 17, 2013. https://web .archive.org/web/20170225151530/https://www.bloomberg.com/news/articles /2013-09-17/heroin-pushed-on-chicago-by-cartel-fueling-gang-murders.

Liu, Baodong, Yehua Dennis Wei, and Christopher A. Simon. "Social Capital, Race, and Income Inequality in the United States." *Sustainability* 9, no. 2 (2017): 248–62.

LockZero.org. "Political History of Bridgeport." University of Illinois, Chicago, n.d. https://web.archive.org/web/20201209161311/http://lockzero.org.uic.edu/V.html.

Lollman, Laura. "4 Arrested in Connection to Deadly Armed Robbery in Mesa." AZ Family, October 27, 2020. https://web.archive.org/web/20210107011354/https://www .azfamily.com/news/4-arrested-in-connection-to-deadly-armed-robbery-in-mesa /article_3978568a-1895-11eb-9045-4fa6d8c66b7a.html.

Lombardo, Robert M. *Organized Crime in Chicago: Beyond the Mafia.* Urbana: University of Illinois Press, 2013.

Lopez-Aguado, Patrick. *Stick Together and Come Back Home: Racial Sorting and the Spillover of Carceral Identity.* Oakland: University of California Press, 2018.

Lupsha, Peter A. "Drug Lords and Narco-Corruption: The Players Change but the Game Continues." *Crime, Law and Social Change* 16 (1991): 41–58.

Lupsha, Peter A., and Kip Schlegel. *The Political Economy of Drug Trafficking: The Herrera Organization (Mexico and the United States).* Albuquerque: University of New Mexico, 1980.

Macedo, Donaldo. "The Colonialism of the English Only Movement." *Educational Researcher* 29, no. 3 (2000): 15–24.

Magaloni, Beatriz. "The Demise of Mexico's One-Party Dominant Regime." In *The Third Wave of Democratization in Latin America: Advances and Setbacks,* ed. Frances Hagopian and Scott P. Mainwaring, 121–46. Cambridge: Cambridge University Press, 2005.

Magaloni, Beatriz, Gustavo Robles, Aila Matanock, Vidal Romero, and Alberto Díaz-Cayeros. "Living in Fear: The Dynamics of Extortion in Mexico's Criminal Insurgency." SSRN, December 1, 2017. https://papers.ssrn.com/sol3/papers.cfm?abstract _id=1963836.

Main, Frank. "'El Vincentillo,' El Chapo's Ex-Logistics Guru, Was a Cartel Big Shot since Teens." *Chicago Sun-Times,* September 14, 2018. http://archive.today/2021.03.07 -054441/https://chicago.suntimes.com/2018/9/14/18385062/el-vicentillo-el -chapo-s-ex-logistics-guru-was-a-cartel-big-shot-since-teens.

Manwaring, Max G. *A Contemporary Challenge to State Sovereignty: Gangs and Other Illicit Transnational Criminal Organizations in Central America, El Salvador, Mexico, Jamaica, and Brazil.* Fort Belvoir, VA: Defense Technical Information Center, 2007.

——. "Security, Stability and Sovereignty Challenges of Politicized Gangs and Insurgents in the Americas." *Small Wars & Insurgencies* 22, no. 5 (2011): 860–89.

Marks, Paula Mitchell. *And Die in the West: The Story of the O.K Corral Gunfight.* Norman: University of Oklahoma Press, 1996.

Marquart, James W., and Ben M. Crouch. "Coopting the Kept: Using Inmates for Social Control in a Southern Prison." *Justice Quarterly* 1, no. 4 (1984): 491–509.

——. "Judicial Reform and Prisoner Control: The Impact of Ruiz V. Estelle on a Texas Penitentiary." *Law and Society Review* 19, no. 4 (1985): 557–86.

Martin, Eric. "Hidden Consequences: The Impact of Incarceration on Dependent Children." *National Institute of Justice* 278 (2017): 2–7.

Martinez, Aaron. "Barrio Azteca Member Sentenced in RICO Case." *El Paso Times*, March 3 2016. http://archive.today/2021.01.11-041344/https://www.elpasotimes.com/story /news/crime/2016/03/03/barrio-azteca-member-sentenced-rico-case/81279358/.

———. "Man Gets Probation in 'Plata O Plomo' Case." *El Paso Times*, January 26, 2016. http://archive.today/2021.01.11-041906/https://eu.elpasotimes.com/story/news /crime/2016/01/26/man-gets-probation-plata-o-plomo-case/79360438/.

Martínez Ahrens, Jan. "El narco impone su ley en la mitad de las cárceles Mexicanas." *El País*, April 15, 2016. http://archive.today/2021.01.14-041813/https://elpais.com /internacional/2016/04/13/actualidad/1460569335_690701.html.

Massey, Douglas S., and Nancy A. Denton. *American Apartheid: Segregation and the Making of the Underclass*. Cambridge, MA: Harvard University Press, 1993.

Mazis, Michael B., and Richard Staelin. "Using Information-Processing Principles in Public Policymaking." *Journal of Marketing & Public Policy* 1, no. 1 (1982): 3–14.

McAllister, Toni. "Tijuana Money Launderer for Sinaloa Drug Cartel Pleads Guilty in San Diego." *Times of San Diego*, April 4, 2019. https://web.archive.org/web /20190408162828/https://timesofsandiego.com/crime/2019/04/04/tijuana -money-launderer-for-sinaloa-drug-cartel-pleads-guilty-in-san-diego/.

McClelland, Edward. "White Flight, by the Numbers." *NBC Chicago*, May 6, 2013. https:// web.archive.org/web/20201204090519/https://www.nbcchicago.com/news/local /chicago-politics/white-flight-by-the-numbers/1951412/.

McCoy, Alfred W. *The Politics of Heroin: CIA Complicity in the Global Drug Trade, Afghanistan, Southeast Asia, Central America*. Rev. ed. Chicago: Lawrence Hill Books, 2003.

McDonald, Colin. "Why Follow the Rio Grande." *Texas Tribune*, February 11, 2015. https://web.archive.org/web/20201214112227/https://riogrande.texastribune.org /blog/2014/9/13/.

McGahan, Jason. "Mexican Drug Lord's Insider Notes May Set Him Free after 10 Years." *The Guardian*, April 11, 2014. https://web.archive.org/web/20201221041444 /https://www.theguardian.com/world/2014/apr/11/mexican-drug-lord-10-years -sinaloa-cartel.

———. "Why Mexico's Sinaloa Cartel Loves Selling Drugs in Chicago." *Chicago Magazine*, September 17, 2013. https://web.archive.org/web/20210118041309/https://www .chicagomag.com/Chicago-Magazine/October-2013/Sinaloa-Cartel/.

McKinley, James C., Jr. "Mexican Cartels Lure American Teens as Killers." *New York Times*, June 23, 2009.

McNevin, Anne. *Contesting Citizenship: Irregular Migrants and New Frontiers of the Political*. New York: Colombia University Press, 2011.

Meisner, Jason. "14 Years for Chicago Brothers Turned Informants in Takedown of Cocaine Cartel." *Chicago Tribune*, January 27, 2015. https://web.archive.org/web /20201108102954/https://www.chicagotribune.com/news/breaking/ct-flores -brothers-cartel-sentencing-met-0128-20150127-story.html.

Meisner, Jason, and Annie Sweeney. "Wives of Chicago Twins Who Cooperated against El Chapo Arrested on Money Laundering Charges." *Chicago Tribune*, June 15, 2021. https://web.archive.org/web/20210721235048/https://www.chicagotribune .com/news/criminal-justice/ct-pedro-margarito-flores-wives-money-laundering -el-chapo-20210615-7okzn54m7nfd3kem23woktzdhm-story.html.

Merton, Robert King. *Social Theory and Social Structure*. New York: Free Press, 1968.

"Mexico Arrests 'Money Launderer' for Drug Lord Guzman." BBC, March 28, 2016. http://archive.today/2021.03.12-065537/https://www.bbc.com/news/world-latin -america-35909667.

México Evalúa. "Índice de inseguridad ciudadana y violencia." *México Evalúa*, November 10, 2010. https://www.mexicoevalua.org/indice-de-inseguridad-ciudadana-y-violencia/.

Miller, Marjorie. "Suspected Drug Lord Shot to Death at Mexican Resort." *LA Times*, April 15, 1993.

Miller, Richard Lawrence. *Drug Warriors and Their Prey: From Police Power to Police State*. Westport, CT: Praeger, 1996.

Miroff, Nick, and Carolyn Van Houten. "The Border Is Tougher to Cross Than Ever. But There's Still One Way into America." *Washington Post*. October 24, 2018. https://www.washingtonpost.com/graphics/2018/national/border-asylum-claims/.

Mitchell, Kirk. "Colorado's Supermax Prison Now Occupied by El Chapo Is 'Worse Than Death,' Ex-Warden Says." *Denver Post*, July 27, 2019. https://web.archive.org/web/20201127071538/https://www.denverpost.com/2019/07/27/supermax-el-chapo-escape-mentally-ill/.

——. "Two Denver-Area Mexican Restaurants Tied to Drug Lord Joaquin 'El Chapo' Guzman's Money-Laundering Enterprise, Federal Suit Says," *Denver Post*, March 2, 2019. https://web.archive.org/web/20201116112053/https://www.denverpost.com/2019/03/01/el-chapo-denver-mexican-restaurants/.

Molzahn, Cory, Viridiana Ríos, and David A. Shirk. *Drug Violence in Mexico: Data and Analysis through 2011*. San Diego: University of San Diego, 2012.

Montenegro, José Luis. "Californian, Businesswoman, 'Narco Junior': El Chapo's American Daughter." *The Guardian*, March 4, 2016. https://web.archive.org/web/20201109060123/https://www.theguardian.com/world/2016/mar/04/el-chapo-daughter-joaquin-guzman-california.

Montoya, Luis. "Cuellar: Latest FBI Report Shows Border Cities to Be Safe." *Rio Grande Guardian*, November 15, 2015. https://web.archive.org/web/20201115205050/https://riograndeguardian.com/cuellar-latest-fbi-report-shows-border-cities-to-be-safe/.

Moore, Lindsay, and Joseph Flaherty. "The Friday Surprise: Donald Trump Pardons Sheriff Joe Arpaio." *Phoenix New Times*, August 25, 2017. https://web.archive.org/web/20200914091421/https://www.phoenixnewtimes.com/news/sheriff-joe-arpaio-gets-pardon-from-donald-trump-9606956.

Moore, Natalie Y., and Lance Williams. *The Almighty Black P Stone Nation: The Rise, Fall, and Resurgence of an American Gang*. Chicago: Chicago Review Press, 2011.

Moreno, Carolina. "Enrique Peña Nieto's TIME Cover Sparks Outrage in Mexico." *Huffington Post*, December 7, 2014. https://web.archive.org/web/20200805001042/https://www.huffpost.com/entry/enrique-pena-nieto-time_n_4803677.

Moser, Whet. "Illinois Is in the Middle of America's Meth Belt." *Chicago*, March 14, 2013. https://web.archive.org/web/20201112025355/https://www.chicagomag.com/Chicago-Magazine/The-312/March-2013/Illinois-In-the-Middle-of-the-Meth-Belt/.

Mosher, Clayton J., and Scott Akins. *In the Weeds: Demonization, Legalization, and the Evolution of U.S. Marijuana Policy*. Philadelphia: Temple University Press, 2019.

Mosso, Rubén. "Cae en Michoacán 'El Tablas,' uno de los 10 más buscados por FBI." *Milenio*, June 26, 2018. http://archive.today/2021.01.11-061017/https://www.milenio.com/policia/cae-michoacan-tablas-10-buscados-fbi.

Nagle, Luz E. "Corruption of Politicians, Law Enforcement, and the Judiciary in Mexico and Complicity across the Border." *Small Wars & Insurgencies* 21, no. 1 (2010): 95–122.

National Drug Intelligence Center. "Arizona Drug Threat Assessment." December 2003. https://www.justice.gov/archive/ndic/pubs6/6384/overview.htm.

Naylor, R. T. *Wages of Crime: Black Markets, Illegal Finance, and the Underworld Economy*. Ithaca, NY: Cornell University Press, 2002.

Neumayer, Eric. "Unequal Access to Foreign Spaces: How States Use Visa Restrictions to Regulate Mobility in a Globalized World." *Transactions of the Institute of British Geographers* 31, no. 1 (2006): 72–84.

Newcomb, Brent K. "Immigration Law and the Criminal Alien: A Comparison of Policies for Arbitrary Deportations of Legal Permanent Residents Convicted of Aggravated Felonies." *Oklahoma Law Review* 51 (1998): 697–725.

Nye, Joseph S., Jr. *Soft Power: The Means to Success in World Politics*. New York: Public-Affairs, 2004.

O'Brien, Benjamin Gonzalez, Loren Collingwood, and Stephen Omar El-Khatib. "The Politics of Refuge: Sanctuary Cities, Crime, and Undocumented Immigration." *Urban Affairs Review* 55, no. 1 (2019): 3–40.

Olate, Rene, Wilson Alvarado, Christopher P. Salas-Wright, and Michael G. Vaughn. "Evidence-Based Community Interventions for Tackling the Problems of Youth Gang Violence and Delinquency in Central America." In *Human Rights and Social Equality: Challenges for Social Work*, Vol. 1, *Social Development*, ed. Sven Hessle, 106–13. Surrey, UK: Ashgate, 2014.

O'Neil, Shannon. "The Real War in Mexico: How Democracy Can Defeat the Drug Cartels." *Foreign Affairs* 88, no. 4 (2009): 63–77.

O'Neill, Kevin Lewis. "The Reckless Will: Prison Chaplaincy and the Problem of Mara Salvatrucha." *Public Culture* 22, no. 1 (2010): 67–88.

O'Rourke, Ciara. "Cornyn Says Spillover Violence in Texas Is Real and Escalating." *PolitiFact*, March 27, 2010. https://web.archive.org/web/20210112053344/https://www.politifact.com/factchecks/2010/mar/27/john-cornyn/cornyn-says-spillover-violence-texas-real-and-esca/.

Ortiz Uribe, Mónica. "Barrio Azteca Gang Shows How Crime Transcends Borders." *Fronteras*, March 24, 2014. https://web.archive.org/web/20160901050406/http://fronterasdesk.org/content/9564/barrio-azteca-gang-shows-how-crime-transcends-borders.

——. "Eating Ice Cream with a Gangster in Jail." Borders Are Meant to Be Crossed, July 20, 2010. https://web.archive.org/web/20190407192547/https://bordereporter.wordpress.com/2010/07/20/eating-ice-cream-with-a-gangster-in-jail/.

Pager, Devah. *Marked: Race, Crime, and Finding Work in an Era of Mass Incarceration*. Chicago: University of Chicago Press, 2008.

Paoli, Letizia. *Mafia Brotherhoods: Organized Crime, Italian Style*. Oxford: Oxford University Press, 2003.

Paoli, Letizia, Victoria A. Greenfield, and Peter Reuter. *The World Heroin Market: Can Supply Be Cut?* Oxford: Oxford University Press, 2009.

Papachristos, Andrew V., Anthony A. Braga, and David M. Hureau, "Social Networks and the Risk of Gunshot Injury." *Journal of Urban Health* 89, no. 6 (2012): 992–1003.

Papachristos, Andrew V., and Chris M. Smith. "The Embedded and Multiplex Nature of Al Capone." In *Crime and Networks*, ed. Carlo Morselli, 97–115. New York: Routledge, 2014.

Paral, Rob. "Chicago's Immigrants Break Old Patterns." Migration Policy Institute, September 1, 2003. https://web.archive.org/web/20201115113637/https://www.migrationpolicy.org/article/chicagos-immigrants-break-old-patterns.

Park, Robert, and Ernest W. Burgess. *Introduction to the Science of Sociology*. Chicago: University of Chicago Press, 1921.

Pasternak, Judy. "U.S. Moves to Crack Powerful Chicago Gang." *Los Angeles Times*, September 1, 1995. https://web.archive.org/web/20160819163212/http://articles.latimes.com/1995-09-01/news/mn-41129_1_chicago-s-gangster-disciples.

Patenostro, Silvana. "Mexico as a Narco-Democracy." *World Policy Journal* 12, no. 1 (1995): 41–47.

Pearce, Matt. "When Martin Luther King Jr. Took His Fight into the North, and Saw a New Level of Hatred." *Los Angeles Times*, January 18, 2016. https://web.archive.org/web/20210116190842/https://www.latimes.com/nation/la-na-mlk-chicago-20160118-story.html.

Pelz, Mary E., James W. Marquart, and C. Terry Pelz. "Right-Wing Extremism in the Texas Prisons: The Rise and Fall of the Aryan Brotherhood of Texas." *Prison Journal* 71, no. 2 (1991): 23–37.

Pérez Esparza, David, and Eugenio Weigend. "The Illegal Flow of Firearms from the United States into Mexico: A State-Level Trafficking Propensity Analysis." *Journal of Trafficking, Organized Crime and Security* 1, no. 2 (2015): 115–25.

Peron, Thomas Kauê Dal'Maso, Luciano da Fontoura Costa, and Francisco A. Rodrigues. "The Structure and Resilience of Financial Market Networks." *Chaos: An Interdisciplinary Journal of Nonlinear Science* 22, no. 1 (2012): 013117. http://aip.scitation.org/doi/10.1063/1.3683467.

Pettit, Becky, and Bruce Western. "Mass Imprisonment and the Life Course: Race and Class Inequality in US Incarceration." *American Sociological Review* 69, no. 2 (2004): 151–69.

Pew Research Center. "What Census Calls Us: A Historical Timeline." Social & Demographic Trends, 2015. https://web.archive.org/web/20201101112913/https://www.pewresearch.org/wp-content/uploads/2020/02/PH_15.06.11_MultiRacial-Timeline.pdf.

Phillips, Brian J. "Inequality and the Emergence of Vigilante Organizations: The Case of Mexican Autodefensas." *Comparative Political Studies* 50, no. 10 (2017): 1358–89.

Phippen, Weston. "Inside an Arizona Drug Smuggling Gang." *Phoenix New Times*, March 7, 2013. https://web.archive.org/web/20201111215524/https://www.phoenixnewtimes.com/news/inside-an-arizona-drug-smuggling-gang-6457630.

Pierce, Sarah, Jessica Bolter, and Andrew Selee. "US Immigration Policy under Trump: Deep Changes and Lasting Impacts." *Migration Policy Institute* 9 (2018): 13209–19.

Piketty, Thomas. *Capital in the Twenty-First Century.* Translated by Arthur Goldhammer. London: Belknap, 2014.

Police Accountability Task Force. *Recommendations for Reform: Restoring Trust between the Chicago Police and the Communities they Serve.* Chicago: Police Accountability Task Force, April 13, 2016. http://archive.today/2021.01.18-043950/https://www.chicagotribune.com/news/breaking/ct-chicago-police-accountability-task-force-final-report-20160413-htmlstory.html.

Pollack, Neal. "The Gang That Could Go Straight." *Chicago Reader*, January 26, 1995, https://chicagoreader.com/news-politics/the-gang-that-could-go-straight/.

Popkin, Susan J., and Mary K. Cunningham. *CHA Relocation Counseling Assessment—Final Report.* Washington, DC: Urban Institute. 2002.

Popovich, Nadja. "A Deadly Crisis: Mapping the Spread of America's Drug Overdose Epidemic." *The Guardian*, 2016. https://web.archive.org/web/20201108103520/http://www.theguardian.com/society/ng-interactive/2016/may/25/opioid-epidemic-overdose-deaths-map.

Poppa, Terrence. *Drug Lord: A True Story; The Life and Death of a Mexican Kingpin.* El Paso, TX: Cinco Puntos, 2010.

Possley, Maurice, and William B. Crawford Jr. "El Rukns Indicted in Libya Scheme." *Chicago Tribune*, October 31, 1986. https://web.archive.org/web/20201104170137 /https://www.chicagotribune.com/news/ct-xpm-1986-10-31-8603210871-story.html.

Provine, Doris Marie, Monica W. Varsanyi, Paul G. Lewis, and Scott H. Decker. *Policing Immigrants: Local Law Enforcement on the Front Lines*. Chicago: University of Chicago Press, 2016.

Public Broadcasting Service. "Thirty Years of America's Drug War: A Chronology." 2000. https://web.archive.org/web/20150303183339/http://www.pbs.org/wgbh/pages /frontline/shows/drugs/cron/.

Purvis, W. E., and R. V. Gundur. "The Drug Trade at a Glance." In *Research Handbook on Transnational Crime*, ed. Valsamis Mitsilegas, Saskia Hufnagel, and Anton Moiseienko, 272–300. Cheltenham, UK: Edward Elgar, 2019.

Pyrooz, David C., and Scott H. Decker. *Competing for Control: Gangs and the Social Order of Prisons*. Cambridge: Cambridge University Press, 2019.

Pyrooz, David C., and Meghan M. Mitchell. "The Use of Restrictive Housing on Gang and Non–Gang Affiliated Inmates in US Prisons: Findings from a National Survey of Correctional Agencies." *Justice Quarterly* 37, no. 1 (2019): 1–26.

Quinones, Sam. *Dreamland: The True Tale of America's Opiate Epidemic*. New York: Bloomsbury, 2015.

Ralph, Paige H., and James W. Marquart. "Gang Violence in Texas Prisons." *Prison Journal* 71, no. 2 (1991): 38–49.

Ravelo, Ricardo. *El narco en México: Historia e historias de una guerra*. Mexico City: Grijalbo, 2012.

Reavis, Dick. "How They Ruined Our Prisons." *Texas Monthly*, May 1985. https://web .archive.org/web/20201027175431/https://www.texasmonthly.com/articles/how -they-ruined-our-prisons/.

Reid, Lesley Williams, Harald E. Weiss, Robert M. Adelman, and Charles Jaret. "The Immigration-Crime Relationship: Evidence across US Metropolitan Areas." *Social Science Research* 34, no. 4 (2005): 757–80.

Reuter, Peter. *Disorganized Crime: The Economics of the Visible Hand*. Cambridge, MA: MIT Press, 1983.

——. "Systemic Violence in Drug Markets." *Crime, Law and Social Change* 52, no. 3 (2009): 275–84.

Rey. "The Latin Kings Speak: Talk by a Latin King Leader." Gangresearch.net, March 28, 2002. https://web.archive.org/web/20150928210239/http://gangresearch.net/Chicago Gangs/latinkings/Rey.html.

Riley, Jack. *Drug Warrior: My Life Bringing Down America's Biggest Drug Lords*. London: John Blake, 2019.

Ríos, Viridiana. "Why Did Mexico Become So Violent? A Self-Reinforcing Violent Equilibrium Caused by Competition And Enforcement." *Trends in Organized Crime* 16, no. 2 (2013): 138–55.

Robins, Lee N. "A Follow-up Study of Vietnam Veterans' Drug Use." *Journal of Drug Issues* 4, no. 1 (1974): 61–63.

Rodríguez Castañeda, Rafael. *El México narco*. Mexico City: Planeta Mexicana, 2010.

Rodríguez Nieto, Sandra. *The Story of Vicente, Who Murdered His Mother, His Father, and His Sister: Life and Death in Juárez*. Translated by Daniela Maria Ugaz and John Washington. London: Verso, 2015.

Rosenbaum, Dennis P., and Cody Stephens. *Reducing Public Violence and Homicide in Chicago: Strategies and Tactics of the Chicago Police Department*. Chicago: Center for Research in Law and Justice, University of Illinois at Chicago, 2005.

Royko, Mike. *Boss: Richard J. Daley of Chicago.* Boulder, CO: Paladin Books, 1971.

Ruggie, John Gerard. *Constructing the World Polity: Essays on International Institution-alisation.* London: Routledge, 2002.

Sabet, Daniel M. "Corruption or Insecurity? Understanding Dissatisfaction with Mexico's Police." *Latin American Politics and Society* 55, no. 1 (2012): 22–45.

Safer, Ronald S., and Matthew C. Crowl. "Substantial Assistance Departures: Valuable Tool or Dangerous Weapon." *Federal Sentencing Reporter* 12 (1999): 41–44.

Saldaña, Juan Diego, and Tony Payan. "The Evolution of Cartels in Mexico, 1980–2015." Rice University Baker Institute for Public Policy, May 11, 2016. https://www .bakerinstitute.org/research/evolution-cartels-mexico-1980-2015/.

Sampson, Robert J. *Great American City: Chicago and the Enduring Neighborhood Effect.* Chicago: University of Chicago Press, 2012.

Sanchez, Gabriella. *Human Smuggling and Border Crossings.* London: Routledge, 2016.

Sánchez-Jankowski, Martín. *Cracks in the Pavement: Social Change and Resilience in Poor Neighborhoods.* Berkeley: University of California Press, 2008.

——. "Gangs and Social Change." *Theoretical Criminology* 7, no. 2 (2003): 191–216.

Sanders, Cynthia K. "Promoting Financial Capability of Incarcerated Women for Community Reentry: A Call to Social Workers." *Journal of Community Practice* 24, no. 4 (2016): 389–409.

Saul, Josh. "Why 2016 Has Been Chicago's Bloodiest Year in Almost Two Decades." *Newsweek,* December 15, 2016. https://web.archive.org/web/20201129144007/https://www .newsweek.com/2016/12/23/chicago-gangs-violence-murder-rate-532034.html.

Saviano, Roberto. "El Chapo's Rise to Power and His First Prison Break." *Time,* July 21, 2015. https://web.archive.org/web/20190612035442/http://time.com/3966611/rob erto-saviano-el-chapo-prison-escape/.

Schaefer Morabito, Melissa. "Understanding Community Policing as an Innovation: Patterns of Adoption." *Crime & Delinquency* 56, no. 4 (2010): 564–87.

Schatz, Bryan. "The Border Patrol Is Setting Itself Up to Hire Some Bad Hombres." *Mother Jones,* March 13, 2017. https://web.archive.org/web/20201206214658/https://www .motherjones.com/politics/2017/03/donald-trump-border-patrol-corruption-use -force/.

——. "New Report Details Dozens of Corrupt Border Patrol Agents—Just As Trump Wants to Hire More." *Mother Jones,* April 24, 2018. https://web.archive.org/web /20201101222933/https://www.motherjones.com/politics/2018/04/new-report -details-dozens-of-corrupt-border-patrol-agents-just-as-trump-wants-to-hire -more/.

Schmidt, Paul Wickham. "An Overview and Critique of US Immigration and Asylum Policies in the Trump Era." *Journal on Migration and Human Security* 7, no. 3 (2019): 92–102.

Schou, Nick. *Kill the Messenger (Movie Tie-in Edition): How the CIA's Crack-Cocaine Controversy Destroyed Journalist Gary Webb.* New York: Nation Books, 2014.

Scott, Michael S., and Kelly Dedel. *Clandestine Methamphetamine Labs.* 2nd ed. Washington, DC: Office of Community Oriented Policing Services, 2006.

Scott, Peter Dale, and Jonathan Marshall. *Cocaine Politics: Drugs, Armies, and the CIA in Central America.* Berkeley: University of California Press, 1998.

Selby, W. Gardner. "Rick Perry Says Violence from Mexico Reaching El Paso, with Bullets Flying and Bombs Exploding," *PolitiFact,* August 5, 2010. http://archive.today /2021.01.12-053735/https://www.politifact.com/factchecks/2010/aug/05/rick -perry/perry-says-violence-mexico-reaching-el-paso-bullet/.

Seligman, Amanda I. *Block by Block: Neighborhoods and Public Policy on Chicago's West Side.* Chicago: University of Chicago Press, 2005.

Shelley, Louise I., and John T. Picarelli. "Methods Not Motives: Implications of the Convergence of International Organized Crime and Terrorism." *Police Practice and Research* 3, no. 4 (2002): 305–18.

Shirk, David A. *Drug Violence in Mexico: Data and Analysis from 2001–2009.* San Diego: University of San Diego, 2009.

Shirk, David A., Duncan Wood, and Eric L. Olson, eds. *Building Resilient Communities in Mexico: Civic Responses to Crime and Violence.* Washington, DC: Woodrow Wilson International Center for Scholars, 2014.

Shoichet, Catherine E. "Mexico's 'Queen of the Pacific' Pleads Guilty in U.S. Drug Case." CNN, April 25, 2013. http://www.cnn.com/2013/04/24/justice/florida-drug-queen -plea/index.html.

Shortland, Anja, and Federico Varese. "State-Building, Informal Governance and Organised Crime: The Case of Somali Piracy." *Political Studies* 64, no. 4 (2015): 811–31.

Shukla, Rashi K., Jordan L. Crump, and Emelia S. Chrisco. "An Evolving Problem: Methamphetamine Production and Trafficking in the United States." *International Journal of Drug Policy* 23, no. 6 (2012): 426–35.

Simon, Jonathan. "The 'Society of Captives' in the Era of Hyper-Incarceration." *Theoretical Criminology* 4, no. 3 (2000): 285–308.

Sinclair, Upton. *The Jungle.* New York: Bantam Books, 1981 [1906].

Skarbek, David. "Governance and Prison Gangs." *American Political Science Review* 105, no. 4 (2011): 702–16.

——. "Prison Gangs, Norms, and Organizations." *Journal of Economic Behavior & Organization* 82, no. 1 (2012): 96–109.

——. *The Social Order of the Underworld: How Prison Gangs Govern the American Penal System.* Oxford: Oxford University Press, 2014.

Skogan, Wesley G. *Police and Community in Chicago: A Tale of Three Cities.* Oxford: Oxford University Press, 2006.

Sloan, Carrie, and Johnaé Strong. "Chicago Has Spent Half a Billion Dollars on Police Brutality Cases—and It's Impoverishing the Victims' Communities." *The Nation,* 2016. https://web.archive.org/web/20210607224829/https://www.thenation.com /article/archive/chicago-has-spent-half-a-billion-dollars-on-police-brutality -cases-and-its-impoverishing-the-victims-communities/.

Smith, Chris M. *Syndicate Women: Gender and Networks in Chicago Organized Crime.* Oakland: University of California Press, 2019.

Smith, Dwight C., Jr. *The Mafia Mystique.* New York: Basic Books, 1975.

——. "Paragons, Pariahs, and Pirates: A Spectrum-Based Theory of Enterprise." *Crime & Delinquency* 26, no. 3 (July 1980): 358–86.

Smith, Luther B., III. *Illegal Immigration: Is It a Threat to National Security?* Carlisle Barracks, PA: US Army War College, 2006.

Snyder, Richard, and Angélica Durán Martínez. "Drugs, Violence, and State-Sponsored Protection Rackets in Mexico and Colombia." *Colombia International* 70 (2009): 61–91.

Søgaard, Thomas Friis, Torsten Kolind, Mie Birk Haller, and Geoffrey Hunt. "Ring and Bring Drug Services: Delivery Dealing and the Social Life of a Drug Phone." *International Journal of Drug Policy* 69 (2019): 8–15.

Solomon, Dan. "The FBI's List of the Most Dangerous Cities in Texas." *Texas Monthly,* January 22, 2015. http://archive.today/2021.01.11-061702/https://www.texasmonthly .com/the-daily-post/the-fbis-list-of-the-most-dangerous-cities-in-texas/.

Spergel, Irving A. *Reducing Youth Gang Violence: The Little Village Gang Project in Chicago.* Lanham, MD: Altamira, 2007.

Spergel, Irving A., and Susan F. Grossman. "The Little Village Project: A Community Approach to the Gang Problem." *Social Work* 42, no. 5 (1997): 456–70.

Spilde, Tony. "Chemical Makes Anhydrous Ammonia Useless in Making Meth." *Bismark Tribune*, October 10, 2006. https://web.archive.org/web/20201206045055/https://bismarcktribune.com/news/local/chemical-makes-anhydrous-ammonia-useless-in-making-meth/article_14044097-8888-5780-9b18-cebef32beccf.html.

Staff and Agencies in Washington. "US Supreme Court Upholds Policy of Making Asylum Seekers Wait in Mexico." *The Guardian*, March 12, 2020. https://web.archive.org/web/20210104064538/https://www.theguardian.com/us-news/2020/mar/11/us-supreme-court-upholds-policy-asylum-seekers-remain-in-mexico.

Steinle, Mia. "13 CBP Employees Arrested for Corruption This Administration." Project on Government Oversight, April 23, 2018. https://web.archive.org/web/20210111215435/https://www.pogo.org/investigation/2018/04/13-cbp-employees-arrested-for-corruption-this-administration.

Street, Alex, Chris Zepeda-Millán, and Michael Jones-Correa. "Mass Deportations and the Future of Latino Partisanship." *Social Science Quarterly* 96, no. 2 (2015): 540–52.

Stumpf, Juliet P. "Crimmigration, Surveillance and Security Threats: Civil Detention and Other Oxymorons." *Queen's Law Journal* 40 (2014): 55–389.

Substance Abuse and Mental Health Services Administration. *Key Substance Use and Mental Health Indicators in the United States: Results from the 2019 National Survey on Drug Use and Health*. Rockville, MD: Center for Behavioral Health Statistics and Quality, Substance Abuse and Mental Health Services Administration, 2020.

Sullivan, John P. "The Barrio Azteca, Los Aztecas Network." *Counter Terrorist* 6, no. 2 (2013): 60–66.

Sutch, Richard. "The One Percent across Two Centuries: A Replication of Thomas Piketty's Data on the Concentration of Wealth in the United States." *Social Science History* 41, no. 4 (2017): 587–613.

Suttles, Gerald D. *The Social Order of the Slum: Ethnicity and Territory in the Inner City*. Chicago: University of Chicago Press, 1968.

Sweeney, Annie, and Jason Meisner. "A Dad's Influence: How the Flores Twins Learned the Drug Trade at Home." *Chicago Tribune*, May 7, 2015. https://web.archive.org/web/20190424040606/https://www.chicagotribune.com/news/ct-father-flores-brothers-met-20150507-story.html.

Szalavitz, Maia. "Commentary: 5 Myths about Heroin." *Washington Post*, March 8, 2016. https://web.archive.org/web/20160318154641/http://www.chicagotribune.com/news/opinion/commentary/ct-five-myths-about-heroin-20160308-story.html.

Tapia, Mike. "Texas Latino Gangs and Large Urban Jails: Intergenerational Conflicts and Issues in Management." *Journal of Crime and Justice* 37, no. 2 (2014): 256–74.

Tapia, Mike, Corey S. Sparks, and J. Mitchell Miller. "Texas Latino Prison Gangs: An Exploration of Generational Shift and Rebellion." *Prison Journal* 94, no. 2 (2014): 159–79.

Taylor, Peter J. "Distance Transformation and Distance Decay Functions." *Geographical Analysis* 3, no. 3 (1971): 221–38.

Texas Department of Criminal Justice. *Statistical Report: Fiscal Year 2016*. Austin: Texas Board of Criminal Justice, 2017. https://www.tdcj.state.tx.us/documents/Statistical_Report_FY2016.pdf.

Texas Department of Public Safety. *Texas Gangs: An Overview of Security Threat Groups and Other Major Gangs in Texas*. Austin: Texas Department of Public Safety, Criminal Intelligence Service, 2007.

——. *Texas Gang Threat Assessment, 2014*. Austin: Texas Department of Public Safety, 2014.

——. *Texas Gang Threat Assessment, 2015*. Austin: Texas Department of Public Safety, 2015.

——. *Texas Gang Threat Assessment, 2018*. Austin: Texas Department of Public Safety, 2018.

Thomas, William Isaac, and Florian Znaniecki. *The Polish Peasant in Europe and America: Monograph of an Immigrant Group*. Boston: Gorham, 1919.

Thompson, Edward P. "History from Below." *Times Literary Supplement* 7, no. 4 (1966): 279–80.

Thomson, Janice E. "State Sovereignty in International Relations: Bridging the Gap between Theory and Empirical Research." *International Studies Quarterly* 39, no. 2 (1995): 213–33.

Thoreson, Karen, Larry J. McCormick, Michael D. Ryan, Cecil Patterson, and Michael D. White. *City of Phoenix Kidnapping Statistics Review Panel*. Phoenix, AZ: City of Phoenix, 2011.

Thrasher, Frederic Milton. *The Gang: A Study of 1,313 Gangs in Chicago*. Abridged ed. Edited by James F. Short Jr. Chicago: University of Chicago Press, 1963.

Tilly, Charles. "War Making and State Making as Organized Crime." In *Bringing the State Back In*, ed. Peter B. Evans, Dietrich Rueschemeyer, and Theda Skocpol, 169–91. Cambridge: Cambridge University Press, 1985.

Tinessa, Giulio. "Marginados, minorías e inmigrantes: Criminalización de la pobreza y encarcelamiento masivo en las sociedades capitalistas avanzadas." *Miradas en Movimiento* 3 (2010): 39–68.

Toll, Eric Jay. "Maricopa County Population Growth No. 2 in Nation, but Far Short of Area's Historic Numbers." *Phoenix Business Journal*, March 26, 2015. https://web.archive.org/web/20201001090510/https://www.bizjournals.com/phoenix/news/2015/03/26/census-maricopa-county-2nd-in-population-growth.html.

Trammell, Rebecca. *Enforcing the Convict Code: Violence and Prison Culture*. Boulder, CO: Lynne Rienner, 2012.

Transparency International. "Mexico, Corruption by Country/Territory." 2019. https://web.archive.org/web/20201201162913/https://www.transparency.org/en/countries/mexico.

Tyson, Ann Scott. "Journey of Chicago's Ultimate Street Tough." *Christian Science Monitor*, December 31, 1996. https://web.archive.org/web/20150924132013/http://www.csmonitor.com/1996/1231/123196.us.us.1.html.

United Nations Statistics Division. "City Population by Sex, City and City Type." United Nations, 2017 and 2020 data. http://data.un.org/Data.aspx?q=city+population&d=POP&f=tableCode%3a240%3bcountryCode%3a484%3brefYear%3a2019%2c2020&c=2,3,6,8,10,12,14,16,17,18&s=_countryEnglishNameOrderBy:asc,refYear:desc,areaCode:asc&v=1.

United States Courts. "Visit a Federal Court." n.d. https://www.uscourts.gov/about-federal-courts/federal-courts-public/visit-federal-court.

US Census Bureau. "Chicago-Naperville-Elgin, IL-IN-WI Metro Area." American Community Survey 1-Year Estimates, 2019. https://web.archive.org/web/20201128020043/https://censusreporter.org/profiles/31000us16980-chicago-naperville-elgin-il-in-wi-metro-area/.

US Department of Commerce. "Quickfacts Beta." Data for 2016 and 2019. https://www.census.gov/quickfacts.

US Department of Homeland Security. *Independent Review of U.S. Customs and Border Protection's Reporting of FY 2013 Drug Control Performance Summary Report*. Vol. OIG-14-40. Washington, DC: Office of Inspector General, 2014.

US Department of Justice, Office of the Inspector General. *Review of the Phoenix Police Department's 2008 Kidnapping Statistic Reported in Department of Justice Grant Applications.* Phoenix, AR: Department of Justice, 2012.

US Department of State. "Mexico Travel Warning." U.S. Passports and International Travel. May 5, 2015. https://web.archive.org/web/20151006020742/http://travel .state.gov/content/passports/en/alertswarnings/mexico-travel-warning.html.

Valdez, Diana Washington. "Las Vegas Man Arrested in Connection with Threatening Billboard Graffiti." *El Paso Times*, May 29, 2014, http://archive.elpasotimes.com /latestnews/ci_25843080/las-vegas-man-arrested-connection-threatening -billboard-graffiti.

Van Koppen, M. Vere, Christianne J. de Poot, and Arjan A. J. Blokland. "Comparing Criminal Careers of Organized Crime Offenders and General Offenders." *European Journal of Criminology* 7, no. 5 (September 1, 2010): 356–74.

Van Koppen, M. Vere, Christianne J. de Poot, Edward R. Kleemans, and Paul Nieuwbeerta. "Criminal Trajectories in Organized Crime." *British Journal of Criminology* 50, no. 1 (2009): 102–23.

Varandani, Suman. "Who Is Jesus Salas Aguayo? Juarez Drug Cartel Leader Captured by Mexican Police." *International Business Times*, April 20, 2015. http://archive .today/2021.01.11-062202/https://www.ibtimes.com/who-jesus-salas-aguayo -juarez-drug-cartel-leader-captured-mexican-police-1888101.

Varese, Federico. "How Mafias Migrate: The Case of the 'Ndrangheta in Northern Italy." *Law & Society Review* 40, no. 2 (2006): 411–44.

Vargas, Robert. "Criminal Group Embeddedness and the Adverse Effects of Arresting a Gang's Leader: A Comparative Case Study." *Criminology* 52, no. 2 (2014): 143–68.

——. *Wounded City: Violent Turf Wars in a Chicago Barrio.* New York: Oxford University Press, 2016.

Varghese, Benson. "ISF: Intermediate Sanction Facilities." Varghese Summersett PLLC, 2015. https://web.archive.org/web/20210127015441/https://versustexas.com/blog /isf/.

Vearrier, Laura. "The Value of Harm Reduction for Injection Drug Use: A Clinical and Public Health Ethics Analysis." *Disease-a-Month* 65, no. 5 (2019): 119–41.

Velasco, José Luis. "Drogas, seguridad y cambio político en México." *Nueva Sociedad* 198 (2005): 89–101.

Venkatesh, Sudhir Alladi. *Gang Leader for a Day: A Rogue Sociologist Takes to the Streets.* New York: Penguin, 2008.

——. "The Social Organization of Street Gang Activity in an Urban Ghetto." *American Journal of Sociology* 103, no. 1 (1997): 82–111.

Venkatesh, Sudhir Alladi, and Steven D. Levitt. "Are We a Family or a Business? History and Disjuncture in the Urban American Street Gang." *Theory and Society* 29, no. 4 (2000): 427–62.

Vijayan, Sunita. "Monterey County Charges Northern Riders as a Gang for the First Time in State." StreetGangs.com, May 7, 2010. http://archive.today/2021.01.12-052049 /https://www.streetgangs.com/news/051010_monterey_county_charges/.

Villazor, Rose Cuison, and Kevin R. Johnson. "The Trump Administration and the War on Immigration Diversity." *Wake Forest Law Review* 54 (2019): 575–616.

Vulliamy, Ed. *Amexica: War along the Borderline.* London: Bodley Head, 2010.

——. "How a Big US Bank Laundered Billions from Mexico's Murderous Drug Gangs." *The Guardian*, April 3, 2011. https://web.archive.org/web/20210228083142/https:// www.theguardian.com/world/2011/apr/03/us-bank-mexico-drug-gangs.

——. "How Will El Chapo's Recapture Affect Mexico and Narco-Trafficking?" *The Guardian*, January 11, 2016. https://web.archive.org/web/20160308143346/http://www

.theguardian.com/world/2016/jan/11/el-chapo-capture-joaquin-guzman -mexico-government-drug-war-cartel-violence.

Wacquant, Loïc. *Las cárceles de la miseria*, Vol. 1. Translated by Horacio Pons. Buenos Aires: Manantial, 2000.

Wainwright, Tom. *Narconomics: How to Run a Drug Cartel; What Big Business Taught the Drug Lords*. New York: PublicAffairs, 2016.

Ward, Thomas W. *Gangsters without Borders: An Ethnography of a Salvadoran Street Gang*. Oxford: Oxford University Press, 2013.

Webb, Gary. *Dark Alliance: The CIA, the Contras, and the Cocaine Explosion*. New York: Seven Stories, 2011.

Weber, Max. *The Theory of Social and Economic Organization*. Translated by Alexander Morell Henderson and Talcott Parsons. Glencoe, IL: Free Press, 1947.

Weide, Robert D. "The Invisible Hand of the State: A Critical Historical Analysis of Prison Gangs in California." *Prison Journal* 100, no. 3 (2020): 312–31.

Welch, Michael. *Detained: Immigration Laws and the Expanding INS Jail Complex*. Philadelphia: Temple University Press, 2002.

Werb, D., K. D. Wagner, L. Beletsky, Patricia Gonzalez-Zuniga, Gudelia Rangel, and S. A. Strathdee. "Police Bribery and Access to Methadone Maintenance Therapy within the Context of Drug Policy Reform in Tijuana, Mexico." *Drug and Alcohol Dependence* 148 (2015): 221–25.

Wilson, Christopher E. "Crime Data and Spillover Violence along the Southwest Border." Washington, DC: Woodrow Wilson International Center for Scholars, n.d.

Wilson, David P., Braedon Donald, Andrew J. Shattock, David Wilson, and Nicole Fraser-Hurt. "The Cost-Effectiveness of Harm Reduction." *International Journal of Drug Policy* 26 (2015): S5–S11.

Wilson, Nana, Mbabazi Kariisa, Puja Seth, Herschel Smith IV., and Nicole L. Davis. "Drug and Opioid-Involved Overdose Deaths—United States, 2017–2018." *Morbidity and Mortality Weekly Report* 69, no. 11 (2020): 290–97.

Winslow, Don. "The Dirty Secret of El Chapo's Downfall." *Vanity Fair*, February 1, 2019. https://web.archive.org/web/20201118134037/https://www.vanityfair.com/news /2019/02/the-dirty-secret-of-el-chapo-downfall.

Witte, Eric A. *Undeniable Atrocities: Confronting Crimes against Humanity in Mexico*. Open Society Justice Initiative. New York: Open Society Foundations, 2016.

Wolf, Brett. "El Chapo Renews US Law Enforcement Concerns about Money Laundering via Prepaid Cards." Reuters, March 4, 2019. https://web.archive.org/web /20210308041920if_/https://www.reuters.com/article/bc-finreg-money -laundering-idUSKCN1QN218.

Wolf, Sonja. "Mara Salvatrucha: The Most Dangerous Street Gang in the Americas?" *Latin American Politics and Society* 54, no. 1 (2012): 65–99.

——. "Maras transnacionales: Origins and Transformations of Central American Street Gangs." *Latin American Research Review* 45, no. 1 (2010): 256–65.

Wolff, Edward N. "Wealth Trends in the United States during the Great Recession and Recovery, 2001–2016." In *Wealth(s) and Subjective Well-Being*, 485–503. New York: Springer, 2019.

Wolff, Michael Jerome. "Violence and Criminal Order: The Case of Ciudad Juarez." *Urban Geography* 39, no. 10 (2018): 1–19.

Woodiwiss, Michael, and Dick Hobbs. "Organized Evil and the Atlantic Alliance Moral Panics and the Rhetoric of Organized Crime Policing in America and Britain." *British Journal of Criminology* 49, no. 1 (2009): 106–28.

Woody, Christopher. "The US Sanctioned a 'Smooth as Butter' Cartel Operator and a Mexican Soccer Star Allegedly Working with Him." Business Insider Australia,

August 10, 2017. https://web.archive.org/web/20210426072938/https://www.busin
essinsider.com.au/us-sanctions-raul-flores-hernandez-and-rafael-marquez-2017
-8/?r=US&IR=T.

Young, Gay, Robert H. Schmidt, Oscar J. Martinez, and Kathleen A. Staudt. *The Social Ecology and Economic Development of Ciudad Juárez*. New York: Routledge, 2019.

Yllanes Ramos, Fernando. "Social Rights Enshrined in the Mexican Constitution of 1917." *International Labour Review* 96 (1967): 590–608.

Zibell, Amanda, Jayde Ely, Jasmine De Los Rios, Sacha Ten, and Tony Vidale. *Enhanced Drug and Gang Enforcement (EDGE) Report*. Phoenix: Arizona Criminal Justice Commission, 2014.

Zilberg, Elana. *Space of Detention: The Making of a Transnational Gang Crisis between Los Angeles and San Salvador*. Durham, NC: Duke University Press, 2011.

Zorbaugh, Harvey Warren. *The Gold Coast and the Slum: A Sociological Study of Chicago's Near North Side*. Chicago: University of Chicago Press, 1929.

Zust, Barbara L. "Assessing and Addressing Domestic Violence Experienced by Incarcerated Women." *Creative Nursing* 14, no. 2 (2008): 70–72.

Index

Page numbers in *italics* refer to figures.

CPSIA information can be obtained
at www.ICGtesting.com
Printed in the USA
LVHW031917300323
743031LV00002B/320

9 781501 764479